CADOGAN GUIDES

"Cadogan Guides really need no introduction and are mini-encyclopaedic on the countries covered ... they give the explorer, the intellectual or cultural buff—indeed any visitor—all they need to know to get the very best from their ~~visit~~ ... by the many inveterate armchair travellers ..."

"The quality of writing in this British serie~~s~~ ... history, customs, sightseeing, food and lodg~~ing~~ ... for interesting detail and informed recomm~~endation~~ ..."

"Standouts these days are the Cadogan Gu~~ides~~ ... ~~many~~ written books."

—American Bookseller Magazine

"Entertaining companions, with sharp insights, local gossip and far more of a feeling of a living author ... The series has received plaudits worldwide for intelligence, originality and a slightly irreverent sense of fun."

Daily Telegraph

Other titles in the Cadogan Guides series:

vertical City

'*New York*—mecca which lures the brightest minds, the most brilliant writers, the most masterful artisans to its gates!'

—W. Parker Chase, *New York, the Wonder City*, 1931

CADOGAN CITY GUIDES

NEW YORK

VANESSA LETTS

CADOGAN BOOKS
London

THE GLOBE PEQUOT PRESS
Chester, Connecticut

Cadogan Books Ltd
Mercury House, 195 Knightsbridge, London SW7 1RE

The Globe Pequot Press
138 West Main Street, Chester, Connecticut 06412

Cover design by Ralph King
Cover illustration by Angela Wood
Maps © Cadogan Books, drawn by James Soane
Index by Dorothy Frame

Editor: Victoria Ingle
Series Editors: Rachel Fielding and Paula Levey

First published in 1991

British Library Cataloguing in Publication Data

Letts, Vanessa
   New York. – (Cadogan guides).
   1. New York (City)—Visitors' guides.
   I. Title
917.4710443
ISBN 0–946313–99–7

Library of Congress Cataloging-in-Publication-Data

Letts, Vanessa
   New York / by Vanessa Letts: illustrations by Charles Shearer.
      p.   cm. – (Cadogan guides)
   Includes index.
   ISBN 0–87106–322–0
   1. New York (N.Y.)—Description—1981—Guide books.
   I. Shearer, Charles.   II. Title.   III. Series.
   F128.18.L44   CIP
   917.47'10443–dc20   90–21788

Photoset in Ehrhardt on a Linotron 202
Printed on recycled paper and bound in Great Britain by
Redwood Press Limited, Melksham, Wiltshire

CONTENTS

Walk III: The Lower East Side and East Village *Pages 130–49*

Orchard Street—Eldridge Street Synagogue—Clinton Street—Essex Street Market—Anshe Slonim Synagogue—Marble Cemetery—Little Ukraine—Astor Place and Cooper Union—St Mark's Place—St Mark's-in-the-Bowery—Tompkins Square

Walk IV: Bohemian Squares: the Flatiron District and Greenwich Village *Pages 150–72*

Flatiron Building—Madison Square—Ladies Mile—Gramercy Park—Union Square—14th Street—University Place—Washington Square—St Luke's Place—Christopher Street—Jefferson Market Courthouse—Patchin Place—Gansevoort Meat Market—Hoboken, New Jersey

Walk V: Vertical City *Pages 173–94*

Empire State Building—Garment District—Time Square—Sin Street—New York Public Library—5th Avenue—Diamond Row—Rockefeller Center—Radio City—MoMa

Walk VI: The Upper East Side *Pages 195–214*

Metropolitan Museum—Guggenheim Museum—Cooper Hewitt—Reservoir—Conservatory Garden—Carl Schurz Park—Municipal Asphalt Plant—Temple Emanu-El— Central Park Zoo—Plaza—Tiffany's—Trump Tower

Walk VII: The Civic Center, Chinatown and SoHo *Pages 215–35*

Woolworth Building—City Hall—Foley Square Courthouses and Night Courts—First Shearith Cemetery—Chatham Square—Mott Street—the Bowery—Little Italy—Canal Street Casbah—Greene Street—Broadway—Bayard-Condict Building—West Broadway

Walk VIII: Midtown East *Pages 236–53*

Roosevelt Island Cable Car—Bloomingdale's—57th Street—Park Avenue—Waldorf-Astoria—Grand Central Terminal—Chrysler Building—Automat—Tudor City—United Nations Building—East River Heliport—Beekman Tower—Sutton Place

Museums *Pages 254–61*

The Heights and the Harlems *Pages 262–77*

El Barrio and La Marqueta—Central Harlem—North Harlem and Hamilton Heights—Morningside Heights and Columbia—Washington Heights, Fort Tryon Park and The Cloisters

Food and Drink *Pages 278–306*

LIST OF MAPS

ABOUT THE AUTHOR

Vanessa Letts was born and brought up in South London, and educated at Cambridge University where she read English. She has lived and worked in New York on several occasions, and in 1990 she won the *Spectator* magazine's Shiva Naipaul Memorial Prize for travel writing.

ACKNOWLEDGEMENTS

Heartfelt thanks go to Michael Pauls, collaborator and conspirator, without whom the Vanessa would have been a goner. Special thanks also go to William Olivieri, from the Port Authority of New York, and Robert Mantho, who both gave inspiring advice; to Bonnie Mark and Heather Carr, who carried my suitcases; to Randy and Bunny Williams, Debs and Joe Trump, Christopher Ash, Matthew Barac, Ritu Birla, Frank Chirico, Sam King and James Soane, who all looked after me while I was in New York; to my mother, who was foolish enough to let me borrow her study; and finally, to the forbearance and patience of my editor, Vicki Ingle.

The publishers would particularly like to thank Jane Shaw, Dorothy Frame and Felicity Carter for respectively copy-editing, indexing and proof-reading this book.

PLEASE NOTE

INTRODUCTION

'*New York*—synonym for big, great, astounding, miraculous!'

'*New York*—home of the world's greatest captains of industry, the world's most stupendous structures, the world's richest business institutions—veritable center of our country's wealth, culture, and achievement!'

—W. Parker Chase, *New York, the Wonder City*, 1931

In the middle of the Great Depression, W. Parker Chase—self-made impresario, master of hyperbole, and owner of several troupes of show-girls—wrote a Vision of New York in the Future for his panegyric, *New York, the Wonder City*. By 1990, the book concludes, New York will bulge and groan with a population of 50 million; buildings will soar 250 stories into the air; New Yorkers will crunch up their meals and cocktails in pills and pellets; ladies will fling away their skirts for bathing costumes; roadways will be noiseless; and 'business depressions, Wall Street crashes, Communistic upheavals and other disturbances will be a thing of the past'. Best of all, scientists will have perfected a life-perpetuating serum.

Not one prediction has come true. Spirited into the future with a dollop of serum, the great Parker Chase would find a New York as maddening, as temporary, as unspeakable as it always has been. The Wonder City of the 1990s is dirty, nasty, and noisy; its streets smell of chocolate bars and cowpats; its inhabitants are cocky and razor-edged; its buildings are monstrous, impossible and disheveled; even its flora and fauna are unusually devious and brutal. And yet it captivates instantly; inspires and elevates one minute; alarms and depresses the next. People love the Wonder City and they hate it: their reactions are deeply ambivalent; so much so that the city elicits gushes of hyperbole and torrents of invective, in roughly equal quantities.

No wonder, for New York is cloudland and rathole, paradise and pandemonium; imperious Empire State and idiotical Gotham*; oxymoronic, the best and worst of cities, depending on your mood. It can't be summed up, except in statistics—7.5 million New Yorkers, anything between 8 and 15 million rats, 2.4 million trees, 1 million illegal immigrants, 865,000 buildings, 12,000 miles of streets and sewers, 600–1000 people *per acre*, 17 million tourists and 2000 murders a year, 3.5 million commuters (the population of Havana) and 30,000 tons of trash a day. From a distance the Wonder City makes a kind of sense. Close to, it is preposterously lopsided; not a single entity but a fascinating jumble of hundreds and thousands of incompatible elements—neighborhoods, buildings and people, squashed together so that the streets and avenues hum with life, and everything seems louder, brighter and more important than almost anywhere else you can think of.

Happily for the visitor, New York is surprisingly un-touristy. There are sights in abundance, but they are generally upstaged by distractions around them—by the streets and sidewalks, which shudder and quake with traffic and noise; by the seaside-light, which transfigures towers and scrapers into pink, lemon and lime-green ice-cream confections; and, of course, by New Yorkers themselves, who wisecrack, curse and flirt their way around the city with astonishing panache. They make it an incredibly verbal city. Keep your ears pricked at all times, and you will be as entertained by what you hear as much as by what you see. Behind a gruff exterior, New Yorkers are a warm, wistful, open-hearted lot. Perhaps because over 40 per cent of the resident population are immigrants, they make lifelong friends instantly, on the first acquaintance, and their favorite pastime is muscling a stranger into conversation.

The world's metropolis is a curiously homely, even parochial place, and the best entertainments in the city are the most simple—the neighborhood bars and diners where solitary New Yorkers champ on the ice in their drinks and wolf down huge breakfasts; the shops where they catapault themselves into battle as though they were in a Middle Eastern bazaar; the buses and subways where they grumble and complain to their hearts' content; or the brickloads of Sunday papers which they dutifully lug back to their apartments and pore over for the next week.

Finally, before you venture forth remind yourself that the very things that make New York unbearable—the incivilities, the dunghill smells, the grime, the tension, the hurry and the congestion—are the ones that make it the most exhilarating, the most energetic, and the most challenging Wonder City in the world. After you have been there, nowhere else will make your heart thump, zoom, flutter and whirr in quite the same way.

* New York was first christened 'Gotham' by Washington Irving, in honour of the old nursery rhyme and the English village of Gotham in Nottinghamshire, proverbial for the folly of its inhabitants.

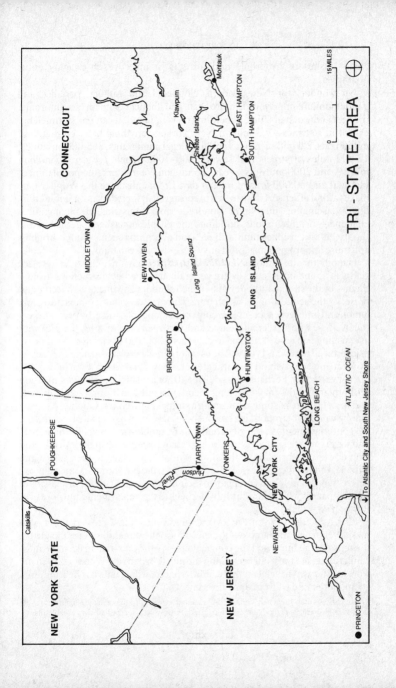

TRI - STATE AREA

0   15 MILES

NEW YORK STATE

CONNECTICUT

NEW JERSEY

LONG ISLAND

ATLANTIC OCEAN

Catskills

POUGHKEEPSIE

MIDDLETOWN

NEW HAVEN

BRIDGEPORT

Long Island Sound

TARRYTOWN

YONKERS

HUNTINGTON

NEW YORK CITY

NEWARK

PRINCETON

LONG BEACH

Klawpum

Shelter Island

Montauk

EAST HAMPTON

SOUTH HAMPTON

Hudson River

To Atlantic City and South New Jersey Shore

To Dibbs Locksmith

Travel

Getting to New York

By Air: New York has two main international airports, John F. Kennedy (JFK) and Newark. A third, LaGuardia, is mostly used for domestic flights. JFK and LaGuardia lie to the east of Manhattan in Queens, and Newark to the west in the state of New Jersey. All three are about a 30-minute taxi ride away.

By Air from the UK: Heathrow and Gatwick have the most frequent direct flights to JFK and Newark. Twice-weekly flights leave from Manchester and Glasgow, and once-weekly flights from Prestwick. Flights are crowded during the peak traveling season (between June and September), and it is always a good idea to book well in advance because standbys can be few and far between.

Flights to the US come in a bewildering variety, and prices vary wildly according to season and competition. All the major airlines – British Airways, TWA, Continental and Virgin Atlantic – do standard (APEX) fares which have to be booked between 21 and 30 days before departure. The high season lasts from late-June until mid-September and the low season from mid-September until mid-April, with the exception of the 10 days before Christmas which count as high season.

One of the best deals is offered by Virgin Atlantic (tel 0293 562000) which now does daily flights to JFK as well as to Newark. Their Late

Saver fares can only be booked within 3 days of departure, but you can book your return flight at the same time. Slippers, headsets, scones and jam, and an in-flight magazine about Richard Branson are thrown in with the cost of the ticket. British Airways offer a more expensive standby fare which can be booked up to 48 hours before departure. For the latest bucket-shop prices, which can be incredibly low, it's worth having a look at the *Evening Standard*, *Time Out* or the Sunday papers. Also, the Air Travel Advisory Board (tel 071 636 5000) gives numbers of travel agents currently offering good deals.

The flight takes between 7 and 8 hours. Make sure you drink plenty of water, and ask for a window seat so you have something (rather than someone) to lean against.

Airlines in London
Air India: tel (071) 493 4050
Air Canada: tel (071) 439 7941
British Airways: tel (071) 897 4000
British Caledonian: tel (071) 668 4222
Pan-Am: tel (071) 409 0688
TWA: tel (071) 636 4090
Virgin Atlantic: tel (0293) 562000

Courier Flights: CTS, tel (081) 844 2626, recruit couriers on Concorde for around £450, but they must be booked between 2 and 3 months in advance.
TNT Skypak: tel (081) 861 2345.

By Air from the US and Canada: Practically all the big US airlines offer flights to the New York area. Before booking, make sure you know whether flights include stops or changes of aircraft, which may reduce the price of your ticket but greatly increase the length of your journey. Check in at least half an hour before departure.

Major US Carriers Serving New York
America West: tel 800 247 5692
American: tel 800 433 7300
Braniff: tel 800 BRANIFF
Continental: tel 800 525 0280
Delta: tel 800 221 1212
Midway: tel 800 621 5700
Northwest: tel 800 225 2525

Pan Am: tel 800 442 5896
TWA: tel 800 221 2000
United: tel 800 241 6522
USAir: tel 800 428 4322

By Sea from Southampton: If you have lots of big ones, a harp and a Mercedes to transport, and want to brush up on your deck-quoits, then traveling by sea is the obvious alternative. You can take an unlimited amount of baggage, eat an unlimited amount of food, and join classes in bridge, waltzing and the delights of feeding royal jelly to your dog. A one-way 5-day trip from Southampton to New York in the most expensive suites on the QE2 can cost up to £8700, or about £2250 for a first-class double cabin, deck-quoits and food included. Off season, a transatlantic double cabin is around £850. Make reservations through a travel agent or directly through Cunard (in New York, tel 880 7500; in London, tel (071) 491 3930).

Passports and Visas for EEC Citizens: Take a valid, 10-year passport (a Visitor's passport will not suffice), or you will spend the rest of your holiday in the airport. If you are staying for less than 90 days and have a return ticket on a major airline, you do not need a visa. To stay on for longer, however, you will have to apply for a visa from the US Embassy. (In London, from the Visa and Immigration Department, 5 Upper Grosvenor Street, London W1A 2JB, tel (071) 499 3443). Unless you queue up outside the embassy and get your visa in person, a written application takes four weeks. You need a passport, a passport photograph and evidence that you are going to return to your native land (a note explaining that you have are tied to a job, college, child or doggie is usually enough). On the application form, you must swear that you're not a communist, fascist, criminal or drug-dealer, and if customs find any incriminatingly subversive literature on you, they can refuse admission, on the grounds that you swore falsely. This peculiar ruling is the result of the McCarran-Walter Act, a McCarthy-era leftover that has become a national embarrassment (though not yet embarrassing enough to get it repealed).

Customs: Foreigners are allowed to enter with duty-free gifts valued at up to $100, plus 200 cigarettes, 50 cigars or 3lbs of tobacco, and 1 liter of alcohol. Returning Americans may bring gifts worth up to $400.

If you have a foreign passport and make it conspicuous, customs officials are inclined to give a less rigorous inspection – although they still won't be impressed by drugs, or even plants, fresh food (especially fruit and meat), chocolate liqueurs, obscene publications and (of all things) lottery tickets.

On Arrival

Arriving in New York is not a soothing experience. If you are arriving after 10 pm, make sure you have some American currency on you because the *bureaux de change* will be closed.

Immigration is the first obstacle, and unless you hurtle out of the plane to the start of the queue, you should allow at least an hour to get through. The immigration officers are bullies: their job is to make the innocent visitor stammer and sweat. As always, politeness makes a good impression. Even so, if you don't have traveler's cheques, credit cards, or cash to prove you have enough money to stay in the country unaided (calculated at about $200 a week), you may find your visit is restricted to 3 months or even 6 weeks, especially if you don't have a return ticket. The officials are bound to ask where you are staying, so have the name, address and telephone number of your hotel, or of friends in the city to hand.

Transport from the Airports: Getting to the city is the next hurdle. Unless you are very exhausted and disorientated, your best bet is to go by bus. The **Carey Bus System** (tel 718 632 0500) leaves Kennedy and La Guardia every 20 minutes between 6 am and midnight, and drops passengers at Grand Central Station on the east side of midtown on 42nd Street and Park Avenue. From Grand Central you can easily get a cab to your hotel. (Cabs are yellow, and a lit sign on the roof means they are vacant. Get straight in and then tell the driver where you are going.) From Newark buses run by **Olympia Trails** (tel 212 964 6233) every 15 minutes between 6 am and midnight to the World Trade Center in downtown Manhattan, or else to Grand Central Station in midtown. It costs $8 to go on a Carey bus from JFK, $6 from La Guardia, and $7 to go on an Olympia bus from Newark. Allow 45 minutes for the trip, but up to 1½ hours during rushhours.

Although the buses are infinitely preferable, from Kennedy you can take the **JFK Express** – a subway and bus ride which takes at least an hour and costs $6.75.

The third, more expensive, way of getting into the city is to take a **cab**. These cost around $25 from JFK and around $30 plus a few dollars for state tolls from Newark. You can quarter the price by asking the taxi dispatcher to fix you up with a group of people who want to share. More simply, you can make friends with the lonely person standing in the queue next to you, and ask if they mind sharing.

If you want to arrive in the city in a hurry, you can take a **helicopter** from Kennedy for about $58. The ride takes 10 minutes, choppers leave JFK terminals for the East Side Heliport on 34th Street and the East River in midtown every half hour between 1.30 pm and 7.30 pm. (Call New York Helicopter, tel 800 645 3494 for more information.)

If you have 90 minutes but no money to spare, you can take the **Q10** green bus from JFK to the Union Turnpike-Kew Gardens subway station, and then catch an E train into the city. It costs $2.50.

Transport to the Airports: Do the above backwards, remembering to add extra time for traffic jams, tantrums and confusion. JFK is enormous, and at *both* international airports most airlines have their own terminals. If your airline is at the end of the line, add an extra 15 minutes to your journey. If it is raining, add another $1/2$ hour. For up-to-date information on traffic and weather conditions call (1 800) AIR RIDE. Trying to find out about flight arrivals and departures can be an infuriating business, especially if you are traveling on one of the more obscure airlines, because there is no central bureau of information. Most of the major carriers have their own numbers, but they will not be able to tell you about any of their rivals.

Airlines in New York

Air France: tel 247 0100 (reservations) or 1–718 917 2410 (flight information).

British Airways: tel 1–800 247 9297 (reservations) 1–718 397 4397 (flight arrivals), or 1–718 917 5500 (departures).

Continental: tel 319 9494 (domestic flights) or 1–800 231 0856 (international flights).

Pan Am: tel 687 2600.

Swissair: tel 1–718 995 8400 (reservations), or 1–718 995 5112 (flight information).

TWA: tel 290 2121 (domestic flights), or 290 2141 (international flights).

Virgin Atlantic: tel 1–800 862 8621.

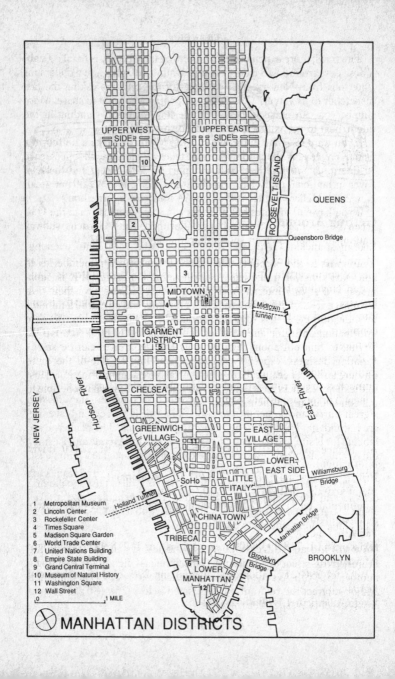

UPPER WEST SIDE

UPPER EAST SIDE

QUEENS

ROOSEVELT ISLAND

Queensboro Bridge

1

10

2

3

MIDTOWN

7

Midtown Tunnel

4

9

GARMENT DISTRICT

8

5

CHELSEA

GREENWICH VILLAGE

EAST VILLAGE

LOWER EAST SIDE

Williamsburg Bridge

SoHo

LITTLE ITALY

NEW JERSEY

Hudson River

East River

Holland Tunnel

CHINATOWN

TRIBECA

Manhattan Bridge

Brooklyn Bridge

BROOKLYN

6

LOWER MANHATTAN

12

1 Metropolitan Museum
2 Lincoln Center
3 Rockefeller Center
4 Times Square
5 Madison Square Garden
6 World Trade Center
7 United Nations Building
8 Empire State Building
9 Grand Central Terminal
10 Museum of Natural History
11 Washington Square
12 Wall Street

0   1 MILE

⊗ MANHATTAN DISTRICTS

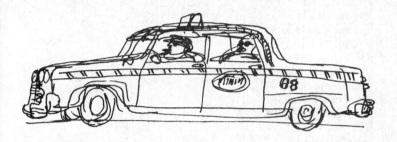

Getting Around

Like most ancient Greek and Roman cities, and 13th-century Peking, Manhattan is built on a grid. This makes getting around on foot easy as pie, except in certain anarchic areas such as Brooklyn and Lower Manhattan (anything below 14th Street) where the grid goes temporarily haywire. Fifth Avenue runs straight down the middle, dividing the island into east and west. Broadway, following an Indian trail, is the only real confusion, since it runs diagonally from top to bottom and slices up avenues.

Before you venture forth, remind yourself that cars drive on the righthand side of the road. Luckily, most streets are one-way; even-numbered streets run east, and odd-numbered streets run west.

New Yorkers are usually happy to proffer directions, but they do so in a great hurry, and sometimes in code. The words 'street' and 'avenue' are redundant. Thus '42nd bet. Park 'n' Lex' means 'The place you are looking for is situated on 42nd Street, between Park Avenue and Lexington Avenue.' Be prepared, as well, for directions reduced to a minimalist, utterly unintelligible 'srinkydinkdinkeyony'.

Once you have been in the city a few days, you will get used to judging distances in blocks. Blocks in Manhattan are rectangular, and it takes about 1½ minutes to walk along a short side, and about 3–5 minutes to walk along a long side, between avenues.

How to Find an Address: There is a magical system for locating the nearest cross-street to a building. Cancel the last digit of the building's number (328 8th Avenue becomes 32), divide it by two (16), and then add or subtract the relevant number listed below (26). (So the nearest cross-street is West 26th Street.)

Avenue A: add 3
Avenue B: add 3
Avenue C: add 3
Avenue D: add 3
1st Avenue: add 3
2nd Avenue: add 3
3rd Avenue: add 10
4th Avenue: add 8
5th Avenue: 1–200 add 13
201–400 add 16
401–600 add 18
601–775 add 20
776–1285 subtract 18
1287–2000 add 45
2000+ add 24
6th Avenue: subtract 12
7th Avenue: add 12
8th Avenue: add 10
9th Avenue: add 13
10th Avenue: add 14
Amsterdam Avenue: add 60
Audubon Avenue: add 165
Broadway: subtract 30
Columbus Avenue: add 60
Convent Avenue: add 127
Central Park West: divide by 10 and add 60
Edgecombe Avenue: add 134
Lenox Avenue: add 110
Lexington Avenue: add 22
Madison Avenue: add 26
Manhattan Avenue: add 100
Park Avenue: add 34
Riverside Drive: divide by 10 and add 72
St Nicholas Avenue: add 110
West End Avenue: add 59
York Avenue: add 4

Maps. It is quite important to get hold of a decent street map as soon as possible. The best, by a long way, is the purple plastic-covered *Streetwise Manhattan* map, published by Streetwise Maps Inc. It is small and sturdy, and stands up to rain storms. But most important of all, it shows the locations of subway stations. You can get Streetwise maps in most bookshops (and discounted along with detailed *Rand McNally* maps in the Strand Bookstore on 12th Street and Broadway). The other alternative is the excellent *Van Dam* fold-out map, and the *Flashmaps Instant Guide to New York* which comes in the form of a pocket book. Some shops also sell irresistible thumbnail-sized maps and magnifying glasses. Don't buy them. They are completely useless, since even with the help of the glasses the details are still too minute to make any sense at all. Rand McNally and **Geographia** do football-pitch-sized maps of the boroughs.

Next, get yourself subway and bus maps. These are free from token booths (but they tend to run out), from tourist information centers, and from the information booths at Grand Central and Penn Stations.

Subways are best used in the daytime and early evening; buses and taxis later on.

By Subway: Unfortunately much of the subway's unenviable reputation is deserved: there *are* strange excrescences on the walls, unsavory pools on the floors, and unmentionable smells. And the whole system is fiendishly confusing: there are *no maps* on platforms, and stations like Times Square and 14th Street resemble Escher drawings. Announcements, when you get them, are indecipherable; and even though the graffiti has been eradicated, the stations are still dirty (you come out the other end looking as though you've spent the day in someone's fireplace).

Nevertheless you *will* end up using the subway, whether you like it or not. It is the fastest, cheapest and most convenient way of getting round the city, and every day 3.5 million passengers lurch along its 700 miles of track. If you are lucky, you will find yourself a nice, clean air-conditioned car, which whisks you from 14th Street to 96th in less than 10 minutes. Some people even enjoy the ride: the subway has 10 separate fan clubs; architecture critics enthuse over its labyrinths; there is Jim Dwyer and his mackintosh, New York's own subway correspondent; and there are the best subterranean buskers in the world.

You will manage perfectly well as long as you have a map, and you know whether you are traveling uptown or downtown. The fare (presently $1.25) is the same, no matter how far you go. Each station has a booth where you buy single tokens (brass coins 'good for one fare') or packets of 10. Deposit them in a slot in the turnstile and then make your way down to the track, unless you are traveling late at night, in which case you

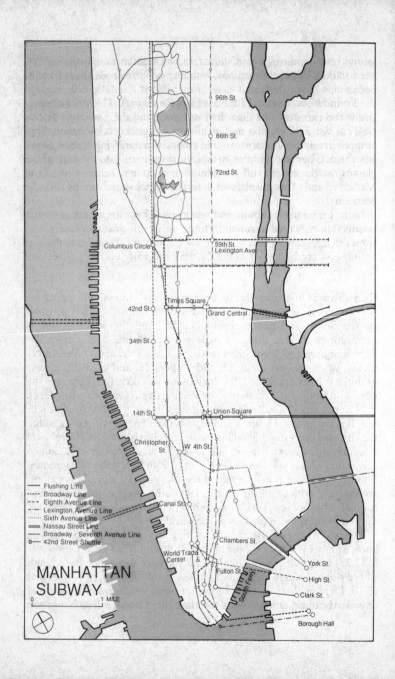

MANHATTAN SUBWAY

Flushing Line
Broadway Line
Eighth Avenue Line
Lexington Avenue Line
Sixth Avenue Line
Nassau Street Line
Broadway - Seventh Avenue Line
42nd Street Shuttle

0   1 MILE

96th St.
86th St.
72nd St.
Columbus Circle
59th St.
Lexington Ave.
Times Square
42nd St.
Grand Central
34th St.
14th St.
Union Square
Christopher St.
W 4th St.
Canal St.
Chambers St.
World Trade Center
Fulton St.
South Ferry
York St.
High St.
Clark St.
Borough Hall

should stay in one of the off-hours waiting areas marked in yellow. It is easy to hurdle over the turnstiles without paying and cops, waiting on the other side, know this.

Trains are referred to by a letter (A–S) or a number (1–7). They have a thousand other names (like the *Lexington Avenue Express*, the *IRT*, or *BMT*), but it's best just to concentrate on letters and numbers. The express trains are useful for getting around in a hurry, but make sure you don't miss your stop and end up God knows where. Take an express train to a stop near your destination and then swop to a local, which usually runs from an adjacent platform. Keep your wits about you, however, as express trains are notoriously capricious. They will suddenly start making local stops only, and vice versa. That was what the unintelligible station announcement was all about.

By Bus: New York's buses are schizophrenic: in the daytime they creep through the traffic at a snail's pace and it takes about a year to get from one end of 14th Street to the other; at night, Paris–Dakar racing drivers take over the wheel and you zoom along at breakneck speeds. Still, if you have time to spare, buses are the best way of seeing the city and getting to know New Yorkers. Cross-town buses can be deathly slow, but buses traveling up and down avenues are a little more bearable.

There is a special etiquette attached to boarding a bus. First of all, bus drivers will be mortally offended if you do not rush up and salute them like old friends, then thank them as you disembark, even though, strictly speaking, talking to the driver is against the law. (One is said to greet his passengers with 'Get'cher smile on, folks; nobody rides dis bus today widdout a smile . . .') Do not rashly jump the queue in your haste to greet him, however, or the other passengers will gang up and throw you off. Once inside *you must have a subway token or exact change.* (The fare is the same as for the subway. Unless you buy something – a packet of gum will do – shops and newsagents refuse point blank to give out change.) As you pay your fare, ask the driver for a free transfer, so you can change from a north-southbound to an east-westbound bus, or vice versa. The transfers last for about half a day, so you can get off, do some shopping, and then board your next bus for free. You exit from a door in the middle, which you push open yourself. Note that if you do not keep a tight hold on it, it is liable to swing back and knock you out.

Bus and subway information: tel 330 1234.
Lost and found: tel 625 6200.

By Taxi and Limousine: Taxi medallions cost a fortune (nearly

$100,000), but fares are about half what they are in London or Paris, and if there's no traffic it can be cheaper to share a taxi between four than to travel by subway. Legitimate taxis are yellow with a medallion on top; gypsy cabs are banned below 79th Street, but many are OK as long as you negotiate in advance. Many yellows refuse to go to places like Harlem and the Bronx (though legally they have to).

When a taxi is empty the central light on the roof is illuminated and you can hail it from the street. Get in, and then tell the driver your destination. It helps to have an idea of where you're going, because many New York taxi drivers are new to the city, and they can be vague about addresses. Apparently they don't carry maps on principle. Tips are 15 per cent.

If it starts to rain, go to a coffee bar and wait, in a philosophical frame of mind, for the rain to stop. You won't get a taxi even if you pray.

Limousines are not really limos at all, but elongated cars (with up to eight doors) run by cab companies for airport service.

NYC Taxis and Limousine Commission (complaints): tel 382 9301.

By Car: Even New Yorkers avoid driving in the city. Parking is a nightmare. If you do find a space, remember that it is illegal to park in front of a fire hydrant, and that parking often alternates from one side of the road to the other from morning to evening. The companies listed below hire cars:

Avis: tel (1 800) 331 1212.

Budget Rent-a-car: tel 807 8700.

Thrifty Rent-a-car: tel 325 West 34th Street, (868 6888).

By Bicycle: Most New York cyclists are a serious danger, to themselves and to others. Bicycle messengers bike the wrong way down streets at breakneck speeds. Make a mental note to look the *other* way when you cross the street. If you too have the death wish you can pick up second-hand bikes very cheaply from junk and charity shops.

Bicycle Hire

Metro Bicycles: 1311 Lexington Avenue, at 88th Street, tel 427 4450.

Pedal Pusher: 1306 2nd Avenue, between 68th and 69th Streets, tel 288 5592.

Travelers With Disabilities

A few years ago, a Federal judge ordered the transport system to provide complete access for the handicapped. The city facetiously proposed instead providing a chauffeur-driven limousine for every handicapped citizen—and they proved it would be cheaper than remaking all the buses and subway stops. Subways are still off limits, but there *are* excellent 'kneeling' buses equipped with hydraulic lifts to raise wheelchairs in and out of the bus. Most public buildings in New York now have ramps and facilities for the disabled, and of course nearly all of them have elevators. For information about public transport call (718) 596 8585. For more general information, contact the Mayor's Office for the Handicapped, at 52 Chambers Street, Office 206, New York NY 10007, tel 566 3913. There is also a special Theater Access Project for the disabled at 1501 Broadway, tel 221 1103.

Guided Tours

If you are new to New York, the best way of orienting yourself in the city is to take the Circle Line boat trip round the island (about $15), or, more expensively, a helicopter flight over the top. Otherwise, taking an ordinary bus from one end of Broadway to the other will be illuminating and cheap ($1.25).

Circle Line Cruise: leaves from West 42nd Street and the Hudson River at regular intervals, tel 563 3200, 3 hours.

Island Helicopter: leaves from the heliport at 34th Street and the East River. From $30 upwards, tel 683 4575.

Gray Line: 900 8th Avenue, between 53rd and 54th Streets, tel 397 2600. Bus tours. Long tours are very exhausting and the shortest trips are the best value.

Specialist Tours

Grand Central Terminal: organized by the Municipal Art Society, 457 Madison Avenue (tel 935 3960). The best tour in New York. Tours last an hour, are free and meet every Wednesday at the station at 12.30 pm at the Chemical Commuter Bank. The Municipal Art Society also organizes tours of all sorts of other Manhattan curiosities, including abandoned subway tunnels and the meat market (see p. 171).

Radio City Music Hall: 50th Street, at 6th Avenue, tel 246 4600 ext 263. Tours of Radio City's extraordinary interior leave at frequent intervals (see pp. 191–2.)

Federal Reserve Bank of New York: 33 Liberty Street, tel 720 6130.

Intriguing tour of the largest underground gold vault in the world. You must phone ahead, at least a week in advance (see p. 107).

Wild Man Steve Brill: tel (718) 291 6825. Botany courses **in the field**, in parks throughout New York including Central Park. Eccentric, but never boring.

The 92nd Street Y: Lexington Avenue, at 92nd Street, tel 427 6000. An excellent ever-changing program of tours all over the city: from visits to the Hasidic community in Williamsburg, photographers' studios in the Flatiron District, and Channel 13's television studios; to jaunts over the George Washington Bridge into New Jersey.

Park Rangers: tel 397 3080. Free tours of Manhattan parks. Highly recommended.

New York Stock Exchange: 20 Broad Street tel 656 5168, free (see pp. 104–5).

Art-Deco Society of New York: 145 Hudson Street, tel 385 2744.

Harlem Your Way!: 129 West 130th Street, tel 690 1687. Walking tours in Harlem of all shapes and sizes.

Harlem Spirituals: 1457 Broadway, tel 308 2594. Trips to gospel services, nightclubs, restaurants, shops and museums.

Penny Sightseeing Company: 1565 Park Avenue, tel 410 0080. Owner-operated coach tours of Harlem.

Barry Lewis: tel (718) 849 0297. Tours all over the city, by an architectural historian known as the king of Manhattan guides.

NBC Studio Tour: 30 Rockefeller Plaza, tel 664 4444.

Practical A–Z

Calendar of Events

NB: to the British, Americans write dates backwards, so 5/20/92 means 20 May 1992.

For precise dates, times and details, consult the *Village Voice*, the Metropolitan section in the Friday edition of the *New York Times* or contact the Visitors and Conventions Bureau (tel 397 8222).

September
The year starts in September. New York suddenly revives after the long, steamy, catatonic summer: everyone scurries back to work, and the city feels almost spring-like as the racing, football, hockey, theater, opera and art gallery seasons get off the ground.

First Monday: **Labor Day Weekend**. Supposed to honor the American worker, Labor Day signifies the end of the summer, and is observed religiously, whatever the weather. Crowds mob the beaches on Long Island, which by the following weekend will be deserted—even in sweltering temperatures—until the next Memorial Day in May. On the Saturday there is **Wigstock**, a transvestite version of Woodstock in Tompkins Square on the Lower East Side. The audience wears wigs, and drag queens sing along to back-up tapes under an outdoor bandshell. In Brooklyn there is the very festive **West Indian Carnival** with floats, dancing and concerts.

19: **Feast of San Gennaro**, in Little Italy on Mulberry Street, for 10 days. An effigy of the saint, stuck with dollar bills, is paraded down the street, but apart from that, the crowds, burgers, goldfish bowls and doughnuts don't seem especially Italian.

Late Sept: **New York Film Festival**, until early October. It's worth making a point of visiting the city especially for the festival which in the past has had the premieres of Bertolucci's *The Conformist*, Būnuel's *The Discreet Charm of the Bourgeoisie* and Truffaut's *Day for Night*. To be sure of getting tickets, you should apply to Lincoln Center in advance, though often it is easier to get returns on the day of a showing than people imagine (tel 369 1911).

Last Sunday: **Atlantic Antic**, along Atlantic Avenue in Brooklyn. A proper *casbah*, courtesy of Brooklyn's exuberent Middle Eastern neighborhood on Atantic Avenue. There are belly dancers, *durbek* drums and even camels, as well as exotic foods and spices—*babaganouj*, myrrh, frankincense, and pastries streaming honey.

October
12: **Columbus Day**. New York's Italians are proud of their ancestor, though to their fury the Spanish-Americans persist in claiming him as theirs. Nevertheless, the parade up 5th Avenue from 44th Street to 72nd is really an Italian event. There are usually about 20,000 marchers, 28 marching bands and 18 floats as well as a tableau of Ligurian flowers. The quincentennial in 1992 is beginning to loom.

Third Sunday: **New York Marathon**. Watching the thousands of sweating legs and pale faces on television, you will be relieved to be left out. The joggers puff 26.3 miles through all five boroughs.

31: **Hallowe'en**. Children dress up in grotesque costumes and pelt each other and passers-by with eggs and shaving foam. Trick-and-treating is thought dangerous in Manhattan but is quite common in Queens, the Bronx and Brooklyn. All over the city, residents decorate their houses with pumpkins, seasonal bunches of red maize and, sometimes, cobwebs and ghoulish mannequins of ghosts and witches. If you are in the city do not miss the night time **Hallowe'en Parade**, in which an extraordinary array of revoltingly freakish costumes somehow threads a lunatic way through the West Village to Washington Arch at the bottom of 5th Avenue.

November

Last Thursday: **Thanksgiving**. Macy's department store organizes a parade of rubber blow-up cartoon characters and celebrities, which goes from the Natural History Museum down to Herald Square. Rather than attend the parade, watch the surreal proceedings the night before when grotesque Donald Ducks and Minnie Mouses are inflated with helium in the park next to the museum. Thanksgiving is supposed to commemorate the first harvest of the European settlers, but it has turned into a dress rehearsal for Christmas. Families get together to tell each other what they want for Christmas, and eat turkey, cranberry sauce and pumpkin pie (which can taste like a cross between mashed swede and baby food). After Thanksgiving, New Yorkers give up working and brace themselves for the party-going and present-buying lead up to Christmas.

Last Friday: the day after Thanksgiving, and the biggest shopping day of the year in America (which is why Macy's throws a parade).

December

New Yorkers get noticeably more hysterical as shopping for presents turns into a city-wide obsession.

Early Dec: At some point over the first few days of December (consult the newspapers for details) there is the ritual **lighting of the Christmas tree** in Rockefeller Center. Fifth Avenue is spruced up with the country's classiest Chistmas decorations, including the massive 57th Street illuminated snowflake and the Rockefeller Center angels. Window decorations in shops like Lord & Taylor's and Bergdorf Goodman's are superb.

31: On **New Year's Eve** revelers gather to watch a peculiar ritual in which a Big Apple descends from the top of Times Tower, in Times Square, to the bottom. People get very drunk, and the New York Roadrunners Club organizes a **midnight run** in Central Park. In **St Marks Church** on 10th Street and 2nd Avenue about a hundred poets read in the New Year with extracts from their own work (tel 228 9682).

January

First week: The **Winter Antiques Show** at the Seventh Regiment Armory, Park Avenue at 67th Street (tel 665 5250 for more details).

Last week: **Chinese New Year** (tel 267 5780 for exact date and further details). Parades, firecrackers, dancing dragons and restaurants fit to burst.

February
22: **Sales** in stores on Washington's birthday. More sales on 12th February (Lincoln's birthday) and 14th February (St Valentine's).

March
Mid March: **New Directors, New Films**: a festival of 25 new films at the Museum of Modern Art (tel 708 9480 for more details).

17: **St Patrick's Day Parade**. Now one of the biggest holidays in US cities—a substitute for a carnival in which New York's rowdiest Irish-Americans paint their faces green and descend on 5th Avenue and the bars in Manhattan. Not a good day for political discussions.

25: **Greek Independence Day Parade**. A rather more sober affair.

April
Easter: New York celebrates **Easter** with typical gusto and yet another parade. Children hard-boil eggs and color them with special dying kits, and on the Saturday before Easter there is an **egg-rolling contest** on the Great Lawn in Central Park.

Mid April: **Cherry tree blossom** in the Conservatory Garden in Central Park and the Brooklyn Botanical Gardens.

15: Income-tax deadline: on the steps outside the General Post Office, Hebrew National hand out free **hot dogs** at midnight to anyone making a last-minute submission.

Last weekend: **Gramercy Park Flower Show**.

May
Second Sunday: **Brooklyn Bridge Day** and **Mothering Sunday**. Hallmark, the greetings card company, has also created Father's Day, Grandmother's Day and Mother-in-Law's Day. There are celebrations on the bridge.

Mid May: **Ukrainian Festival** on East 7th Street between 2nd and 3rd Avenues. One of the city's jolliest street festivals with tombolas, Ukrainian wooden toys, Ukrainian food and painted eggs, known as *pysanky*.

17: **Martin Luther King Jr. Memorial Day Parade**, to celebrate the achievements of the civil rights leader.

18

Third week: **9th Avenue Food Festival**. An unmissable two-day street festival of food. Stalls and shops between 37th Street and 54th sell food made by communities from all over the city—Italian, Argentinian, Greek, Indian, Ukrainian, Mexican, West Indian, Spanish, Japanese and Haitian. Not surprisingly, the event, attended by thousands, is immensely popular.

Last Monday: **Memorial Day**. Beaches officially open and summer begins in earnest.

June

All month: **Metropolitan Opera** puts on free performances in the Sheep Meadow in Central Park attended by over 100,000 people (tel 360 8211 for more details). Also in Central Park, the outdoor Delacorte Theater puts on two plays for its **Shakespeare in the Park** festival. Free tickets are distributed at 6 pm on the day of the performance, one per person (tel 535 5630). Bring a picnic.

First Sunday: **Puerto Rican Day Parade**, one of the more raucous parades, though with so many different nationalities now at large in the city it sometimes seems as though hardly a day goes by without someone having a march down 5th Avenue. (The only people who don't are Wasps.) For dates and times of all parades tel 397 8222.

10: **Feast of San Antonio**. A smaller version of the Feast of San Gennaro in September.

Late June: **Lesbian and Gay Pride Day Parade**. Marchers make their way down 5th Avenue to Washington Square, and thence all over the West Village.

July

As the heat builds up, New Yorkers get increasingly irritable.

All month: Julliard School students perform a mixed bag of **garden concerts** for free at the Museum of Modern Art (tel 708 9480).

4: **Independence Day**. Organized firework displays all over the city, and in the Lower East Side, highly disorganized firecracker wars. Try to view it all from a rooftop, or from Riverside Park. The next day most people abandon Manhattan for beaches on Long Island.

Second Sunday: **Fiestas de Loiza Aldea**. A version of the Festival of St James the Apostle held in the Puerto Rican town of Loiza Aldea. Mass is held at the Church of San Pueblo on Lexington Avenue and East

117th Street, and an effigy of St James is carried to Ward's Island via the footbridge on 102nd Street. After the procession there is a Latin American festival on the island.

Full Moon: **Feast of O-Bon**: Japanese festival of music and dancing held in Riverside Park on the Saturday nearest the Full Moon, moongazers gather in Central Park.

August
As humidity levels rise, most New Yorkers leave the city. The ones who stay behave in an erratic, rather eccentric manner—some say because the psychiatrists are all on holiday.

Last week: **Harlem Week**. Parades, exhibitions and sports events in Harlem.

Climate/Best Time To Go

Extremes of temperature are severe compared to places like London or Paris. Mid-summer and mid-winter are the worst times of the year to visit the city. In the winter it is bitterly cold. It starts snowing well before Christmas, and the first time you mince down an icy sidewalk you will understand why penguins walk on the sides of their feet. There is such a thing as a 'wind chill factor', which means that if you leave a smidgeon of flesh exposed to the wind you will feel a burning sensation, and when you look in the mirror you will see your nose has gone the colour of hot coals. The best way to warm up is to stand in the middle of the road on top of one of the manholes that puff out city steam. New Yorkers, meanwhile, stay ensconced in their boiling apartments, and if they have to go out they generally manage it without stepping into the elements. (It is possible to get from 34th Street to almost as far as Central Park without going outside—through department stores, Rockefeller Center, etc. Most Manhattanites know the route, but it is extremely complex.)

In the summer New York gets unbearably steamy, even in temperatures as low as 75°. If you don't have air-conditioning, you will find yourself hanging about in freezing department stores and restaurants and catching a cold. When it gets tropically humid, electric thunderstorms break out, and that is the best time to rush off to the top of the Empire State Building or onto your roof. You have about half an hour before a monstrous flash flood breaks out and drenches you from head to toe.

If you can possibly arrange it, go in the spring, between middle of April and the end of May, or in the autumn or fall, from the middle of September to the end of November. The seasons change overnight. One day it is snowy and cold, and the next the leaves have all come out, and all the restaurants have moved tables out onto the sidewalk. The light in New York is startlingly beautiful in the spring and autumn.

Americans are just as obsessed by the weather as the British and their weather forecasts are brought to the screens by ultra-sophisticated technology. What's more, they are always accurate. It's worth switching on the weather channel before you venture outside, as air-conditioning and central heating can be misleading.

Consulates

Britain: 845 3rd Ave., tel 752 8400
Australia: 636 5th Ave., tel 245 4000
New Zealand: 630 5th Ave., tel 586 0060
Canada: 1251 6th Ave., tel 768 2400
Ireland: 515 Madison Ave., tel 319 2555
France: 934 5th Ave., tel 606 3688
Italy: 690 Park Ave., tel 737 9100
Portugal: 630 5th Ave., tel 765 2980
Argentina: 12 West 56th St., tel 603 0400
Barbados: 800 2nd Ave., tel 867 8435
Estonia: 9 Rockefeller Plaza, tel 247 1450
India: 3 East 64th St., tel 879 7800
Iceland: 370 Lexington Ave., tel 686 4100
Trinidad and Tobago: 420 Lexington Ave., tel 682 7272

Crime

Organized crime is still big in New York: there is gang warfare in Chinatown, between the Vietnamese and Chinese tongs; and there are thriving Japanese, Cuban, Colombian and, of course, Italian underworlds. In 1989, 30 innocent bystanders – or 'mushrooms' – were shot down by stray bullets fired by drug gangs. And in 1990 homicides topped 2000 for the first time.

If you have never been to New York before, you will be unaccustomed to the tension on the streets. You will also discover that New Yorkers are obsessed with crime stories: the subject dominates day-to-day conversations as well as the media. Nevertheless, New York is not the most dangerous city in the US. The crime that concerns visitors most of all is mugging, although statistically the chances of being mugged are actually quite slim (something like 30,000 to one). You can make them even smaller by using common sense:

Don't wander alone down empty streets at night. When you walk around keep your wits about you and look confident. Sometimes a glum look and highly strung manner can make you vulnerable.

Don't dawdle in areas which are known danger-spots. The Port Authority bus station is the haunt of **chicken-hawks**, named after a kind of vulture from the mid-West which preys on vulnerable animals. Times Square is riddled with **three card monte players** whose stooges pickpocket bystanders, and **hustlers** – kids aged between 9 and 17—who hang out in the video arcades and find easy pickings by rifling through pockets and snatching purses. One trick is to bump into a victim with an ice-cream, mop up his or her jacket and incidentally lift a wallet.

Don't wear conspicuous jewelry.

Carry a spare $20 on your person as 'mugger's money'.

If you are mugged, try to act calmly, and you may avoid violence.

Report any thefts to the nearest police station (call 374 5000 to find out which one is nearest to you). Do not be deterred by the police officers who are daunting figures with riot bats and guns, brusque manners, flabby beer guts and names like Serge, Jesus and Rollo. They will give you a statement so you can claim back the theft from your insurance.

New York has the cleverest confidence tricksters. Don't believe anyone who tells you an intricate story involving lost cars, women or money. Pickpockets have a nasty trick of pointing at a victim and bawling 'Stop, thief!'

Police and Emergency: tel 911
Sex Crimes Report Line: tel 267 7273
Crime Victims Hotline: tel 577 7777

Curtness

In public New Yorkers are infamously curt, and at some point you will brush up against a stereotypically gruff New Yorker. If you are good at being rude, let rip, remembering that New Yorkers are better at being rude than anyone else in the world, and that telling them they are wrong will only inflame their powers of vitriol and invective. Sometimes this can be quite fun. Alternatively, you can take refuge in politeness. The effect is quite astonishing, and confronted with a kindly word the average New Yorker melts like butter.

In private, New Yorkers are spectacularly polite: they open doors for women, shake hands at the slightest opportunity, light your cigarettes and insist on paying for meals. They hardly ever swear in front of ladies, and if they do they apologize. Most New Yorkers are rather flummoxed by the English way of teasing, and sometimes they even mistake an affectionate jibe for rudeness. Luckily they are much too polite to take offence.

Domestic Hazards

For the unitiated, **Bathrooms** are minefields. 'Bathroom' can mean just a loo, or the whole ballgame: showers, bidets jacuzzis, and deluxe loos. 'Restrooms', however, only have lavatories. Often they don't have handles for flushing, but rubberized nobs on the floor which you step on.

Taps, baths and showers are more difficult to understand. The first time you turn on the taps or 'faucets' to have a bath, you will probably get drenched by a torrent from above. Somewhere on the wall, there will be an unlabeled tap which diverts the water from the shower to the bath. Usually the water comes out of one tap, not two, and to change the temperature you turn it. Instead of plugs, many baths have a lever, located somewhere next to the tub, which you have to lift and twist. At the end of your shower it's polite to divert the water supply back to the bath taps, so the next person doesn't get drowned. And watch out for slippery, soapy floors: they cause all sorts of nasty accidents.

American locks are quite tricky. Interior doors have little buttons in the center, which sometimes slip into place and lock you in by accident.

Front doors have at least three different locks, and often special police locks—iron bars which slide into the door as you leave. They are to keep out intruders equipped with battering rams.

For natural hazards, like rats and cockroaches, see pp. 37 and 39.

Electricity

It is difficult to electrocute yourself in New York as the voltage is only 110. You can buy transformers for razors and hairdryers in places like Woolworths and Lamstons, in pharmacies or drug stores. If you are taking a computer, you should purchase an adapter in advance from the company you bought it from. You should also invest in something called a power buster, since New York suffers from power spikes, or surges of electricity, which gradually destroy the brain of the machine till it dies.

To foreigners, light switches can be a bit perplexing. To turn a light on, you put the switch up, not down; bedside lamps have switches that you *turn* in a clockwise direction.

Emergencies

Call 911 for police, ambulance and fire.
Police: tel 374 5000 to find the location of the nearest precinct.

Homeless New Yorkers

Nobody is sure how many people are homeless in the city, but estimates range from 50,000 to 60,000, and sometimes as high as 90,000. You will come across beggars and homeless people whether you walk down the most notorious stretches of the Bowery or past the smartest shops on 5th Avenue. Some are mentally ill or disabled, some are Vietnam War Veterans, and many have simply fallen on hard times. Some New Yorkers give money, and some do not, on the principle that the money would be better spent by a charity for the homeless.

Insurance

It is absolutely **essential** to take out an insurance policy before leaving home. There is no Health Service in the States, and the cost of breaking a leg is something from which you might not recover. Once you are in the US, keep your insurance policy in a safe place, and travel with a credit

24

card so you can be sure of getting immediate medical attention if you fall ill. Most insurance companies will only pay you back your costs after you have applied for the money in writing and the first question you'll be asked, as you stand in front of the doctor dripping blood on his shoes, is whether you have any money. Make sure the policy covers you for at least £150,000. Under the aegis of London Student Travel (tel 071 730 3402), the Campus Travel Group has one of the cheapest deals available, insuring students and anyone aged under 35 for up to £250,000. It has offices, under the umbrella of the USIT travel organization, at the New York Student Center, 356 West 34th Street (tel 239 4247/8).

Lavatories

In the past New Yorkers have relieved themselves with relative ease. During the 19th century, one of the city's most innovative vendors ever patrolled the streets providing customers with a bucket and a billowing cloak. During the LaGuardia administration in the 1940s, there were weekly inspections of 1676 lavatories, and in the final report only 12 were found to be dirty. In recent years, however, the lavatory has become a disappearing species. So much so that in 1990 four homeless people began filing a lawsuit against the city for failing to provide public conveniences. The city is now considering spending $3 million on 100 automatic loos modelled on those in London. For the moment, however, finding a public lavatory involves a tactical maneuver, though being aware of the various euphemisms in use (bathroom, restroom, even sitting room, comfort station and men's/ladies' room) will help.

Scout out WCs in public institutions (libraries, hospitals, museums, universities and municipal offices).

Sneak into the lobby of a big hotel, a department store or a public atrium – like the AT&T Building or Trump Tower. The swankiest loos in New York are in Barney's department store in Chelsea. There are murals painted on the walls and seats covered in a see-through tube of revolving plastic.

Sweep into a restaurant, pretending you belong there. Remember that some restaurants foil this strategy by providing patrons with a key to the loo.

Every time you stop for refreshments, remind yourself to use the lavatory.

Medical Matters

If you need to see a doctor, look up 'Clinics' and 'Physicians and Surgeons' in the Yellow Pages. The Stuyvesant Polyclinic on 2nd Avenue and East 9th Street is one of the cheapest in the city.

Remember that in America, you say 'I am sick', not 'I am ill'; but 'sick' can also means repellent or revolting, as in 'pornography is sick'. Also, 'gas' means wind, 'mucous' means catarrh, 'cramps' are period pains, and 'jock itch' a rash round the testicles. The doctor will send you to a 'pharmacist' or chemist to get 'medication' or medicine.

Police, fire, and ambulances: tel 911
Doctors' Emergency Service: tel (212) 879 1000
Dentists' Emergency Service: tel (212) 879 1000
Doctors On Call: 24-hour house-call service, tel 737 2333
St Lukes-Roosevelt Hospital: has a 24-hour emergency room at 458 West 59th Street, tel 523 4000
St Vincent's Hospital: has a 24-hour emergency room at 7th Avenue and 11th Street, tel 790 7000
Rape Help Line: tel (212) 732 7706
Bellevue Hospital: 1st Avenue and East 29th Street, tel (561 4141)
24-Hour Pharmacy: Kaufman's Pharmacy at Lexington Avenue and 50th Street, tel 755 2266
The Margaret Sanger Center: 380 2nd Avenue and East 17th Street – for sympathetic family planning, contraception and abortion advice, tel 677 6474
Beth Israel Medical Center: Stuyvesant Square, on 19th Street and 2nd Avenue, tel 420 2000, has a 24-hour emergency room
Animal Bites: tel 334 2618
Contagious Disease: tel 566 7132
Food Poisoning: tel 334 7755
Lead Poisoning: tel 334 7893
Fifth Avenue Center for Counseling and Psychotherapy: 43 5th Avenue, tel 989 2990
New York Psychoanalytic Institute: Cheap therapy offered by psychiatrists-in-training, 247 East 82nd Street, 879 6900.

Media

Television
At first watching television in America is quite mesmerizing, but it soon

26

gets boring. One of the problems is that the listings are utterly mystifying – whether you consult an apparently straightforward daily like the *New York Times* or the bible of America, the monthly *TV Guide*. There are scores and scores of channels, and none of the letters and numbers listed seem to correspond to the letters and numbers on the television dial. None of which really matters, because most of the channels show exactly the same menu: commercials, game shows, chat shows, cop shows, soap operas, sitcoms and more commercials. They give you a strange view of the national collective unconscious.

Commercials dominate everything else, which is unfortunate because almost all American advertising is astonishingly artless. Films are chopped up into 15-minute slots so companies can squeeze in as many commercials as possible, and sitcoms and TV dramas have commercials sandwiched *in between* the credits.

CBS, on channel 2, NBC on 4 and ABC on 7 all do news reports, although there is only sketchy coverage of international news. Channel 13, or PBS, the only non-commercial station, shows imports from Britain – quintessentially English costume dramas, Agatha Christies and Sherlock Holmes. Its Macneil, Lehrer Newshour is excellent, and the other popular shows are *Twin Peaks*, Channel 4's *Saturday Night Live*, *The David Letterman Hour*, the American *Blind Date*, and *Lifestyles of the Rich and Famous*.

Television fans can get **free tickets** to game and chat shows from the New York Convention and Visitors Bureau (2 Columbus Circle); from the NBC desk in Rockefeller Center's RCA Building; and from 5th or 6th Avenue, where TV personel shanghai passers-by to top up studio audiences.

Cable

Most apartments and hotels are equipped with cable TV, which is much more watchable than broadcast TV, if sometimes quite bizarre. HBO and MAX show recently released movies, TNT is a blissful channel specializing in old films and revivals, while MTV shows rock videos and interviews round the clock. The other channels are dominated by out-landish Latin American soap operas, featuring television's most stagger-ingly inept actors; and by ranting religious fundamentalists who raise money and draw audiences according to the same premises that made indulgences such a success in the Italian Renaissance. Channel J, the porn channel, boasts Ugly George who scours Manhattan with a video camera in search of ladies who will take off their clothes; Daniel Jay who hosts a live phone-in while sitting naked on a mattress; and Robin Byrd, a chatshow hostess who strips in front of her guests while she lip-syncs to a jingle called 'Baby Let Me Bang Your Box'.

Radio
New York radio is excellent, despite the rather uninspiring names of the stations. AM stations play mostly country music, salsa and religious fundamentalists. Below is a random selection of the most interesting:

FM Stations

WNYC (94 MHz)	The best news bulletins, and informative talks on New York's politics and arts.
WBLS (107.5 MHz)	'Urban Contemporary'. Black-owned disco station currently rivaling WRKS, KISS-98, (98.7 MHz) as the trendiest station.
WCBS (101 MHz)	Rock and roll oldies and the top 40.
WKCR (89.9 MHz)	Columbia University's own station, best for jazz.
WQXR (96.3 MHz)	Conservative classical music station. The main rival to the more adventurous WNCN (104.3 MHz).
WPAT (93.1 MHz)	King of supermarket music: muzak, easy listening, lifestyle and what is known as 'beautiful music'.

AM Stations

WWRl (1600 KHz)	Rhythm and blues, gospel, and the creepy charismatic preacher, the Reverend Ike.
WADO (1280 KHz)	Salsa and Spanish Language.

Newspapers
The two main tabloids are the crime-obsessed *New York Post* and the *Daily News*. The *News* has been the city's best-selling paper for decades and is considered the better of the two, for its crispy headlines; its funnies page with cartoons like Doonesbury; the razor-sharp, impassioned style of the Pulitzer-winning Irish columnist Jimmy Breslin; and its down-to-earth restaurant reviews. The Sunday Entertainment and

Friday Weekend sections have good film reviews and listings of current events. The streetwise coverage of rock and jazz is always spot on, and the Washington column is excellent. Like most tabloids, the *Post* makes gripping reading, even if its politics aren't quite so congenial. The Breslin equivalent is Pete Hamill; there are first-rate drama reviews by the British writer Clive Barnes; and 'Page Six', the gossip column, is always juicy.

The traditionally liberal *New York Times* is the most venerable of all the papers and has the best daily international news, although at first its prehistoric typeface and staid layout make it almost unreadable. Thursday's Science Times is fascinating, and the jazz, classical music and drama reviews are meaty and reliable. Each week, 3754 tons of newsprint are used to create the *Sunday Times*, and a single, gigantic paper feels as though it weighs at least that much. The first edition comes out on Saturday night; reading it keeps you in bed until Sunday afternoon.

New York's only 'alternative' paper, the weekly *Village Voice*, is an excellent introduction to the city. It has comprehensive listings and good coverage of art, film, music and books in the city, alongside sections on international and metropolitan politics. The monthly Literary Supplement is in a class of its own.

At supermarket checkouts, you will see copies of the *National Enquirer*, and battalions of rivals including the *National Examiner* and the *Weekly World News*. They are worth buying for the headlines alone: 'Brave Doctors Remove Live Bomb From Man's Chest', 'JFK Was Related To King Arthur', 'Pit Bull Savages Killer Shark', 'Top Model Eats Herself To Death', and 'Your Shoe Size Tells How Long You'll Live'.

Money

Take double the amount of money you think you need. New York is expensive, and you will find yourself wanting to buy more things than you thought possible. Besides the hotel, $20 a day is the absolute minimum you need to exist, and you will feel more comfortable on $50–60.

The safest way to carry money is in the form of **travelers' cheques**. If you buy them in dollars, you can use them instead of cash in most shops. (If you plan to use them in a restaurant, don't let on until you have eaten your meal, as some waiters snarl at the inconvenience.) Don't bring cheques made out in sterling or other currencies: it is a bore having to change them in banking hours, and you may find that some banks refuse to cash them.

Lost or Stolen Travelers' Cheques
American Express: tel 248 4584
Citicorp: tel 980 9099
Thomas Cook: tel 921 3800

Credit Cards
These are invaluable. Equipped with a credit card, you will be able to bail yourself out of most emergencies. The financial cogs of America turn on plastic, and using cash brands you as an alien.

American **currency** is pretty straightforward. There are $1, $5, $10, $20, $50 and $100 notes or bills. When New Yorkers hand over change, they will say 'six-fifty', and never 'six dollars fifty'. There are 100 cents to the dollar and four principal types of coin:

Penny: small copper coin equal to one cent. It is practically useless, and by the time you go home you will have enough of them jangling around in your pockets to sink an ocean liner. This is because of the $8^{1}/_{4}$ city and state sales tax which is jacked onto everything.
Nickel: zinc-nickel coin worth 5 cents. Almost as useless as pennies.
Dime: silver, much smaller than the nickel, but worth double.
Quarter: large silver coin with rough coppery edges. Save these up, because they are useful for telephones and on buses where you have to pay with change or subway tokens.

Banks are open between 9 and 3 or 3.30, and closed on weekends.

Changing Money Out of Banking Hours
American Express Travel Service: 822 Lexington Avenue, tel 758 6510. There are nine other American Express counters in Manhattan. Call and ask for details of their locations.
Chequepoint USA: 551 Madison Avenue, tel 980 6443. (Open weekdays 8–6, weekends 10–6.)
Deak-Perera: 41 East 42nd Street, tel 757 6915. (Open weekdays 9–5, Saturdays 10–3.)

Harold Reuter & Co: Pan-Am Building, 200 Park Avenue, Room 332 East, tel 661 0826. (Open weekdays 8.30–4.)

Packing

New Yorkers like to dress up, and you will not feel out of place in your snazziest outfit. At work, the dress code is surprisingly formal, and women can raise eyebrows if they wear trousers or skirts above the knee, and don't wear stockings and high heels. Bow ties and braces (in the US: suspenders), are a status symbol, and only those men at the very summit of the corporate ladder wear them. Outside offices, however, you will soon notice that literally anything goes, no matter how sexy or loony. For the daytime, bring lots of layers, so you can strip off in sudden changes of temperature. Above all, bring a pair of comfortable walking shoes like Doc Martens and carry a smart pair around in a knapsack so you can make a quick change. (Similarly, in case you suddenly decide to dash into a fancypants restaurant, men may find it helpful to carry around a jacket and tie.) Many American women wear revoltingly dirty sneakers on their way to work and then do a quick change at the entrance. In the winter people wear an ensemble of black furry hats, pink earmuffs, orange plastic galoshes, yellow raincoats and red balaclavas without a trace of embarrassment. Woolworths sell peculiar plastic skins which fit over shoes and high heels and are very useful in the rain.

You can buy almost anything in New York, except soluble aspirin. Bring opera glasses or binoculars for looking at the tops of skyscrapers and inside apartments. Camera film and medicines are generally pretty expensive in New York, unless you buy them in discount stores or from Canal Street. Plastic knapsacks, earmuffs and collapsible umbrellas are ludicrously cheap, however, and indispensable in the spring, summer and autumn. New York is not sympathetic to insomniacs, light sleepers or nervous dispositions, and if you think you might be woken up by klaxons, police sirens, chomping garbage trucks or loud bangs, invest in a pair of ear-plugs.

Post Offices

The post office is one of America's few nationalized businesses, and it is staggeringly inefficient. Going to the General Post Office on 33rd Street and 8th Avenue can be a harrowing experience: it is a bureacratic labyrinth of over 5000 rooms, including hospitals, wheezing elevators, and the most hopeful inscription in the world, from Herodotus ('Neither snow nor rain nor heat nor gloom of night stays these couriers from the swift completion of their appointed rounds'). It is worth braving the chaos, however, for the **auctions** of year-old unclaimed parcels, which are held in the bowels of the General Post Office building every month (tel 330 2932 for times and dates). Bidders aren't allowed to open the lots, but at the viewing they can shake the parcels and boxes and prod them.

If you are in the city on 15 April at midnight, you can join the impromptu gathering on the steps of the post office when Hebrew National hands out **free hot-dogs** to people dashing in to meet the deadline for their income-tax returns. In the summer, keep an eye out for Manhattan postmen, who look impossibly flash in special-regulation navy shorts and peaked caps.

Some shops, hotels and supermarkets have machines selling stamps, but they cost an infuriating 10 cents extra each, so you are better off going to one of the city's 59 post offices (open Mon–Fri, 9–5, and Sat 9–12). Mail can take three to five days to get from state to state, and there is only one postal delivery a day. Posting a letter is not quite as straight-forward as it sounds, because post boxes are camouflaged as blue rubbish bins. Make sure you write a return address on the top lefthand corner, to avoid your letter or parcel turning up in the auction at the General Post Office. Sending a parcel by surface mail is quite cheap but the speed of its arrival apparently depends on the caprices of the weather. Usually it takes about two months to get to Europe, and in case it doesn't arrive at all, you can insure it. Rules and regulations are dementing: make sure the parcel is wrapped in brown paper and stuck together with gummed paper, or the post office will reject it.

Public Holidays

Contrary to the belief that Manhattan is open all of the time, banks, shops and some businesses are liable to close on the following days:

1 January	New Year's Day
Third Monday in January	Martin Luther King's Birthday
12 February	Abraham Lincoln's Birthday
Third Monday in February	George Washington's Birthday
Third Monday in May	Memorial Day
4 July	Independence Day

32

First Monday in September	Labor Day
Second Monday in October	Columbus Day
11 November	Veteran's Day
Fourth Thursday in November	Thanksgiving
25 December	Christmas Day

Museums are mostly closed on Mondays and open late on Tuesdays, though there are some variations, in particular the Natural History Museum, which is open all week with three late nights, and MOMA, which is closed on Wednesdays and open late on Thursdays. Sadly many churches are kept closed except on Sundays and for weekday evening services. Shops in midtown and the Financial District keep business hours, drugstores are usually open till late, and shops in the East and West Villages stay open until 9 or 10.

Smoking

Smokers are the new pariahs of the city. Anyone who rashly lights up in public can expect torrents of invective, and even punches and swipes. Smoking is banned on all public transport, and in banks, hotel lobbies, sports stadiums, restrooms, theaters and some supermarkets; all restaurants are obliged to have non-smoking sections. Haranguing smokers has become a favorite pastime.

Telephones

Telephone operators treat you like an old chum, they inquire how you are; and they all have names like Dwight, Caspar and Marlon. A ringing tone sounds like a single doleful moan, an engaged tone is fast and chirrupy, and distant crackling classical music means you've been put on 'hold'. Sometimes, in the middle of a conversation, you hear a kind of clucking. This is 'call waiting', telling you that someone else is calling your number. You can put the person you are talking to on hold while you talk to the other caller.

It costs 25 cents to make a local call from a **public telephone**, or a phone booth, and there are pay phones on practically every street corner in Manhattan. None of these are equipped with the indispensable Yellow Pages (businesses and services) or White Pages (private numbers and businesses), and to consult these you will have to venture into a hotel, restaurant or department store.

The **area code** for Manhattan and the Bronx is 212 and the code for Brooklyn, Queens and Staten Island is 718. Whenever you use an area code make sure you preface it with a 1 (i.e. dial 1 (718) to call Brooklyn from Manhattan). 1 800 numbers are 'toll free', which means they cost nothing, and some numbers come in the old-fashioned form of letters corresponding to the alphabet on the dial (there are phone sex lines with numbers like 970 INYA; whereas COP SHOT is a line for people with information concerning the death of a police officer, and the New York Aquarium is (718) 265 FISH).

You can make **international calls** from a public payphone, but you will have to come armed with at least $5.50 in quarters. To make your call you must first dial 0 for the operator, who will tell you the cost of the call and wait for you to deposit the money before making the connection. To reverse the charges, call the operator and ask to make a 'collect' call. Alternatively, there is very useful number for connecting yourself directly to the British operator for free: 1 800 44 55 667. If you have access to a private phone, you can make international calls directly. Dial 011 to connect yourself to an international line, then dial the code for the country you are calling (the UK is 44) and, finally, dial the city code (071 or 081 for London) *without* the 0 (so to call London you punch in: 011 44 71). The cheap rate for international calls is from 6 to 7, although your European friends won't be too pleased if you forget the 5-hour time difference.

Useful Numbers
Emergencies: 911 for police, ambulance and fire.
Police: 374 5000 to find the location of the nearest precinct.
Operator: 0
Directory Enquiries: 411 (Manhattan) 1 555 1212 (local)
   1 + (area code) + 555 1212 (for numbers in other area codes).
Speaking Clock: 976 1616
Sportsphone: 976 1313
Weather: 976 1212
Jokes: 976 3838
Traffic: 830 7666
Dial-a-Dinner: 779 1222
Insomniacs' Hotline: 439 2992
Dial-a-Prayer: 246 4200
Dial-a-Hearing-Test: 737 4000

Time

It is 3500 miles across the Atlantic, and New York is 5 hours behind London. For a few weeks in March, however, it is 6 hours behind, since London changes to Summer time (Daylight Saving Time) about three weeks before America. Chicago, which operates on Central Time, is an hour behind New York and California, operating on Pacific Time, is three hours behind.

Tipping

In America, everyone expects a tip. Remember to tip the good-looking barman who sells you your pint, the grinning bell-hop who carries your luggage, the grouchy concierge who hands you a towel in the restroom, the unctuous *maître d'* who shows you to your table and the chatty taxi driver who drives you to your door (15–20 per cent). Waiters, waitresses and barmen are all underpaid, and rely on tips to top up their salaries. If they don't get a tip they will sometimes abandon their tables and turn nasty. Tips in restaurants are between 15 and 20 per cent, which you calculate in seconds by doubling the sales tax ($8^1/_4$ per cent) and adding or subtracting for good or bad service.

Tourist Information

Contact the New York Convention and Visitors Bureau, 2 Columbus Circle, tel 397 8222. It has free leaflets and subway and bus maps. Or try the information stand at 1465 Broadway in Times Square. The Restaurant Hotline (838 6644) answers questions about prices and menus, and *New York Magazine* has recorded listings about current attractions, tel 880 0755. For listings of theater, film, and the arts and for classified ads see the weekly editions of the *Village Voice*.

Topics

A Bestiary of New York

New York's first beast was *Rutiodon Manhattanensis*, the Manhattan Grubber. An endearing creature resembling a 12 ft long crocodile, it spent most of its time snouting around in swamps for giant worms. In its heyday, about two million years ago, the grubber lived among bisons with 6 ft long horns, beavers weighing as much as overweight truck-drivers, saber-tooth tigers sporting 9-inch fangs and a great number of woolly imperial mammoths.

It is not surprising that these lumbering prehistoric pachyderms are now extinct. Like modern-day New Yorkers, the city's successful species have evolved a preternaturally low profile. Somewhere inside Greater New York there are 15,000 species of insect, 260 varieties of fish, 52 reptiles, (including 14 kinds of snake and two lizards), and 270 different birds, not to mention the ranks of rodents and mammals: chipmunks, beavers, wildcats and bad-smelling opossums and skunks. Not content with these, in the 1970s paranoid New Yorkers invented the ultimate in inconspicuous-but-terrifying monsters—6 ft long alligators which inhabited the sewer pipes in packs, and were hunted down by Public Works Inspectors bearing .22 caliber rifles.

Only two were ever discovered, and they were babies, all of 3 in long. The myth turned out to be a mere distraction from the far more frightening reality of the genus *rattus norvegicus*, 16 in long and a hefty 1 lb on the scales. One of three strains of rat currently at large in the city, the Norwegian cold-water rat has lived in New York with phenomenal success since the first settlers arrived in the 17th century. In recent years, it has even evolved into the 'Super Rat', indigenous to a small area in the South Bronx, and immune to Warfarin, the Bureau of Pest Control's most lethal poison.

Conservative estimates reckon on one rat for every two New Yorkers, although more alarming statistics maintain that rats match humans head for head. Female rats reach puberty at the age of three months, and in less than a year a rat couple is capable of rearing over a hundred babies. Families occupy territories about one and a half times the length of the average tenement apartment. They are apt to move house as often as their human counterparts, swimming across the Hudson and the East River in robust pairs, or running in gangs, like the group of Harlem rats who upped sticks for Midtown in 1959, and set up a thriving colony in the middle of Park Avenue and 58th Street.

Population densities vary a great deal, of course, and most rats prefer areas like the Lower East Side, where the subways, pipes, drains and sewers are the most ancient, rusting and cramped. The city's grandest rats, meanwhile, spend the springtime courting and nesting in Central Park, and the autumn gathering their wits for a mass migration into the basement snuggeries of the swanky apartments on Central Park West.

Apart from the odd eel, jellyfish or trout which occasionally turns up in gutters and drains, rats enjoy a monopoly over underground New York. But Manhattan is above all a vertical city, and its wildlife has adapted itself to a suitably vertical lifestyle—a colony of ants thrives on top of the Empire State Building, a pair of peregrine falcons builds a nest on the roof of Riverside Church and a lady on the Upper East Side keeps a chicken run on a balcony overlooking East 57th Street. At the southernmost toe of Manhattan, moreover, bats dangle from the cables of Brooklyn Bridge, mice hitch rides up the elevators to their home in the Statue of Liberty's torch, and dogs and cats take walks on the roofs of tenement buildings on the Lower East Side. On their great journey south, black swarms of migrating Monarch butterflies have even been known to take a pitstop *en masse* on the crown of a Wall Street skyscraper.

Birds ought to be the best adapted to vertical life, but after a record 1400 dead magnolia warblers were found at the base of the Statue of Liberty, most skyscrapers now turn down their lights during the migration season so that some 400 species can navigate their way through the city without any mishaps. The avians that do best are the agressive, violent types: in Central Park, the most vicious crows in the country have taken to attacking red-tailed hawks, toy dogs and even babies; and a force of vigilante owls, faster killers than most manmade poisons, has been installed by the Parks Department in a vain attempt to keep down the rats.

New York's most hated birds of all, however, are two British exports: the sparrow and the starling. Sparrows first came to New York in the 1850s, thanks to the misguided Honorable Nicholas Pike, and his fellow directors from the Brooklyn Institute. In 1863, 14 sparrows were loosed in Central Park—they were an immediate hit. Elaborate sparrow houses were set up all over the park and people took to keeping them as pets. In a space of only a few years, however, they had bred into a multitude, and O. Henry was cursing the 'confounded little squint-eyed yawping nuisances' of Madison Square.

Starlings arrived a few years later, courtesy of a mad poet called Eugene Schieffelin who was obsessed with the idea of populating the country with every bird mentioned in Shakespeare. In 1890 he released 60 in Central Park, and a few months later the first breeding pair was discovered nesting in a bush near the Museum of Natural History. Over a century later, America's starling population is teetering on the 200 million mark. Starlings are disliked by country and city alike: a single flock can gobble up 20 tons of potatoes in an afternoon; and the droppings which spatter streets, sidewalks and sculptures harbor lethal diseases.

Strange as it may seem, Manhattan has a dozen bird-watching clubs and New Yorkers in general are relatively keen on wildlife. In one case a few years ago, the Parks Department discovered a shy 16-year-old who was so fed up with his urban living quarters that he went native, living in treehouses which he built in the north end of the Central Park. He was duly taken to court, and then offered a job pruning trees. All over the city there are closet gardeners tending allotments hidden away on rooftops, on vacant lots, or even in Central Park (where a policeman was once caught nurturing a secret patch of marijuana). As far as pets go, despite rigidly enforced pooper-scooper laws, dogs outnumber cats by three to one, probably because the fiercest breeds are such an effective deterent against muggers.

Even the ugliest, nastiest bull terrier, however, won't protect its owner from the city's most daunting beast of all: the species of *blatta* or cockroach that infests every nook and cranny of Manhattan, from the fanciest Upper East Side dining room to the dingiest diner, and from the tallest scraper to the darkest sewer. An abundance of cockroaches lived in jungles 250 million years ago, before reptiles, mammals or rubbish bins even existed, and though the unappetizing beetle and its horrid waggling antennae are still basically prehistoric in design, it is easily the best adapted to life in a 20th-century metropolis.

Scientific studies have shown that while the Manhattan cockroach is basically vegetarian, it can adapt its diet to almost any kind of digestible matter, and is especially partial to cream buns and éclairs. In addition it has a morbid penchant for dark, confined spaces and generally adopts a particular crack as a favorite lair (the toaster, the oven, or, best of all, the underside of a kitchen drawer).

Almost impossible to eradicate, the cockroach is a supreme test of the most hard-boiled New Yorker. It is quicker off the mark and faster on its pins than practically any living creature in the city, and in extremity it can jump into the air like a grasshopper. Ignored and left to its own devices, it quickly becomes tame, and instead of running away when disturbed, will flock to greet its host in ever increasing numbers. There is nothing quite like the experience of waking up in the middle of the night and stumbling across a cockroach party in the kitchen.

For New Yorkers who wish to rid themselves of these uninvited guests, there is a considerable variety of options: sprays which kill the roaches instantaneously (satisfying to inflict, but ineffectual in the long run); Roach Motels, (cardboard boxes full of glue where 'roaches check in, but they *don't* check out'); poisons (with names like Combat and Black Flag); and finally the exterminator, who arrives dressed in astronaut's gear and fumigates the whole apartment until it reeks of meths. Recently New Yorkers have even resorted to hunting down cockroaches with geckos imported from Java and Malaysia. Blue-skinned and orange-spotted, with suction-pads for feet, the 8 in long lizards are allowed to roam free in apartments and munch up stray cockroaches. The ever-resilient New Yorker, meanwhile, is getting used to the distant sounds of crunching beetle-carapaces, and the eerie gecko bark, which sounds like a cross between a lamb's bleat and a Yorkshire terrier's yap.

In the end, however, most New Yorkers nurture a secret respect for the city's most ubiquitous and successful living creature. Even in literature the cockroach has found itself an immortal niche as Don Marquis's Archy, the maudlin office cockroach, who typed with his head and never used capitals because he couldn't manipulate the shift key. And of course it is Archy who has the last word in any Manhattan Bestiary:

i do not see why men
should be so proud
insects have the more
ancient lineage
according to the scientists
insects were insects
when man was only
a burbling whatisit

Garbage

New York is built on garbage; its wildlife thrives on garbage; its 'chief production', as the artist Claes Oldenburg put it, is garbage; and, according to the last Commissioner of Sanitation, ultimately it will be engulfed by garbage.

Every 24 hours, the subway produces 32 tons of trash, 2000 tons of newspapers and 1000 50 lb bags of dust; and every year ASPCA officials have to dispose of 300,000 stray cats and dogs. In all, New York produces more waste in one day than the cities of London and Tokyo combined—some 26–30,000 tons, not counting sewage.

Rubbish is everywhere in the city, transforming its flat streets and avenues into an undulating terrain composed of little heaps, mounds and rivulets of litter. New Yorkers, meanwhile, are strangely passionate about their trash. They like foraging and scavenging for it almost as much as they like throwing it away. There are shops on Canal Street which specialize in recycled rubbish. There are outdoor sculptures which are made of garbage—a lamppost draggling a hundred pairs of sneakers on Tompkins Square; sidewalks and street signs plastered with a mosaic of broken china on St Mark's Place; and a brownstone fire escape bulging with 38 giant teddy bears in East Harlem.

Garbage has been an inspiration to New York's artists since Jean Tinguely created his *Homage to New York* in 1964: assembled out of junk foraged from a dump in New Jersey and doused in gasoline, it spontaneously combusted in the sculpture garden of the Museum of Modern Art. And in 1981 the Sanitation Department appointed its own artist-in-residence, Mierle Ukeles, whose performance pieces included shaking the hands of each of the 10,000 department members.

The most rubbish-obsessed New Yorkers of all, however, were the legendary Collyer brothers of 5th Avenue, whose brownstone mansion was barricaded five floors deep with the accumulated junk of 38 years. On 21 March 1947, police stormed the house. Tunneling up to the second floor, searchers found the frail body of Langley, wrapped in a faded gray dressing gown, and dead in his bed. Three weeks later, after the removal of 100 tons of newspapers, 17 pianos, 5 violins, thousands of cardboard boxes and a Model T Ford, they located Homer Collyer, starved to death under one of his own booby-traps.

Historically speaking, garbage has played a crucial role in the growth and development of the city. City Hall and Manhattan's criminal courts stand on the site of the first unauthorized dump, a 16 ft hillock that 17th-century New Yorkers dumped in the Collect Pond, New York's only accessible source of fresh water. In the years that followed, many of the communities founded in Greenwich Village and the Upper West and East Sides sprang up as the result of an exodus of the well-to-do from untreated garbage, which made disease spread like wildfire. In the reeking civic center downtown, devastating epidemics of yellow fever and cholera raged as New York evolved into one of the most dangerously unsanitary cities in the world. It was not until the 1920s that the city built proper sanitation plants, powered by sewage gas. And even then, there was an outbreak of cholera less than 20 years ago, when untreated sewage leaked into wells on Long Island.

The main problem facing New York today, however, is the sheer quantity of its waste. In a city constrained by an acute shortage of space, the task of disposing of some 30,000 tons of garbage every day is no small matter. From the beginning, land in New York has been at an absolute premium; so much so that on Hart Island, where the city buries paupers and unidentified corpses, bodies have to be dug up every 15 or 20 years to make room for new arrivals. In 1901, when someone calculated that there was space for only 10 bodies per square foot, a New Yorker named James O'Kelley patented a device for burials in the air. An egg-shaped rocket, the 'Navohi', it was filled with acid and gas, and launched into the heavens like a hot-air balloon on fire.

No one has ever thought of sending garbage into the stratosphere, and the city's traditional method of waste disposal has been landfill. New land, made out of trash, muck and treated sewage, has been swelling Manhattan's shoreline since the 17th century. A section of the East River Drive near the United Nations Building, for example, sits on a chunk of the bombed British city of Bristol, which US troopships brought back as ballast in World War II. The most recent addition is the million cubic yards of debris taken from the foundations of the World Trade Center, making up the 25 acres of Battery Park City. A fair number of Manhattan's most daunting skyscrapers, what's more, stand on an un-bio-degradable bed of nappies and newspapers, not to mention shredded money which the Federal Reserve Bank compacts in bales and gives away to construction companies at the rate of $20,000,000 a day.

And so, while Venice sinks under pollution, Manhattan rises on trash and sewage. Of course the island alone could never absorb all the rubbish it produces, and most of it ends up in dumps (euphemstically called landfills) out in the boroughs and in New Jersey, where it is sprayed with disinfectant, or 'bubble-gum', and covered in sand. Mercifully, dumps soon sprout ailanthus and ginkgo trees, introduced to New York in the 19th century because they thrive on rubbish and smog (poplars were banned from the city at about the same time, because their roots punctured sewer mains). When it ran out of space, the Eastchester Bay landfill in the Bronx started growing vertically, into a miniature Alpine range with promontories offering grand views of Manhattan. The Fountain Avenue landfill in Brooklyn, on the other hand, grew into such a tall mound that it got in the way of the flight path into JFK airport in Queens: eventually the landfill had to be closed when engineers became nervous that the vortex of seagulls flying around the top of the mountain peak would suck itself up into propellers and ground incoming planes.

Most city trash ends up at the largest landfill in the world, the 3000 acres of Fresh Kills in Staten Island. With its 550-ft Himalayan peaks, the dump boasts the highest points on the Eastern Seaboard south of Maine. Here, 18 barges work round the clock ferrying in enough garbage to fill the Empire State Building every month. A machine called the Rex Compactor crushes and compacts, and in its wake a truck spreads the ground with a thin layer of soil. In the oldest, most fermented parts of the dump the Getty Synthetic Fuel Company has sunk wells 100 ft down into the rubbish, and it extracts enough methane and carbon dioxide to supply 15,000 ovens on Staten Island.

Meanwhile Fresh Kills is running out of space. As an alternative, the city has suggested building eight 'resource recovery centers' starting with the abandoned Navy Yard in Brooklyn, where rubbish will be incinerated to make steam and electricity for Consolidated Edison. No one likes the idea of fumes containing the carcinogen found in Agent Orange wafting across their front doors, and opposition has been predictably fierce (an attempt to open up a sewage plant on the Upper West Side in the 1970s led to riots). By the year 2000, however, Fresh Kills will be full, and the city will have to think of another way of disposing of its trash, if it is not to be transformed into a nightmarish landscape of stinking black plastic.

The Man Who Lit New York

Sadly the great heyday of neon is past. The famous signs of Times Square, where the art form reached its apotheosis, have gradually been replaced by bland billboards lit from within. Nevertheless, determined neon enthusiasts can hunt out relics of the golden age all over New York: a glowing squirl of tubing at the J. Soane Wig Shop on 14th Street, for example, or the bedraggled, multi-colored curls and extrusions saying 'Chinese Dragon Restaurant' that cover two sides of a sign on Mott Street. The most extravagant illuminated signs of all, however, are outside Manhattan, on the riverside edges of Queens, Brooklyn and New Jersey, where they stare across at the island and tempt Manhattanites. The easiest way of seeing them is to take the Circle Line tour round Manhattan at dusk. Working anticlockwise, the best are:

'Good to the Last Drop': the giant cup of Maxwell House coffee eternally emptying and refilling itself in New Jersey.

'Read the Watchtower': the creepiest sign of all, provided by the Jehovah's Witnesses, along with a digital clock which sits on top of a former pharmaceuticals factory on Brooklyn Heights.

'Dominos': magnificent twirling red tubes belonging to the venerable sugar factory in Williamsburg.

'Silvercup': newly refurbished neon *tour de force* now advertising the film studios based in the old Silvercup bakery in Long Island City.

'Pepsi-Cola': the largest and most famous of all, courting residents of the United Nations and the Upper East Side from its home in Queens.

The lost neon extravaganzas which 50- to 60-year-old New Yorkers remember with such nostalgia were largely the creation of one person: Douglas Leigh, the 'Man Who Lit Up New York'. Even before Leigh's arrival, however, Times Square twinkled with what G.K. Chesterton sniffed at as 'a glorious garden of wonder ... to anyone who was lucky enough to be unable to read'. Broadway's first proper electric sign, encouraging New Yorkers to 'Buy Homes on Long Island Swept By Ocean Breezes', went up in 1891. A decade later Coney Island's 'Electric Eden' of $2^1/2$ million lights could be seen 38 miles out to sea where it dazzled ships sailing into the harbor. Back in Manhattan an advertising man called Gude dubbed the stretch of Broadway between 14th and 33rd Streets the 'Great White Way', but it wasn't until after World War I that the neon billboard really came into its own and Times Square blazed in a mesmerizing scintillation of light.

Douglas Leigh came to New York in 1929, just in time for the Wall Street Crash; and he was the man responsible for relighting Times Square after the lights went out in the Depression. In the twenties glowing peanuts had showered the square and a luminous Highlander had danced a whiskey fling, but in Leigh's hands the neon signs of the thirties rose to a new level of sophistication. His first creation, for A&P the supermarket chain, was a 25 ft cup of coffee that billowed out steam. It was followed by a blinking penguin who smoked Kools, an enormous Wilson whiskey sign which used up enough electricity for a small town, and a Pepsi-Cola waterfall which sprayed pedestrians on windy days. His masterpiece, however, was the Camel-smoker who changed clothes and identity every three months, and blasted steamy smoke down an 8 ft long cone for 17 years.

After the War, Leigh took to fixing neon signs on dirigibles and touring them round the countryside. Meanwhile, television gradually brought about the demise of the neon billboard, and the end of a glorious era was signaled when the Camel-smoker was finally dismantled in 1967. Seven years later, however, Leigh was invited to light up the Empire State Building in red, white and blue for the American Bicentennial. It was a turning point for the Manhattan skyline, which had lost its charm since skyscraper glass boxes blunted it in the sixties. In 1977 Leigh designed an entirely new lighting system for the Empire State using 204 metal halide lamps, which were four times as bright as floodlights, and colored gels made of Lexan, the strongest plastic available. Soon Leigh was transfiguring skyscrapers all over the city, and by the end of the 1970s the Manhattan skyline had a renaissance of colored light.

In 1984 Leigh finished off his transformation of the Empire State with 880 colored flourescent tubes installed on the mast. Thanks to Leigh the skyscraper is now a kind of litmus paper for the city, changing color at least a dozen times a year. For the bemused, the guide below explains all:

Red, green and black: Martin Luther King, Jr. Day
Red and white: St Valentine's Day
Red, white and blue: Washington's Birthday
Green: St Patrick's Day
White and yellow: Easter Week
Red: Memorial Day
Red, white and blue: Independence Day

Blue and white: Steuben Day
Red and white: Pulaski Day
Red, white and green: Columbus Day
Blue and white: United Nations Day
Red, orange and yellow: Halloween
Red and green: Christmas to New Year.

Stoops and New Yorkers

Stoops are more than just steep flights of stairs leading up to houses and tenements. In a city as overcrowded as New York, the stoop is the single most important 'room' in the house. An outdoor front parlor with air-conditioning, it functions as a stage where neighbors gather to watch and be watched, to show off and gossip, to fight and canoodle. No platform could be more perfectly suited to the streak of exhibitionism latent in every New Yorker. Sometimes such a large crowd attaches itself to one stoop it is practically impossible to get in the front door, and irritable residents put up signs pleading 'No sitting on the stairs please'. The stoop crosses all barriers of class and race: well-off young couples like sitting out on their stoops in Greenwich Village as much as the gangs of kids in Alphabet City. Where a stoop doesn't already exist, moreover, it is invented: New Yorkers simply plant their armchairs on the sidewalk, sit themselves down on an imaginary staircase, and watch the rest of the world go by.

The stoop has an illustrious pedigree dating from the arrival of the first Dutch settlers in the 17th century. In Holland houses traditionally had a flight of steps or *stoep* leading up to the best rooms, which were raised well above the level of the street and thereby protected from flooding. Leaking dikes and floods were not a particular threat in Manhattan, of course, and the first stoops served no function other than to remind the colonists of the fatherland. They must have been a homesick and rather impractical crew, for they built the first settlement on flat, swampy land resembling Holland, in preference to the far more suitable fertile meadows nearby. Soon they had constructed a miniature replica of Amsterdam, complete with windmills, canals and the inevitable stoop.

New Amsterdam has long since disappeared, but the stoop lives on as the most visible sign that New York is a Dutch city at heart. Indeed, apart from his liking for the stoop, the New Yorkers's appetite for speculation and real estate, and his strange infatuation with baths, showers and personal hygiene are all traits that date back to the original Dutch settlers. For centuries, Dutch dynasties dominated the city's trade and commerce. The phenomenonly prosperous Vanderbilts, for example, emigrated from Bilt in Holland in the 17th century, started the Staten Island ferry, and ended up owning the largest network of railroads in America. The Roosevelts, who arrived at about the same time, eventually produced two American presidents in the space of 24 years. Stoops themselves owe their very survival to real estate moguls instilled with the Dutch spirit of enterprise. These canny developers encouraged architects to incorporate stoops into brownstones, realizing that a double entrance up to the parlor and down to the kitchen dispensed with the need for an alley leading to a tradesman's entrance at the back, so saving a few feet of precious space.

In fact, anyone who looks closely can find traces of the Dutch settlers all over the city. Most place names are anglicized forms of the Dutch: Wal Streit, Bowerij, Breukelen, Haarlem, Boswijck, Bronck, Jonkheers, and Konijn Eiland. And even Peter Stuyvesant, the prickly Dutch governor with a peg leg who stumped around New Amsterdam for 17 years before surrendering to the British, is curiously commemorated in scores of New York businesses—not to mention a park, a hospital, a housing estate, a beauty salon, a coin-op laundry, and a brand of cigarettes.

The most curious Dutch hieroglyph of all is found in the silhouettes of the old water tanks scattered on rooftops all over the city. The tanks (along with stoops and fire-escapes) are a familiar sight to New Yorkers, but an oddity in the eyes of most foreigners. Indeed, they look most peculiar, like rockets about to take off; some emit exhaust steam from the heating system, and others sit on a perch of huts, ladders and scaffolding. Most were made in the 19th century by a Mr Rosenwach, whose grandfather manufactured barrels for sauerkraut and pickles. Ostensibly they exist to store water for the building below, but what few visitors or even New Yorkers realize, is that they are windmills without sails. Along with the stoop, they are the most atavistic throwbacks to Dutch New Amsterdam in the city.

Sucking Subways

The subway has been a thorn in the side of New York for years. In the 1980s Mayor Koch turned the campaign against subway graffiti into a $30-million crusade, and in 1981, while transit workers went on strike, passions rose to such a pitch that there was a bizarre assassination attempt on the chairman of the city's transportation authority. The system is massively underfunded, so that as New York's water table goes on rising, whole sections of subway tunnel are now floating on water.

Even so, every day half the population of a disgruntled New York dives underground and hurtles across the city in subway trains. Few remember that New York was once proud of what was the most extensive subway system in the world, covering more than 815 miles and carrying over two billion passengers a year.

New York got its first proper subway in 1900, (long after London, Glasgow, Budapest, and Berlin), but historically it is the home of the world's first underground railway—under Atlantic Avenue in Brooklyn. Built in the 1840s, the 21 ft wide tunnel was half a mile long and operated for 11 years before it was covered up and forgotten by everyone except mushroom-growers and bootleggers.

Thirty years later New York's second 'subway' was dug out on Broadway and Murray Street. The tunnel was a block long and trains were blown and then sucked along it at the speed of 10 miles an hour by a Force Blast wind-machine nicknamed the Western Tornado. To avoid the crippling costs of purchasing a franchise from Boss Tweed, who captained the city's most corrupt administration ever, Alfred Beach constructed the tunnel in deadly secret, stealthily removing the earthworks at night. In the end Tweed's scheme for a network of elevated railroads or 'Els' killed the project, and the dream of belching passengers at 60 miles an hour from Wall Street to Central Park was shattered. Like its predecessor, Broadway's pnuematic subway was forgotten, until 1912 when subway construction workers cut through it and discovered a perfectly preserved waiting room decorated in opulent style, with cobwebby frescoes and a goldfish tank.

By 1875 the fish-spine girders of the Els overshadowed 2nd, 3rd, 6th and 9th Avenues. The system gave passengers romantic, roller-coaster views of the city, but its steam locomotives showered New York with thick clouds of grime, cinders and soot. Though sections of aerial track still exist in parts of Brooklyn and Queens (the J and L trains still offer the best panoramas of Manhattan in the city), the subway eventually won the day, and in 1938 Mayor La Guardia took an acetylene torch to the 6th Avenue El and began its demolition. Only the 2nd Avenue El, which was one of the last to go, had an after-life when it was bought by the industrialist Henry J. Kaiser during World War II, and transported to California where it carried war-workers to the Alameda shipyards.

The subway system that New York finally built itself in 1904, was the most technologically sophisticated in the world, with parallel tracks for express and local trains. It was constructed in record time, thanks to an enormous workforce of nearly 10,000 immigrants; but there were a great many fatalities: 18 deaths a year in the period between 1914 and 1937 alone. One of the strangest accidents occurred in 1905 during the construction of the IRT tunnel linking Manhattan and Brooklyn. One of the laborers or 'sandhogs' building the underwater tunnel was sucked up through the shield chamber and catapulted through the mud of the 30-ft deep riverbed like a human cannon ball, and from there up into the East River where he was picked up uninjured by a passing tug.

Until the great decline of recent years, traveling on the New York subway was an urbane affair. Carriages had handsome wood paneling, seats were covered in wicker-work, and subway kiosks on the street resembled oriental temples. The privately operated IRT company marked their stations with illuminated blue-and-white globes, the BMT with illuminated green-and-white hexagons, and the city-run IND with blue street lamps. Inside, stations were decorated with mosaics, illustrated panels and friezes of terracotta, majolica and tilework.

Today it is almost perverse to talk about the beauty of the New York subway system, but miraculously many of these splendid tiles and panels survive, adding a sprinkling of charm to the general grime and gloom. As you judder around the murky depths keep an eye out for the following:

Beavers—decorating Astor Place station in bas-relief, in deference to John Jacob Astor, who made his first forture selling beaver furs.

Sloops—at South Ferry, commemorating the boats which sailed to markets up the Hudson in the 1850s.

Crowstepped gables—at Wall Street station, showing Dutch gables and the wooden fence or 'wall' built to keep the Indians out in the 17th century.

Peter Stuyvesant's house—in a mosaic at Whitehall Street station. Originally whitewashed, it was derided as the 'White Hall' by the English Governor.

Steamboats—at Fulton Street station, actually the *Clermont* which Robert Fulton designed in 1807, six years after he invented the submarine.

Blue ceramic plaques—at Bleecker Street, the only station with blue tiles.

The City Gaol—depicted at Christopher Street, originally home to New York's penitentiary before it moved to Sing Sing.

Brooklyn Bridge—in bas-relief at Chambers Street Station.

Underground Manhattan

To the uninitiated, the only clue to the city below the city is the wispy steam which wafts out of manholes and escapes through ruptures in the tarmac, at the rate of 15 million lbs an hour. Few New Yorkers have any idea of the immense and complex underworld which puffs, trickles, throbs and sputters under their toes. Below them is the tubular chaos of subterranean Manhattan; a knotted mess of pipes, drains, sewers, tunnels, cables and mains that enable New Yorkers to flush the loo, cook a meal, live in tropical heat and get themselves to work: 38 miles of water tunnel, 50 miles of steam pipe, 134 miles of subway track, 6000 miles of sewer, 7800 miles of gas mains, 62,000 miles of electrical cable, 500,000 manholes and 20 million miles of telephone wire. No other city has such an ungovernable jungle of underground conduits.

New Yorkers take it in their stride, even though they know the ground beneath them has an alarming tendency to erupt in lethal explosions of steam, gas and water. In 1989 a jet of steam (which heats the city via a network of 19th-century pipes) gorged through concrete and paving on Gramercy Square causing several injuries, denting cars, and coating an apartment and a tree with asbestos snow. On average, a water mains bursts somewhere in New York every 24 hours, and in 1957 there were a record six bursts in five hours all on one stretch of 39th Street. Every week city workers are supposed to fill in 30,000 pot-holes, (of such phenomenal dimensions that Jaguar have built a special pot-hole obstacle course to test their cars' suspension for the New York market).

Electricity failures also take their toll, and during the great blackouts of 1965 and 1977 New York was paralyzed. The power cut of 1965 swept across the city just as the rush hour was getting under way at 5.27 pm. New York ground to a halt under the full moon: 800,000 people were marooned in the subway, aeroplanes had to be redirected to New Jersey, 96 people were trapped on elevators in the Empire State Building, and hundreds more spent the night in restaurants and department stores. At breakfast the next day there were no newspapers. It was calculated that businesses had lost $100 million overnight.

Not surprisingly, the city's inhabitants like to build their nests high up, in skyscraper forests; but they do spend an abnormal amount of their lives grubbing about below ground. Rockefeller Center, Grand Central, Penn Station and the World Trade Center all have vast, sprawling underground concourses where New Yorkers gobble down oysters and coffee, shop, bet, play the stock exchange and tennis, and work-out. The subway even has its own force of over 3000 armed police; a fearsome lot, who swagger about flaunting guns and truncheons. In the bitter cold of winter, however, they are forced to turn a Nelson's eye to New York's latter-day cave dwellers: homeless people who move into mains tunnels under Grand Central and onto the sidings along underground tracks all over the city. Recently one man was found living in a tent in a subway tunnel along with his family of pet birds and rabbits, and in 1966 Consolidated Edison workers, who make sure New York gets its steady fix of electricity, steam and gas, came across someone living in a manhole under the Bowery. The 6 by 8 ft room had its own electric light, a hotplate attached to the cables running through the vault, and a clothes rack hung with coats.

The true masters of subterranean New York are the engineers and splicers who have to navigate their way underground every time someone asks for a new telephone line, a rat chews through a cable, or vibrations from cars and subway trains destroy some vital connection. Incredibly enough, no map or key to underground New York exists, and today's engineers rely on their own ingenuity to burrow a way through the tangle of pipes, drains, cables and mains. Vertical New York can soar upwards, concertina-style, but the underground city is always thirsty for space, so that even telephone lines, which normally sit 4 ft under the streets, sometimes have to be dug as deep as 50 ft.

The city is riddled with abandoned tunnels, and if a utility company is lucky it can appropriate one of these, as ConEd did to an old gas tube which now carries steam from Manhattan to Astoria in Queens. The Transit Authority reckons that somewhere in the city there are 23 deserted stations and almost 6 miles of unused tunnels, although diggers occasionally stumble on a 19th-century tunnel which has somehow been forgotten. Sometimes someone unexpected has got to it first. During the campus riots of '68, students invaded Columbia University via defunct coal transportation tunnels, and Andy Warhol once requisitioned the disused private railway spur under the Waldorf Astoria for a dusty Halloween party, during which supper was served from derelict subway cars. So far, no one has found a use for the spaghetti of pnuematic tubes that used to convey mail and post around the city at 30 miles per hour.

Apart from strange pipes and tubes, New York conceals swamps, ponds, quicksands and creeks; extraordinary vestiges of the virgin New Amsterdam which the Dutch settlers found when they first arrived in the 17th century. Great Kill still flows into sewers under 42nd Street, Minetta Brook and supposedly a few gasping trout dribble under Greenwich Village, and Turtle Creek floods Upper East Side mansions on its way to the East River. And of course, at the very bottom of the city is the 225 million-year-old bedrock of schist which made Manhattan possible in the first place. Without its unusually robust and stable formation the world's heaviest city could never have existed.

Water

Purity and cleanliness are words so seldom mentioned in the same breath as New York, that it comes as rather a shock to learn that the city boasts the most wholesome water of any municipality in the world. According to official samplers, it tastes of balsam and sweet chrysanthemums; and it arrives in New York in such pristine condition that it requires no chemical treatment other than chlorination. New Yorkers love water. They use and consume $1^1/_2$ billion gallons of the stuff every day; around 207 gallons per person, or double the amount of Paris or London. Strangely, in a city not noted for its smoothly oiled administrative machinery, New York is home to one of the cheapest, most innovative and efficient water supply systems anywhere. Water has flowed into the city without a single interruption since the first Croton Aqueduct was built in 1842; 95 per cent is conveyed by gravity, and only 5 per cent has to be pumped.

In fact, New York's water tunnels are the most impressive of all its engineering feats. Most cities simply quench themselves at the nearest river, but New York, which still flushes raw sewage straight into the Hudson, has its water diverted from sources as far as 125 miles away, and from three great systems—the Croton, Catskill and the Delaware. The Catskill system, which dates from 1907, has a total storage capacity of 190 billion gallons. To build it, nine villages were submerged, 2850 people moved out of their houses, and 4000 bodies were disinterred from 39 cemeteries. The largest system of all, the Delaware, has a capacity of 330.4 billion gallons. On its way to the city it travels through three states via the longest tunnel built anywhere, dropping from 295 ft above sea level to 1114 ft below, which is the equivalent of the fall from the top of the World Trade Center to 59 ft under the sidewalk.

More alarmingly, New York's two gigantic water tunnels have not been inspected since they were first installed in 1910. It is said that if one were to crack, a geyser would shoot 300 ft into the air, washing out the foundations of surrounding skyscrapers and causing them to topple onto the streets below. Taking this frightening scenario to heart, in 1954 the city embarked on City Tunnel No. 3, an Olympian plan to satisfy the city's ever-increasing thirst, and allow City Tunnels 1 and 2 to be shut down for essential renovations.

The project has been described as the greatest engineering wonder of the world, and the largest construction project in the Western hemisphere, with the exception of defense contracts. Work finally began in 1970, just before the city went bankrupt, and after years of economic and political wrangles Stage 1 has only just been completed.

The site lies at the north end of Van Courtlandt Park. Here, close to the Bronx-Yonkers border is Hill View, a reservoir sitting 300 ft above sea level from which water flows via either City Tunnel 1 or 2 into the Bronx, Manhattan, Queens, Brooklyn and Staten Island. Nearby, under a grassy hillock and a white cross, is the first valve chamber built for City Tunnel No. 3.

It is a spectacular sight. Eight hundred foot down is a clammy chamber the size of two football pitches, filled with 17 pipes, a narrow-gauge railway, concrete stalactites and clouds of steam. From here, water is blasted down a 24 ft-diameter tunnel which dives between 200 and 800 ft below the surface and runs from Van Courtlandt Park in the Bronx south to Central Park, and then east under Roosevelt Island to Long Island City in Queens. So far the project has cost $200 million, and 21 lives; and though the expense of Stages 2, 3, and 4 is bound to be greater, no one has even hazarded a completion date.

History

New York 1650

New York sits on a bed of three-billion-year-old rock. You can see hunks of it in Central Park, where black Manhattan schist surfaces for air; slivers of mica make it glint in the the sun like the plastic boulders used in zoos. Around it buildings, fashions and cultures spark up and fizzle out with each generation. The rock underneath, however, is close-packed, dense and hard; it is practically the only thing in the city that is sturdy and durable.

In the Pleistocene Period two glaciers steam-rollered down from the Arctic and ground to a halt over Manhattan. Later on, saber-toothed tigers, giant beavers, bisons, sloths and tapirs meandered up from the tropics. Not long ago workers dug up the remnants of a mastodon, a kind of 15 ft long elephant with tusks the same length and shaggy auburn hair, at what is now 141st Street and Broadway.

Discovery, and Early Profiteering

Nearly one and a half million years after the glaciers and the mastodons, the ancestors of the American Indian emigrated to America via the Bering Straits. They made themselves at home in Manhattan for several thousand years—until **Giovanni da Verrazano**, searching for the fabled Northwest Passage to the East, stumbled on New York Bay. There, he found 'a very agreeable place between two small but prominent hills', populated by friendly 'Indians' dressed in birds feathers who 'came towards us joyfully, uttering loud cries of wonderment'. About six different **Algonquin** tribes lived in the area, planting maize, beans and tobacco, and hunting down reindeer, bobcats, otters and wild turkeys. Virgin New York had fish, game and berries in abundance: at the south end of the island were flat salt marshes; in the middle, hills, forests and streams; and at the far end in Harlem, fertile plains and meadows.

Strong currents forced Verrazano back to his caravel before he had a chance to step ashore, and nearly a century passed before the first European actually set foot on the island. On 6 September 1609, **Henry Hudson** anchored the *Half-Moone* in the Lower Bay. He was an Englishman, working for the Dutch East India Company, though the first tribe he encountered imagined he was a Supreme Being who lived in a floating house. 'Strong drink was offered which made all gay and happy', and the island was therefore christened Mannahattanink, or 'the island of general intoxication'. So runs the delightful but fanciful story told to a credulous Moravian missionary by a tribe of Delaware Indians in 1790. The genuine derivation is much more dull, and comes from an Algonquin term which probably means 'island', or 'Island of the Hills'.

Hudson was more intent on discovering a passage to the Orient than finding land, so he immediately sailed up-river, charting its course as far as the present day state capital, Albany. He did not find the spice route, but he did find something just as precious: beaver, mink, and otter furs, and Indians willing to trade them. It was enough to convince the Dutch that the area was worth colonising, and in 1610 and 1614 a group of Amsterdam merchants dispatched several boats on forays into the area, and a trading post was established at Fort Nassau in Albany. Hudson himself returned in 1610 under the British flag, only to find himself icebound with a starving crew who finally mutinied and abandoned him to a chilly death in the depths of New York Bay.

The first settlers came over in 1619 and 1624. In all, there were 30 families, a mixture of Dutch, French-speaking Walloons and black slaves. The main settlement was upstate, at Fort Nassau, but eight families and some cattle were left behind under the walnut trees on Nut Island, which is nowadays known as Governors Island. In 1625 a larger group moved onto Manhattan's toe, and in 1626 **Peter Minuit**, the Director-General of the Company, purchased the island for trinkets worth 60 guilders, which 19th-century historians calculated as worth $24. The deal was hardly a purchase, however, since the tribe Minuit dealt with didn't come from Manhattan, and anyway the Indians, who had land in abundance, had utterly different notions of ownership to Europeans.

Speculation became and remained the city's *raison d'être*. While the rest of the early colonies were started by settlers escaping religious and political intolerance abroad, the New Netherlands was founded on hopes of commerce and trade. Its first, urbanized settlers immediately set about establishing Nieuw Amsterdam in the image of the fatherland. They could have picked a better spot on the island—with brooks, ponds and lakes—but instead they chose flat and swampy land which reminded them of home. The infant city had a windmill, a canal, (the Heere Gracht or Gentleman's Canal), and narrow crow-stepped houses built gable-end to the street, with Dutch *stoeps*, or stoops: steep-stepped porches to a raised ground floor.

Colonial New York: Free Trade, Strong Drink and Riots

By the 1660s, Dutch New York was already a busy trading post. In 1644 the West Indian Company opened up the station to traders outside the corporation. Eight English merchants emigrated to the city, and the first black settlement, owned by freed slaves, grew up in today's SoHo. The next year a Jesuit missionary was told that 18 languages were spoken on the island. The early colonists paid scant attention to the strictures of their governors, and were just as indifferent to religion, so exasperating one pastor that he denounced them all as 'uncivil, and stupid as garden poles'. Trade thrived, however, and the Dutch set in motion the sudden transformation of the island from a natural Eden into a prospering, entirely man-made city. By 1670, the Englishman, Thomas Denton, was eulogizing about a new commercial Canaan 'where the land floweth with milk and honey'.

In the 1640s a number of bloody wars broke out with the Indians as a result of the high-handed policies of the governor, **William Kieft**. He started a protection racket, imposed a tax on the Indians, and eventually built a barrier, actually a wooden fence, across today's Wall Street to protect the city. To set things to rights, in 1647 the Company sent in **Peter Stuyvesant**, who sneered at the colony as 'more a mole hill than a fortress'.

Stuyvesant came hot foot from the Dutch colony in Curaçao where the Portuguese had blown off his leg with a canon ball in a naval tussle. Nicknamed Old Peg Leg behind his back, he tramped around Nieuw

Amsterdam on a wooden stump which had silver attachments for cer-emonial occasions. Authoritarian, priggish and quick-tempered, Stuy-vesant administered the colony with a rod of iron. His first act was to close pubs on Sundays and at 9 on other nights, a reckless move, since the settlers were great drinkers and nearly a quarter of the colony's businesses were grog shops. Shortly after, Stuyvesant tried to exile a group of Brazilian Jews who arrived in the colony in 1653 and had Quakers lashed and beaten, but commerce was king in Dutch New York, and the Company insisted on religious tolerance. Still, under Stuyve-sant's 17-year administration Nieuw Amsterdam matured into a city, and in 1653 got its first rudimentary form of representative government when a common council was set up under orders from the Hague.

In 1664, in the middle of the Dutch trade wars with England and France, Charles II granted the colony to his brother, the Duke of York. In March a 'ragged troup' of British warships began raiding Dutch towns on Long Island. They justified the assault on a dodgy claim based on John Cabot's voyages in 1498. Eventually a fleet under **Colonel Richard Nicolls** blockaded the harbor and demanded surrender. Stuy-vesant defiantly tore the letter into shreds and held out for 11 days, but the city's fortifications were in a wretched state, its citizens phlegmatic and impassive. On 8 September, the British took the city without a shot; New Amsterdam became New York; and a disconsolate Stuyvesant retired to his farm on the Bowery.

Under the English, the city kept its a reputation for slipshod morals and loose lifestyles. In 1692 a shocked Anglican chaplain described a city addicted to flip (a rum and beer hot toddy that smelt of ammonia) and 'cursing & Swearing... some doing it in that frequent horrible & dreadfull manner as if they prided themselves both as to the number and invention of them'. Apparently, people lived together out of wedlock, and in conversation they spoke in loud voices and constantly interrupted one another. Governors were notoriously spineless and lackadaisical, especially **Edward Hyde**, who went about dressed as a woman and had his portrait painted wearing a décolleté gown in the latest fashion. Eventually he was arrested and ended his days in a debtor's gaol.

In 1688, inspired by the Glorious Revolution, **Jacob Leisler** and a group of Protestant radicals seized the fort. The group took over govern-ment of the city for a period of nearly two years, during which they called its first municipal elections. Although Leisler had been an unflinchingly loyal partisan, when William of Orange finally sent over a new governor in 1789, he was unfairly tried and hanged for treason.

In the next few years rumbling dissatisfaction with the administration voiced itself in uprisings, fires and robberies which were blamed on Negro slaves. The most important event of the period, however, was the trial of the newspaper editor, **Peter Zenger**. In 1725 the city's first newspaper, the *New York Gazette*, was published, but in no time at all it turned out to be merely a mouthpiece for Willam Cosby, the city's corrupt Governor. Zenger and his colleagues formed an oppositional faction, and retorted with a newspaper of their own, the *New-York Weekly Journal*. When the *Journal* took to satirizing government officials as circus animals and exposing the desperate poverty of the city, Zenger was clapped into gaol. Andrew Hamilton, Pennsylvania's brilliant attorney general (and also, incidentally, the architect of Independence Hall), came to his defence, acquitted Zenger, and struck a crucial blow for freedom of speech in the country.

Revolution and its Rewards

As the colonies edged towards revolution, the population of New York swelled to 20,000. In 1763 the Treaty of Paris concluded the Seven Years' War with the French, who conceded most of their American possessions to England. Relieved of the French menace, the colonies were suddenly united by resentment of the English. New York had more Tories than any of the other colonies, but it also had a vociferous contingent of militant patriots. When the British tried to pay off debts from the war with provocative new taxes like the Sugar, Stamp and Townshend Acts, New York's **Sons of Liberty** took to the streets. They declared independence in City Hall Park, burnt up an effigy of Governor Colden, and ripped up and melted down the statue of George III that stood on Bowling Green. Finally, in January 1770, a few days before the Boston Massacre, the Battle of Golden Hill broke out near Wall Street. Though it was really no more than a scuffle, New Yorkers like to claim it as the first engagement of the American Revolution.

New York occupied a critical position between the southern colonies and New England, and the British went all out to take it. In the spring of 1776, while **Washington** made his headquarters in Greenwich Village, General Howe moved 200 ships into the harbor. Later that summer the two sides met near Brooklyn Heights at the Battle of Long Island in which Washington's troops were outnumbered by two to one. Under the cover of a dismal fog, Washington managed to retreat up Manhattan Island to Washington Heights, while a tricksy Quaker matron called

Mrs Murray supposedly distracted Howe and his troops with her hot cakes and songs. At the next confrontation, the Battle of Harlem Heights, Washington beat the British and escaped into White Plains with his ragged troops.

The British occupied the city, and did so for the next seven years. New York became a thriving Tory town. The Brits played cricket, went whoring, listened to concerts and watched plays. They kept thousands of the rebel soldiers in prison ships moored on the Hudson, where many starved to death in intolerable conditions. In 1781 there was great excitement when the first member of the royal family to set foot in America, Prince William Henry, paid a visit to the garrisoned city. At last, in 1783, **Lord Cornwallis** surrendered and Washington triumphantly marched from Harlem down to the Bowery. As British troops evacuated, their parting gesture was to grease the flagpole, to prevent the Revolutionaries raising the flag of the new Republic.

Congress came to New York, and for a short time it became the capital of the US. Members met in the old City Hall, which was revamped by **Pierre L'Enfant** (who later designed Washington DC). In 1789 George Washington was elected and inaugurated in the new, Federal Hall as President. The capital moved to Philadelphia, but in the next decade the population doubled to 60,515, and New York became the largest city in the nation. The first stock exchange and the first bank were organized, and Tammany Hall, founded in 1786 as a friendly society, began to develop into the powerful Democratic party machine which later came to dominate New York politics.

At the same time **Alexander Hamilton** published *The Federalist* with John Jay; 85 essays on the new democracy that have become part of America's secular scriptures. An outstanding figure in New York's life in this period, Hamilton was as romantic a figure as any Treasury Secretary could be (he was America's first, and his face is on the $10 bill). Born in the West Indies, and meeting an untimely end in a famous duel with Aaron Burr, in his brilliant career he oversaw the beginnings of American industry, and he personally did much to ensure that New York, and not Philadelphia or Boston, would become the nation's financial capital.

By 1809, New York's population had topped 100,000. The city continued to prosper in spite of the 1812 War, when a British fleet once again blockaded the harbor and cut off foreign trade. To direct its growth, in 1811 the commissioners came up with the Randel Plan, and laid out the city in a chequerboard of 2028 rectangular blocks. At that point practically the whole of the city north of City Hall and Chambers Street was still rural, and the report coyly admitted '... it may be the subject of merriment that the Commissioners have provided space for a greater population than is collected in any spot this side of China.' Anticipating that most of the traffic would run between the docks on the east and west sides of the island, the commissioners laid out 155 cross-streets with only 12 north-south avenues along its length. The only vestige of the original Manhattan they retained was the Broadway spine, an old Indian trail.

Dawn of the Metropolis;
Immigrant Waves and Tammany Sachems

The Erie Canal, which cost $7 million to build, opened in 1825. Connecting Albany and Buffalo, it gave the east coast access to trade with the Midwest and the Great Lakes, and gave a massive boost to the economy of New York Harbor, making it outstandingly the most important port on the eastern seaboard. By the middle of the century, according to one recent historian, maritime trade had made New York 'the unchallenged metropolis of America'.

While the port expanded and prospered, it also began to bear the brunt of the first of the great tides of European immigrants that swept into America via New York from the early 19th century until the 1920s. In 1819 the first 19,000 immigrants, mostly Irish Catholics, appeared on the scene. Between 1840 and 1857 another 3 million, Irish escaping the potato famines and Germans fleeing the failed Revolution of 1848, followed in their wake.

The city was dismally unprepared for the sudden influx of people. Slums mushroomed all over the city, thanks to the acute shortage of housing, and there were a series of disastrous yellow fever and cholera epidemics between 1818 and 1840, brought on by completely inadequate water supplies and sewage systems. Although business thrived, the gap between rich and poor widened, and in the financial panic of 1837 50,000 became unemployed, and there were a series of riots in which thousands of people convened on City Hall and then ransacked a warehouse, tumbling barrels of flour onto the streets.

Between 1840 and 1860, with the population more than doubling again, a committee including **William Cullen Bryant**, the newspaperman and nature poet, pressed for the building of a Central Park to relieve the congested city. But in the same year as work began on the park, there was another financial crisis, which left 40,000 unemployed. In Tompkins Square, on the Lower East Side, there were hunger demonstrations, and elsewhere troops and howitzers were brought out to protect buildings like the Customs House and the Subtreasury from looters led by violent Irish gangs, like the Dead Rabbits, the O'Connell Guards, the Hudson Dusters, and the Gopher Thugs.

The gangs flourished under the thumb of **Fernando Wood**, so-called grand sachem, or leader, of Tammany Hall, and Mayor from 1850 until the outbreak of the Civil War in 1861. Wood made politics into a profession, and was one of the first in a long line of Tammany bosses who got into power by exploiting the enormous immigrant vote, at a time when a third of the voters in the city were Irish. He was a shifty character, who entered the city on the back legs of an elephant in a circus procession and went on to make his fortune selling bootleg liquor in the Gold Rush.

In the Civil War, the city divided between Wood's Democratic faction, which opposed the war since the immigrant vote was reluctant to serve in the military, and those who sided with the Union against the Confederates in the South. While **Abraham Lincoln** enthused Abolitionists with his famous 'Might Makes Right' speech against slavery at the Cooper Union, Fernando Wood gave his full-hearted support to the South and even went to such ludicrous lengths as proposing New York's secession from the Union.

Disaffection with the war finally erupted in the Draft Riots after Congress passed a compulsory Conscription Act in 1863. The rioters were incensed by a clause in the act exempting the well-off from compulsory military service upon payment of $300 for a substitute. Street battles with the police raged for four days, during which a rabble rampaged the city, burning down the enrolment office, sabotaging telegraph wires and storming the Colored Orphan Asylum. Meanwhile businesses and banks shut down and public transport ground to a halt. In all, about 50,000 rioters took to the streets, bringing New Yorkers face to face with its own hoi-polloi. Over a thousand people were killed and property worth between $2 and $5 million was destroyed.

After the war, Wood was soon upstaged by the most spectacularly crooked of all Tammany's bosses, **William Marcy 'Boss' Tweed**. During his six-year reign, the Boss and his accomplices pocketed something like $200 million between them. Tweed shot up the ladder of caucus politics. He left school at 14, joined a tough gang of riff-raff and a volunteer fire company, the 'Americus'. By the time he was 21, he was thoroughly ensconsed in the Tammany machine. He became an alderman, won a seat on the corrupt City Council dubbed the 'Forty Thieves', and eventually got himself elected as grand sachem.

At last, in 1871, the system of kickbacks, graft and bribes which Tweed had nurtured for so long was exposed by George Jones, the editor of the *New York Times*, and Thomas Nast, the cartoonist, who lampooned Tammany mercilessly with 'those damn pictures', as Tweed called them. He was tried and sent to jail, but escaped and made off for Chile and Cuba. Finally, in Spain, Tweed was re-captured by the Spanish authorities, who sent him back to the prison he had built himself in New York where he died of double pnuemonia.

1865–1918: The Four Hundred and the Four Million

After the Civil War, New York matured into a full-blown metropolis. It was a land of opportunity not just for Tweed and his plundering crew, but also for go-getters who ranged from Eastern European immigrants to parvenues and robber barons who made their fortunes out of commodities like sugar, rubber and gas. Central Park, the Metropolitan Museum, Brooklyn Bridge, New York Public Library and the laying of the Atlantic Cable were all completed in the years before the turn of the century.

By 1863 there were several hundreds of millionaires living in the city, whereas two decades previously there were twenty in the whole nation. In these halcyon days before taxation, the rich indulged themselves in conspicuous consumption as well as philanthropy. New York's new department stores, (A T Stewart's, Arnold Constable's, Macy's and Lord & Taylor's), began catering to the first consumers. By 1900, New York gobbled up four times as much electricity and five times as much water as London. Châteaux and mansions had started their northern march up 5th Avenue, pushing back the shantytowns on the fringes as far as 89th Street.

Society moulded itself into the Four Hundred, the maximum number of guests who could squeeze into Mrs Astor's 5th Avenue ballroom. The Astors, Vanderbilts and Whitneys were the film stars of their day, and their parties were written up in salivating detail for the general public to relish. One report describes an affair at Sherry's Restaurant hosted by C. K. G. Billings, who had supper served to his guests while they sat on horses and sucked champagne through rubber tubes.

A new wave of immigrants, this time from Southern and Eastern Europe and China, swept into the city around the turn of the century, and in 1907 a record 1,285,349 were admitted in a single year. Most of those who stayed in New York found themselves in the Lower East Side, where there was a population density of 330,000 to a square mile. Despite the appalling conditions, the Jewish Lower East Side evolved an intellectual and cultural life of its own. Workers, who were more politically aware than ever, began publishing their own newspapers and striking, though in the end it was a tragic fire at the Triangle Shirtwaist Factory in SoHo in 1911 which killed 145 sweatshop workers, that finally forced through the first legislative reforms. At the same time, a book called *How the Other Half Lives* by a Danish immigrant, Jacob Riis, brought photographs of the slums, sweatshops and street urchins into the front parlors of the well-to-do.

Congestion became such a problem that in 1870 someone called Melville Smith suggested the city build elevated pedestrian walkways or 'arcades' over the streets. The bizarre idea was rejected, but in the 1880s New York got a 'vertical railway', known as the El or Elevated, and in 1904, an infant subway system, the IRT. The subway opened up great expanses of the city to the commuter, in particular Brooklyn, Queens and the Bronx, which had been consolidated into the city in 1898. A construction boom followed, and in 1913 the Woolworth Building became the tallest in the world. New Yorkers began moving into apartment houses and working in skyscrapers, and the skyline metamorphosed into the toothy jaw of the 1930s.

When America entered the war in 1917, one and a half million soldiers were dispatched from New York Port and a steel net was laid across the Narrows to keep out German U-Boats. Flags flapped from every window and the city bubbled with patriotism: New York became the headquarters of US propaganda, and there were attacks on German Americans on the Upper and Lower East Side.

The Twenties: New York at the Top of the World

America emerged triumphantly from the war as a world power, but her policy remained strongly isolationist, and new immigration laws in 1921 and 1924 put such a tight squeeze on quotas that immigration all but ceased until 1965. In New York, however, Harlem suddenly doubled its population from 83,000 to over 200,000, as black people flocked to the city. Most came from the rural south, where farmers were devastated by a world surplus of grain and other agricultural products. Although Harlem was overcrowded with a population density twice that of the rest of Manhattan, it flourished. The next decade saw the Harlem renaissance when writers, artists and musicians like the poet Langston Hughes and the novelist Claude McKay gravitated to what became the capital of black America.

Twenties America was a curious mixture of morality and decadence. Women got the vote, while an alliance of the Women's Christian Temperance Union, the Anti Saloon League and the Methodist Church succeeded in imposing Prohibition of the 'manufacture, sale or transportation' of alcohol, on the whole country. New Yorkers responded with characteristic gusto. One hundred thousand speakeasies opened up for business, and liquor was just as easy to come by as before, except that the lucrative trade was controlled by the criminal underground, and made the fortunes of big-time gangsters like Big Bill O'Dwyer, Dutch Schultz, Lucky Luciano and Louis Lepke. One of the more expensive speakeasies, the 21 Club on 52nd Street had an underground labyrinth of cellars holding 5000 cases, and an automatically disappearing bar.

Embodying the optimism, insouciance and buoyancy of post-War New York was **Jimmy Walker**, its raffish, dandified new mayor. The author of 'Kiss All the Girls for Me', and 'In the Valley Where My Sally Said Goodbye', 'Beau James' was easily the most charming in the city's history. Having started as a happy-go-lucky songwriter on Tin Pan Alley, he moved in much the same milieu during his administration, indulging his passion for nightclubs, sports, gambling, showgirls and clothes (he designed his own clothes, changed as many as five times a day, and once packed 100 ties and 20 new waistcoats on a trip to Europe). Another Tammany man, Walker immediately won the heart of New York when he legalized boxing. Indeed, he was still remembered with affection although an investigation covered his administration in a cloud of scandal and corruption and he resigned in 1932.

In the twenties New York became a fantastical city, obsessed with spectacle. At Rudolph Valentino's fortnight-long funeral in 1926, huge mobs turned out to cheer on the stars and the rose-strewn coffin. On the weekends millions left the city for Dreamland and Luna Park at Coney Island. They canoodled in the Tunnel of Love, laid bets at a 25-acre mechanical race course, went to Midget City, inhabited by 300 dwarfs, and gaped at a lifelike reconstruction of the Creation. In Manhattan, the entertainment king was Samuel Lionel Rothapfel, or 'Roxy', who opened chains of bowling alleys and cleaners, and hosted his own radio show, 'Roxy's Gang'. In 1926, he spent $15 million building his Cathedral of the Motion Picture, the Roxy, which transported New Yorkers into an air-conditioned arcadia of electric fountains, multicoloured flickering lightbulbs, and luxurious Louis Quatorze furniture.

Alongside the rollicking jollity was the drunken economic boom which engendered the Chrysler Building, the Empire State and Rockfeller Center. By 1929 the national income of the US was greater than that of Britain, Germany, Japan, France and 18 other countries put together. Money saturated the stock exchange, and speculation fed on a mixture of its own momentum and cheery events like Lindbergh's Trans-Atlantic flight in 1927. In 1929 tickers were unable to keep up with the pace of business as the market reached an all-time peak. Then suddenly it lost its nerve and the bubble burst. On Black Thursday 13 million shares were sold and 11 speculators killed themselves; five days later, on Tuesday, 29 October, another 16.4 million shares were dumped as Wall Street crashed.

The Thirties: The Little Flower and the Evil Gnome

For the next six years New York was throttled by the worst economic depression in its history. By 1932, one in three New Yorkers in the workforce were unemployed, and 1.6 million on public relief. Many found themselves in shantytowns branded 'Hoovervilles' after the US President. They slept in 'Hoover blankets' made of newspaper, and rummaged in garbage bins for scraps of food. One of the biggest Hoovervilles, with a main thoroughfare dubbed Prosperity Street, was next to the Reservoir in Central Park. Another at the foot of East 10th Street was so well-organized it elected its own mayor and laid on special police and sanitation services.

Coincidentally, in 1934 the city elected **Fiorello La Guardia** as mayor. It was a timely move, since the 'Little Flower' is remembered to this day as the most clean-cut mayor New York ever had. (And also as the stocky, fatherly figure wearing an enormous Stetson who chatted to New Yorkers over Sunday radio broadcasts, and dramatized the comics in a squeaky voice to the children during a newspaper strike.) The son of a Jewish mother and a Protestant Italian father, La Guardia lived in Italian East Harlem and spoke six languages, which he used at Ellis Island where he worked as an interpreter earning money to support himself at law school.

As soon as La Guardia moved into office he had Lucky Luciano arrested and set about cracking down on the criminal underworld, cleaning out the police, and breaking Tammany boss rule. Most importantly of all, however, he got money flowing back into the city from the New Deal, Franklin D. Roosevelt's reform package to set the country back on its feet again. The deal laid down $500 billion dollars for emergency relief and allocated the colossal sum of $4.8 billion to WPA or Works Project Administration to create new jobs.

In New York, WPA soon became the most vigorous engine for economic recovery, creating as many as 7000 assignments and jobs a day, from street cleaners and park laborers to artists and writers. Roosevelt saw New York as a prime testing ground for his New Deal programs, and his support was unstinting. Along with the president and his wife, La Guardia was at the forefront of a new era of liberal politics in America. Between 1934 and the end of his administration in 1945, he pumped dollars into welfare, housing, highways, parks and a new airport. The reforms were massive, ranging from the confiscation of salacious magazines and organ grinders from the street, to the creation of tens of thousands of acres of new parks.

Overseeing the latter was La Guardia's right-hand man, the civil servant **Robert Moses**. While mayors merely came and went, Moses stayed. He stayed for nearly four decades, assuming La Guardia's mantle of reform in the 1940s, and keeping a vice-like grip on it until 1968 by which time he was one of the most powerful and power-hungry men in the city. In the end the imperious Moses emerged as an extraordinary kind of angel-devil, a paradoxical figure compelled at once by misplaced vision, zeal and megalomania. He is sometimes said to have been the greatest single influence over the (car-ensnared) shape of American cities today, and certainly he did more than any other person to recast physical New York into the city we see today.

The achievement was immense. During Moses' half-century reign the city got 627 miles of roadways, seven bridges, Lincoln Center, the World Trade Center and the parks and beaches of Long Island. All worthy causes, but at the cost of laying waste whole expanses of the Bronx and Brooklyn for freeways, uprooting and evicting an estimated quarter of a million people from their homes, blitzing whole neighborhoods, and replacing them with inhuman tower blocks, vertical slums where covers for toilets were considered an unnecessary expense. 'No law, no regulation, no budget stops Bob Moses in his appointed task,' La Guardia had once remarked in admiration.

The Post-War Period: Decay and Bankruptcy

Between the 1939 and 1964 World's Fairs, both Moses' babies, New York plumped out with a population of 7.5 million people. Exhibits in the 1939 World's Fair heralded the triumph of the consumer society—of televisions, sheer nylon stockings, cars, and the family—but it took World War II to create the right economic conditions for the dream to become a reality. During the war, New York once again became the take-off point for American troops and soldiers. The lights were dimmed in Times Square, but most importantly at Columbia University a nuclear experiment by Dr Robert Oppenheimer codenamed the 'Manhattan Project' led to the atomic bomb which ended the war against Japan in August 1945.

In the same year, La Guardia stepped down, and a Democratic candidate, **William O'Dwyer**, became mayor. After the War, the city became suddenly affluent, and naturally there was a burst of construction. Moses talked O'Dwyer into giving the United Nations a permanent home in Manhattan, saying it would fix New York as the capital of the world, and in 1948 the complex was built on land worth $8.5 billion which John D. Rockefeller bought and donated.

In the next decade, the neo-classical residences along Park Avenue were bulldozed and replaced by a slick new boulevard of glass skyscrapers with plazas and concourses like Lever House and the Seagram. In 1947 Stuyvesant Town and Peter Cooper Village were built as middle-income housing, initially for war veterans on the Lower East Side. They proved such an inspiring success that the city brought in huge tax abatements to encourage similar schemes like the Manhattan Urban Renewal Project on the Upper West Side, which all but collapsed in a scandal over finances and tax abatements. O'Dwyer himself resigned in disgrace over his connections with the criminal underground and a crooked bookie called Harry Gross—though ironically, years before he became mayor, O'Dwyer the District Attorney had helped crush crime syndicates including the Brooklyn hit squad, Murder Inc.

O'Dwyer left for Mexico with his tail between his legs, while New York braced itself for a third tidal wave of immigration. Between 1950 and 1970 1.6 million new faces arrived in the city, many of them black, Hispanic and Puerto Rican. The combination of oafish urban planning and the construction boom in the business sections of Manhattan drove the newcomers into a shrinking pool of run-down housing in the inner-city ghettoes, and entangled them in a vicious circle of poverty.

Crime and vandalism escalated, and the middle classes and families left in droves. In the great 'White Flight' of the 50s and 60s more than a million people fled New York and big corporations like Mobil and Union Carbide decamped for the suburbs. The city erupted in a series of terrible riots in Harlem and Bedford-Stuyvesant in 1964 and East Brooklyn and the South Bronx in 1967, part of the wave of violent battles between the police and the ghettoes which devastated cities all over America in the 60s. Molotov cocktails and bottles filled with gasoline were thrown in the streets, buildings and refuse bins were incinerated, and everywhere there were allegations of police brutality.

New York staggered through a number of strikes, including a transit strike by 34,400 workers in 1966 which cost $70 million to resolve. Spending on social welfare rocketed, and the city imposed higher and higher taxes, only to find that the exodus of businesses and middle classes had shattered the tax base. Though the mayor, **Abe Beame**, was an accountant, by 1975 he was spending $12.8 billion and taking only $10.9 billion. By 15 October, New York seemed hours away from bankruptcy. As panic struck, everyone looked to the White House to bail them out, but an intractable Ford administration sat on its hands and refused absolutely to part with a cent of federal aid, prompting the famous *Daily News* headline: 'Ford to New York—Drop Dead!'.

In the end the city was rescued by last minute loans from the teachers and sanitation unions. In the next few months the city got a new fiscal programme courtesy of Big MAC, or the Municipal Assistance Corporation, which was formed to act as a watchdog over the spendthrifts at City Hall. Washington was sufficiently impressed, and finally came up with a short term loan of two and half billion, and the next year a consortium of bankers headed by David Rockefeller raised a further $600 million.

New York in the Eighties: A Tale of Two Cities

Crestfallen, New York hobbled through the next three years with a drooping morale. More than 65,000 workers lost their jobs in municipal government; teachers, police and firemen took wage freezes, and the poor were especially hard hit by drastic cutbacks in basic services and welfare allowances. It was only with the election of **Ed Koch** in 1978 that the city revived a little. It was not so much that Koch saved the city from insolvency, but more that his readiness to smash crime, get tough with the unions and tighten the belt everywhere else won back the confidence of the economic kingpins: the real estate boys, Wall Street's money men and Washington.

With a newly robust economy, Koch miraculously paid back federal loans a year ahead of schedule, and in 1985 he announced a budget surplus. This was at the height of another construction boom, subsidized by more tax abatements and low interest loans, in which 60 new skyscrapers burrowed up into the Manhattan skyline, including the quirky AT&T Building, the grotesque, golden Trump Tower, and the three gleaming blue-glass prongs of the World Financial Center in Battery Park City.

A Jewish boy from the Bronx, Koch cultivated a brash, wittily outspoken style which won admirers. He was maniacally patriotic about his own city, and during his three-terms he commissioned the song 'I Love New York' and wrote two books about himself, one of which was turned into a Broadway musical. He even managed to survive the bureaucratic scandal which blew up around him after the Democratic borough president of Queens, Donald Manes, committed suicide in 1986.

By 1990, New York had lost patience and was ready for a less pugnacious and more sympathetic kind of administration; Koch finally fell from power, and his place was taken by **David Dinkins**, the city's first black mayor. Manhattan had boomed in the eighties; huge areas of the city were gentrified and spruced up with restaurants and shops, but it was at the expense of the poor, who only got poorer. Today, one in four New Yorkers live below the poverty line. In Harlem the infant mortality rate is the same as a Third World country and there is a 70 per cent drop-out rate in high schools. In the city as a whole there are an estimated 90,000 people who are homeless, and in the last few years crack has been blamed for increases in violence and crime, and AIDS has put an extra strain on health services.

With MAC once again warning that a recession is looming, Dinkins has a daunting task ahead of him. In the eighties, New York's compressed mixture of opulence and squalor became a symbol for a nation increasingly divided into haves and have-nots. Rebuilding a sense of community in this city will prove as difficult a job as the more concrete problems of the schools, social services and the collapsing infrastructure. On the other hand, Dinkins can rely on the energy of the million new immigrants speaking more than 128 languages who have arrived in the city in the last decade. The Manhattan founded by a group of settlers who spoke 18 languages between them, is still a city of transients and newcomers, and somehow their spirit and flair keep the wheels grinding in this most impossible of cities.

An Architectural Compendium

decoration on Grand Central Terminal

'A town that eats up its own tail every five or ten years'.
—Jerome Charyn, *Metropolis*, 1986

'Overturn, overturn, overturn! is the maxim of New York.
The very bones of our ancestors are not permitted to lie
quiet a quarter of a century and one generation of men seem
studious to remove all relics of those who precede them'.
—Philip Hone, *The Diary of Philip Hone*, 1845

In one of the most transient cities in the world, buildings are doomed to
an anxious existence. The wrecker's ball lurks around every corner, big
buildings prey on small buildings, giant buildings prey on big buildings,
and the average New Yorker outlives all of them. In other cities, buildings stand for endurance and stability; in New York they remind you of
your own impermanence.

The architecture of Manhattan comes as a delightful shock. Instead of
neatly proportioned rows of sleek skyscrapers, the first thing that im-
presses outsiders is a sense of planned chaos; what Le Corbusier called
the 'beautiful catastrophe'. Here, buildings have zest—they can be
uplifting, squalid, shabby, modern, brutal, hideous, illogical and over-
powering—all together in a jumble. On paper, Manhattan is impossible,
but somehow it exists; an anarchic pandemonium contained within the
geometry of an invisible two-dimensional grid.

70

From the moment the colony started raising revenue by selling off water lots to merchants, the architecture of Manhattan has been the by-product of commerical enterprise. In the 17th century, the word 'speculation' meant astronomy, star-gazing and heavenly contemplation. Today, of course, it has split into two, referring at once to the enterprises of the down-to-earth real estate developer and to the lofty conjectures of philosophers and thinkers. Speculation does not account for the evolution of a settlement of 200 Dutch gable houses into a man-made mountain range of 100-story shimmering glass skyscrapers. But it helps to explain how the curious mixture of the utilitarian and the wildly whimsical came to be so characteristic of Manhattan's architecture.

The compendium sketches a brief chronology of Manhattan's architecture from the Dutch settlement onwards. The Manhattanite's traditional disrespect for the past has meant that the survival of specific architectural styles has been a distinctly haphazard affair. It is partly through neglect, that ghostly remembrances of old New York hang on in little pockets of low-rise buildings all over the city. Miraculously, many of the styles and buildings mentioned below are still there, though in some cases finding them requires more than a little detective work.

New Amsterdam

New Amsterdam was a congested little town, hemmed in by a ramshackle wooden fence which became Manhattan's first cross-street and is nowadays known as Wall Street. The settlement was homely, rather than pioneering, and full of comforting reminders of old Amsterdam—canals and windmills, clogs and neat rows of traditional Dutch houses built

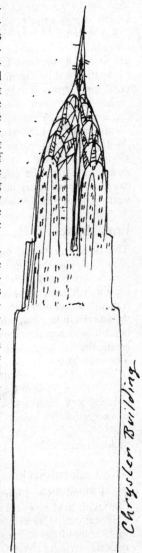

Chrysler Building

gable-end to the street with steeply pitched crow-stepped roofs and Dutch 'stoeps' or stoops.

It is often said that New York's best structures (Brooklyn Bridge, Grand Central Terminal, Central Park, the Statue of Liberty, the Grid) are first and foremost feats of engineering, so it is appropriate that Manhattan's first architect—**Cryn Fredericksz**—was actually an engineer. He was sent in 1623 by the East India Company to lay out a typical Dutch town of tidy rectangular plots for farms, gardens and orchards, plus an intimidating fort. The plans made no allowances for the topography of the island, however, and New Amsterdam settled for the higgledy-piggledy medieval street plan which survives to this day, along with a modest and rather flimsy fort which was liable to collapse in rainstorms. Nevertheless, maps and pictures were dutifully sent back to the Hague portraying the settlement, with shameless exaggeration, as a walled city of Renaissance grandeur.

English New York

The British destroyed most of Dutch New Amsterdam, and English New York was then, in its turn, almost entirely obliterated during the Revolution. New Yorkers recall the Dutch settlement with affection, but the English presence is seldom mentioned, except by some people who remember that pigs were allowed to roam free to eat up the garbage in the streets. In fact it was the English who in 1664 initiated the practice of landfill, which persists to this day. In 1664, to raise revenue from real estate, the city began selling off 'water lots' on land exposed at low tide. The merchants who bought them built cribs which they sunk into the swampy soil below and filled with 'landfill' consisting of debris, soil and ship's ballast. Most of English New York became landfill itself, and the only pre-Revolutionary building remaining from British rule is St Paul's, an exceptionally elegant Georgian church built in fields next to Broadway in 1766 by Thomas McBean, a pupil of the great English church builder James Gibbs.

The Federal Style

The Federal Style, a more classical, Americanized version of English-Georgian, held sway over the city between the 1760s and the 1830s. Classical details harked back to the Roman republic, making it perfect for civic buildings and monuments. Indeed, the supreme example of the Federal style in Manhattan must be **Joseph Mangin** and **John**

McComb's City Hall (see pp. 221–2). An engineer from France, Mangin had worked on the Place de la Concorde in Paris, and the final exterior of City Hall, reminiscent of a château, smacked more of Mangin's native panache than of the Scotsman McComb's more restrained hand. The interior is outstanding: filled by a great cantilevered marble staircase with coffered dome and Adam-style decoration.

Apart from its civic buildings, the Federal style produced some of the most charming townhouses the city has known. The semidetached houses were a model of simplicity, perhaps because most were assembled by carpenters (rather than architects) who took details at random from English pattern books. Two or three stories tall, the row house's most typical characteristics were its two 'eyes', a pair of dormer windows peeping out of a pitched roof, and its entrance consisting of a stoop and a front door decorated with classical columns and a fan-light illuminating the hallway inside. The best examples today can be found in TriBeCa's Charlton, King and Vandam Streets, and in parts of Brooklyn Heights.

Eclecticism: Mixed-up New York

New York is mixed-up! The confusion of styles can be mad and dynamic! And it is exactly this which demonstrates the creative power of the city.'
—Reinhart Wolf, *Interview with Andy Warhol, 1980*

The Classical Revival of the 18th century and the Greek War of Independence in 1821 naturally appealed to Jeffersonian ideals of democracy and to architects searching for a distinctively American style. Translated to the New World, the 'Greek Revival' caught on in the climate of economic euphoria that followed the opening of the Erie Canal in 1825. The style itself was democratic, in that its columns, porticoes and pediments could be tacked on to all sorts of buildings—from courts, churches, banks and businesses to well-to-do town and country houses—and immediately conferred dignity, urbanity and confidence. Perhaps the best example of Greek-Revival New York is 'The Row', the fleet of aristocratic townhouses connected by an unbroken cornice on Washington Square, developed in the 1830s and home to Henry James' grandmother.

The American Greek Revival sparked off a silent 30-year war of styles and a succession of neo-Gothic, Romanesque, Renaissance, Italianate, and even Federal Revivals. 'Though New Yorkers imitate the dead and gone of Italy and Greece,' wrote one commentator, 'they will not copy their next-door neighbors'. Practically all the different styles are contained in Brooklyn Heights, which was divided up and sold off in lots from the 1820s until the end of the century, and remains New York's finest encyclopaedia of the 19th-century townhouse.

The New York Brownstone

By the 1850s Italianate styles came out on top, and the New York brownstone, which Edith Wharton referred to as a disgusting kind of cold chocolate sauce, triumphantly dribbled its way through Manhattan. Though nowadays it is regarded with great affection and priced accordingly skyhigh, the poor old brownstone was snubbed as the worst kind of architectural parvenu right up until the 1950s.

Mined in New Jersey and Connecticut, brownstone was cheap to quarry and easy to carve, and could be slapped like veneer onto an even cheaper brick structure below. Brownstone lots were narrow and deep, and because space was limited, they filled up the whole area available. Instead of back entrances and alleys, their fronts were equipped with stoops—steep flights of steps leading up and down to entrances on the ground and basement floors. Originally descended from the Dutch *stoep*, as an anti-flooding device, the stoop was useful in New York because it meant that tradesmen and guests could use the same entrance and a saving could be made on valuable real estate.

Another advantage was that once he had the basic template, the client could tart up his brownstone with all sorts of grandiose appendages, such as enormous overhanging Renaissance cornices (resembling the eaves on a traditional Dutch farmhouse) and fancy cast-iron railings, lamps and bannisters (some even lost the stoops in an attempt to look fashionably English). The carving on the communal-garden brownstone, however, is pretty clumsy, and fire escapes are often the brownstone's most conspicuous feature.

Eventually, in the 1880s, the brownstone was superseded by the more sophisticated Queen Anne and Romanesque townhouses of the Upper West Side. Finally, it was demolished to make way for the rise of apartment houses and department stores in the thirties. Still, a good deal survive, especially on Lexington and 3rd Avenues, in Harlem, and on the east and west fringes of Midtown. Indeed, the style has come to seem so

74

ubiquitous in the city, that the term 'brownstone' often refers to any old townhouse, whether it is faced with brownstone or not.

Geometrical New York: The Grid

> The chequerboard blocks, the recurrent regularity of the
> streets, you admit, point to something planned: but the
> buildings are eruptive and the whole city abnormal—
> something again that apparently just 'happened'.
> —John Van Dyke, *The New New York*, 1909

In 1811 New York's commissioners devised the grid: a chessboard superimposed on a ghost city that did not yet exist. 'It may be a subject of merriment', the report admitted, 'that the Commissioners have provided space for a greater population than is collected on any spot this side of China'. It was the most reckless real estate venture in the history of New York. At the time the island was rural, and although there was a smattering of hamlets in Greenwich Village and Harlem, the town proper occupied a space barely a mile long at its butt-end (to skimp on costs, the back of the new City Hall at the northern frontier was faced in brownstone rather than marble, because no one imagined that the city could grow any further).

An engineer, **John Randel Jr.**, was contracted to survey Manhattan. Though he was attacked several times for trespassing and was once arrested by the sheriff, he managed to cover the whole island, and came up with a plan imitating 13th-century Peking. Ignoring the natural terrain of hills, valleys and lakes, Randall sliced up the land into a horizontal plane of 2028 rectangular blocks of busy avenues (for commerce and business) and quieter cross-streets (for residences). And so Manna-hatta, the Indian 'island of hills', evolved into today's geometrical mountain range of buildings.

The commissioners were not interested in planning a beautiful city of parks and boulevards in the style of Sixtus V's Rome, or Haussmann's Paris, and made no provision for today's Central Park, except for a meagre 'Parade' on 34th Street. Like those of their Dutch forebears, the concerns of New Yorkers were the practical matters of real estate and economy. As the report put it, 'a city is composed principally of the habitations of men, and straight sided, and right-angled houses are the most cheap to build and the easiest to live in'.

On the other hand, because it laid down no aesthetic restrictions whatsoever, the grid gave free rein to architectural improvisation. This affected the development of New York in two ways. First the grid encouraged vertical growth: creating a ladder which New York's more intrepid social pioneers climbed in society's relentless attempt to flee the encroachment of commerce and business. And secondly it functioned and still functions as the rigid skeleton of city which is permanently changing; where buildings gobble each other up and seem to float, like Madison Square Garden which has changed its location four times in the last century. 'Within the grid architectural conformity to a general design is something not required, not planned, not even contemplated,' wrote the impassioned architectural critic Van Dyke, 'nothing shall be like anything else, nothing shall conform except by the law of contrariety'.

Central Park

By the middle of the 19th century the only large-scaled formal recreational space in New York was Green-Wood Cemetery, a romantic 478-acre landscape of rolling hills and lakes in Brooklyn which was popular with strollers and tourists on weekends (see p. 125). Central Park, on the other hand, was planned at the last minute 18 years after Green-Wood in 1858, when Manhattan looked as though it was about to be engulfed in a sea of real estate. The work of two great landscape architects—**Frederick Law Olmsted**, (another engineer), and the English designer, **Calvert Vaux**, Central Park is an extraordinary creation: an 840-acre carpet of countryside rolled out in the heart of the city, containing a range of sample landscapes for the urban rambler. Though it looks natural, the park is entirely synthetic, carved out of scrubland previously used by squatters. The project was a feat of engineering: 10 million cartloads of earth and stone were removed for the landscaping, and transverse roads from the west to the east side of Manhattan were sunk into the ground, so pedestrians were hardly aware of them (see p. 126).

Red New York: Apartment Houses and Tenements

The origins of New York's mythically palatial apartment houses are distinctly lowly. They lie in tenements built from the 1840s onwards to contain the great 19th-century influx of immigrants from Ireland, Germany, Italy and Eastern Europe, a good deal of whom found themselves in the squalid slums of the Bowery and a dingy disreputable area known as the Five Points.

The first tenements striped New York in horizontal bands of red brick and green cornices, like an Edward Hopper painting. Nice to look at, but ghastly to inhabit, they would have been more bearable had they not been so horrendously congested. Five- or six-story walk-ups took up 90 ft of the standard 100 by 25 ft lot enforced by Randel's grid plan. Ventilated by a narrow airshaft (which stank because it was used as an unofficial garbage dump), each building held at least 20 families, with a shared bathroom on each floor and lavatories in the basement aerated by grates in the street. The worst horrors of the slums were the tenement-lodging houses; impossibly overcrowded, signs outside advertised 'Standing Room' and space in hallways for 5 and 3 cents a night.

In 1901 a law was passed on these 'Old Law' tenements demanding stricter regulations on air, light, and density. It was pusillanimously enforced, and in the end it was the more stringent legislation of 1929 that fazed out tenement construction altogether. Even so, great numbers of tenements survive all over the city, particularly on the less well-off perimeters of the city, in the Lower East Side, Alphabet City, Harlem, Amsterdam Avenue and the Bronx. Many have been gentrified, many remain hopelessly overcrowded, and some in the most desperate areas are simply empty shells, blackened and gutted by fire. Typically, façades are wreathed in a jungle of fire escapes (Henry James described them as a ghastly 'little world of bars and perches and swings for human squirrels and monkeys'); and the roofs, New York's own 'costa del tarmac', are blanketed in a seaweed of wires, cables and television aerials. Underneath all this trim, you can occasionally make out fine plaster carvings and gargoyles over the entrances executed in the 19th century by Italian immigrants.

By the turn of the century, congestion and real estate prices had reached such a pitch that the middle classes reluctantly vacated their brownstones. Instead of tenements, they moved into Parisian 'apartment-hotels' or 'French flats'. Although the first proper apartment house was built down on East 18th Street in 1869, the city's pioneering apartment dwellers settled the Upper West Side. Here, establishments like the Ansonia, the Dakota and the Dorilton imitated French châteaux and Baroque castles, but their interiors were equipped with all mod-cons, from the usual central heating, primitive air-conditioning and

77

refrigerators, to pnuematic pipes for polishing top hats, bakeries, restaurants and servants.

After the First World War it was the turn of the rich to evacuate their free-standing mansions on 5th Avenue and squeeze into 22-room apartment-palazzi on the newly created Park Avenue, then known as New York's 'gold-digger's lane'. These buildings were conservative in design, but during the twenties massive Art-Deco apartment houses were developed on Central Park West. The twin-pronged towers of the Majestic, the Beresford, the San Remo, the Eldorado and the Century Building studded the twenties skyline with the theatricality of a stage set.

The Chicago World's Fair and Beaux-Arts Civic Monuments

Orchestrated by **Daniel Burnham**, who designed the Flatiron Building on Madison Square, the Chicago World's Fair of 1893 envisioned an American renaissance of buildings designed in richly classical beaux-arts styles, with cities laid out according to the rather urbane beaux-arts ideals of pomp and circumstance. The Fair had an immense impact on New York. The influence of the more radical Chicago school of skyscraper architects was quashed, and New York turned into a sugar-white city of civic buildings and monuments. This style dominated the period between the 1890s and the 1920s when Manhattan got its most magnificent and aristocratic civic architecture, from the great public library on 42nd Street to Park Avenue to the aptly named Grand Central Terminal (see pp. 247–8).

One of the quirks of these buildings is that they are so well versed in the art of surprise. Because the grid precludes the vistas which beaux-arts buildings rely on for a truly grandiose impact, Manhattan's civic monuments lurk round corners, and then leap into view. The only New York building with a proper approach is **Cass Gilbert's** Custom House, a stupendous Paris Opéra adapted for commerce, which sits on Bowling Green on the layout devised for 17th-century New Amsterdam (see pp. 100–1). The grid plays strange tricks on conventionally beaux-arts designs, most spectacularly on the sumptuous façade of **Warren & Wetmore's** Grand Central Terminal, where the three great arched windows and the central sculpture group are almost entirely upstaged by a great tongue of Park Avenue viaduct sticking out of the middle.

Spurring on the New York renaissance were a clutch of American architects who had trained at the École des Beaux Arts in Paris, and most of whom had exhibited at the Chicago World's Fair. One, **Richard Morris Hunt**, had actually worked on the north façade of the Louvre, before he embarked on several 5th Avenue mansions, including Mrs Astor's gargantuan ballroom on 61st Street; a swaggering baroque front for the city's stately home of culture, the Metropolitan Museum of Art (see pp. 200–4), and an enormous pedestal for the Statue of Liberty (see pp. 98–9).

The designs of the beaux-arts school of architects drew on an eclectic range of European styles, interpreted them with far more verve than the originals, and then adapted them to an extraordinary variety of functions. For example, **George Post** designed a sturdy Roman temple for Wall Street's Stock Exchange (see p. 105), and a replica of the Château de Blois for Mrs Vanderbilt. The team of **Carrère & Hastings**, produced a version of Charles Girault's Petit Palais in Paris for a beaux-arts swimming pool which is still open in Hamilton Fish Park on the Lower East Side; and a second look at their most famous work, the New York Public Library, reveals that it is actually a free-wheeling Versailles (see pp. 184–5). Sometimes designs became downright eccentric, as in **Whitney Warren's** batty New York Yacht Club on West 44th Street, with its three bay windows carved to resemble the sterns of 18th-century clippers and gushing stone waves.

New York's pre-eminent civic architects were the McKim, Mead and White triumvirate: **Charles Follen McKim**, the austere classicist of the group, **Stanford White**, the brilliant, romantic genius with a flair for the picturesque and a penchant for chorus girls (he died in suitably flamboyant style when he was shot on the roof of one of his own buildings by the deranged husband of an ex-mistress); and **William Rutherford Mead**, a relatively pedestrian worker, doomed to obscurity by his more colorful partners.

Although this odd trio worked outside the city (the Mall in Washington DC, a rebuilding of the White House, and the campuses of Harvard and the University of Virginia), they were firmly rooted in New York. Scores of projects commissioned for the city included churches, mansions and hospitals, stations, offices and restaurants. Perhaps their greatest work of all, alas no more, was Penn Station, an immensely grand space based on the Roman Baths of Caracalla, and replaced by the new Madison Square Garden jukebox-oil drum in 1966. Nevertheless their impact on New York is still highly visible—from the clubs based on outsized Florentine palazzis on 5th Avenue, to Washington Arch in Greenwich Village, Brooklyn Museum, Columbia University, and the towering Municipal Building on Centre Street which so impressed Stalin's architects.

Embryonic Skyscrapers

> This is the first sensation of life in New York—you feel that
> the Americans have practically added a new dimension to
> space. When they find themselves a little crowded, they
> simply tilt a street on end and call it a skyscraper.
> —William Archer, *America Today*, 1899

When it rose up to loom down Wall Street in 1846, the 284 ft Gothic Revival spire of Trinity Church was the tallest in the city, and tourists were encouraged to climb to the top, where the great height made 'the people in the streets seem like pygmies, and the vehicles like so many toys'. Seven years later, Manhattan got its first prototypical skyscraper: the Latting Observatory, a 350 ft tower of timber and iron, erected on 42nd Street along with a Crystal Palace as part of the World's Fair of 1853. Taller than the Statue of Liberty, it was one of the highest structures ever built in Manhattan (until the contruction of the 390 ft 31-story Park Row Building in 1899). The Observatory was equipped with a steam elevator and in the style of the Empire State Building today, tourists bought ice-creams from shops at the base and then took elevators to telescopes on the first and second floors.

It was the invention of the elevator, with the introduction of cast and wrought iron, that made skyscrapers feasible; and both came together in New York in 1857. Peter Cooper, the iron-works owner and developer of the *Tom Thumb* locomotive, installed wrought-iron railway tracks as beams in his building on Astor Place, the Cooper Union For the Advancement of Science and Art (see p. 143). In the same year, Otis installed the first safety elevator in the new Haughwout Building, a cast-iron palazzo-department store in SoHo. The Haughwout was one of hundreds of cast-iron warehouses built in SoHo from the 1850s onwards. Cast-iron was quick to assemble and cheap to manufacture, and unlike traditional load-bearing walls, the frames were strong enough to support an infinite number of stories.

Manhattan's first elevator building and skyscraper proper was the 12-story Tower Building, constructed in 1889 at 50 Broadway. Most New Yorkers now spend about a week every year traveling in

Manhattan's 32,000 elevators, but when the Tower Building was completed people were so nervous that the architect was forced to live on the 11th story to prove it was safe. It was not the tallest building on the island, but it was the first to use a steel skeleton and stone curtain-wall construction. Other pioneering scrapers, like the Park Row Building of 1899, shot up near City Hall on Printing House Square.

In 1898 Chicago's most radical skyscraper designer, **Louis Sullivan**, designed the Bayard-Condict Building on Bleecker Street. It was an iconoclastic work, rejecting the neo-classical rules expounded by the Chicago World's Fair of 1893. Instead it fulfilled Sullivan's dictum that 'form follow function': that buildings should express their purpose (in this case offices) and their structure (a steel-cage skeleton). This form of anti-historical functionalism did not go down well with staid New Yorkers, and Sullivan received no more commissions in Manhattan.

Evolution of the Skyscraper I: Sodom by the Sea

New York's infant scrapers are peculiar beings, based loosely on the classical column, with sensible bases and trunks topped by fantastically flamboyant capitals. The fancy hats are shamelessly eclectic. Stolen from Gothic, Romanesque, Renaissance and beaux-arts styles, their creators cared little about aesthetic integrity.

The architectural historian, Rem Koolhaas, has put forward the delightful theory that Coney Island's fantastical architecture influenced Manhattan's early scrapers. Dubbed a latter-day 'Sodom' by its detractors, Brooklyn's Coney Island's acquired massive amusement parks around the turn of the century. The first developer, George Tilyou, started in 1881 with an Observation Tower he had bought from the 1876 Centennial Exhibition in Philadelphia. At 300 ft, the skeletal structure was taller than anything in Manhattan. It was accompanied by Brazilian and Japanese pavilions from the same exhibition, a hotel constructed in the shape of a 150 ft elephant, and a replica of a ferris wheel built for the Chicago World's Fair of 1883.

The island's second developer was the showman Fred Thompson, a drop-out from the École des Beaux Arts in Paris. In 1903 he designed Luna Park, an extraordinary premonition of the finialed Manhattan that emerged in the twenties, complete with 1214 electrically illuminated minarets and towers, and a skyline straight out of *The Arabian Nights*. Anticipating the eclecticism of Manhattan's early scrapers, Thompson declared that his buildings rejected all the set forms of architecture, and

81

that the architect 'must dare to decorate a minaret with Renaissance detail or to jumble Romanesque with *l'art nouveau* always with the idea of keeping his line constantly varied, broken, and moving, so that it may lead gracefully into the towers and minarets of a festive sky-line'.

A year later the erstwhile state senator and real estate promoter J. R. Reynolds opened Dreamland, with its million electric lights and a Renaissance tower which soared 375 ft into the air, bearing an uncanny resemblance to the Metropolitan Life Tower built five years later on Madison Square. For Dreamland, Reynolds employed a New York architectural firm who produced a white city resembling the 1893 Chicago World's Fair (see Beaux-arts, above, for its influence on Manhattan architects). Completing the circle, a quarter of a century after Dreamland, Reynolds was the developer responsible for Manhattan's most whimsical Christmas tree of all, the Chrysler Building.

Evolution of the Skyscraper II: Manhattan Palazzi

Meanwhile, in Manhattan the race to build the tallest building began in earnest. In 1902 **Daniel Burnham**, the great skyscraper builder from Chicago and director of the World's Fair, built one of Manhattan's most irresistible skyscrapers on Madison Square. An inflated Renaissance palazzo, it was constructed out of a steel cage and stood on a triangular site. Looking like an ocean liner sailing up Broadway, it was immediately nicknamed the Flatiron Building after its peculiar shape. At 300 ft it was a little shorter than the Park Row Building on Broadway, but it still dwarfed its neighbouts and many New Yorkers found its shape so disturbing they were convinced it would collapse in the wind.

The Flatiron was followed in 1908 by another composite palazzo-tower, **Ernest Flagg's** great Singer Building, double the height of the Flatiron and, unfortunately, a magnet for suicides. Demolished in 1970, it still holds the record as the tallest building ever blown up. A year later, however, in 1909 the Singer was beaten in height by the Metropolitan Life Tower, a bizarre 712 ft version of the Campanile of St Marks in Venice which stood opposite the Flatiron and dwarfed it.

By 1908 skyscrapers were being touted as miniature cities: the idea had been a New York obsession ever since Melville's Bartleby the Scrivener, who preferred not to move out of his Wall Street office. In the skyscraper, architects had at last created a totally autonomous environment which rivalled nature.

In 1913, the skyscraper reached maturity in the form of **Cass**

Gilbert's Woolworth Tower, the tallest building in the world at 792 ft, and a monumental advertisement for Frank Woolworth's great chain of five-and-dime stores (see pp. 220–21). A fan of Napoleon and of Barry's Houses of Parliament in London, Woolworth commissioned and received a Gothic Revival masterpiece of imperial proportions.

Zoning

In 1915 the Equitable Building loomed up on Broadway, containing offices for 15,000 workers and 45 acres of space on a plot just bigger than an acre. It was so blatantly greedy, screening out all light and air from the streets around it, that it precipitated the Zoning Law of 1916.

The zoning laws introduced a vertical grid plan. Instead of rising sheer from their sites as the Equitable did, at a certain height buildings had to step back from the plotline, or area on which they stood. A tower could then rise as high as the builder could take it, so long as it filled no more than 25 per cent of the plot. For the next half century, the laws transformed the skyline of Manhattan along the lines of the finials, pyramids and ziggurats of Luna Park on Coney Island.

Art-Deco Aerodynamics

Despite the world-beating height of some of its towers, New York was palpably slow in catching up with the design innovations taking place in Chicago and Europe at this time. The catalyst for change was a combination of the zoning laws, and the launch of Art Deco at the Paris *Exposition des Arts Decoratifs* of 1925. The skyscrapers that resulted were new and imaginative in style and decoration, and they gave New York its extraordinary skyline, although they were not fundamentally iconoclastic.

The obsession was with aerodynamics; and, like fireworks, nearly all the futuristic scrapers of the twenties and thirties unwittingly imitate rockets, or refer to flight. Most famously, the Empire State Building was equipped with a mast for dirigibles, hyped as the transport of the future. Similarly, the American Radiator Building caught a green-colored fire at the top, like an upended firecracker; while the Waldorf-Astoria had an electrically retractable roof, and stood on stilts wedged between the tracks of Grand Central. The architect of the Chrysler hid a spire in the roof, tacked on at the last minute to beat the briefest Tallest Building in the World, at 40 Wall Street, and the Chrysler itself was tricked out in icons of the automobile. Four years later, Walter Chrysler brought out the streamlined and finned 'Airflow' model which looked like a speed car (it was also available as with the same engine and chassis, and a 'traditional' body).

New York's architects began experimenting with the zoning laws; and one, **Hugh Ferriss**, actually gave up architectural practice in order to concentrate on drafting an imaginary New York of the air, with the tops of skyscrapers as hangars, airports and runways. Likewise, in 1923 **Harvey Wiley Corbett** (who later worked on Rockefeller Center) proposed a scheme for the Regional Plan Association of New York for 'a modernized Venice'. Pedestrians were elevated onto overhead bridges and walkways, and surface levels were abandoned to trucks and cars. Six years later **Raymond Hood** proposed a city of apartment houses built along the spans of the East River bridges.

Rockefeller Center: New York's City-within-a-city

The various plans for a new New York eventually merged in the city's unparalleled example of urban planning: Rockefeller Center, which surfaced in the midst of the Depression in the years between 1931 and 1938 (see pp. 188–9). Here at last New York had created the true city-within-a-city: an organic complex whose underground concourses magically absorbed pedestrians, cars, tourists, delivery trucks and businessmen, and whose scrapers functioned as offices, theaters, cinemas, museums, television studios and plazas which were showcases for modern sculpture.

It was a brilliant achievement that vindicated the dreamy, whimsical reputation of Art Deco.

Raymond Hood and the International Style

In the 1930s **Raymond Hood** emerged as New York's most innovative skyscraper architect. His two most remarkable scrapers, the Daily News and the McGraw-Hill (see p. 250), stood as sentinels of the avant-garde at either end of 42nd Street. The Daily News Building at the east end is New York's earliest (and many would say superior) version of the slabs that proliferated across post-war Manhattan. It is pinstriped in brown and white brick, with spandrels set close together, emphasizing the vertical thrust of the building in a way that obviously inspired New York's supreme skyscraper, the soaring RCA Building in Rockefeller Center, designed a few years later by a consortium including Hood.

The McGraw-Hill Building, likewise, spans the gap between pre-war Art Deco and modernism. It is also one of the city's most appealingly extravagant skyscrapers, with a sleek Art-Deco lobby, and a matchless glimmering green terracotta exterior tipped with gold which turns from a greeny-blue at the bottom to a lighter leafy green at the top, making the scraper look taller than it really is.

Though they piously denounced its Deco details, the architect Philip Johnson, then only 26, and the critic Henry Russell Hitchcock, hailed the McGraw-Hill as the only New York building to merit inclusion in their compendium of 1932 called *The International Style*. Their own coinage, the 'international style' referred loosely to the work of the Viennese architects Loos and Hoffmann, the radical Dutch group, de Stijl, and also to the founder of the Bauhaus, Walter Gropius—all of whom were rejecting ornament and decoration for abstract and cubist designs, curtain walls and corner windows well before the First World War. Hitchcock and Johnson welcomed the new movement as a universal style; a successor to the anonymous but standardized architecture of the Middle Ages. Scandalized by the brazen caprice of Art Deco, the authors proclaimed the McGraw-Hill as the only structure in Manhattan which—thanks to its horizontal bands of windows—came close to 'achieving aesthetically the expression of the enclosed steel cage'.

The Rise and Fall of the Glass Box

Along with the exhibitions organized by Philip Johnson at New York's temple of modernism—the new Museum of Modern Art on 53rd Street—*The International Style* paved the way for the supremacy of the glass slab. The war, of course, brought construction to a halt, but it also prompted an influx of architects fleeing Europe. In the hiatus, the Bauhaus boys infiltrated all the important American schools: Gropius became head of architecture at Harvard; Mies van der Rohe (at that time Johnson's mentor) took a similar position at the Illinois Institute of Technology; while Moholy Nagy founded the Chicago Institute of Design, and Josef Albers became a director of Yale.

After the war, the architecture of Manhattan was transformed. The marriage of reinforced concrete and air-conditioning created office space which was infinite, and in which only the top nobs got to sit next to a window. In 1952 the first International Style glass curtain-wall arrived, (courtesy of the new United Nations buildings, a project initiated by Le Corbusier), and Manhattan's first fully fledged glass box was born. Slabs invaded Midtown and Lower Manhattan's streets and avenues, and blunted the elegantly jagged skyline of the pre-war years. The only exception to their homogeneity was **Frank Lloyd Wright's** enigmatic white snail-shell, the Guggenheim Museum (see pp. 204–6), the second and last of his commissions in Manhattan (which was still twice as many as his mentor, Louis Sullivan, had received half a century earlier).

Not all the boxes were bland, however, and pioneers like **Mies van der Rohe's** Seagram Building and **Skidmore, Owings & Merrill's** Lever House (see pp. 242–3) stand tall among the ranks of New York's finest. Unfortunately for such buildings, imitation has been the sincerest form of insult: in the fifties and sixties whole avenues of New York filled up with queues of catastrophically second-rate replicas. Done on the cheap, such slipshod clones simply couldn't compete with buildings like the suave Seagram which relied on the highest quality materials (bronze and walnut panelling), meticulous detailing (window blinds could only be drawn half-way, or completely, to preserve the uniformity of the exterior), and a definite sleight of hand to 'express' the internal construction of the scraper.

Finally, in 1977, New York got the ultimate in glass boxes, the gigantically boring, though technologically innovative twin sticks of the World Trade Center, begun in 1962 and finished 15 years later, at unthinkable cost.

Post Modernism

In Manhattan, Post Modernism was a wonderful catch-all term for buildings built in the seventies and eighties which weren't glass boxes. Conveniently for both the critic and architect, it described what the new buildings were not, rather than what they were.

By the mid-1970s, some areas of Midtown New York had turned into a Hall of Mirrors where glass skyscrapers were endlessly repeated and distorted in each others' reflecting skins. Manhattan was slow to rebel against the transparent curtain wall, and the first serious challenge came in the form of the Citicorp Building (see pp. 243–4), a chisel-shaped scraper dressed in a sheath of white aluminum and standing on stilt-like columns, which appeared in Midtown in 1977.

In the past decade, for the first time in ages, newly acquisitive architects reverted to what New York has always done best: extravagant, feckless eclecticism. Once more, skyscrapers became playful and fantastical. **Philip Johnson**, once the star jockey in the International Modern stable, turned coat and designed the Madison Avenue AT&T Building—with an enormous un-proportioned Gothic/Romanesque atrium topped by a crown stolen off a Chippendale highboy (see pp. 241–2). It was followed by a clutch of similar eccentricities: from 385 Third Avenue, a beige-pink office building designed in the shape of a lipstick, to **Kevin Roche's** new E. F. Hutton building with a serrated top hat and ground floor neo-Egyptian columns.

In the thirties writers had predicted an uncompromisingly futuristic New York: H. G. Wells thought it would go underground, and others thought it would shoot 250 stories into the sky. But if anything the buildings of recent years make Freudian gestures to the past. In 1989 **Skidmore, Owings & Merrill** designed a pioneering new skyscraper for Citicorp in Queens. At 663 ft, it immediately became the tallest structure outside Manhattan. Land has always been plentiful outside the island, and space within has never been at such a premium, and for some extraordinary reason, few scrapers have ever been built outside its perimeters. The new Citicorp is crow-stepped exactly like a massively elongated Dutch gable house. More Dutch allusions are embedded in the ziggurats and pyramids making up the hats of **Cesar Pelli's** new and unlovely World Financial Center, which is part of a new commercial, recreational and residential complex in Battery Park City.

The Future

The bizarreness of the Post-Modern Metropolis, and the peculiar, atavistic allusions to the past, are strangely suited to a city where economics and planning have scarcely had any influence over the psychology of its architecture. No one has any idea how Manhattan's architecture will develop. The only certainty is the immutable grid; and the impossible, protean city on top of it, living cannibalistically on the moment and fueling itself on change.

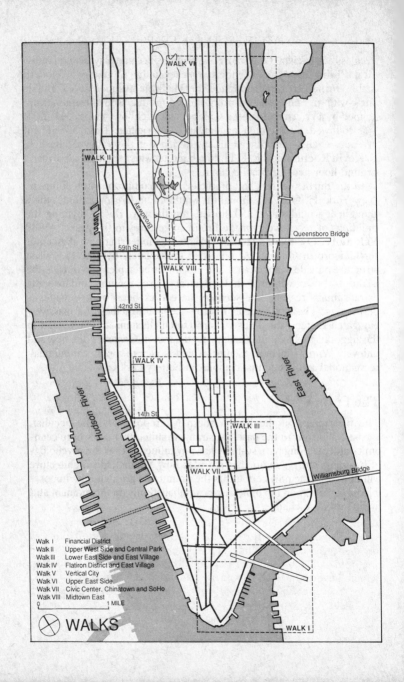

WALK VI

WALK II

Broadway

WALK V

59th St

WALK VIII

42nd St

WALK IV

14th St

WALK III

WALK VII

Queensboro Bridge

Hudson River

East River

Williamsburg Bridge

WALK I

Walk I   Financial District
Walk II   Upper West Side and Central Park
Walk III   Lower East Side and East Village
Walk IV   Flatiron District and East Village
Walk V   Vertical City
Walk VI   Upper East Side
Walk VII   Civic Center, Chinatown and SoHo
Walk VIII   Midtown East

0   1 MILE

⊗ WALKS

Manhattan Walks

In New York a walk invariably turns into an adventure. At the end of it, your face will probably be smudged with dirt, your ears will be ringing with the sound of klaxons and hooters, and your feet will throb with unfamiliar vibrations. Somewhere along the way, however, you will always have stumbled on something utterly unexpected.

New York is not, like most other cities, an amorphous sprawl. Instead it is divided up into scores of principalities and kingdoms—the 'neighborhoods'—each no bigger than a small hamlet, and each wildly different. Broadway, for example, crosses roughly 17 separate neighborhoods on its journey from the bottom of Manhattan to the top, and it undergoes at least 17 drastic character changes along the way. Many of the walks in this book include two or even three neighborhoods.

Something that may take longer to get used to is having to re-adjust the way you look at things. In New York, streets and avenues are deep gullies filled with sky and lined by mountainous buildings. You can look at the architecture close to, or from miles away, but you won't be able to see anything in between; and you certainly won't find any European-style vistas. To help you see the city, the walks whisk you up to the tops of skyscrapers and hurl you under sidewalks. At various times, you will find yourself floating in New York Bay on a ferry or above it in a helicopter; scrambling over the East River across an elevated walkway, or dangling over 1st Avenue inside a cable car. Binoculars or opera glasses are invaluable.

There are eight walks, and all are biased towards architecture and food. Vertical City, the Financial District and Midtown East (Walks V, I, and VIII), are all rather glamorous skyscraper walks with breathtaking views of the city from down below and on high. The Lower East Side, Chinatown and the West Village (Walks III, VII, and IV), take you through a more charming and unexpectedly low-rise Manhattan, crammed with neighborhood shops, restaurants and bars, where eating and drinking can be extraordinarily entertaining. The walks on the Upper West and Upper East Sides (Walks II and VI), focus on architecture and food in roughly equal quantities, as well as an abundance of stupendous museums, and parks for picnicking. They are good on a sunny day *or* a rainy day, though on really dismal day you should head off to the Financial District which comes into its own in depressing or stormy weather conditions.

At the beginning of each walk you will find a list of main sights, followed by a couple of paragraphs explaining where to start and how to get there, where to eat, and when to go. The walk through the Flatiron District and the West Village (Walk IV), for example, is most fun in the evening, when the bars, clubs, billiard parlors and bookshops are open, and the meat market is getting under way. The Lower East Side (Walk III) is exciting at lunchtime on Sunday when the Jewish shops and markets, and the East Village bars and restaurants seethe with activity; the Financial District (Walk I) is most interesting early on a weekday morning (for the fish market and the office-workers); Vertical City (Walk V) is best in the afternoon and early evening; and the Upper East Side is fine on any day of the week *except* Monday, when most of the museums are closed. With regard to timing, however, as Groucho Marx put it: when it's 9.30 in New York it's 1937 in Los Angeles; so if opening times, admission charges and restaurant prices have altered, take it as a healthy sign of New York's legendary appetite for change.

As far as the practicalities of walking around New York go, remember that when you emerge from the nether regions of the subway it is often difficult to work out whether you are facing uptown or downtown. Also note that signs that say 'Don't Walk' mean 'don't walk or you will get mown down and taken to hospital'. Throughout the book, directions are given New York-style in 'blocks'. Blocks between avenues take about 4 minutes on foot; blocks between streets, about $1^1/_2$.

Pick of Manhattan

Views: Grand Central Concourse at rush-hour from the rooftop glass catwalks; midtown from the Empire State Building at midnight; the wall of skyscrapers round Central Park, from the sculpture garden on the roof of the Metropolitan Museum.

Walks and Rides: Brooklyn Bridge and Promenade at sunset; Staten Island ferry at 2 am; Marriott Marquis Hotel elevators; J train over Williamsburg Bridge; front carriage of the express A train, from 125th Street to Columbus Circle.

Architecture: Rockefeller Center; Flatiron Building; New York Yacht Club; Upper West Side Rotunda; Municipal Asphalt Plant; Anshe Slonim Synagogue.

Lobbies: Ravenna Mosaics in the Woolworth Building; butterfly-wing mosaics and stained glass in the Irving Trust Co. Building; Chrysler Building automobile murals and mahogany elevators; Radio City.

Museums: Museum of Natural History; Frick Collection; MoMA; Isamu Noguchi Garden Museum; Police Academy Museum.

Fantastically Ugly Buildings and Nightmare Places: Astor Plaza; inside the Trump Tower; Grace Building; New York Visitors and Conventions Bureau; St Vincent's Hospital; New York Vehicle Licensing Bureau; Penn Station; Post Offices.

Retreats: Conservatory Garden, Central Park; Frick Collection; Broadway Buddhist Temple.

Shops: Maxilla & Mandible (bones and stuffed animals, Upper W. Side); Strand Bookshop (Union Sq.); Zabar's Delicatessen (Upper W. Side); 47th Street Photo (electronics); Canal Street Casbah (industrial junk and flea markets); MoMA Design Store.

Bars: Grand Central Oyster Bar; Beekman Tower Cocktail Bar; Holiday Cocktail Lounge (E. Village); Rainbow Room (RCA).

Dancing: Sound Factory (Chelsea); Roseland (Midtown); Save the Robots (Lwr E. Side); Carmelita's (14th St.); The World (E. Howston St.).

Entertainment and Spectator Sports: New York Public Library Reading Room; East River Park baseball games; short-order chefs in diners and cafés; grand opera in Central Park; Post Office monthly auctions of unclaimed parcels; Roller Skaters' Disco in Central Park; evensong at St Thomas'; rush hour in 42nd Street; Times Square cinema audiences; the Sunday *New York Times*; bowling; betting parlors and bars; Fulton Fish Market and Gansevoort Meat Market, very early in the morning; New Yorkers eating.

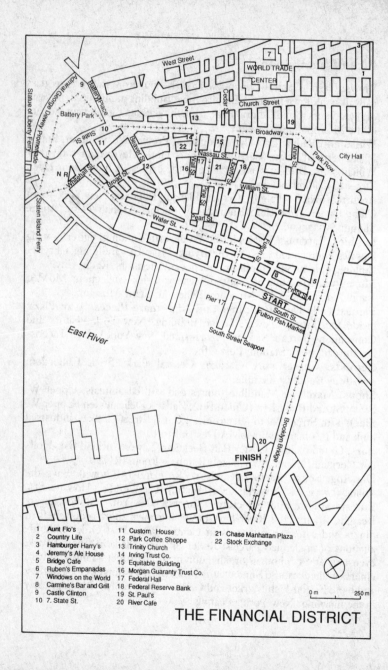

THE FINANCIAL DISTRICT

1 Aunt Flo's
2 Country Life
3 Hamburger Harry's
4 Jeremy's Ale House
5 Bridge Cafe
6 Ruben's Empanadas
7 Windows on the World
8 Carmine's Bar and Grill
9 Castle Clinton
10 7. State St.
11 Custom House
12 Park Coffee Shoppe
13 Trinity Church
14 Irving Trust Co.
15 Equitable Building
16 Morgan Guaranty Trust Co.
17 Federal Hall
18 Federal Reserve Bank
19 St. Paul's
20 River Cafe
21 Chase Manhattan Plaza
22 Stock Exchange

Walk I
The Financial District

Brooklyn ferry before 1883

Fulton Fish Market—Staten Island Ferry—Statue of Liberty and Ellis Island—Bowling Green—Wall Street—Stock Exchange—Federal Reserve Bank—World Trade Center—Brooklyn Bridge

This short walk of tall buildings and wide views takes in some of the most historic sites in New York.

Wall Street means everything between City Hall and the tip of the island. It includes the Fulton Street Fish Market, the skyscraper-fortress of offices in the Financial District, where Melville's Bartleby the Scrivener incarcerated himself, Brooklyn Bridge, which has the single most exciting walkway in the city, and the toe of Manhattan, where the first Dutch settlement was built and the ferries now leave for Staten Island and the Statue of Liberty—the first glimpse 19th-century immigrants had of their promised land.

A special Congestion Committee once calculated that if all the workers left their offices at one time, the streets would need six layers of sidewalks. Today, even the rush hours have to be staggered; Wall Street is the most congested area in the city, and the most thrilling time to visit is in a torrential rainstorm when the streets are more crowded than ever. Umbrella stands sprout like mushrooms, and you can dodge in between plazas and lobbies without getting wet. With luck, the clouds will part for a theatrical sunset as you walk over the Brooklyn Bridge at the end of the walk. This is very much a business center—so *don't* come on a weekend when Wall Street is spookily deserted but still warm from the week's influx of humanity.

Start: the walk starts at the fish market, and anyone who can make it there by 6 am should take the **M1**, **M6** or **M15** bus to Broadway and Fulton Street. (The subway is dangerously empty so early in the morning). Otherwise, start at the Staten Island Ferry (p. 97). By subway, take the **1** or the **N** and **R** trains to **South Ferry**, or the **4** train to **Bowling Green** and by bus, take the **M1**, or **M15** to South Ferry. The ferry leaves from Battery Park at the bottom of Whitehall Street.

Walking Time: allow at least 4 hours. The Staten Island ferry takes an hour, and so does the Stock Exchange tour.

LUNCH/CAFÉS

Aunt Flo's, 79 Warren St., near West Broadway. Soul food with wonderful homely breakfasts of grits and hot sausages, and enormous lunches of barbecued ribs and curried chicken.

Country Life, 48 Trinity Place, at Rector St. Vegetarian buffet run by 7th Day Adventists, with excellent breakfasts and lunches of nut roasts and vegetarian *enchiladas*.

Hamburger Harry's, 157 Chambers St., near Greenwich St. Huge hamburgers.

Jeremy's Ale House, 254 Front St., at Dover St. The best fish and chips in New York.

Bridge Café, 279 Water St., near Dover St. More fish but much more expensive ($22 for supper).

Ruben's Empanadas, 64 Fulton St., near Gold St. *Empanadas* to take away.

Windows on the World, 1 World Trade Center, 107th Floor. Brunch/breakfast is a great bargain: $8 buys a smoked salmon omelette and a continental breakfast. Supper comes at a *prix fixe* of $77 for a seven-course meal, with five wines chosen from a list 800 items long. If you just want a drink there is the **City Lights Bar**, and if you want a snack and jazz too there is the ghastly-named **Hors d'Oeuverie**, all on the same floor.

> Mammon, n. The god of the world's leading religion. His chief temple is in the holy city of New York.
> —Ambrose Bierce, *The Devil's Dictionary*

There is something satanic about the temples of Mammon on Wall Street. On the sunniest days, the skyscrapers darken the streets with an artificial night-time, and even the news stands have to be lit with little electric bulbs. In the winter the streets are warm where city steam, smelling of sulphur and bitumen, seeps out from cicatrices in the tarmac, and spectral bodies spew out of revolving doors and eight tunnels of subway. The crowd, like Mammon, keeps its eyes on the sidewalk: the streets are so medievally narrow, and the scrapers so tall, that you strain your neck when you look up, and in any case, the tops are too far away to make out.

Nevertheless, it is here, at the butt-end of Manhattan, that the history of the city began, with the first Dutch settlement of 1624. Nieuw Amsterdam was set up as a business venture by the Dutch East India Company, and the concept remains little changed to this day. Speculation and commerce is still the *raison d'être*, and economic power is still based on Wall Street, originally the northernmost wall of the Dutch colony.

Physically, however, the city has metamorphosed several times over. The Dutch settlement was obliterated by a wave of speculative construction, spurred on by a catalogue of fires in the 18th and early 19th centuries. An 1866 guidebook reckoned the city was entirely rebuilt once every seven years: 'The denizens of New York are such utilitarians,' the author moaned, 'that they have sacrificed to the shrine of Mammon almost every relic of the olden time'. Today, the only relic of Dutch Nieuw Amsterdam, which was built in the image of the fatherland with windmills, stoops and canals, is a kind of X-ray: a negative, etched onto the medieval street plan, with roads and sidewalks displacing canals.

As you walk down to the Fulton Fish Market (on South Street between Beekman and Fulton Streets) note that all the land east of Pearl Street—which was once the pearly riverside edge of the island—is manmade.

In 1684, the English began raising revenue from real estate by selling 'water lots' on land revealed at low tide. Instead of foundations, New York's first property developers sunk cribs into the waterlogged earth which they filled with debris from demolished hills and buildings, and with garbage and ships' ballast. The practice, peculiar to Manhattan, was known as landfill. Ultimately it consumed not just Dutch New Amsterdam, but also the natural contours of the island, its hills, valleys and shoreline, and to this day it is still used for massive schemes like Battery Park City.

*Most New Yorkers have never seen the **Fulton Fish Market**, and wouldn't dream of going, but if you can make it before dawn (ideally by 4 or 5 am) it is a really thrilling sight, and the only one that has survived the demise of New York Harbor since containerization killed off boat traffic after the War.*

The fishy stench, which supposedly can cure a cold in less than 20 minutes, reeks as far as the M15 bus stop at City Hall. Down on Fulton Street are the market's two enormous warehouses, each bathed in a theatrical blaze of football lights. In between tottering mountains of boxes, fish and ice, gum-booted jobbers and truck drivers gather round for the warmth. They are a very jovial lot—'How do you stop a fish from smelling? Cut off its nose', is their best joke. Inside, they will sell you the odd clambering lobster, a shark with a matt-dry rhinoceros hide, or a bag of severed fins, snappers, or soft-shell crabs. It's a good idea to bring a plastic bag.

Except for fish, the market has nothing to do with the sea. The 19th-century catch was shipped in and included delicasies other than fish—squirrel, raccoon, ground-hog and opossum. Today, fish comes on consignment from Florida, Boston and Maine by truck. These are monstrous, futuristic machines with locust-like bonnets, sinister, waggling antennae for headlights, and carapaces delicately painted with seals, mermaids and sharks. Apart from the lorries, the market is still completely unmechanized, and huge crates of fish are ferried about by man-dwarfing trolleys.

*Next door to the fish market are the schooners, clippers and barks of **Pier 17**. They are actually floating museums, part of a new development, a bizarre kind of pastiche harbor called **South Street Seaport**. The maritime themepark has an abundance of suburban clothes shops, dozens of wine bars and pricey restaurants. The riverside view is rather nice and you may want to come back here for a drink at suppertime, although on Friday evenings and at the weekend there are too many tourists and Wall Street types for it to be very agreeable.*

Things were more lively in the 19th century when this part of South Street was notorious for what an English traveler described as its 'deeds of violence, flagrant vice, and scenes of debauchery': sailors' lodgings, liquor stores, dance houses, and brothels 'of the worst description'. Worst of all, there were man-eating wharf rats, and a bar called the Hole in the Wall which boasted two beefy female bouncers who bit patrons' ears off.

> *As the sun rises over the Brooklyn Bridge, the first batch of office workers descends on Wall Street and the fish market disbands. Before anyone goes to work or to bed, however, they eat breakfast at* **Carmine's Bar and Grill** *on the corner of Front and Beekman Streets, which is what you will need before making the 15-minute walk down to the Staten Island Ferry terminal.*
>
> *From the fish market, walk down to the end of Water Street, and turn right onto Whitehall Street. The shabby* **Staten Island Ferry** *terminal is at the foot of Whitehall Street. (Ferries leave every half hour, day and night; after years of stagnation, the fare has recently increased by a hundred per cent to 50c, which is still less than a cup of coffee.)*

As Brendan Behan put it, Staten Island is not exactly Monte Carlo, and the fun of going on the ferry is mostly the breathtaking backwards view, of Manhattan. Apart from commuters, the intrepid few who set foot on the island are Buddhists and film buffs on pilgrimages to the Museum of Tibetan Art (see p. 259) and Todt Hill where Coppola filmed *The Godfather* (and Marlon Brando, a little tipsy, unwittingly bared his bottom to real members of the Mafia employed as extras on the cast).

Just as the Brooklyn Bridge has its 'jumpers', the ferry is famous for kissers. Although it's infinitely more romantic at night-time, when the boat creeks and slides through New York Bay's eerie black waters and fog horns bellow in the Atlantic, the ferry has become such a fashionable place to kiss that gangs of smoochers hog the deck in the daytime as well. Spiro, the ferry's shoeshiner and Charon, has made the trip to Staten Island over 100,000 times since 1951, and says that American girls kiss like heavyweight boxers.

In the summer the ferry is a respite from the sticky New York heat, and at lunchtime it is thronged with flocks of office workers, eating their sandwiches, and exhausted pigeons, who prefer to hitch a ride, rather than leg the 5 miles between islands. Everyone gazes exhaustedly at the breathtaking view. Before the Second World War it was even better: there were no skyscraper boxes in Manhattan; the tops were jagged and the skyline was even more picturesque, a floating alpine range, fenced in by a 4-mile wall of ships.

> *After the ferry trip, turn left onto the* **Admiral George Dewey Promenade**. *If you are pressed for time, the promenade is the best*

place for looking at the Statue of Liberty, rather than visiting it. To the west you see the 25-year-old **Verrazano-Narrows Suspension Bridge**, **Governors Island** *(now a Coast Guard's installation) and* **Ellis Island**, *which processed and sifted over 12 million immigrants between 1892 and 1954. Paupers, prostitutes, 'ill people', the varicose-veined, and anyone with a ticket paid for by someone else, were amongst those sent back home as undesirables. The abandoned Receiving Station, an enormous ghost-ridden barn, is currently being renovated at a cost of $140 million and the long-promised* **Museum of Immigration** *will be open and well worth a visit by 1991 (see p. 255).*

Lastly, of course, there is the icon which saluted the immigrants as they sailed into New York, the **Statue of Liberty***. In the opening of Kafka's comic novel* America *the salute is terrifying; an awed Karl Rossmann, Kafka's preternaturally innocent hero, sees Liberty suddenly illuminated by a great shaft of light, and wielding a sword rather than a torch. Kafka himself had never visited America.*

In fact the portly matriarch, properly addressed as 'Liberty Enlightening the World', is a likeness of the sculptor's formidable mother. Auguste Bartholdi's *forte* was monumental sculptures, and his penchant was for ladies of enormous proportions. Originally he had in mind a lighthouse for Egypt in the form of a torch-bearing woman symbolizing Progress; a second Pharos to go at the head of the Suez Canal. In the meantime, however, French republicans came up with the notion of giving the Americans a Centennial present, a Statue of Liberty, identifying France with its more sprightly twin republic.

Bartholdi simply transferred his idea from Egypt to America. The prototype Liberty was enlarged three times in his Paris studio (one version stands on a bridge over the Seine), and for the final stage the statue was constructed as if it were a skyscraper, with an interior steel pylon built by Gustave Eiffel. In 1886 all 225 amply endowed tons were presented to the US Ambassador in Paris, dismantled, and then transported to New York. During the re-assembly on Liberty Island, however, Congress ran out of funds and to New York's eternal shame, San Francisco, Cleveland and St Louis all put in offers for the statue. Eventually a rather sheepish New York agreed to take her in, persuaded by a publicity campaign launched by the newspaper man, Joseph Pulitzer, and of course Emma Lazarus' sonnet:

Keep, ancient lands, your storied pomp!' cries she,
With silent lips, 'Give me your tired, your poor,
Your huddled masses yearning to breathe free...'

The sonnet is *not*, as most people imagine, inscribed on the tablet Liberty grasps in her left hand.

About 300 yards along the promenade from the ferry terminal is a round, sandy-colored bunker called **Castle Clinton** *which sells tickets for the boat to the Statue. Unless you get here very early in the morning or in the depths of winter, be warned. At the height of the tourist season the trip can take up to 3 hours, and the authorities advise you not to go the whole way up if you suffer from crowd-phobia, heart trouble, or varicose veins. The elevator half-way up the statue is all right, but even if you suffer from none of the above, you may get queasy climbing the 171 steps up a single-file staircase to the crown. Luckily the 42 ft ladder to the torch was closed in 1916 when it was deemed too narrow and frightening for visitors.*

Reduced to a ticket office and lavatories, and denuded of its roof, doors and façade, Castle Clinton barely lives up to its name. Pathetic as it looks, few buildings in the city can have served more purposes. First it was an anti-British fort, put up in 1807; then it turned into a theater called Castle Garden, and next an immigration station which served the city for 50 years before Ellis Island. Most New Yorkers remember it nostalgically in its penultimate incarnation, as New York Aquarium. They have never forgiven the Parks Commissioner, Robert Moses, who had its contents, electric eel and all, carted off to Coney Island as an act of spite when his plans to build a tunnel from the Battery to Brooklyn were thwarted.

Battery Park, *named after the battery of canons which protected the tip of the island before the shoreline was extended to Castle Clinton, is another hunk of landfill. Walk across it, to* **Bowling Green**, *where Battery Place meets State Street, and Broadway begins.*
    The Georgian house at **7 State Street**, *a lone survivor from the 1800s when it stood on a fashionable promenade at the edge of the water, is now, bizarrely, a shrine to the first American-born saint, Elizabeth Seton, canonized in 1975. A sinister fellow selling pieces of Berlin Wall, Jerusalem Earth and other religious paraphenalia lurks near the entrance—a sweet little portico with wooden columns*

supposedly carved out of a ship's masts. Inside, is the shrine, containing the saint's relics, where Mass is held before and after work.

Next to the shrine, on State Street between Bowling Green and Bridge Street, is the **US Custom House**, *a swaggering beaux-arts granite pile sporting lovely dolphins, tritons, waves, masts and anchors. Rather snootily, it turns its back on the harbor from which Customs extracted so much loot in the form of import duties that at one time it was the Federal Government's chief source of income.*

In front of the entrance are superb, anthropomorphized sculptures of the four continents by Daniel Chester French, best known for his Lincoln Memorial in Washington, DC. The allegory is pretty blunt: Europe, equipped with the icons of education, looks fuddy-duddy; Asia is slothful; Africa is asleep; while America, stamping down an Aztec ruin and brandishing a sheath of Indian maize, is imperial and youthful. Cass Gilbert, the architect, designed a sophisticated steel skeleton to support the building (later he used the same technique to build the tallest tower in the world, the Woolworth Building), and then dressed it up in all the trappings of high culture as the Paris Opera.

Inside, don't bother with the boring **Museum of Financial History**; immediately in front of you are 16 tremendous murals in a rotunda, painted in poster-paint colors by the WPA (Works, Progress, Administration) artist Reginald Marsh in 1937 (see p. 65). They narrate the arrival of a passenger liner, and one, on the righthand side at the far end of the hall, shows Marsh's favorite movie star, Greta Garbo, beseiged by reporters and flashbulbs, while an unctious publicity man liberates a pair of doves. In 1973 the customs men upped sticks for the World Trade Center, and the spectacular, ghoulish lobby, with its 16 kinds of marbles including *cipollino* ('sliced onion') columns, has more or less been abandoned since then. There is a plan to put the Smithsonian's Museum of the American Indian in the building, which is not without its ironies, considering the bombastic statuary outside.

It stands on Manhattan's first colonized site, **Fort Amsterdam**—or James, Willem Hendrick, Anne, George, depending on whether the Brits or the Dutch were calling the shots. The East India Company sent along an engineer to build a grand pentagonal fort measuring 1600 by 2000 ft. The actual fort was much smaller and surrounded by a stumpy cedar fence, although the illustrations sent back to the colony depicted it with hefty stone walls and all sorts of grand elaborations and accoutrements.

Directly opposite is **Bowling Green**, Manhattan's only circular park, laid out in 1732 when the English leased it for the rent of one peppercorn and used it for bowling. The iron fence was put up in 1771, to stop people using it as a municipal garbage dump. It is still intact except for the finials which were melted down in 1776 and fired back at the English, along with the park's centerpiece, a gilded statue of George III sitting on a horse and dressed in a toga, like Marcus Aurelius in Rome. In a fit of pique the English knocked down a nearby statue by the same sculptor— one of William Pitt who opposed the Stamp Act, by which a tax was levied on the colonies to support the British army.

Next, walk to the north end of the park, to Cunard's old booking offices on the lefthand side at 25 Broadway.

Go inside, into what is one of the best lobbies in the city, a cavernous, echoing dome based on Raphael's Villa Madama in Rome (itself inspired by Nero's monstrously opulent Golden House). It is now, of all things, a post office, though the red, blue and green mosaics and murals have all been left just as they were. Showing frigates and brigs, mermaids, maps, and porpoises, together with racy friezes of smouldering ladies and cavorting cupids, they describe a lost world of glamorous steamship travel for the uppercrust.

As you come out, look out for 26 Broadway on the other side, which was built as a home for John D. Rockefeller's corporate giant, Standard Oil; the tower, in fact a chimney, was designed to look like an oil-burning lantern, and the entrance is surrounded by dragons snorting fire.

By now, you must be hungry, and you can stop off for a Wall Street-style breakfast at the Park Coffee Shoppe on the corner of Beaver and Broad Streets. Here, the short-order chefs carve up 20-egg omelettes with mathematical precision, and fry, toast and grill with more gusto than demons stoking the fires of hell. If anyone looks dozy, the waitresses hurl cartons of milk to wake them up.

After breakfast, walk back to Broadway and then two blocks north up Broadway, a grim fortress of grey skyscrapers, to Trinity Church, the landmark standing on the lefthand side of Broadway at the top of Wall Street.

A century and a half of pollution has completely blackened the Gothic façade of Trinity Church, one of the oldest and gloomiest in the city, and one of the wealthiest landowning ministries in the world. Until 1892, Trinity was also the tallest building: its 264 ft tower could be seen 15 miles out to sea, and sightseers were encouraged to climb it for the view. Nowadays, no one could possibly miss the symbolism of Trinity's black spire engulfed by Wall Street's great gully of temple-skyscrapers— impious heirs to the Gothic attempt to build towers that really did aspire to God.

Do go inside if you get here at lunchtime, when there are weekday concerts, although the interior is no great shakes. (Tours weekdays at 2, concerts Tues at 12.45, adm free). More interesting is Trinity's **cemetery**, a little patch of green and sometime drug-dealing spot, usually obscured from Broadway by a human wall of cross-looking financiers perched on elevated shoe-shining thrones. The headstones are blackened too, like rotten teeth, but you can still make out the carvings, which include a good selection of skull and cross bones, death masks, coffins, angels' wings and masonic symbols.

'Reader reflect how soon you'll quit this stage: you'll find but few attain to such an age...' is a most alarming inscription, just near the entrance to the cemetery. It refers to William Bradford, who brought the printing press to New York. Bradford printed the city's first Bible in the same year as he printed its virgin money, epitomizing Trinity's ambivalent relationship with Wall Street. The cemetery's other two notables are Alexander Hamilton, the first US Secretary to the Treasury (and the fellow on the $10 bill), and Robert Fulton, who started as a painter and lived in a *ménage à trois* in Paris as 'Toot', with two Americans, 'Wifey' and 'Hub', before 1804 when he invented a submarine and the steam ferry that linked Manhattan to Brooklyn.

> *Opposite Trinity, on the righthand side of Wall Street as you look down, is a skyscraper parody of a church, the* **Irving Trust Company**. *One of the most sumptuous scrapers in the city, it was built in 1932, in the midst of the Great Depression, when New York was filling up with soup kitchens and shanty towns dubbed Hoovervilles.*

Ralph Walker, the architect, pared the skyscraper down to an elongated white limestone spire, which soars so high, the top can't be seen from the bottom. What you do see, is rippled and fluted like a curtain, with oversized entrances similar to the porches of a Gothic cathedral, and slim windows, latticed like butterfly wings. The glass is not stained, but early in the afternoon it burns vermillion red, as though a fire is blazing

102

inside. This happens when the lights are turned on in the lobby, a cathedral vault that dwarfs the bankers and is decorated with a flamboyant gold-and-red mosaic that seems wonderfully inappropriate for a bank.

You should definitely walk through here, and it is worth taking along some convincing disguise, such as a pinstripe and a briefcase, and risking prosecution, to see the most grandiose section of all: the private dining room in the top of the tower. It was built on palatial proportions: three stories high, with slender butterfly-veined windows stretching from top to bottom, a baronial marble fireplace, and a mother of pearl fish-scale ceiling.

> *From the Irving Trust Company, you can see another one of Wall Street's supremely vainglorious edifices, the* **Equitable Building** *which is a block north on 120 Broadway, between Pine and Cedar Streets.*

This colossos indirectly determined the shape of the Irving Trust's jagged spire, and those of all New York's scrapers built between 1916 and 1962. Containing 1.4 million sq ft of office space, and 16,000 workers, it rises a sheer 40 stories from the ground with no setbacks. It ate up so much light and air that it prompted the Zoning Laws of 1916, which restricted the bulk of skyscrapers by drawing up what was essentially a vertical grid plan for New York. When they reached a certain height, depending on the size of their plot, scrapers had to step back like pyramids from the street although towers could rise to an infinite height.

> *Walk two blocks down Wall Street to Broad Street. If you stand on the southeast corner, all you see is a solid wall of* **Wall Street** *temples; Corinthian columns on the Stock Exchange opposite, Doric on Federal Hall on the north side of the Street, and Ionic on the building right behind you, 23 Wall Street.*

In fact Wall Street takes its name not from these more recent fortifications, but from an anti-British oak fence put up by the Dutch governor, Peter Stuyvesant, in 1653. The original plan called for a palisade of sharpened tree trunks, but an Englishman, Thomas Baxter, supplied flimsy 13 ft planks instead. These were immediately pinched for firewood and lumber, so the fortifications were useless. The Nieuw Amsterdam of those days was more congenial than today's Wall Street: covered with neat farms and gardens, with a canal on Broad Street, named the 'Heeren Gracht' after one in Amsterdam.

This is a good moment for a close inspection of 23 Wall Street, the **Morgan Guaranty Trust Company**.

The pock-marks on the outside walls were made by flying debris from a horse-drawn wagon which mysteriously exploded outside the building in 1920, killing 38 and wounding a hundred. The perpetrator was never discovered, although Wall Street had more than even its fair share of self-proclaimed enemies, and Morgan Guaranty, right in the nerve center of Mammon's citadel, was an obvious target. A private bank for banks, it was a symbol of the immense economic power wielded by an élite of financiers.

J. P. Morgan Jnr, at whom the bomb was directed, raised loans for the British during the First World War, while his father, the one with the enormous red swollen nose, founded America's giant shipping and railway corporate monopolies, as well as US Steel, the country's first billion-dollar company. By 1929, a coterie which made up five per cent of the population were receiving a wopping third of all personal income. It was a turning point in Wall Street's history: after the stock market crash, Roosevelt's New Deal reforms put a stop to the autonomy of private banks. Wall Street suffered such a fit of hysteria that at the Pecora Hearings into the crash, a press agent had a midget sit on Morgan's lap in the witness stand.

> *Across the street, at 28 Wall Street, the Greek temple confusingly known as* **Federal Hall** *is in fact the old Custom House and Subtreasury, (open Mon–Fri 9–5, adm free). It is actually two temples in one: the outside a replica of the Parthenon, the inside the Pantheon's domed cockpit.*

During the economic panic of 1873 Wall Street had a characteristic attack of paranoia, and the whole building was fortified against a siege, with turrets on the roof, bullet-proof shutters, three Gatling machine guns and a stack of grenades. Before 1842, the original Federal Hall stood on the site. Washington was inaugurated on its steps in 1789, when New York was capital for a brief year before the Federal government moved to Philadelphia. On the steps outside, a huge pigeon-spattered statue of Washington commemorates the occasion and inside is a small, dull museum about Washington.

> *Facing Federal Hall, at 8 Broad Street, on the righthand side of the street, is Wall Street's most famous temple of all, the* **New York**

Stock Exchange. (*Open Mon–Fri 10–4, adm free, visitors' entrance at 12 Broad Street.*)

An 1869 guide book called the exchange the seat of 'all device and deception, ingenious invention and base fabrication'. The most blatant piece of invention of all is the classical façade, serving precisely the same function as a stage curtain. The sculptures on the pediment are just as theatrical: Integrity, with winged ears, steps fearlessly out of the frieze, although when polluted vapours began eating her away, the marble was secretively replaced with metal, so that, as one architecture critic put it, 'the public would not know that any facet of the Stock Exchange was vulnerable'.

Today, the exchange admits the public to a special viewing balcony. One visitor in 1909 likened the trading floor to Bedlam, except that the exchange members seemed 'freed from the restraint of their keepers'. Though it starts the day swept clean, the trading floor is soon covered in a carpet of scraps of paper, while the grand coffered ceiling is covered by a knot of sinister black pipes connecting to each one of 22 electronic stick-insects, or trading posts.

Although a mysterious voice spells out what is going on in words of one syllable, the chaos is at first so hypnotic, and then so utterly bewildering, that the conclusion—the stock exchange is 'a public market: fair, orderly and regulated'—is not exactly convincing. The description omits the crashes of 1989 and 1987, the strange statistic that nevertheless the average income of Wall Street's investment bankers has increased over the last decade by 21 per cent. The crash of 1929 is skimmed through as the product of 'reckless speculation of the margin'. On that day, tickers could not keep up with the speed with which 16 million shares were traded in a few hours, heralding the Depression. It is one of the great Wall Street myths, however, that the streets were littered with bodies hurled from skyscraper windows. Although two bankers with a joint bank account jumped hand in hand from the top of the Ritz, and the Spanish playwright Lorca described how he saw the crash 'amid suicides and groups of fainters', the suicide rate did not rise in 1929, and those who did kill themselves used guns rather than jumping out of windows.

From the Stock Exchange, walk a block north up Broad Street to Pine Street and **Chase Manhattan Plaza**. *Immediately to your right on the plaza is Jean Dubuffet's witty black-and-white sculpture, the* Group of Four Trees *stranded in a great expanse of concrete.*

Behind it is the bank itself, which David Rockefeller turned into the biggest in the world, and, with the same instinct for expansionist enterprise as the Dutch plutocrats, into a virtual right-arm of American foreign policy in developing nations from Chile, South Africa and Vietnam to Yugoslavia. Like the buildings on Wall Street itself, this skyscraper, a spandreled office block soaring 813 ft into the air, is another brow-beating totem of power. It was the first glass box to be built in Lower Manhattan by Skidmore, Owings & Merrill, whose Lever House in midtown spawned the fever of glassboxes and plazas which so radically transformed Manhattan's jagged skyline in the 1960s. In the middle is a sunken rock garden created by the Japanese sculptor, Isamu Noguchi, from misshapen meteoric basalt extracted from a riverbed near Kyoto. Down below is a dystopian scene: office workers sitting at a grid of desks, and staring at Noguchi's dribbling fountain, whose fish, poisoned by coins and noxious fumes, have long since abandoned their pond for Elysian fields.

*Nevertheless this is a good moment to have a sit down and reach for your binoculars, since Chase Manhattan's elevated plaza is an excellent platform for viewing the tops of some of the nearby scrapers that are otherwise invisible. To the south is a verdigris pyramid tipped with a needle, the ziggurat crowning the first headquarters of Chase Manhattan at **40 Wall Street**. It was just pipped to the post by the Chrysler Building in the race to build the tallest building in the world in 1930, so it seems most unjust that an aeroplane collided into this building, just after the Second World War, instead of its rival on 42nd Street.*

*To the east down Pine Street is the lunatic Gothic spire of **70 Pine Street**, which went up in 1932 and is easily the most beautiful Art-Deco building in the area. If there are clouds in the way, you can walk down to the building itself, a block east on Pine and Pearl Streets, and inspect the pair of three-dimensional miniature replicas which the architect installed above the entrances on Pine and Cedar Streets. Have a good look as well at the aluminum revolving doors which are exquisitely decorated with butterflies resting on stylized flowers.*

Forget skyscrapers for the moment. Turn left onto William Street and then left again onto Liberty Street. Immediately behind Chase Manhattan Plaza, there is more gold than in Fort Knox, lurking underneath an enormous Florentine palazzo built for a medieval-style assault: the **Federal Reserve Bank of New York**.

You need to telephone for a ticket a week in advance to see the vaults, which contain gold reserves of 75 different nations worth a sum total of $144 billion (tel 720 6130). Whenever an international transaction is made on the market, the Federal Bank acts it out by moving the gold, a bar at a time from one compartment to another, at a cost of $1.70 an ingot. Five floors down, you see two workers performing this bizarre ritual: one who counts aloud and one who weighs, both wearing magnesium clogs in case they drop one of the 28lb bars on their toes. Upstairs, dollar bills are sucked up into a vacuum cleaner at the rate of $40 million a day; deteriorated and counterfeit notes are shredded and used as stuffing, landfill or presents for visitors.

Now go back to Broadway, which is one block to the west on Liberty Street. On the way, you cross the intersection of Liberty and Nassau Streets.

This corner was the home of a cigar girl, Mary Rogers, the victim of a particularly nasty murder in 1842. When her lacerated body was discovered in New Jersey the mystery became a *cause célèbre* and although it was never solved, Poe came up with his own solution in the short story 'The Mystery of Marie Roget', which was set in Paris as the sequel to *The Murders in the Rue Morgue.* Today **Nassau Street** seems cheery enough, and the shoetricians all display signs saying 'If you don't come in at least smile as you walk past'. It is a good street to get all kinds of discounted goods: cameras, pantyhose and, for $5, personalized birthday poems written by computer in iambic pentameters.

*On the left as you reach Broadway, is Isamu Noguchi's absurdly elegant 28 ft high '***Red Cube***', executing a pirouette in the plaza of the* **Marine Midland Bank***, at 140 Broadway.*

Lower Manhattan's most poised and superior modern skyscraper, the bank is also by Skidmore, Owings & Merrill, the largest architectural practice in the country. Built in 1967, it has an inscrutable skin of dark-tan glass which reflects all the buildings around it.

On the other side of Broadway is **One Liberty Plaza**, yet another scraper by the same firm, but not nearly so good. It replaced the largest scraper ever to be demolished, the Singer Building. Built in 1908 with all mod-cons, including a set of vacuum pipes for polishing top hats, the

Singer Building was New York's tallest building, and quickly became a magnet for suicides. 'It seems to have a strong appeal to those who were soured on life', ruminated W. Parker Chase in 1932, the manager of a troupe of chorus girls and the author of *New York, the Wonder City*. 'Cheer Up Everybody,' the book insists, 'And try and peg along until 1940 when that life-perpetuating serum thing will be perfected'.

Right in front of you, are the unbeautiful 110 stories of Minoru Yamasaki's **World Trade Center**, *the second tallest tower in the world after the Sears Tower in Chicago. The towers are only a block to the west, between Church, Vesey, West and Liberty Streets, but in the tourist season there will be crowds, and you may prefer to press on to the Brooklyn Bridge. The number 2 tower has the observation deck on the 107th floor, but you can avoid the queues by going to the number 1 tower's* **City Lights Bar**, *or* **Windows on the World**, *an excellent, expensive restaurant on the 110th floor.*

Even though you can't escape one or other of the towers, the view is fairly staggering, and the Observation Deck (open Mon–Fri 9.30–9.30), 1350 ft up, is so high that the city seems two-dimensional. The thought of the coup orchestrated by Philippe Petit, the French acrobat who crossed from one tower to the other on a steel tightrope cable, disguised as a construction worker, makes you feel sick.

If you don't like the building, you can at least admire its sophisticated engineering. Instead of the steel cage conventionally used for skyscrapers, the entire weight of the building is borne by its outside walls, really a fence of closely spaced aluminum piers, so there is no need for any columns inside. An unfortunate side effect is that the windows are only a foot wide and can't be opened. When the Center was finally completed in 1982, at a cost of over a billion dollars, more than a million cubic yards of muck had been removed from the site. It was dumped on the nearby wharves as landfill, and now the 92-acre extended shoreline is a complex of condominiums and offices called Battery Park City.

Now dash up Broadway, past **St Paul's** *which is on the lefthand side between Fulton and Ann Streets.*

The architect, Thomas McBean, was a pupil of James Gibbs who designed London's St Martin's in the Fields. Originally, it too stood in wheat fields, and today it is the only pre-Revolutionary church in Manhattan. The Georgian interior, painted pink and blue, is rather pretty, thanks to a golden starburst by Pierre L'Enfant, who laid out Washington, DC. In the 19th century it faced Barnum's American Museum, a tourist attraction that had a bear chained to the roof, an anatomical freak show, a cow with four horns, a 'Feejee' mermaid assembled out of a fish tail and a monkey's torso, and the celebrated midget *ménage à trois*, General Tom Thumb, Commodore Nutt and Lavinia Warren.

*Turn right off Broadway and walk up Park Row to the **Brooklyn Bridge**. On the way you pass the Woolworth Building and City Hall which begins Walk VII (see p. 215). The pedestrian entrance to the Brooklyn Bridge is on the right, just past the point where Park Row joins Nassau Street.*

The view backwards, framed by the cat's cradle of suspension cables, is New York's finest. If you can arrange it, it is nicest to cross the bridge in the evening. The city's sunsets are famous for their unnatural redness: a special effect that, thanks to the chemicals and fumes which spew out of New Jersey and filter out every color except red, transforms Manhattan into a glowing inferno.

The walkway itself is much touted as a romantic spot, and although John Travolta certainly danced across with gay abandon in *Saturday Night Fever*, the way it shudders and rattles 12 ft above the noisy roadway can be quite nerve-racking. Venture here alone, and you can expect to be besieged by cyclists, Samaritans and gangs of burly secretaries jogging in sneakers. The men who are repairing the bridge, moreover, insist on pointing out the rusty remains of one of the cables which snapped a few years ago and killed a tourist taking photographs.

The feat of engineering was the handiwork of John Augustus Roebling, who maintained that even if all the suspension cables should break at once, the bridge would merely sag. A keen student of Hegel, Roebling was a German immigrant who came to America in 1831 to live on a utopian farming community near Pittsburgh. But he never even saw what he called his 'East River Bridge; the greatest engineering work of this age': whilst reconnoitering a site for the Brooklyn Tower, Roebling's foot was crushed against the pier by a vengeful Fulton ferry, which the bridge was putting out of business.

His toes were amputated, but his foot became gangrenous, and a week before the bridge got planning permission, lockjaw set in and Roebling died of tetanus. More tragedies ensued. His son Colonel Washington

Roebling took over, but was crippled three years later by an attack of the bends. The divers' disease is caused by air decompression, and was contracted by over a hundred men during the laying of the foundations for the two granite towers. The human 'sandhogs' actually dug the foundations 75 ft underwater, inside inverted boxes which were gradually filled with concrete. Washington Roebling eventually retired to a sickroom in Brooklyn Heights, supervizing work on the bridge through a telescope.

In the end the bridge took 14 years and 600 men to build, and as Roebling predicted, it became an icon for the city. The poet Hart Crane wrote an invocation, 'O Harp and Altar', exalting it above God, and the bridge inspired the abstractionist painters, John Marin and Joseph Stella who both exhibited in the Armory Show (see pp. 153–4).

But as usual in New York, where there is myth, there is the publicity stunt. In 1884 P. T. Barnum led 24 of his elephants across the walkway to prove it was safe, and a Bowery boy called Steve Brodie launched a whole career on the basis of his orchestrated 'jump' from the bridge in 1886. Sceptics insisted that he merely swam into the middle of the river and surfaced just as a dummy hit the water from above, but Brodie immediately became a celebrity. He gave lectures in museums, opened a saloon on the Bowery, and toured the States with a show in which he plunged through a trap-door into a shower of rock-salt spray to rescue his 'Bowery goil', Blanche, 'a corkin' good looker' who was pushed off the Brooklyn Bridge by the blackguardly Thurlow Bleeckman. Years later he even starred with Bugs Bunny in a cartoon in which he gets twicked by the scwewy wabbit.

> *The steps to the right on the Brooklyn side of the bridge land you on Cadman Plaza West, and the A and C train subway stops—**High Street Brooklyn Bridge**—are right in front of you across the patch of grass on Cadman Plaza West and Cranberry Street. (It is one stop to Manhattan where you can change to the 4, the 2 or the J train.)*
>
> *Before you go home, you might like to wander down to the **River Café** for a cocktail. Walk down Cadman Plaza West, which turns into Fulton Street, to the river. The restaurant is right next to the bridge at the foot of Fulton Street, on 1 Water Street.*

Walk II
The Upper West Side and Central Park

Central Park West and the Dakota—Broadway in the Seventies—Zabar's—Riverside Park and the Boat Basin—the Natural History Museum—Central Park—the Frick Collection

This is rather a leisurely walk, suited to ramblers and idlers. In fact this is the only walk in the book which is really perfect for picnics, since the route takes in the glutton's paradise of Zabar's delicatessen and two of the city's choicest parks—Riverside and Central. If there is a freak flash flood (and the rain in New York really is like the preposterous stuff that falls in bad movies: suddenly, and in vertical sheets), you can always take refuge in the Frick Collection and the Natural History Museum.

If you only see one art gallery in your life, perhaps it should be the astonishing collection of old masters in the Frick; and if you only visit one museum, it would be very tempting to make it the Natural History Museum. Unedifying in all the best possible ways, it contains what must be the world's most shamelessly theatrical collection of stuffed animals. The museum is open late until 9 on Wednesdays, Fridays and Saturdays, and actually it is best seen at night, because by day it can be a positive madhouse of screaming children. After the nippers have gone home for tea, however, its halls are transfigured and appear vast, gloomy and sepulchral. **Start**: by subway, take the **1**, the **A** or the **D** train to 59th Street and Columbus Circle, or the **N** or **R** train to 57th Street and Broadway and

111

THE UPPER WEST SIDE AND CENTRAL PARK

0 m   250 m

1 Good Enough To Eat
2 Flor de Mayo
3 Sarabeth's Kitchen
4 Popover
5 Sakura
6 Famous Dairy Restaurant
7 American Diner Royale
8 Indian Kitchen
9 Ansonia Hotel
10 Carnegie Deli
11 Hearst Magazine Building
12 Visitors Bureau
13 Gulf and Western Building
14 Tavern on the Green
15 Cafe des Artistes
16 Hotel Belle Claire
17 Apthorp Apartments
18 Flea Market
19 Roller Skaters' Disco

Lincoln Center

W 62nd St.
Columbus Circle
59th St.
Seventh Ave.
START
Eighth Ave.
W 57th St.
W 55th St.

then walk to 57th Street and 7th Avenue. By bus, take the **M6**, the **7**, or the **M104** to 55th Street.

Walking Time: with museums, 4 hours, although it only takes about 30 minutes to walk from Riverside Park on the east side to Central Park on the west.

LUNCH/CAFÉS

Good Enough to Eat, 424 Amsterdam Avenue, near 80th St. American 'home cooking', with vast breakfasts including the colossal 'Lumber Jack', served until 4.

Flor de Mayo, 2282 Broadway, near 82nd St. Hong Kong, Cantonese and Cuban cuisine all mixed together, and very good too.

Sarabeth's Kitchen, 432 Amsterdam Avenue, between 80th and 81st Sts. American cooking and good brunches, although some of the eaters are rather prissy.

Popover, 551 Amsterdam Ave., near 87th St. Burgers, what they call 'creative' sandwiches and impeccably cooked scrambled eggs which are forced down a cappuccino jet and steamed. 'Popovers' are little buttered dough parcels, a bit like croissants.

Sakura, 2298 Broadway, at 83rd St. First class *sushi*.

Oyshe, 199 Columbus Ave., at 69th St. Japanese cooking (*Oyshe* means 'delicious'.)

Famous Dairy Restaurant, 222 72nd St., between Broadway and West End Ave. Ancient Jewish dairy restaurant with brunches (blintzes, potato pancakes, cream cheese cakes) served until 3.

American Diner Royale Bake Shop and Café, 237 72nd St., between Broadway and West End Ave. Jewish café and bakery with perfect bagels and lox.

Broadway Cottage II, 2492 Broadway, between 92nd and 93rd Sts. Excellent, MSG-free Szechuan and Hunan cooking, and unlimited free wine with dinner.

Indian Kitchen, 2200 Broadway, near 78th St. For curry.

When Central Park was finished, everyone assumed that the Upper West Side would turn into a carbon copy of the Upper East Side: prim, established and stinking rich. Smart people did come—as you can see from the stage-set apartment buildings lining Central Park West and Riverside Drive—but the West Side never developed in predictable ways, and instead it became a kind of Left Bank rebuke to the establishment tastes of the other side of the park.

114

You get a good idea of the Upper West Side's maverick edge from its architecture. It is completely irresistible—exuberent, fanciful, and sometimes frankly daffy—ranging from the flash Art-Deco apartment houses on Central Park West to the Ansonia Hotel on Broadway, a beaux-arts confection of carbuncles, pimples and boils. Even Manhattan's silliest building—the pseudo-Islamic cheese-grater on Columbus Circle—raises smiles of affection. Westsiders, moreover, are perfectly suited to the architecture. In fiction, they include Saul Bellow's Mr Sammler, J. D. Salinger's Glass family and Walter Matthau and Jack Lemmon's 'Odd Couple'. Stereotypically, they are liberals, Jewish intellectuals, gay doctors and lawyers, writers, actors, musicians, and the cultural cognoscenti of the city.

In the sixties, the Upper West Side got its own cultural campus in the shape of the Lincoln Center, a complex harboring the Philharmonic, two opera companies, the ballet, an arts cinema, a theatre and no end of plazas. It was built on the site of some of New York's shabbiest slums—the ones used for the filming of *West Side Story*—and since then its presence has slowly but surely transformed the Upper West Side into a fashionable neighborhood. The poorer Hispanic Westsiders have upped sticks for cheaper areas to the north, and whole stretches of Broadway and Columbus Avenue are swamped with shops and restaurants. Though the West Side old guard staunchly denounce it, the process of gentrification, which has become a pattern all over the city, now seems unstoppable.

> *Start with a pastrami on rye in the* **Carnegie Deli** *on West 55th Street and 7th Avenue. The Carnegie ranks among New York's legendary delicatessens, and Woody Allen paid homage to it in his film* Broadway Danny Rose *in which the late owner, Leo Steiner, describes the time Kruschev came in to buy a sandwich. Since Steiner's death, rumor has it that the coleslaw is not so crispy as it used to be, although to a layman everything still tastes completely delicious. The helpings are the biggest in New York, and the menu is definitely the corniest ('Carnegie Haul', 'Tongue's for the Memory' and 'Beef Encounter' are the least horrid).*
>
> *From the Carnegie, walk a block west, turn right onto 8th Avenue and then walk four blocks north to Columbus Circle. Immediately on your left on 57th Street, and impossible to miss, is the* **Hearst Magazine Building***.*

There is something odd about this building. It is not just the Hollywood schmultz, the Viennese Secessionist details, the peculiar, outsized columns, or even the sinister cowled statues on the corners. Look at it some more, and you suddenly see that it is a skyscraper base without a skyscraper—as though the top had taken off, like a rocket from a launching pad. It was half-built in 1928 for the newspaper, film and real estate giant, William Randolph Hearst. With characteristic cheek, Hearst chose one of his own art directors—the set designer Joseph Urban—and not an architect to design the building—although why the whole skyscraper never materialized is a mystery.

> *Carry on up 8th Avenue to Columbus Circle. Its white marble centerpiece is the* **New York Visitors and Conventions Bureau**, *a monument to the American Tasteless movement of the 1960s.*

It was built originally as a Gallery of Modern Art to house the collection of Huntington Hartford, the A&P supermarket heir. Hartford was a rebel, set on bringing about a revolution in art: a move away from the abstract and post-modern, to what he called the 'beautiful'—pre-Raphaelites, Salvador Dali and Bouguereau. The gallery was a spectacular flop, and the building itself was derided by the whole of New York as 'Kitsch for the Rich' and 'Marble Lollipops'. It was designed by Edward Durrell Stone, a one-time prophet of the international style (he designed its American flagship, the Museum of Modern Art), who seriously deviated during the 1960s into Middle Eastern-style motifs and Islamic grilles after he built the American Embassy in New Delhi.

> *At the hub of Columbus Circle is a sculpture of Christopher Columbus, and opposite, on the north side of the circle is the* **Gulf and Western Building**, *a 44-story skyscraper containing the corporate headquarters of the rapacious conglomerate formed in the 1970s. One of its properties is Paramount Pictures, and the tower contains a special screening room on the 30th floor, as well as a cinema for the hoi-poloi in the basement.*
>
> *Cross Columbus Circle and keep walking north up 8th Avenue. At this point it becomes Central Park West, one of Manhattan's really fashionable addresses, and one which seethes with celebrities scuttling in and out of side-entrances.*

It was rechristened in 1876 by real estate developers who knew that the prestige of a Central Park address would lure people into the area. As elsewhere in New York, the by-product of speculation was spectacular architecture, and the 10-minute walk from here to 72nd Street and the Dakota building takes you past the most impressive line-up of Art-Deco apartment houses in the world. Each building has a pair of twin towers, and together they make up the peculiarly toothy skyline of Central Park.

> *Walk two blocks north from the Gulf and Western building to 62nd Street, and the first Art-Deco beauty, the Irwin Chanin company's* **Century Apartments**. *Its two towers look like Mayan/Art-Deco versions of an animal's front teeth. Ask the doorman if you may look round the lobby. It is stuffed with lovely underlit ashtray-tables, salmon-pink Art-Deco sofas, and shell-shaped light fittings, with an inner courtyard filled with four funny little Art-Deco igloos for storing tools.*
>
> *Next, walk up to 65th Street. On the way you pass a miniature* **Statue of Liberty**, *a rather unassuming 55-ft replica that has been quietly perching on top of the Liberty Warehouse at 3 West 64th Street since 1902. Walk past it to 65th Street and* **55 Central Park West**, *the next extraordinary Art-Deco apartment house on the avenue.*

It was in this apartment house that a fridge exploded over Sigourney Weaver in *Ghostbusters*. In the film, a pre-Columbian temple was superimposed onto the roof of the building, turning it into one of the Mesopotamian ziggurats which the skyscrapers unwittingly imitate. If you look up, you will see that the brick on the outside changes from peach-red to tan, mimicking a ray of sun falling across the façade.

> *Walk up another block to 67th Street. To the right in Central Park itself is the horrendous* **Tavern on the Green**, *one of the tackiest smart restaurants in Manhattan, full of chandeliers, fairy lights and customers stooping under vast shoulder pads. It's an amusing place to drop in for a cocktail, as is the* **Café des Artistes**, *a restaurant and bar exactly opposite at 1 West 67th Street.*

Compared to the Tavern, the inside of this restaurant is hugely tasteful, even down to the mildly naughty murals by Howard Chandler Christy, who was a resident in the **Hotel des Artistes** above. The interior, decorated like an Elizabethan manor, with shields, gargoyles, dragons, a Tudor porter's lodge, beams and knobbly armchairs, was originally built for artists. It soon became too expensive and celebrities like Noel

Coward, Rudolph Valentino, Isadora Duncan and Mayor John Lindsay moved in instead.

*From here you get a good view in profile of the Art-Deco twin-towers of the **Majestic** apartment building up on 71st Street. From the side, they look like streamlined jelly moulds. Also from Chanin's stable, the design was actually meant seriously as an expression of futuristic Machine Age aesthetics; the towers concealed water-tanks and were therefore functional as well.*

*Walk up past the Majestic to 72nd Street and the Upper West Side's first and greatest luxury apartment building, the **Dakota**. You can see, but not touch it, thanks to a pseudo-moat cordoned off by some handsome cast-iron railings of dragons, griffins and Zeuses, and some aggressive porters stationed in sentry boxes.*

The dour, peculiarly blackened fortress is really quite creepy, and you can see exactly why Polanski chose it as a setting for *Rosemary's Baby* and Boris Karloff as a place to live (he so terrified the children in the building that they spurned his sweets at Halloween). The charred façade is actually salmon-coloured brick, and originally the building must have looked much jollier. Henry Hardenburgh, who also designed the Plaza Hotel on 59th Street, intended it to look like a pretty château surrounded by its own moat and set in the picturesque 'grounds' of Central Park. When it was finished, it stood alone in a part of the city as remote, one critic quipped, as the Dakota Territory. The owner of the building, the Singer-sewing-machine heir, Edward Clark, was taken with the idea, and got Hardenburgh to add ears of corn, arrowheads and an Indian's head above the entrance.

In the end, the Dakota made living in apartment buildings respectable. It became one of the most prestigious addresses in the city, and over the years has acquired enough mystique to have had a book written about it. The tourist bus loads all stop off to see the place where its most famous resident of all, John Lennon, was shot by Mark David Chapman in 1980. Annually, on 8 December, faithful Beatles fans congregate outside the building and in **Strawberry Fields**, a section of Central Park opposite set aside as a memorial to Lennon.

*Retrace your steps back to 70th Street, turn right and walk across Columbus Avenue past a forest of high-stooped brownstones, to Broadway. On your way, keep an eye out for one really astonishing eccentricity: the jazzy **Pythian Temple** at 135 West 70th Street,* *just before Broadway. This was built in 1926, four years after the discovery of Tutankamen's tomb in Thebes, and the freemasons who commissioned it were clearly having an attack of Egyptian Revival fever. The inscription on the cornice is wonderfully embellished with lotus leaves in green- and blue-glazed terracotta, gold hieroglyphs, and (you risk a crick in the neck looking at these), two pharaohs in yellow headgear, perched on thrones on top of a crenellated roof.*

As soon as you hit Broadway the West Side suddenly gets chaotic. The sidewalk is an obstacle course of second-hand books on polythene sheets and wobbly trestle tables covered with African paraphernalia.

The odd little Dutch cottage with gables in the middle of Broadway is one of New York's two remaining **subway kiosks**, or 'control houses'. The subway came here around the turn of the century, and ultimately it was responsible for the development of what was originally a remote hamlet called Harsenville where an exiled Talleyrand sought refuge during the Reign of Terror ('I found there a country with 32 religions and only one sauce,' he exclaimed indignantly on his return to France.)

*Turn right, and start walking north up Broadway. At 70th and 73rd Streets and Amsterdam Avenue, Broadway slashes the grid into slivers and shreds, creating theatrical vistas and corners for two more snazzy apartment houses, the **Dorilton** on the righthand side of 71st Street and Broadway, and the neo-Baroque **Ansonia** on the lefthand side at 73rd Street. The Dorilton's scantily clad amazons and cupids caused an uproar when it was built in 1900, and one critic even claimed 'the sight of it makes strong men swear and weak women shrink afrightened'. From the Dorilton you get the best view of the corner towers of the grandiose **Ansonia Hotel**.*

For all its French foppishness—domes, mansards, turrets and fancy balustrades—it still resembles a British seaside hotel. It was here, however, that Bette Midler was discovered dancing in the hotel's 'Continental Baths', a gay spa in the basement. The architect was a Frenchman, Paul Duboy, and when the residential hotel first went up it was one of the most luxurious in the city with two swimming pools, air conditioning, a pnuematic message system, and seals splashing about in the lobby fountain. It is most famous, however, for its extra-thick walls, a fire precaution that incidentally soundproofed the rooms and attracted a distinguished succession of musical visitors including Toscanini, Stravinsky, Ziegfeld, Yehudi Menuhin and Caruso, who gave impromptu

119

concerts from the balconies even though his voice penetrated the thickest walls.

> *Close to, the Ansonia is incredibly shabby. Walk past it and onwards to 76th Street and the* **Citerella Fish Bar** *at 2135 Broadway, for a half-dozen oysters. When Dickens came to New York he found its cubicled oyster bars particularly sinister. The Citerella, however, is very jolly and the fish displays are quite lovely. Peer down 75th Street towards Central Park and you see the double classical water towers of the* **San Remo** *apartment house. More pseudo-ziggurats, these towers are in fact temples, filched from one properly called the Choragic Monument of Lysicrates in Athens.*
>
> *Continue climbing Broadway. On the left, you pass the* **Hotel Belleclaire** *at 77th Street.*

Maxim Gorki stayed here briefly in 1906 after the failed Revolution of 1905. The visit was not a hit: he was set upon by the newspapers and evicted from the Belleclaire after it came out that the depraved Bolshevik was not in fact married to his mistress. Incensed and splenetic, Gorki avenged himself in a superbly vitriolic account of the city. New Yorkers were 'insignificant and enslaved', he vituperated, because the city itself was monstrous, like the 'voracious and filthy stomach of a glutton, who has grown into an imbecile from greed and, with the wild bellowing of an animal, devours brains and nerves ...'

> *Just one block away, between 78th and 79th Streets, you can look in at William Waldorf Astor's elegant Renaissance-style* **Apthorp Apartments**, *occupying a whole city block and reeking with the opulence despised by Gorki. The limestone palace, which went up a year after Gorki's literary assault, is one of New York's very grandest.*
>
> *From here you are only a block away from Zabar's Delicatessen on 80th Street, but on the way keep an eye out for the* **First Baptist Church** *on 79th Street. According to the pastor, the missing righthand spire, which looks as if it has just been lopped off by a gust of wind, awaits the return of Christ so the congregation and the church can be completed. Even though it is unfinished the vaguely Art-Nouveau church is extremely pretty, especially the colonial interior.*
>
> *Next door, on a Saturday afternoon, nearly 10,000 West Side epicureans pass through* **Zabar's**, *which stands on the lefthand side*

of Broadway and 80th Street in a bizarre mock-Tudor manorhouse.

Originally kosher, the West Side Zabar's dates from the 1930s, when it moved here from Brooklyn. Everything is incredibly cheap, but absolutely the best buy is the smoked salmon, which is handpicked by the Zabars themselves. You will have to push and shove to get it. On a weekend, the shop sells over a ton of smoked fish, and you can purchase 142 kinds of French cheese. Zabar's challenges its female customers—over a booming loud-speaker system—to think of something it doesn't stock. All you will be able to think of, however, is sausages. They are everywhere you look: 15 kinds of salami hang from the ceiling like fleshy stalactites, while others lie in rows along the floor, like ammunition.

If the sausages maelstrom is all too much, go up to the mezzanine where Zabars sell bargain crockery, Sabatier knives, vacuum cleaners and lovely machines called Osterisers. Otherwise you can stop off at Zabar's coffee shop for a take-away cappuccino which tastes more of cinnamon than coffee, and a bagel from the **H & H** bakery nextdoor on 80th Street and 2239 Broadway. The largest manufacturer in the city, it sells 70,000 bagels a day.

> *Now go back down to 79th Street and turn right; Riverside Park is a short two blocks away, down a steeply sloping hill. At the foot of 79th Street you will inevitably find yourself caught up in an elegant and intricate concrete structure known as the* **Rotunda**.

All sleek curves and articulated concrete lines, this is a quiet triumph of engineering. Anyone who likes the exquisitely elongated pedestrian bridges built over English motorways in the 1970s will understand its peculiar beauty. It is actually an interchange, part of the West Side's Henry Hudson Parkway. The design works on three levels, incorporating a parking space, walkways and auto ramps. To get to the waterfront, walk through the centre, a concrete arena encircled by colonnades. This rather theatrical space is used for occasional jazz concerts and as shelter in the winter to a number of homeless people and some winos. One, urbane and garrulous, claims he has written the musical score of *Murder on the Orient Express* as well as Mendelssohn's Violin Concerto. 'Agatha Christie?', he says, 'she was a peach of a girl'.

> *A grand classical staircase leads out of the Rotunda to the* **79th Street Boat Basin**, *a tiny marina of jangling yachts and houseboats. To the south, between 59th and 72nd Streets, are 76 acres of*

*industrial wasteland: abandoned railroad, colossal wrecks and col-
lapsing wharves, originally New York Central Railroad's freight
yard. Donald Trump bought the site in 1983 for $95 million, but his
proposal for the construction of 'Television City', comprising the
headquarters of NBC, shopping malls and the world's tallest tower
of 150 stories, was quashed by a public outcry in 1986.*

*A walk north from the boat basin shows you more of the park and
the frill of Gothic palazzi along* **Riverside Drive**.

Note that the drive itself, designed in 'English picturesque style' in 1880,
is the only truly curved street in the city—the sheer waste of space
involved in a curve brands it as the stamping ground of the conspicuously
rich. Chagall, Runyon, the Gershwins (together), Hearst and his mistress Marion Davies (separately), all lived here in no mean splendor.
Less splendidly, Edgar Allen Poe hung out on Mount Tom, a rocky
promontory he supposedly used for writing on the Hudson between 83rd
and 84th Streets. (Just next to this outcrop, through an unlocked door,
you can get underneath the Hudson Parkway, and explore the abandoned freight tracks that were concealed when the 4-lane highway was
added in 1937.)

Between 83rd and 90th Streets the park has pretty flower gardens, and
is a good spot for picnicking, with a nice view of the **Soldiers and
Sailors Monument** on the waterfront at 89th Street (yet another copy of
Lysicrates' temple in Athens), and George Washington Bridge in the
distance.

*After lunch, go back along 80th Street in the direction of Central
Park. Anyone who likes à la mode shopping should do it now, on
Columbus Avenue, and even those who don't should pay a brief visit
to* **Maxilla and Mandible**, *on the righthand side of Columbus
Avenue and 81st Street.*

Maxilla and Mandible stuff anything in the dramatic pose of your choice,
and they claim their range of skeletons and stuffed animals is unique.
Customers, for some reason usually soigné young ladies, can purchase
anything from pouncing antelopes, sleeping bats and 4 ft wide moose
antlers, to alligator, rat and beaver skeletons and (not so nice) baby's
skulls and human pelvises.

The smell in the shop is very disconcerting: a mixture of illness,
fermented fruit and vinegar; putrid and slightly nauseating, like miasmic
vapors.

*On Sunday mornings this stretch of Columbus has a **flea market*** *that outsharks the sharks on Madison Avenue, but it is interesting to look round; and if you need a French Empire* siège d'amour *or a damp Bauhaus* chaise longue, *this is the place for you.*

*From 81st Street, walk down Columbus Avenue to the entrance to the **Natural History Museum** (open Sun–Tues and Thurs 10–5.45; Wed, Fri and Sat 10–9), on 77th Street between Columbus Avenue and Central Park West. On the way you pass a small park in the museum grounds. Every year, on the night before Thanksgiving, it becomes the setting for a Dali-esque nightmare. In the gloom, chimerical Snow Whites and Donald Ducks are slowly inflated with helium and heave into grotesque rubber balloons for the Macy's Thanksgiving Parade the next morning (see the City Calendar, p. 17)*

When work began on the massive Museum of Natural History in 1872, it was the only building in what H. G. Wells called 'a waste of rubbish dump and swamp and cabbage garden'. The curators started with an enormous collection of 10,000 specimens acquired from two European naturalists. The idea was to build the largest museum on the continent, and horses and carts collapsed transporting chunks of granite to the site. The museum, however, grew in its own way, mushroom-like, over a period spanning 63 years, into a labyrinthine complex of 22 different buildings covering four blocks, and housing 34 million exhibits.

Made of pink Vermont granite and looking more like a fairytale castle than a museum, the 77th Street wing sprouts stalactites at its entrance. Just inside is an authentic 65 ft sea-going war canoe filled with models of a Chilkat chief and his followers in the Haida tribe. This sets the tone for the rest of the museum, in which real and fake exhibits are presented within superbly painted dioramas, and all confused, so you are never quite certain whether you are looking at a model, a work of art or the real thing.

*Pick up a floor plan and set off without delay for **Ocean Life and Biology of Fishes**, to the right on the ground floor. The ladies on the door recommend this gallery, and they know best.*

On the way you pass North American Forests which contains an enormous cross section of a Giant Sequoia tree. The rings are annotated in a most eccentric manner, from AD 550 when the tree was a sapling, to 1891, when 'Conan Doyle published Sherlock Holmes *and the zipper was invented'. This was the year of the tree's nemesis, when two unnamed men mysteriously spent 13 days hacking it down. Just to the left is a disgusting giant model of a millipede and*

123

its repulsive larvae, and round the corner in Invertebrates there is a 39 ft squid suspended from the ceiling, a 34 lb lobster, and the entrance to Ocean Life.

Here is a really tremendous sight. Bathed in an outlandish blue light, a 94 ft, 10 ton whale swoops across the whole gallery in a nose dive, casting dramatic shadows in every direction. The blue whale is the largest creature known to man, and this replica is the largest museum exhibit in the world. Moulded out of fibreglass and polyurethane foam, with a steel skeleton, it cost $300,000 to make. The dioramas round about are disturbingly gruesome. A polar bear, with its maw all bloodied, has just killed a ribbon seal; while its neighbor, a huge sperm whale with a devil-may-care look in his eyes, is busy munching on a trembling squid.

*Now take the elevator to the 3rd floor and walk through African Mammals to the balcony of Hall 7. From above, you see seven furious elephants stampeding the center of the **Akeley Gallery** below.*

These were collected by Carl Akeley, after he was very nearly gored to death by an elephant in Africa in 1911, and rescued himself by swinging his body between the brute's tusks. On another occasion the redoubtable explorer strangled a leopard after he ran out of bullets. He finally died from a gnat bite which brought on a fever during an expedition to the Belgian Congo in 1926. Akeley is also renowned as a sculptor, an author, and the inventor of the panoramic motion picture camera, the cement gun and several revolutionary techniques in taxidermy, practised to great effect on the life-like elephants in front of you.

*Go back to the ground floor and choose between the **Biology of Man**, where you may illuminate the Visible Woman, and the **Minerals and Gems Hall** which is thronged with rather freakish followers of the New Age cult for crystals and minerals. Although nearly the whole haul was retrieved, in 1964 a Californian beach-bum dubbed Murph the Surf managed to break in and escape with the Star of India saphire (the world's largest) and the DeLong star ruby, on a day when the burglar alarm wasn't working. Today the exhibits are worth over $80 million.*

If you are going to spend more time in the museum, there are a number of awe-inspiring experiences in store. The first is Burt Lancaster's disembodied voice relating the Seven Wonders of the Universe under the dome of the **Hayden Planetarium**. Three-dimensional planets and stars appear in the heavens and smoke billows out of the artificial firmament, but the extravaganza's earth-shattering climax, in which it turns out that the eagerly anticipated Seventh Wonder is the human eye, is definitely a let-down. To make up for it, there is **Naturemax**, a cinema which shows movies on a screen four stories high and 66 ft wide with a six-channel sound system. The films themselves are basically incomprehensible (in one the camera suddenly lurches down the ear of a mountain climber, while another explores the circulation of an anaemic ballet dancer), but the overall effect is quite overwhelmingly realistic. You will have to come back in the evening for the Planetarium's late-night show, in which laser beams groove and jive to a rock soundtrack.

Central Park

Leave the Natural History Museum, and walk across **Central Park** *in a south-easterly direction to the Frick Collection on East 70th Street. The nearest entrance to the park is on 81st Street. The center path takes you to the Shakespeare Garden, a scrubby rock-garden, mostly scrub, and, up a steeply winding pathway, to* **Belvedere Castle***. (Open during daylight hours, free adm.)*

The castle looks like something you find in Disneyland, although in fact it was built in 1858 and New Yorkers take it very seriously. At any rate, from the top there is a tremendous view of the whole park and its Belvedere-less skyline, allowing you to get your bearings (the weather station inside the castle has a jolly useful free map for this).

Up here, the first thing you notice is a swarm of black dots; a sea of humanity illustrating Brownian motion. The park is so congested and convivial that any solitary soul who has come here seeking rustic tranquility might as well jump now. Central Park is stuffed with flirts and chatterboxes, and hail-fellow-well-met New Yorkers have scant respect for the unaccompanied reader or sketcher. In fact you should count yourself unlucky if you haven't had a proposal of marriage before you go home.

Although the idea of a New York without this lovely rectangular expanse of green carpet is rather frightful, it very nearly became a reality. In the original gridplan of 1811, the surveyors provided for a park called the 'Parade' below 34th Street, between 3rd and 7th Avenues. Of course the speculators devoured it, and it looked as though they would munch up the rest of the island as well, until the poet and newspaperman William Cullen Bryant launched a campaign for a park in his *New York*

Post, in the 1850s. The city bought 80 acres of land, while Frederick Law Olmsted and Calvert Vaux, the greatest landscape architects of the century, (also responsible for Prospect Park, Boston's Fenway and the garden boulevards of Kansas City), were commissioned to design the park.

From a height, the park looks utterly artificial: the rocks, Manhattan schist that glisters in the sunlight, seem moulded out of some kind of synthetic rubber; and the landscape, its lawns and hillocks scorched and torn with overuse, resembles the model scenery used for train sets.

The fact is, there *is* nothing natural about Central Park. In the 1850s it was a wasteland harboring over 300 shanty huts, a garbage dump and sinisterly festering bone-boiling works. 'The valleys reeked with corruption and every possible abomination: it was viler than a hog-pen, and the habitation of pestilence', wrote the gloomy author of *New York in Sunshine and Shadow*. Olmsted and Vaux spent 20 years destroying the natural landscape, and the picturesque frames and views you see now are all man-made. Five million cubic yards of earth were excavated to build what was at the time an engineering wonder, the network of cross-roads running underneath the park, so, as Olmsted put it, it was possible 'even for the most timid and nervous to go on foot to any district of the park...'

> To the right of East Drive is the Metropolitan Museum of Art (see pp. 220 and 256–7), and Cleopatra's **Needle** surrounded by a clump of trees. The 200 ton granite hulk was rolled to this site in 1880 on canon balls. Don't bother taking a closer look: the hieroglyphs on the needle, mounted on verdigris crab claws, have been entirely worn away by pollution. The translation below, inexplicably donated by Cecil B. de Mille, reveals that the message was anyway so verbose as to be practically unintelligible.
>
> For those who like taking part, there are plenty of sports and activities. Down to the left is the open air **Delacorte Theater**, where you can see movie stars performing Shakespeare Hollywood-style between June and September (tel 861 PAPP for details). On the **Great Lawn** there are ballgames, and on June evenings free **Grand Opera**, performed to a massive crowd by the Met (tel 362 6000). On the opposite side of the **Turtle Pond** there are lunatic gatherings of folk dancers every Sunday afternoon, 2–6. To the south, you can join the impossibly named fireman, Nelson Cruise, head of the Empire State's Model Mariners, his fellow sea-dogs and their flotilla of radio-controlled dreadnoughts and man-of-wars on

*the **Conservatory Pond** near 72nd Street and 5th Avenue. Make your way down from the castle and go south via the **Ramble** over Bow Bridge to Bethesda Terrace.*

The dense woods of tulip trees, azaleas and rhododendrons, rushing gorges and intricate paths of the Ramble were intended as a mysterious secluded wilderness of the Jane Austen sort: beyond the perimeter of the formal gardens, where wicked things go on. Nowadays the Ramble is just as congested as the rest of the park, with the addition of a miniature Tour de France of mountain-bikers, and Park Rangers pleading for silence down loud-hailers, so their tour may listen to a reticent woodpecker. The wildest thing you are likely to see, however, is **'Wildman' Steve Brill**.

Following in the footsteps of a 16-year-old who was employed as a tree-pruner after he was discovered living in tree-houses in Central Park, the Wildman was arrested in 1983 for eating berries, which formed a substantial part of his 'half-wild' diet. After an outcry, he was employed by the Parks Department in 1986 to lead foraging tours through the park. He is easy to spot: hirsute and rugged, trousers neatly tucked into socks because he once stepped on a hornet's nest. The tours (tel 718 291 6825 for information) introduce laymen to all kinds of oddities: berries which make your heart stop, and poisonous toadstools which cause death by continuous vomiting unless the victim consumes and holds down eight frozen rabbit brains within 36 hours. 'Ask me any question,' the Wildman chatters on reassuringly, 'and I'll answer it even if I don't know the answer'. You may even get invited to the annual Christmas Wild Party which features Cherokee belly dancing, a lecture on how to survive on lawns, and a banquet of dock curry, five-boro wild salad, and cream of ginkgo-nut* soup.

*At the bottom of the Ramble, cross the Lake via Bow Bridge and make your way to **Bethesda Terrace**. Used as a fake Florentine piazza by the great film director D. W. Griffiths, the Terrace now has a small café and a jazz band; Bethesda Fountain in the middle is probably New York's most famous rendezvous.*

---

* Made from the nuts of ginkgo trees, planted all over the sidewalks of New York because they thrive on polluted air. When ripe, the nuts fall on the ground and the pong of rotting excreta is so strong, you can smell it from a distance of several feet. They are gathered with rubber gloves because they give the skin a nasty rash. Cooked and roasted, however, they are absolutely delicious, tasting of a mixture of swiss cheese and green tea.

*You are now just about parallel with the Frick, but before you leave, do investigate part of Central Park's subculture, the **roller skaters' open-air disco** which starts on Friday evenings and continues until sundown on Sunday. This all goes on **Literary Walk**, about halfway down the Mall.*

Past the statue of Sir Walter Scott and his dog, and under the beady eye of Robert Burns, a small but frantic centrifuge of roller skaters gyrates round a ghetto-blaster in a weird combination of disco, jive, jitterbug and rock and roll. The best ones do the splits and balance cans of Coors and Budweiser on their heads. There is a DJ and about 200 regulars, dressed in spandex bicycling pants and money-belt codpieces.

*Walk across to the eastern edge of the park and 5th Avenue, and then make your way to the **Frick Collection** on East 70th Street. (Open Tues–Sat, 10–6, Sun 1–6).*

The Frick has a policy of only admitting 200 people at a time, and of all the city's so-called retreats, this gallery is the only really effective sedative for anyone suffering from New York Trauma. Even its plush lavatories and telephone booths, upholstered in red velvet, seem reassuring.

Henry Clay Frick was the *bête noir* of the robber barons, which is a bit like being Satan amongst so many devils. The Pittsburgh Gradgrind made his millions out of steel, coke and beating up the labor unions. The most famous instance is the five-day sit-in that took place at the Homestead steel mill in 1892. Frick simply sent in 300 of his thugs, provoking a bloody scrimmage in which 14 people were killed. Two weeks later Emma Goldman's lover, a bookish young anarchist called Alexander Berkman, tried to assassinate Frick in his office.

All of which is at an ironically far remove from the American parvenu's passion for European Old Masters; particularly those depicting the leisured upper classes in emphatically unindustrialized, pastoral settings. Eventually Frick moved his entire collection from Pittsburgh to New York, housing it in 1914 in what one 1930s guidebook refers to as a mansion decorated in the 'neo-classical French eclectic Louis XVI manner'. The Continental mishmash, with its Renaissance furniture and Persian carpets, was grand enough for Frick to swan about in like some crazed Medici prince and make 'Carnegie's place' (his business partner's mansion up the road on 91st Street and 5th Avenue) 'look like a miner's shack'. Every summer, Frick loaded up a custom-built railway carriage with the whole collection and transported it lock, stock and barrel to his estate in Massachusetts. When a journalist inquired whether the tycoon was not concerned about accidents or a train robbery, Frick apparently replied nonchalantly, 'Oh, no. They're insured'.

Although it may be very trying that such a nasty person should have had such good taste, it doesn't really matter one Frick; the collection is quite simply the nicest in the world. This is mostly because it is so small; the paintings are all so well arranged there is no need for a tour, and the selection itself is exquisite. Frick seems to have had a penchant for collecting pairs of anything, as if he were playing Pelmanism. There are Holbein's two fascinating portraits, for example: the virtuous Thomas More hanging next to a supremely shifty Thomas Cromwell, the man who hanged him for high treason. Easily the most stupendous pair of all is El Greco's gaunt and dour *St Jerome* and a terrifying picture of an enraged Christ, casting out the moneychangers in the *Purification of the Temple*. The other rooms contain Vermeers, Goyas, Whistlers, Constables, and Turners. Best of all, there is a self portrait of Rembrandt dressed as an emir, painted when he was in dire financial straits, and his mystifying *Polish Rider*. Opposite this painting, you can't miss Lodovico Capponi's astonishing codpiece in a portrait by Bronzino.

When you have had enough, you can sit in the Frick's courtyard of plants and splashing fountains, contemplate the tulip gardens outside by the landscape architect John Russel Pope, and convince yourself that you have well and truly escaped New York and all its trials and tribulations.

Walk III
The Lower East Side and East Village

Orchard Street—Eldridge Street Synagogue—Clinton Street—Essex Street Market—Anshe Slonim Synagogue—Marble Cemetery—Little Ukraine—Astor Place and Cooper Union—St Mark's Place—St Mark's-in-the-Bowery—Tompkins Square

The unruly, shabby bulge on the east side of downtown Manhattan is probably the part you will like best. At first it takes you aback: there are no skyscrapers, no museums, and few tourist attractions to speak of; some pockets are distressingly dilapidated, while others are well kept and well-to-do.

More than anything else, the people living here give the place its edge and exuberance. Since the Irish came in the 1850s, the Lower East Side has been a refuge for first-generation immigrants, and now, though there is no such thing as a typical Lower East Sider, the area actually feels like a neighborhood. There are tiny Jewish bakeries, selling pumpernickel bread and rugulach, alongside West African groceries, Hispanic bodegas and Chinese hand-laundries, where shirts are starched and stacked in walls of crisp brown-paper parcels. Everyone is fantastically sociable, and it is impossible to go into a shop, restaurant or bar without making a friend.

The area is a promised land for cheap and delicious Jewish food, not to

THE LOWER EAST SIDE AND EAST VILLAGE

1 Ludlow Street Cafe
2 K K's
3 Yaffa Cafe
4 Sapporo East
5 Mary Ann's
6 Little India
7 Veselka
8 Dandi's Cafe
9 Grand Dairy Restaurant
10 Eldridge St. Synagogue
11 Jewish Daily Forward Building
12 Gertel's Bake Shoppe
13 Kossar's
14 Essex St. Market
15 Schapiro's Wine Company
16 Anshe Slonim Synagogue
17 Katz's
18 Bouwerie Lane Theater
19 Souk
20 Theatre 80
21 Counter Point
22 Di Roberti's
23 10th Street Turkish Baths
24 Christadora
25 St. Mark's Church

mention Indian, Italian, Ukrainian, Polish, Mexican, Dominican. Part of the joy of the walk is that you will eat a lot. Come on Sunday, the day after the Jewish Sabbath, when the shops on Essex Street, and the Orchard Street clothes market, are at their liveliest. You will have to wait until lunchtime, however, before the East Village lurches into consciousness.

Orientation: the area splits neatly into two, with Houston Street (pronouced 'Howston') bisecting the waist. Below Houston is the Jewish Lower East Side proper. Above, is the gentrified, arty East Village, a hot-bed of counter-culture in the sixties and seventies, with 'Alphabet City', named after Avenues A, B, C, and D, the more radical and considerably poorer Hispanic area to the east.

Start: by subway, take the **J** or the **F** train to Essex and Delancey Streets, or the **6** to Spring Street and walk east along Delancey Street. By bus, take the **M15** to Delancey and Allen Streets.

Walking Time: 3¹/₂ hours.

LUNCH/CAFÉS

Ludlow Street Café, on the northwest corner of Ludlow and Stanton Sts. Especially good for the Mexican brunch: fresh orange juice, champagne and chicken in peanut sauce, or *Pollo Asano*.

El Sombrero, 108 Stanton St., at Ludlow St. Down-to-earth Mexican food, with extra-strong frozen margaritas.

KK's Polish-American, 1st Ave., between 11th and 12th Sts. Family-run, and best in the summer, when you can eat cold *borscht* (bright pink with a boiled egg bobbing on top) in the backyard, which is eccentrically lit by hundreds of thousands of fairy lights.

Everybody's, 31 2nd Ave., between 2nd and 1st Sts. Tiny French bistro which ought to be much more expensive.

Yaffa Café, 98 St Mark's Place, near 1st Ave. Laid-back neighborhood café, with a lovely garden. Hot croissants with grilled cheese, chilli con carne, etc.

Sapporo East, 245 10th St., at 1st Ave. Superb *sushi*, *sashimi* and *teriyaki* in a restaurant that is sometimes so crowded, the waiters get hysterical.

Mary Ann's, 2nd Ave., near 7th St. High-quality Mexican food. Lunch is always a good buy.

Little India on 6th St., between 1st and 2nd Aves. Sixteen Indian restaurants opened in the 1970s by Bengali students at New York University, who were frustrated by the lack of Indian cuisine in Manhattan.

All are superb, although Panna is my favorite. In the evening, Romna has live sitar and drums.

Veselka, 144 2nd Ave., at 9th St. Good for lunch or breakfast. Delicious Ukrainian stodge: soups, *pierogi*. omelettes, and red Ukrainian *borscht*.

Dandi's Garden Café, 1st Ave., between 10th and 11th Sts. Yugoslavian breakfasts in a jolly pebble garden.

The sheer crush of people and nationalities living cheek by-jowl on the Lower East Side means that most of the action goes on outside, in the streets, and on stoops in front of the tenements.

In the East Village, no one does anything by half measures. Summer starts explosively on 4 July in 'Loisaida', which is the Puerto Rican patois for the Lower East Side, in particular for the stretch of Alphabet City, between Avenues A and D. The first fizzes and crackles begin at dusk, and the fireworks go on all night. Up on the roofs—the 'Costa del Tarmac'—there is carnival fever, and the curious sight of Puerto Ricans celebrating American Independence by bombarding each other with firecrackers. Summer ends just as punctually, on Labor Day, with 'Wigstock'. Decked out in wigs and costumes, an outdoor nightclub descends on Tompkins Square for the East Village parody of Woodstock, mimed to back-up tapes in a bandshell.

In the sixties the East Village took over from the West Village as New York's maverick neighborhood. It became the hub of the city's counterculture as West Village radicals, pioneered by Beat poets like Ginsberg and Kerouac, moved sideways into the cheaper East Village.

In 1981 there was another revolution: artists and art galleries rolled in, reclaiming derelict buildings and launching East Village artists like Keith Haring and Kenny Scharf. Though most of the galleries have now disappeared, they drastically altered the area. In their wake came gentrification, which is now moving inexorably eastwards into Alphabet City. St Mark's Place, the spine of the village, is the New York equivalent of London's King's Road, with token punks and ersatz bohemians.

The area below Houston Street, on the other hand, is the heart of Jewish New York. Between 1881 and 1924 over two million Jews emigrated to America, many escaping the pogroms in Russia. Nearly all passed through the rookeries and sweatshops of the Lower East Side, after they were processed on Ellis Island. Around the turn of the century, the area became a center of Yiddish culture, producing actors and singers like Eddie Cantor, Sophie Tucker and Al Jolson, and artists like the sculptor Jacob Epstein, the painter Mark Rothko, and the writer Henry Roth.

Today, there are nearly as many Jews in New York as in Israel, and although many have long since departed for the suburbs, they come back on Sundays to eat and fight for bargains in Orchard Street's thrilling outdoor market, where this walk starts.

The J and F subway stop on Essex and Delancey Streets lands you in **Spectacle City**: *nearly all the shops on this stretch of Delancey, except for one selling stetsons, are opticians. Giant glasses dangle over the sidewalk, and two opticians in particular, Cohen's and Sol Mascot, make the cheapest spectacles in New York in less than an hour.*

The **Orchard Street Market** *is only a couple of blocks away from the subway. Walk west on Delancey Street to the corner of Orchard Street, where the Kool-Man ice-cream van tinkles out 'Fiddler on the Roof', and turn right.*

On Sunday the whole street is closed to traffic, and stalls selling dresses, socks, fabrics and toys spill chaotically onto the street. You will find yourself bargaining for things you never knew you wanted. The best bargains are at S. Beckenstein's enormous emporium of fabrics, between Broome and Grand Streets. There are also spectacular sequinned dresses in shops with names to match—*Climactic, Glorious* and *H*.

Walk down Orchard Street as far as Grand Street, which is devoted to underwear. If you want breakfast, you couldn't do better than the blintzes at the **Grand Dairy Restaurant**, *a block away to the left, between Ludlow and Orchard Streets, at 341 Grand Street. The waiters here wear bow-ties and crack corny jokes all day long, whether they have an audience or not.*

Walk two blocks down Orchard Street from the intersection with Grand Street to Canal Street.

On the corner is the shell of **S. Jarmulovsky's Bank**, one of the Lower East Side's tallest buildings, topped by an elegant tempietto, actually the guise for a water tower. The private bank faltered in the Panic of 1907 and finally crashed in 1914, causing the ruin of thousands of immigrants and, after a suspended sentence for mismanagement of the bank's assets, Jarmulovsky's death.

From here, turn right onto Canal Street, walk a couple of blocks west and then turn left onto Eldridge Street. On the block between Canal Street and Division Street is the **Eldridge Street Synagogue**.

Built in 1886, the synagogue was abandoned in the 'thirties, and now it is close to dereliction. Even so, it is an amazingly exotic presence on the Lower East Side—a high Victorian mix of Gothic and Moorish styles. The Eastern elements—pastry-cut keyhole windows and pink marble columns—have fared better than the ornate Gothic finials, which have fallen off, and the huge stained-glass rose window, which has been vandalized and boarded over.

If you come on a Sunday and ring the bell, the rabbi will take you on a tour. The magnificent, crumbling upstairs sanctuary reflects the lavish taste of the architects, Herter Brothers, a German firm, which specialized in 5th Avenue drawing-rooms. The rabbi rummages in his waistcoat pocket for a speech, which he delivers in Hebrew and English, explaining the Synagogue Rescue Project and the history of the building which has been 'neglected from behind long time.' At the end, he asks, 'Was that all right?', and then, if you are lucky, bursts into song.

Outside, the synagogue is surrounded by the kind of **tenements** that spread throughout the Lower East Side with vegetable speed in the 19th century. The first thing you notice are the Virginia-creeper fire escapes, which Henry James hated and described at length in *American Notes*. According to Arnold Bennett the tenements seemed to 'sweat humanity at every window and door': there was a population density of 700 people per acre and the death rate in the tubercular 'lung blocks' was twice as high as the rest of the city.

These are copybook examples of tenements—'Old Law' style blocks with dragon-head newels, and a pre-Old Law tenement next to the synagogue at 18 Eldridge Street. Old Law tenements, built between 1879 and 1901, were laid out according to the 'dumbbell' plan, where narrow 90-ft long apartments were constructed sardine-style, with a reeking foot-wide airshaft in between. There were four families to a floor sharing a communal bathroom, and often the whole building had to use lavatories ventilated by street grates in the basement. In 1901, with two-thirds of the population already ensconced in Old Law housing, dumbbell tenements were banned, and minimally better sanitary standards were brought in.

*Make your way back up Eldridge Street to the next block, between Canal and Hester Streets. On the righthand side, next to the Judaica Department Store which sells dusty maccabees and mezuzahs, is the **Chinese Wall Newspaper**, at 52 Eldridge Street. The painted red banners, tied on an iron mesh storefront with purple, red and pink ribbons, are Help Wanted columns—advertisements for local jobs.*

Retrace your steps back to Canal Street and walk four blocks east to Straus Square, where Canal Street runs into East Broadway. On the way you cross Allen Street, with its enormous painted billboard urging passers-by to 'Pray with Dignity in a Ziontalis'.

Before the Rev. Dr Parkhurst's Society for the Prevention of Vice went on the rampage at the turn of the century, Allen Street was a dingy avenue, overshadowed by the El. It was famous for its belly dancers and 'creep houses and panel rooms', brothels equipped with sliding panels so thieves could sneak in and rifle through the victims' trousers.

*Just before you get to Straus Square, you pass the shell of the **Kletzker Brotherly Aid Society** on the lefthand corner of Canal Street at 5 Ludlow Street.*

This is now a Chinese-Italian funeral home, with co-op apartments above. The modest, rather gracious building was formerly one of the Lower East Side's *landsmanshaftn*, associations established by immigrants to support new arrivals from their local *shtetl* (town); in this case, Kletz, in Russia.

> **Straus Square**, *a block to the east from Canal and Ludlow Streets, is the spiritual centre of the Jewish Lower East Side. On the corner of Rutgers Street and 175 East Broadway is the Lower East Side's only skyscraper, the* **Jewish Daily Forward Building***.*

For years, before it moved uptown, the Yiddish newspaper was a cornerstone of Jewish life. It was founded in 1897 by a Lithuanian, Abraham Cahan, who championed the labor movement, as well as Yiddish writers like Isaac Singer and Sholom Aleichem, who found themselves more welcome at the *Forverts* than in book publishing. More than anything else, the paper was respected for its down-to-earth style. One of the most popular columns was the Bintel Brief, or 'Bundle of Letters', which gave straightforward if idiosyncratic advice to readers grappling with life in the New World. They ranged from 'The Sleepless Man', a husband complaining about his wife's 'nocturnal concerts', to people living in such poverty that they wrote in to ask if it was ethical to sell their children to a home where they would get a more comfortable upbringing.

The building is now home to a Chinese association, the Ling Liang, though if you look right up to the top of the west façade, you can just make out a terracotta sign saying *Forverts*. Opposite is the **Seward Park Library** which is topped with a balustrade, the remnants of an idea to build an open-air reading room on the roof, since the interior was too small for the book-hungry immigrants.

In this part of East Broadway there are more than a dozen storefront Orthodox synagogues, many Hasidic. A ritualarium, or *mikveh*, where women bathe themselves every month in rainwater, is still in use at the far east end of East Broadway. Closer to, at 145 East Broadway, near Essex Street, you can peep through louvred shutters into one of the *yeshivas*, where students are trained as orthodox rabbis. Its walls are lined with memorial plaques, each one of which has an electric bulb, illuminated on the anniversary of the rabbi it commemorates.

> *From Straus Square walk a block north along Essex Street to Hester Street. The shops on this block are fascinating. They make and repair* yarmulke, talith *(prayer-shawls)*, bar mitzvah *sets*, mezuzahs, tefellin *(amulets containing prayers on Old Testament parchment) and electrically lit* menorahs. *The Hasidic proprietors close up for afternoon prayers, and in the autumn they set up stalls selling equipment for the High Holy Days.*

137

At the corner of Hester and Essex Streets, is an irresistible nexus of smells.

The seaside whiffs on the northwest corner come from **Guss' Pickles**, whose peppers, half-sours and sauerkraut, cost 50c a go. A few steps away at 5 Hester Street, the air is deliciously scented by the **Kadouri Import Co.**, where spices like cumin and cardamom are arranged in barrels with pistachio nuts and crystallized fruits. A little way down Hester Street is **Gertel's Bake Shoppe**, at No. 53: a bakery run by enormous men and full of comforting smells. You can sit down for a coffee and *rugelach*, and take advantage of the loo in the back.

After Gertel's, go back to the corner of Essex and Hester Streets.

Here (dubbed the **Khazzer-Mark**, or Pig-Market), workers gathered every morning to bargain themselves a job from the contractors known as 'sweaters'. The first unsensationalized account of the sweatshops they worked in was given by the crusading social reformer, Jacob Riis. *How the Other Half Lives* described the furious whirr of sewing machines on every block and the sweatshop interiors—workers ankle-deep in clothes, babies balanced on mountains of material, and faces blackened with cloth-dust.

*Walk one block north up Essex Street to Grand Street and turn right. Immediately on your right, at 369 Grand Street, is **Kossar's**, advertising garlic and onion bialys and bagels in pink-and-blue neon. Every inch of the bakery, which sells some of the best bagels in the world, is dusted in flour.*

While it is certain that the bialy, a kind of onion roll, was invented by the Polish bakers of Bialystok, no one is sure about the origin of the bagel. The mystery has caused furious arguments ever since an article in the *Saturday Review* claimed they were Turkish. K. Jason Sitewell replied with the more dubious theory that a Greek baker called Bagelus accidentally invented the bagel in 381 BC after he wrapped some dough round his feet to cure his gout, fell asleep at midday, and woke up with a bagel on his toe. Others insisted, among other things, that the Dead Sea Scrolls mentioned the 'legab', and that an ossified bagel was discovered in an Egyptian tomb. The most convincing letter came from Harry Bagel, who claimed that his Uncle Morris invented the bagel in 1897.

From Kossar's, walk three blocks east on Grand Street as far as **Clinton Street**, *and turn left.*

Clinton Street is the Hispanic Lower East Side's principal high street. It is at its most energetic on Saturdays when the chihuahuas and ghetto-blasters are out in force. The shops are all colorful, with murals painted on their rolling gates. Most sell bridal wear, and nearly all the signs are in Spanish. Some translate themselves simply as 'Cheap Store' or 'Variety Shop', and sell *productos tropicales*—plantains, mango, *pasteles calientes* (chopped meat wrapped in leaves), and yams—and, less exotically, plastic American eagles, loo seats and chandeliers. Best of all, there are street vendors selling **snow ices**: scraped from a slab of ice, moulded into a cone and doused in flavored syrup, and (occasionally vodka).

Walk two blocks up Clinton Street and turn left at Delancey Street. This end of Delancey is overshadowed by the gray pylons of the **Williamsburg Bridge**, *which links the Lower East Side to the Hasidic community in Williamsburg, Brooklyn. (See 'Day Trips' p. 339).*

When it was built in 1903 the bridge turned Williamsburg into a dormitory for immigrants living on the Lower East Side. Even though it is a suspension bridge, it looks as though it was assembled from a DIY kit, partly because the end spans are supported by stone trusses and piers, rather than being suspended.

Walk three blocks west on Delancey Street back to Essex Street and turn right. The whole of the righthand side of Essex Street between Delancey and Rivington Streets is devoted to the **Essex Street Market**, *a covered market opened in the 1930s after pushcarts were banned from the streets.*

The star of the market is **Julius the Candy King**, who has the first stall on the corner of Delancey and Essex Streets. In summer the King— whose real name is Maurice—is elusive, and all you find is a disappointing sign saying 'Gone Fishing'.

On the next block up between Rivington and Stanton Streets, is the **Essex Street Antiques Warehouse** *where you can pick up some really good bargains, especially 1940s propeller fans. Opposite the antiques market, at 135 Essex Street, is* **Bernstein-on-Essex**, *a delicatessen and kosher Chinese restaurant.*

The customers are as formidable as the waiters, who sport black *yarmulke* with red silk tassles. 'That tongue, it's horry-ble', complains one battle-axe, 'So's yours,' says the waiter, bridling. The restaurant sells wonderful hot pastrami sandwiches.

> *Two doors away from Bernstein's is* **Economy Candy**, *selling kosher marshmallows and Atomic Gum Balls, alongside great barrels of every conceivable kind of nut, halva and candy.*
>
> *Walk back down Essex Street to Rivington Street and turn left. A few steps away at 126 Rivington Street is* **Schapiro's Wine Company**, *selling kosher* 'Wine You Can Almost "Cut with a knife".'

On Thursdays and Fridays its art gallery annex is open, and on Sundays from 10 to 6 there are free guided tours of the cellars which take up an entire block. The grapes are pressed, under the supervision of rabbis, then boiled, and (be warned) the end product is *very* sweet.

> *On the next block east, at 148 Rivington Street, is Manhattan's sole remaining matzoh factory,* **Streit's Matzoh Company**. *Inside, you can peer through a doorway in the shop to the factory behind, where matzoh sheets flop round a conveyor belt, before they are dissected, juddered round in wire baskets and packed in boxes.*
>
> *A block further along, at 166 Rivington Street is the* **Variety Occult Shop**, *one of the* bótanicas, *or religious shops found on the Lower East Side, in Harlem and in parts of Brooklyn. The shops sell a whole range of charms and love potions, including evil eyes and tongues, magnetic Virgins, and good-luck aerosol sprays, a puff of which promises money or love.*
>
> *Retrace your steps to Norfolk Street and walk two blocks north. Just before you get to Houston Street, on the righthand side, at 172 Norfolk Street, is the* **Anshe Slonim Synagogue**.

Sadly, this exquisite building is in a state of colossal disrepair. Modelled on Cologne Cathedral, which had just celebrated its 600th anniversary, it was built in 1849 for a German congregation by Alexander Saeltzer, himself a German Jew. Originally it was even more tremendously Gothic: the towers were crowned by pyramids supporting sculptures and there were lacework traceries and intricate medieval details round the windows. Now the façade is blistering away, and pigeons freewheel in and out of the broken stained glass window at the top.

A few years ago the synagogue was slated for demolition, but execution was stayed, and now there is a clanking sign reading 'Angelo Orensatz, please knock'. Mr Orensatz is an unconventional balding Spanish sculptor, who talks backwards. 'Home my, to welcome yes?', he says, and takes you to the sanctuary inside the church, which he uses as a studio and has been converting into artists' apartments since 1986. Painted banners and metal sculptures dangle from the ceiling, and up in the crumbling gallery is a display of clay sculptures, resembling parts of the body. 'Expression the like, you do. Yes?', he asks, and if you recklessly nod, he says, 'You love I. Yes?'.

After you have escaped from the synagogue, walk north to the end of Norfolk Street, turn left down Houston Street and walk three blocks to the west, past a Puerto Rican bar whose domino players compete on the sidewalk all through the summer.

East Houston Street is an excellent place for lunch.

At 205 East Houston Street, on the corner of Ludlow Street, is **Katz's 'That's All!' Delicatessen**. Inside, ancient signs swing from the ceiling, urging you to 'Send a Salami to your Boy in the Army' which rhymes, in New York, and in fact there is still a special mailing counter. The waiters keep sharpened knives in their jacket pockets for hacking up monstrous sandwiches.

If you want a picnic, there is gastronomic heaven at **Russ & Daughters**, a little way down from Katz's, at 179 Houston Street. Their *Novie* (Nova Scotia salmon) and dried apricots are incomparable. If you just want a snack there is **Yonah Schimmel's**, further down at 137 Houston Street and their knishes are the best in New York.

*After lunch you can start exploring the **East Village**, which is the area north of Houston Street. Walk along Houston as far as Allen Street, which changes its name to 1st Avenue at the invisible frontier with Houston. Cross the Paris-Dakar Rally on Houston, and walk north up 1st Avenue.*

*Three blocks north on your left, on 3rd Street, at 49¹/₂ 1st Avenue is the Lower East Side's self-proclaimed campest of camp shops, **Little Rickey's**, 'Where Elvis is your cashier in the cathedral of kitsch'. If you are looking for an Elvis suspender belt, a Virgin Mary*

141

*scatter cushion, or a Felix the Cat wagging clock, Little Rickey's will
have it.*

*Go back to East 2nd Street and walk west, towards 2nd Avenue.
On the righthand side of the block is the* **New York City Marble
Cemetery** *which was opened in 1830.*

This is one of the most peaceful spots in the city: the gates are permanently locked, so only squirrels patronize it. President James Monroe
was here briefly in 1832, but he was soon removed, and the only resident
of note is the unfortunately named Preserved Fish, a merchant from a
prominent family of lawyers. Even so, the tall, unnaturally white obelisks
on pristine lawns are a haunting sight in this grubby area.

*Keep walking west on 2nd Street, past 2nd Avenue, until you get to
the Bowery. Between 1st and 2nd Streets, you can see the* **Bouwerie
Lane Theatre**, *built in 1874 as a German bank, across the street
near Bond Street. This is one of the city's loveliest trompe l'oeil
palazzi. The whole thing is constructed of cast-iron rather than
stone, and it is only the sharpness of the angles that gives it
away.*

This part of the **Bowery** *is New York's skid row. The area is not
dangerous, and if you walk south down the Bowery you can investigate the collection of shops selling* **commercial kitchen-
equipment**, *including the standard cinammon dispensers, and the
heavy Buffalo china coffee mugs used in coffee shops.*

*Now walk east again, back down 2nd Street to 2nd Avenue, turn
left, and walk north up 2nd Avenue as far as 7th Street. At 7th
Street, turn left into* **Little Ukraine**, *the stretch of 7th Street that
lies between 2nd and 3rd Avenues.*

If you are in the city in May, do not miss the Ukrainian Street Festival,
during which the whole block is closed to traffic and taken over by
tombolas, stalls selling handmade Ukrainian toys and great spreads
of Ukrainian food. On the righthand side, at 11 East 7th Street, is
Surma, one of several Ukrainian shops which come into their own at
Easter, when they decorate and sell *pysansky*, hand-painted eggs. On the
other side of the street, is the onion-domed **St George's Ukrainian
Catholic Church**, built here in 1977 by a large and wealthy
congregation.

Directly opposite the church, at 15 East 7th Street, is **McSorley's Old Ale House**, which says it is the oldest saloon in New York, although it is not. Until 1970 McSorley's was a male sanctuary, and 'Good ale, raw onions, and no ladies' was its motto. They still brew their own ale, and the best time to drink here is on a weekday lunchtime, when it is quiet.

Walk to the end of the block and turn right onto 3rd Avenue. On the left, marooned in an island between 3rd and 4th Avenues, is the **Cooper Union Building***, looking very like a beached brownstone whale.*

Cooper Union was founded in 1859 by Peter Cooper, the entrepreneur, and offered free technical and scientific courses to anyone 'of good moral character'. Cooper himself was uneducated, and made his million twice over in the glue and iron trades. He then invented one of the first steam engines, the *Tom Thumb*, as well as an automatic cradle, which rocked and fanned itself, and played music.

Today, Cooper Union is one of the most progressive architecture schools in America. The building itself is of architectural interest because it was the first in the world to be constructed with wrought-iron beams. Cooper developed and built them out of railway tracks at his own ironworks, and eventually the idea metamorphosed into the steel frameworks used for holding up skyscrapers. There are still public lectures in the Great Hall, where Abolitionists spoke against slavery before the Civil War.

Walk a block north up 3rd Avenue and turn left on **Astor Place***, which is named after New York's first multi-millionaire, John Jacob Astor, who built a mansion nearby and owned all the land along Lafayette Street.*

Between midday and midnight the sidewalk in front of Cooper Union turns into a **souk**, which comes and goes according to the movements of the police. The stuff on sale ranges from junk extracted from garbage cans to stolen bicycles. When the police descend, the whole flea market magically disappears, except for the book and porn-magazine peddlers who don't need licenses.

Walking west on Astor Place as far as Lafayette Street, you can't miss Bernard Rosenthal's huge 15 ft tall steel cube, the

143

'Alamo', on the traffic island to your right. It is balanced on one side, and is supposed to pirouette when pushed, although the 'weathering' apex is now so rusted you need to give it a really good shove to make it budge.

Behind the cube at Astor Place subway station is a replica of one of the elegant, almost oriental, beaux-arts **subway kiosks** used all over the city in the 19th century. Down below, the station is decorated with ceramic tiles of beavers, another salute to John Jacob Astor who made his first fortune trading beaver furs.

*Now retrace your way east on Astor Place and cross 3rd Avenue. On the other side of the avenue, Astor Place turns into **St Mark's Place**, which is the hub of the East Village.*

The street draws a whole spectrum of exhibitionists, from cultured New Wave punks to college-types riding motorized skateboards with more nerve than skill. Everyone who comes here thinks St Mark's Place is the most fashionable street in the world, and beleaguered residents have painted signs on their stoops saying 'Do not sit on the stairs, please', which you can't see, because so many people are sitting on them.

For walkers, the pink, red and blue pyjama-striped street is crammed with interest. Look out for the mosaics by **Joe Power**, who has encrusted all the lampposts, walls and spare crevices with pieces of colored broken glass, china and Dutch tiles, like an outdoor grotto. The buildings here are set back, so the extra-wide sidewalk is carpeted in second-hand books, weird magazines, and stalls. In the middle of the block is a community centre, offering craft and theater classes. The rest of the street is jam-packed with basement stores, in particular leather shops (dealing in Doc Marten's, Harley-Davidson belts, gauntlets and studs), and restaurants which move their tables onto the sidewalk in the summer, infecting the street with Mediterranean *joie de vivre*.

In the 19th century, St Mark's Place was well-to-do; the wealthiest of the Lower East Side's Eastern European communities lived in its elegant Federal houses and the street had several social clubs, including a German marksmen's club. In the fifties, West Village radicals arrived in the East Village via St Mark's Place. A bizarre collection of poets and writers—Jack Kerouac, Allen Ginsberg, Frank O'Hara, William Burroughs and Norman Mailer—all moved in, exclaiming on the 'Pierre-of-Melville goof and wonder of it all'. In their wake came the hippies, Bill

Graham's Fillmore East concerts, and the rock group Electric Circus, at 23 St Mark's, where the community center is now.

*On the righthand corner of St Mark's and 2nd Avenue, drop into the **Gem Spa** newsagents for one of their famous egg creams. They contain neither egg nor cream, but frozen milk, seltzer (soda water), and syrup.*

If you walk east to the next block, between 1st and 2nd Avenues, on the gateposts outside 73 St Mark's you pass some lion-gargoyles with human features.

Two doors east at **77 St Mark's** is W. H. Auden's house where the poet lived from 1953 until 1972, over the basement where Trotsky printed *Novy Mir*. Auden's pokey apartment evolved into an alpine range of abandoned, egg-encrusted plates, and the whole place was apparently beseiged by such a populous 'vertical nation of cockroaches' that the walls seemed to be moving.

On the righthand side of the street, near the corner of 1st Avenue is **Theater 80 St Mark's**, which has the handprints and autographs of Myrna Loy, Gloria Swanson and Joan Crawford, among others, inscribed on the sidewalk outside. The cinema shows double-bills of revival movies from midday to midnight. Inside, is a sacred niche for Joan Crawford's portrait, and a café, with packets of candies arranged by some creative hand into pyramids, and illuminated by blue paraffin lamps.

*Walk back to 2nd Avenue and turn right. On the left, at 135 and 137 2nd Avenue, is the **Ottendorfer Library**, and the **Stuyvesant Polyclinic**, two majestic remnants of Deutschländle, the German community living here in the 19th century. The clinic, which is still in use, has busts of the doctors and scientists, Hippocrates, Galen, and Harvey on the porch and under the cornice.*

*Continue two blocks north, to 10th Street. To the left, the block of 9th Street between 2nd and 3rd Avenues is turning into a miniature Japanese enclave. There is a Japanese café, a Japanese video shop and a Japanese bar called **Counter Point**, at 237 East 9th Street.*

If you have time, pop in and ask for a blow-fish *sake* chaser and a pint of Guinness: the barman warms up some *sake*, drops in a blow-fish fin, and then theatrically sets fire to the whole thing. You down the fishy liquid and, if you are really brave, you bite on the fin, which is supposed to give you the precipitous rush of adrenalin you need for the Guinness.

145

Go back to 2nd Avenue and walk north to 10th Street. Set back from the avenue at a diagonal angle is the city's most handsome and second-oldest church, **St Mark's-in-the-Bowery***.*

The church is a mongrel in terms of style; a 1799 Federal body is topped by an 1828 Greek Revival steeple by Ithiel Town (who designed the houses on Washington Square), while the pretty Italianate cast-iron portico over the entrance dates from 1858.

It was probably built on the site of Peter Stuyvesant's chapel, which stood here in 1660, in the middle of his 62-acre farm, or 'bouwerie'. After he surrendered New Amsterdam to the British in 1664, the Dutch governor spent the last eight years of his life stumping around the farm on his silver-capped wooden leg. His statue is on the righthand side of the entrance, and his remains lie in a vault in the graveyard behind.

On the lefthand side of the entrance is a sculpture of an American Indian, with hands that are much too big, and a body that melts into its own sandstone. If the style looks familiar, it is because it was sculpted by Solon H. Borglum, whose more famous brother, Gutzon, carved Mount Rushmore. St Mark's main cemetery is to the left, past the American Indian, but you will have to ask at the church office if you want to look round. In 1878 it was the scene of a macabre kidnapping, when body-snatchers disinterred the body of department store millionaire A. T. Stewart, and held it for a ransom of a quarter of a million dollars. Two years passed before Stewart's widow, worth $50 million, was persuaded to relinquish $20,000 for her husband, whose putrifying remains were eventually reburied in Garden City.

In the twenties the church became a center for even more unusual events under the ministry of Dr William Guthrie, who worked out his own system of holistic faith, and introduced parishioners to the delights of American Indian chanting, Eastern mantras and a Body and Soul Clinic. Sadly, the pagan-style frescoes which he had painted on the pediment have long since disappeared. The church still has a reputation for being radical, however, and it is always hosting some sort of theatrical, literary or musical event. (See the *Village Voice* for listings).

A little way west on 10th Street from St Mark's, is the **'Renwick Triangle'***, a wedge of exquisite wisteria-shaded brownstones, which James Renwick, who did Grace Church on Broadway and 10th Street, designed in Italianate style in 1861. The wedge is* *formed at the point where 10th Street is bisected by Stuyvesant Street, named after the driveway to Stuyvesant's mansion.*

Go back to St Mark's Church, and walk a block north up 2nd Avenue to East 11th Street.

In 1901, Butch Cassidy lived round the corner in a boarding house on 12th Street. At that time, 2nd Avenue was dubbed the **Jewish Rialto** because it contained so many Jewish theaters. For 2nd Avenue's writers, actors and directors, life revolved around the Café Royal on 12th Street, which closed down in 1953 and became a dry cleaners.

At East 11th Street turn right and walk east as far as 1st Avenue, a little Italian enclave of delicatessens, shops and patisseries. It is time for some tea.

Just before 1st Avenue is **Veniero's Café**, specializing in thousands of miniature pastries, and round the corner, on 1st Avenue, is the **Black Forest Pastry Shop**, which has delicious (take-away) crème caramels.

Across the road, at 176 1st Avenue, **Di Roberti's Pasticceria** is my first choice. The tea rooms, built in 1904, are the finest in New York. The walls are tiled in white and inset with sparkly green and gold Art Nouveau mosaics, and the eternally grim proprietor looks as though he dates from the same era. The cappuccino, half-froth, half-cinnamon, and the *cannoli*, tubes of brittle pastry filled with ricotta, are wonderful.

Now walk down to 10th Street, turn left, and walk a block east to Avenue A. Traditional steam baths, or shvitz, *the Yiddish for sweat, used to be scattered all over the Lower East Side. The sole surviving example is the* **Tenth Street Russian Turkish Baths**, *on the righthand side, at 268 10th Street (open until 10, and later by appointment). You may see a beetroot person emerging from a massage in the Russian Radiant Heat Room, or perhaps from the bar, which serves mainly Stolichnaya vodka.*

Keep going down 10th Street until you get to Gothic Revival **St Nicholas' Greek and Russian Orthodox Church**, *on the corner of Avenue A, and* **Tompkins Square Park**, *which fills up four city blocks, between 7th and 10th Streets, and Avenues A and B.*

Tompkins Square is the East Village's forum. Everyone uses it: Puerto Ricans from Loisaida, West Africans and WASPS, drug-dealers and children, punks and radicals, poets and ancient Ukrainians and Poles. If there is one particular place in the whole of New York that sums up the hundreds of different worlds carrying on at the same time in the same city, then it is Tompkins Square.

The first thing you notice is the distressing sight of 300 homeless people who live in a shanty town of makeshift tents in the middle. Gentrification over the past five years has caused enormous acrimony: in that time the East Village has become expensive; some rents are on a par with SoHo, and the clash between rich and poor is more blatant than ever. When police tried to rid the park of its homeless in 1988 and 1989 serious riots ensued, and the tension is still palpable. The riots were prefigured more than a century ago in 1874: in the wake of the financial panic of 1873, German socialists held a demonstration against unemployment which the police broke up so violently, it was dubbed the 'Tompkins Square Massacre'.

Today, the buildings round the square are a motley bunch. The north side has a row of elegant houses with high stoops built in 1846, 12 years after the park was laid out in the style of a Bloomsbury square. On the corner of 10th Street and Avenue B you can't miss the mural by Chico, *Say no to Crack*, and round the corner on 11th Street there are more murals by other Loisaida artists. To the west on Avenue B the tall 12-story Art-Deco building is the **Christadora**. Originally a settlement house where George Gershwin gave his first recital, the tower was converted into luxury condominiums in 1987, and was the focus of the recent riots.

The west side facing Avenue A is the most lively. It has a curious mixture of gentrified restaurants, diners and brightly painted bodegas whose window displays of washing powders and cereal packets are supposedly a code for the drugs available inside. On the corner of 7th Street and Avenue A, you can drop into the Polish diner, **Leshko Coffee Shop**, which is a rallying point for people living in the neighborhood. It looks onto a street lamp which has been turned into an impromptu sculpture, and hung about with nearly 200 sneakers and plimsolls.

*Tompkins Square is officially the end of the walk. The **M13** bus will pick you up from Avenue A and 9th Street and take you back to the **6** subway at Astor Place (it takes 10 minutes to walk).*

If you want to stay on for a bar crawl, however, you couldn't choose a better starting point. There is the **Aztec Lounge** *on the corner of East 9th Street and Avenue A, which shows up dandruff on black clothing, the* **Horseshoe Bar** *on the corner of Avenue B and 6th Street,* **Mona's Bar** *on Avenue B and 13th Street, where they have cider on draught, and lastly the* **Gas Station** *down on Avenue B and 3rd Street, a wrecked garage used as a performance art venue as well as a bar.*

Walk IV

Bohemian Squares: the Flatiron District and Greenwich Village

Washington square Arch

Flatiron Building—Madison Square—Ladies Mile—Gramercy Park—Union Square—14th Street—University Place—Washington Square—St Luke's Place—Christopher Street—Jefferson Market Courthouse—Patchin Place—Gansevoort Meat Market—Hoboken, New Jersey

Greenwich Village gloats at the top of every sightseer's list, while the Flatiron District, if it is included at all, hovers uncertainly at the bottom. The first is New York's darling neighborhood, crammed with the most picturesque streets in Manhattan; the second is a more oddball district, filled with mysterious, forgotten architecture and quirky backwaters. The two go well together, since the Flatiron District dilutes the sickly bijou charm of Greenwich Village.

There is a lot to do: shooting, bowling and playing billiards; buying fake perfumes, novelty toys and secondhand books; visiting the meat market, cruising bars and clubs, and diving under the Hudson on the PATH train for a backwards view of Manhattan. Nearly all of this can be done at night, when the illuminated skyscrapers of the Flatiron District look eerie and outlandish, and the crowds start posing in earnest in the streets, bars and clubs of Greenwich Village. The afternoon or early evening is an excellent time to do the walk, although you will have to get your skates on to catch the Police Academy Museum which closes at 3.

150

THE FLATIRON DISTRICT and
GREENWICH VILLAGE

1   John's Pizzeria
2   Waverly Coffee Shop
3   Florent
4   White Horse Tavern
5   Metropolitan Life Insurance Co.
6   New York Life Insurance Co.
7   Barnes and Noble
8   National Arts Club
9   Police Academy Museum
10 Farmers Market
11 Strand Book Store
12 Bowlmor Lanes
13 Washington Mews
14 "The Row"
15 Judson Memorial Church
16 Provincetown Playhouse
17 St. Luke's
18 Northern Dispensary
19 Balducci's
20 Jefferson Market Courthouse

0 m   250 m

Orientation: named after one of New York's best-loved skyscrapers, the **Flatiron District** covers a small area east of 5th Avenue from 14th to 26th Streets encompassing Union, Madison, Gramercy and Stuyvesant Squares. **Greenwich Village** (also known as the West Village), on the other hand, is a notorious jumble of streets, where the grid goes temporarily haywire.

Start: take the **N** or **R** train to 23rd Street and 5th Avenue, or the **6** to 23rd Street and Park Avenue South. By bus take the **M2, M3** or **M23** to Madison Square.

Walking Time: 4 hours.

LUNCH/CAFÉS

Curry in a Hurry, 130 East 29th St., at Lexington Ave. In 'Little India', an area based around 29th and 28th Streets, between Madison and 3rd Avenues.

Choshi, 77 Irving Place, at East 19th St. *Sushi*.

Cucina Stagionale, 275 Bleecker St., near Jones St. A scrum for pasta, though at lunchtime things are decidedly calmer.

Waverly Coffee Shop, 11 Waverly Place, near 6th Ave. Muffins, omelettes, and fries.

Violeta's Mexican Restaurant, 220 West 13th St., near Greenwich Ave. *Tacos*, *nachos*, *enchilidas*, *chilli*, *mole*, *burritos*, *chilaquiles*, *tortillas*, and Mexican beer.

John's Pizzeria, 278 Bleecker St., between 6th and 7th Aves. The most famous pizzas in New York, and very good too.

Caribe, 117 Perry St., near Greenwich St. Caribbean, Creole and West Indian cooking in the New York equivalent of London's Kew Gardens. Try the jerk chicken.

Gulf Coast, 489 West St., at West 12th St. Cajun-fried alligator and catfish with hushpuppies.

Benny's Burritos, 113 Greenwich Ave., near Jane St. Delicious *tortilla* envelopes filled with beans, beef and cheese, *guacamole*, and sour cream.

Florent, 69 Gansevoort St., between Washington and Greenwich Sts. Fashionable meat market restaurant open 24 hours. French food on the pricey side, with freezing refrigerated-lorry air-conditioning.

Tortilla Flats, 767 Washington St., near West 12th St. Depraved Tex-Mex.

Bellisima Café, 418 6th Ave., near West 9th St. Hot-sausage pizzas.

Dragon Burmese Restaurant, 557 Hudson St., near West 11th St.

Curious mix of Indian, Chinese, and Thai, with hot sauce and Chinese beer or jasmine tea.

Bruno Bakery, West Broadway, between Bleecker and Houston Sts. An Italian bakery where you can contemplate the *Time Landscape* opposite: a 'sculpture' of oak, sassafras and maples, recreating Manhattan as a pre-colonial rain forest.

White Horse Tavern, 567 Hudson St., at West 11th St. Where Dylan Thomas drank himself under the daisies. Cheeseburgers and hard-boiled eggs.

At first glance the Village and the Flatiron District could not be more unalike. Full of wholesale novelty toy shops, photographic agencies and publishing houses, the Flatiron District usually gets dismissed as a mere appendage to midtown. The Village, on the other hand, is known as the mecca of gay New York: a flamboyant neighborhood which comes into its own on the evening of 31 October when 50,000 boisterous revelers dress in cowls, sheets and gore, and parade through the twisty streets of the Village until late into the night.

Historically, however, the two districts come from the same stable: both began in the last century as sanctuaries for the affluent, and yet, by 1900, both had been transformed into bastions of radical art and politics. Literary salons, left-wing clubs and a mixture of revolutionary socialists and cloudland Bohemians gravitated towards the Village, while Union and Madison Squares became platforms for mass meetings and political rallies. In 1913 the neighborhoods collided in the Flatiron District with two memorable events—the Armory Show and the Paterson Strike Pageant.

The pageant, depicting the terrible plight of strikers at the Paterson silk mills in New Jersey, was an extraordinary occasion. It was presented, under the banner of the radical IWW union (Industrial Workers of the World), by 1200 textile workers who walked from Paterson to Madison Square, accompanied by the journalist John Reed (the only American to be buried in the Kremlin) and the 'Ashcan' artist, John Sloan.

The Armory Show was organized and attended by the same caucus of Villagers as the Paterson Pageant, and it was the first exhibition in America of Cézanne, Van Gogh, Gauguin and the avant-garde. Though it was aimed at the effete middle classes of New York, it soon became a national cause célèbre. After the *New York Times* had described it as part of a general movement to 'destroy' society (as well as 'art' and 'literature'), it was seen by a quarter of a million people. When it got to

153

Chicago, effigies of Matisse were burnt in the street and, rather hilariously, the Vice Commission sent in a senator to view Marcel Duchamp's abstract painting of a *Nude Descending a Staircase*.

Since the demise of Bohemianism and bobbed hair, the Flatiron District and the Village have moved on and apart. The fact that they were both real estate boneyards until well after the War, means that each contains rare pockets of 19th-century architecture. Amazingly, New Yorkers have only recently begun to appreciate the tremendous cast-iron chateaux of Ladies Mile, the Art-Deco scrapers of Madison Square, and the well-bred brownstones of Gramercy Square. Likewise, the modest, unpretentious cottages, brownstones and villas of the shabby old Village were scoffed at for years. Now, hallowed and restored to pristine neatness, they sell at $2–5 million a piece. They can seem impossibly twee, but their human scale makes the Village seem far more intimate and homely than the rest of Manhattan.

People in the Village these days fall into five distinct sects: gay, (four out of five of the men on Christopher Street); journalists (in the bars); very rich (actors and stockbrokers living in brownstones); tourists (dragged round in posses of up to a hundred) and B&Ts ('Bridge and Tunnel' suburbanites from Long Island, Westchester and New Jersey who pour in on weekends to the undisguised dismay of everyone else). An oil and water combination perhaps, but one that definitely makes the neighborhood festive and convivial.

*The walk starts in the southwest corner of Madison Square at its extraordinary landmark, the triangular-wedge of **Flatiron Building** which hovers over the slice of island made by 5th Avenue and Broadway at 23rd Street.*

Designed in 1902 by the Chicago architect, Daniel Burnham, the Flatiron has one of the earliest steel skeletons of any skyscraper in New York. It is often wrongly cited as New York's first skyscraper—the first was the Tower Building built in 1889 on Broadway.

Though it is tempting to take an elevator to right up to the top for a view, it is not advisable: the elevator deposits you, somewhat embarassingly, in the middle of someone's office. Seen head-on, the cake-slice shape of the Flatiron is one of the strangest sights in New York: on the one hand it looks two-dimensional, like a pop-up palazzo, and on the other oddly adrift, as though it has cut its moorings and is coolly floating up Broadway. People noticed its oddness straight away and, though properly titled the Fuller Building, it was instantly nicknamed the Flatiron.

Indeed, it seized the city's imagination: Edward Steichen and Alfred Stieglitz photographed it obsessively—in snow, rain and fog—comparing it to a 'monster steam-liner' advancing on the onlooker. Ford Madox Ford and H. G. Wells described the way its prow ploughed up traffic on Broadway and 5th Avenue. It was especially fascinating, however, for the peeping-toms who flocked to what was reputedly the windiest corner in the city for a flash of calf, stocking and ankle. Policemen would shoo them away—hence the origin of the expression 'twenty-three skidoo' (scram)—and in 1905 someone even shot a racy docudrama—*The Flat-iron Building on a Windy Day*.

Today the voyeurs have departed, and no one will arrest you if you go and stare in at the Astra Trading Co.'s showroom in the Flatiron's prow. It is filled with a permanent Christmas display of dusty toy soldiers and cobwebby singing teddy bears. Madison Square has somehow become the center of the New York novelty toy industry, and all around the area you see similar wholesale and retail novelty shops.

> *From the Flatiron, walk over to the middle of* **Madison Square Park**, *a patch of grass which is of sentimental value to most New Yorkers because in the 1840s it was used as a prototype pitch for the newly invented game of baseball.*

The park was formally laid out in 1847. Soon, however, it was at the hub of fashionable New York, as a batch of expensive hotels and restaurants like the palatial Fifth Avenue Hotel

Flat iron building

155

and Delmonico's grew up around it. Round about were battalions of the 'chocolate-coated' brownstone mansions so loathed by Edith Wharton (who was born in one on 23rd Street, in 1862).

In the 1880s the arm and torch of the Statue of Liberty were a strange sight in the middle of the square, plonked there as part of the campaign to raise money for the statue's plinth. Inevitably, in 1891, this stretch of Broadway was the first to be illuminated, with an electric sign telling people to '*Buy homes on Long Island swept by ocean breezes*'.

> *From the middle of the square you get a good view of the two screwy skyscrapers on its east side: the Metropolitan Life Insurance Company Building, between 23rd and 25th Streets and the New York Life Insurance Building, between 25th and 26th Streets. If the great white tower of the* **Metropolitan Life**, *looks disconcertingly familiar, it is because it is a wildly outsized version of the Campanile in St Mark's Square in Venice.*

As the Flatiron had been, it was briefly the tallest building in the world when it shot up in 1909. The three-story clock, which plays snatches of Handel, is still the world's largest. At the very top is *The Light That Never Fails*, (the company slogan)—a glowing nipple which flashes ruby red on the quarter hour, and white on the hour.

> *Next to it, the* **New York Life Insurance Building** *is another colorful sight, topped by a glittering golden pyramid. A Cass Gilbert Gothic extravaganza of 1928, the scraper is impressive, though it pales in comparison with the same architecture's infinitely more elegant Woolworth Tower of 1913 (see pp. 220–1).*

It replaced Stanford White's Madison Square Garden, one of the most fanciful confections New York has ever seen. A Spanish Renaissance pleasure-palace used for boxing shows, concerts and horse-races, it was commissioned by the New York Horse Show in 1890 and served a number of purposes (including the staging of the Paterson Pageant in 1913). It had yellow and white walls covered with *fleurs-de-lys*, little turrets, a Moorish arcade cloistering the sidewalk, gondolas and a tower copied from the Giralda in Seville. On top was a revolving golden statue of Diana by Saint-Gaudens, which scandalized 1890s New York, even though it was too high up for a truly anatomical inspection.

Living under Diana in his own building was Stanford White, the most prominent member of McKim, Mead & White, the pet architects of New York's turn-of-the-century *beau monde*. A conspicuous man-about-town, White came to a suitably theatrical end when he was shot watching *Mamzelle Champagne* at the Garden. His assassin was the cuckolded husband of a former mistress, Evelyn Nesbit. With his red hair and short legs, White had seduced the chorus girl when she was 16 in his lavish pied-à-terre. Inside were mirrored walls, a sumptuous green velvet sofa, sketches of nudes in suggestive poses, and a red velvet swing trailing smilax, on which Nesbit reeled up to the ceiling to kick out the panels of a rotating paper parasol. Next door was a red velvet room with a mirrored four-poster bed illuminated by multicolored fairy lights. 'It's all over kittens, don't cry', White said when she came to, 'Now you belong to me'.

After the murder, White's assasin was committed to an asylum, a second Madison Square Garden was built on 9th Avenue, and Nesbit became a heroin addict, eventually dying in 1966 in a Panama brothel. Also in 1966 McKim, Mead & White's *pièce de resistance*, Penn Station, a tremendous edifice based on the Roman Baths of Caracalla, was demolished and replaced by New York's 'jukebox', the hated *third* Madison Square Garden, on 8th Avenue and 33rd Street.

Stanford White is currently having a kind of posthumous revenge as the third Madison Square is being demolished, replaced by a high-rise tower designed in the form of a fish, and moved to a new location two blocks east.

Now go back to the Flatiron, take the lefthand fork down Broadway on its eastern flank, and make your way south down **Ladies Mile***, a stretch of grand department stores catering to society ladies in the 19th century and then forgotten in the 20th.*

As you walk you see what amounts to a Grand Canal of semi-detached châteaux. The stores now sell toys and discount carpets, and though their façades are blackened with grime, the buildings themselves are remarkably intact. They look best as a group, but two king pins, facing each other on the south side of 20th Street, stand out. The one on the left is a McKim, Mead and White creation, of salmon-pink brick with swooping Romanesque arches and a magisterial corner entrance, and the one on the right is the old Lord & Taylors, a beautiful cast-iron palace with a Second Empire mansard roof built in 1869.

A block down, on the righthand side of 19th Street, is **The Last Wound-Up***, a deranging shop specializing in clockwork toys and musical boxes. Opposite, housing what claims to be the world's largest carpet store, is a vast cast-iron palace with a huge French-*

Empire mansard roof by Griffith Thomas, the man responsible for some of the grandest cast-iron fantasies in SoHo.

Step inside, pretend you are shopping for carpets, and walk in a westerly direction all the way through the building past row after row of spindly iron columns to the west entrance on 5th Avenue.

You surface on 5th Avenue more or less opposite the **Barnes & Noble Annex** on 18th Street and 105 5th Avenue, which has so many discounted books that customers trawl round with supermarket trolleys. Nearby is a clutch of men's boutiques, and, just off 5th Avenue at 20th Street, the **West Side Rifle and Pistol Range** (open weekdays till 11).

Stop off for a quick round if you wish, and then walk three blocks east on 20th Street, crossing Broadway and Park Avenue South. Near the latter you pass the site of the old Kenmore Hotel, where Dashiell Hammett once registered under the name of T. Victrola Blueberry, wrote The Maltese Falcon, *and did a moonlight flit without paying his bill. Keep on east for a few yards till you collide with* **Gramercy Park***.*

In 1831 what had been a marshy hinterland ('Gramercy' is pidgin Dutch for 'Crooked swamp') was transformed overnight into what is still one of the most fashionable addresses in New York. Bought and laid out by the real estate dealer, Samuel Ruggles, it was New York's only private square, and today residents rent keys for $175 while outsiders make do with staring through the railings. If you peer through, you can see a statue of the 19th-century actor, Edwin Booth, playing Hamlet, as well as droves of nannies and their chubby wards. 'They're the fat cats,' explains a cheerful man who stands outside feeding the squirrels walnuts through the railings, 'they're crummy with money'.

The park is surrounded by exquisite houses. Easily the most eccentric, at **36 Gramercy Park East***, is a 1920s Gothic apartment tower which is guarded by two life-size statues of silver-armored knights. Opposite, on the west side,* **3 and 4 Gramercy Park West** *is a lovely but more sober pair of Greek Revival brownstones sharing a filigree cast-iron verandah covered in wisteria. On the south side of the park is the most famous pair of all, the* **National Arts Club***, at number 16, and the* **Players Club***, at number 15.*

The former was revamped in Victorian dress as a residence for Samuel Tilden, the presidential candidate in 1876. During a time when New

York was panicked by riots, Tilden took the precaution of fitting the house with steel rolling gates and an escape tunnel linking it to 19th Street. The Players Club was also remodeled in Renaissance style by Stanford White, after Edwin Booth bought the building in 1888 and founded the club to boost the profession's prestige. Alumni have ranged from Irving Berlin and Laurence Olivier to Richard Gere and Frank Sinatra—any lurking fans are discreetly wafted away.

From the square, carry on walking east down 20th Street to the block between 3rd and 2nd Avenues. On the lefthand side of the street, at 235 East 20th Street, is the fascinating **Police Academy Museum**. *(Second floor, open weekdays 9–3, closed Wed, adm free).*

The displays range from the usual police memorabilia (police hats from all over the world) to enthralling explanations of counterfeiting, ballistics, and the Bertillon Phrenological Identification Method, used for 30 years to detect criminal tendencies by measuring the shape of the head before someone proved it was utterly spurious. Another interesting exhibit describes the history of New York's organized crime networks, and at the back are various odd display cases containing Al Capone's machine gun and a number of 'Recently acquired contraband weapons' including a dagger disguised as a fountain pen, an umbrella sword, and a silk-stocking blackjack.

Now retrace your steps to 3rd Avenue, turn left, and walk down to 17th Street. On the way you pass **Fat Tuesday's**, *an old German beer-garden with an unusual Baroque façade at 190 3rd Avenue. Today it houses a jazz club where a spritely Les Paul, who invented the electric guitar out of a piece of railway track and some telephone wires, plays every Monday night.*

Turn right onto 17th Street, and then walk west as far as Irving Place. A block north, on the righthand corner of 18th Street and Irving Place, you can stop off for a drink at **Pete's Tavern**, *which has been going for 127 years as the self-appointed oldest bar in the city.*

William Sydney Porter wrote his short story *The Gift of the Magi* in a booth at the back, under the pseudonym of O. Henry which, the barmen will inform you, was stolen from one of the screws at the Texas gaol where he was imprisoned for embezzlement. O. Henry lived in a large apartment nearby, downed a quart of whisky a day, and a couple of beers a night.

> *From Irving Place, walk a block west along 17th Street to* **Union Square**.

A drug-pusher's paradise only 10 years ago, Union Square is now a pleasant place teetering towards gentrification. Around it is an odd mix of glamorous restaurants, like the Union Square Café, and greasy spoons and cheapo shops, like the row of shops on 17th Street between Broadway and 5th Avenue which sell fake perfumes and imitation Gucci bags. If you come on a Wednesday, Friday or Saturday, the square itself seems strangely pastoral thanks to the **Farmers Market**, a mass of stalls selling homemade cider and pretzels, as well as fruit, vegetables, plants and flowers from New Jersey and Long Island. In the summer there are lunchtime jazz concerts next to the book and postcard stall, which is a permanent fixture on the west side.

From before World War I until the end of World War II, Union Square was a center for illegal demonstrations, marches and soap-box orators. In 1927, police mounted machine guns on the roofs when an enormous gathering protested about the execution of the anarchist labor agitators, Nicola Sacco and Bartolomeo Vanzetti. Accused of murder and robbery in 1920, they were executed seven years later in spite of circumstantial evidence, and the fact that another man had confessed to the crime. Three years later, in the midst of the Depression, a demonstration by 35,000 ended in another bloody confrontation with the police. As a result meetings were legalized, and in the next few years the Socialist party, the Communist party, several labor unions and the *Daily Worker* all established their headquarters nearby.

> *Union Square's two most interesting buildings are next door to each other, at* **31 and 33 Union Square**, *on the west side between 16th and 17th Streets.*

Both are extremely narrow. Now a restaurant, 31 Union Square is a slim Renaissance palazzo, opened as a bank in 1902, while number 33 is a crazed mixture of Venetian Gothic, Moorish and classical styles as interpreted in 1893. Although now a shabby outlet selling 'Athletic Apparel', it had a suitably exotic past when it served as the 'Factory', one of Andy Warhol's underground production studios, where he made *Blow Job*, *Flesh* and *Sleep*. In June 1968 a young woman called Valerie Solanis strolled into the studio and took a shot at Warhol, who had turned down her screenplay.

Walk down to the south end of the square and **14th Street***, which separates midtown from the villages below.*

Frantic, grubby, and a bit grotty, 14th Street is a fascinating consumer's paradise, crammed with shops and trestle tables selling discount hi-fi, radio-controlled toys and mouthwash. Nearly every shop seems to be in a permanent state of cataclysmic liquidation: '*This is it!,*' the signs wail, '*We Have Made Our Decision* and *Are Forced! To Sell* entire *Stock!!*'. As well as the discount stores there are scores of wig shops, tarot readers and Korean manicure parlors. This is the time to get your hand read or massaged, since 14th Street gives the best value for money in the city.

Up until a few years ago, it was packed with peep shows and porno parlors and this part of 14th Street was prime stamping ground for prostitues. In 1892 Emma Goldman, the Russian-born anarchist, took herself off here, and, inspired by *Crime and Punishment*, joined the other street-walkers, in an attempt to raise money to assassinate Henry Clay Frick. She finally pulled a 60-year-old gentleman, who took her off to a bar, bought her a drink, pressed $10 into her hand and then left, saying she didn't have the knack.

A block to the east, between Irving Place and 3rd Avenue, you can make a short detour to the **Palladium***, at 126 14th Street. This is a nightclub, converted by the Japanese architect, Arata Isozaki, in 1985, from an old movie palace. Next door, oozing clouds of cigarette smoke, is* **Julian's Billiard Academy***, a venerable establishment with a dishevelled look about it which stays open and busy into the small hours. It was used for shooting the remake of* The Hustler *starring Paul Newman.*

Head back to 14th Street, turn left onto Broadway, and walk south as far as East 12th Street. This section of Broadway has a mass of interesting antiques warehouses which usually auction off everything in lots on the weekend. On the left at 828 Broadway and 12th Street is the dusty **Strand Bookstore***, with its 8-mile labyrinth of secondhand books, supposedly the largest in the world.*

The best discounts are proof copies, review copies and hardbacks, often reduced by as much as 50 per cent. Those who venture in don't surface for several hours, though sometimes they do get picked up.

Push on, walking east along 12th Street to University Place. If you have time, make another little sports detour a block north to the **Bowlmor Lanes** *(open weekdays 10–1, Fridays and Saturdays 10–4) at 110 University Place.*

Bowling is great fun, mainly because it needs luck and hardly any skill. However, the people at the Bowlmor would have it the other way around, and they show off with all kinds of fancy spins and lobs. The Bowlmor is the largest of only three bowling alleys left in the city; it has 44 lanes, a bar, a grill and cocktail waitresses.

Now walk four blocks south down University Place, and then turn right onto **8th Street**.

In recent years, to the distress of Villagers, 8th Street has gone down-market, and on the weekends it overflows with loud-mouthed B&Ts. Still the street has a flourishing streetlife, the shops deal in an amazing range of cowboy boots and tacky novelty items, as well as T-shirts citing '10 reasons why a pint of beer is better than a woman'.

Continue walking for one block west along East 8th Street to 5th Avenue. On the corner is an enormous tan Art-Deco apartment tower, **1 Fifth Avenue**. *Looking rather like a sandcastle covered with Gothic gargoyles and pointy arches, it is a good landmark for orientating yourself in the Village.*

Inside, is a smart bar and restaurant, **1/5**, decked out with Art-Deco remnants from the wrecked Cunard Liner the SS *Caronia*. The people who drink here epitomize the chasm between the suburban crowd thronging 8th Street and the more sophisticated residents of the Village.

From this corner, turn left onto 5th Avenue. A little way down on your left is the entrance to **Washington Mews** *which once served as stables and servants' quarters for 'The Row' (see below).*

Typically, this once-grotty backwater has slowly evolved into one of the most exclusive streets in Manhattan, and now the visitor sees a chocolate-box scene of prettified mews houses, flower boxes, creepers and expensive German-made cars.

Have a nose round and then return to 5th Avenue and turn left. Twice a year on this part of 5th Avenue, the Village has an open-air art show, apparently devoted to New York's most atrocious painters. Hurry past to **Washington Square Arch**. *The gateway to Greenwich Village—actually a 77 ft high triumphal arch built on*

the same scale as those of antiquity—is directly ahead of you at the
foot of 5th Avenue, in Washington Square.

Fred Astaire danced on top of it, in an otherwise forgotten film, *The Belle of New York*; and in 1916 John Sloan and Marcel Duchamp, the Dada artist, climbed up the stairs inside the arch with four other revelers, and proclaimed the secession of the Village from the US, and an independent republic—'New Bohemia'. They lit a bonfire on top, ate a picnic, hung up Chinese lanterns and red balloons, and fired toy pistols, until they were disbanded by the militia.

Today, the door to the stairs inside the arch is kept decidedly locked, and according to one of the park keepers there is a collection of 28 footballs on top. Under the arch, you will notice various lost souls clutching copies of *New York Magazine*, for along with the New York Public Library on 42nd Street, this spot is renowned as the city's most popular rendezvous for blind dates.

The arch was designed by Stanford White in 1892 to commemorate the hundredth anniversay of Washington's inauguration. He based it on one in wood that he had designed for Washington Square in 1889. This was a bizarre construction—150 ft in height, illuminated by hundreds of tiny lightbulbs and crowned by a statue of Washington painted cerrulean blue. It was so much admired at the time, however, that Villagers commissioned a permanent monument.

On the other side of the arch lies **Washington Square Park**, *which is always full of people: blubbery joggers, outcasts, and, in the summer, cheery crowds and various performers who take over the space in the middle. The latter come in all shapes and sizes, including an octogenarian who juggles rabbits and spoons.*

Originally a swamp, the park first served as an execution ground, then as a paupers' graveyard for victims of the yellow fever epidemics that blitzed the city in the early 18th century. Some people say 22,000 bodies still lie under the park. In 1965 Con Edison workers unhappily stumbled on 25, wrapped in yellowed shrouds.

During the worst epidemic, in 1822, the streets round City Hall were barricaded, and the business community upped sticks and fled with their offices, banks and grog shops to the fields along the Hudson. They returned six months later, but the upheaval spurred on the development of fashionable Greenwich Village, which duly sprouted a mass of grand brownstones and row-houses between 1820 and 1850.

163

At one time, Washington Square was surrounded by these. Now only the north side of the square has its original Greek Revival row-houses. The red-brick terrace to the east of 5th Avenue, **1–13 Washington Square North**, comprises the 'very solid and honorable dwellings' Henry James described in *Washington Square*, though number 18, the house belonging to his grandmother on which he based the novel, has long since been demolished.

Today, terraces are a rarity in New York and the houses of 'The Row' seem exceptionally handsome, with their statuesque porticos, elongated sash windows, lofty stoops and elaborate wrought-iron balustrades and railings. The only intruder is number 3, revamped in Queen Anne style as an artist's studio in 1884, and home to Edward Hopper and John Dos Passos who wrote *Manhattan Transfer* here in the 1920s.

> *Have a brief look round, and then make your way to the south side of the square, which has an extraordinary unattributed sculpture of elephant's feet carved out of a dead elm:* Tribute to Hannibal. *In the middle of Washington Square South, on the southwest corner of Thompson Street, is Stanford White's other great contribution to the square of 1892, the **Judson Memorial Church**.*

White was ambidextrous as far as styles went, and this concoction is basically Romanesque Revival, with a mass of Classical and Gothic details. Inside it is cool and quiet, and there are some superb pink-and-blue stained-glass windows by John La Farge, (and also some lavatories, though they are not of artistic interest). The tower of the church resembles the one in Hitchcock's *Vertigo*, and contains dormitories for New York University—NYU.

The university has had an unenviable reputation as a rapacious land-grabber ever since the 1960s, when Philip Johnson and Richard Foster were employed to work on a series of buildings to unify the campus. The two architects came up with the trio of red-sandstone monoliths you see to the left of the Judson Church, between LaGuardia Place and Mercer Street. Dubbed the 'Redskins', they so horrified preservationists that the plan to re-face the east side of the square in red sandstone was eventually scrapped.

> *Walk over to the southwest corner of the square, and turn left onto Macdougal Street. John Barrymore, the brother of Ethel and Lionel, who once slept through a San Francisco earthquake in a drunken*

daze, had an aerial bolt-hole just off this corner in the form of a
palatial roof garden of wisteria, cherry trees and grapevines.
As you walk down Macdougal Street you probably won't notice
the plain brick building at number 133 on the righthand side.

This is the **Provincetown Playhouse**, home to the experimental theater group which injected a shot of new life into American theater after World War I. In 1916 the group took up Eugene O'Neill, produced his first play, and moved to New York from Cape Cod. O'Neill lived nearby in a room he called the 'garbage flat' and got embroiled in an affair with Louise Bryant, John Reed's wife, which is supposed to have formed the basis for his stream-of-consciousness play *Strange Interlude*.

At this point, a welcome place to stop for cakes and coffee is the **Caffè**
Reggio, *at 119 Macdougal Street, a little way further down*
between West 3rd Street and Minetta Lane.

The interior resembles the set from a Jacobean revenge tragedy: in one corner is an Egyptian inglenook and some quotations from the *Divine Comedy*; in another, a portrait of Cesare Borgia and in another, a silver *macchina* trickling inky coffee and puffing little jets of steam.

Next door is **Mamoun's Felafel**, which dispenses delicious take-away pitta bread sandwiches stuffed with *felafel* (deep-fried spice balls) and *tahini*. Further down, facing each other on the intersection of Macdougal Street and Bleecker, you can sit down in the **Café Borgia**, where Ginsberg and Kerouac gave poetry readings during the sixties.

A few steps down from the Reggio is **Minetta Lane**, *pidgin Dutch*
for the brook which still dribbles under the pavement, and originally
flowed west from Madison Square through the Village to the Hudson
River. On the corner, at 113 Macdougal Street, is the **Minetta**
Tavern.

A flash place these days, the bar is plastered with memorabilia recalling its most famous patron, Joe Gould. A poet and self-professed Bohemian, Gould spent years prowling the Village and cadging drinks off tourists while compiling his opus magnus, the 11-million word *Oral History of Our Time*. He befriended Malcolm Cowley, William Carlos Williams, Hemingway and e. e. cummings, who wrote a poem about him and was one of the few people to have read snatches from the *Oral History*. Gould kept it in two dirty suitcases, but when he died in an asylum in 1957 these had mysteriously vanished.

Now turn right onto Minetta Lane and then immediately left onto **Minetta Street**, *a tiny road which does a dog-leg bend round to 6th Avenue.*

Originally these two streets comprised the 'Minettes', slums chronicled in a number of Stephen Crane's short stories. In the 1920s, both streets were lined with speakeasies, one of which housed a printing press used, rather unsubversively, to launch the first issue of *Reader's Digest* in 1922.

At its south end, Minetta Street runs into 6th Avenue, which scythed its way through an old Italian neighborhood in the 1920s creating an intersection known as **Father Demo Square**. Directly opposite you is the **Church of Our Lady of Pompei**, whose services, held in Italian, are so raucous that you can hear them from the other side of the street. A Greek temple on the outside, the church is a suitably jazzy blend of blues, pinks and golds inside.

Walk across Father Demo Square towards the church, and turn right onto Bleecker Street. Between 6th Avenue and 7th Avenue, this section of **Bleecker Street** *has a batch of hopelessly tempting Italian butchers, bakeries, pasticcerias and cafés.*

Zito's, at 259 Bleecker, has hot, crunchy bread which Sinatra gets sent to his hotel whenever he visits the city, and it is well worth investing in some now (in general, New York has disgusting bread). You can sit down to bowls of homemade soup at the **Bleecker Luncheonette**, on the corner of Bleecker Street and Carmine Street, go for a coffee at **Rocco's Pastry Shop**, at number 243, and then pick up an ice from a French intruder, the **Lafayette Bakery**, at number 298.

At 7th Avenue, turn left, walk south down the Avenue for three blocks and turn right onto **St Luke's Place**.

Behind a row of ginkgo trees is the Village's most beautiful terrace of Italianate row-houses. Built for affluent merchants in the 1850s, each has an immensely steep stoop, a massive portico and extremely elegant French windows.

At number 6 are two 'Lamps of Honor', posted outside the house when James J. Walker, songwriter and dandy who became mayor in 1926, moved in. The author of the big hits 'There's Music in the Rustle of a Skirt' and 'Will you Love me in December as you do in May?', Jimmy Walker's spirited *joie de vivre* was peculiarly suited to New York in the twenties. The wisecracking Irishman certainly cut a dash through the

166

city, tricked out in pearly spats, dainty cravats and svelte suits which he designed himself and changed as often as five times a day. He won the hearts of New Yorkers after he legalized boxing and Sunday baseball, and remained popular even when a series of Tammany scandals over graft and bribery crumpled his administration. He died fourteen years after his resignation and was given a requiem mass with all the trimmings at St Patrick's Cathedral.

At the end of St Luke's Place is **Hudson Street**, *which once ran alongside the riverbank, but is now three blocks west of the Hudson.*

It is well worth making a short diversion to the Hudson, via either Morton or Barrow Streets. In 1938, when New York Harbor was the busiest in the world, you could hardly see the river for boats, docks, and shipping sheds. Since containerization and the death of the harbor, the riverside is now an outlandish terrain. Body beautifuls preen along the abandoned piers, used as a cruising ground by gays and sunbathers, while West Street has a clutch of hard-core leather clubs and bars with names like 'Spike' and 'Ramrod'.

From Hudson Street, walk north two blocks to the corner of Barrow Street. On the left, take a look round the wild and jungly **St Luke's Church Garden**, *jam-packed on Sundays with New Yorkers reading the papers. Then walk a few steps north along Hudson Street to* **St Luke's-in-the-Fields**, *a country church which did stand in the middle of fields when it was built in 1822. It is a good-looking, modest church with a plain square tower and louvred windows.*

Walk back to Barrow Street, past the Hudson Diner, which does wonderful chilli hot dogs, and turn left. The next few streets are almost too quaint to be true. Walk a block east along Barrow Street and turn right onto Commerce Street. On the corner, 19 and 20 Commerce Street is a curious twosome nicknamed the **Twin Houses**, *and supposedly built by a sea captain for his difficult daughters.*

A few steps down, on the bend of Commerce Street, is an old box factory housing the **Cherry Lane Theater**.

The experimental theater was founded in 1924 by Edna St Vincent Millay, the charismatic poet and playwright who burnt her candle so successfully in the twenties and thirties. Born in Maine, she was named after St Vincent's Hospital in the Village when its doctors saved the life of her uncle. (In a drunken stupor, he had fallen asleep in the hold of a ship leaving New Orleans and was discovered nine days later in New York.) The Cherry Lane eventually became an Off-Broadway theater, premiering plays by Beckett, Albee and Ionesco. It also landed Barbra Streisand her first job, as an usherette.

Continue walking along Commerce Street to the intersection with Bedford Street.

On the corner is the **Isaacs-Hendricks Residence**, a clapboard house which claims to be the oldest house in the Village. Next door, is the Village's narrowest house, **75¹/₂ Bedford Street**, built in a 9¹/₂ ft wide alley in 1873. John Barrymore lived here first, then Edna St Vincent Millay, and finally Cary Grant.

From here, walk north along Bedford Street, only 24 ft wide in some parts and revered as the most beautiful street in the Village, to the next corner, where Barrow Street crosses Bedford Street.

On the righthand side, you can stop off for a pint at **Chumleys**, an old speakeasy which has an unsignposted entrance at 86 Barrow Street, and an escape route round the side to a courtyard on Bedford Street. Filled with tourists and the members of the US Chess Federation, the inside walls are covered with the book-jackets of the various Village writers who have been regulars over the years.

Next, walk north a block on Bedford Street, to the intersection with Grove Street. Down to your left, between 10 and 12 Grove Street, are the locked gates of **Grove Court***.*

All you can make out is a thick curtain of ivy and railings. Part the curtain of ivy and you will see another genteel mews, originally a group of rough and ready workingmen's houses built in the 1850s, when it was known as 'Pig's Alley'. Either side of the entrance is a row of pretty Greek Revival houses, built between 1827 and 1834 by carpenters and masons who worked from English builders' copybooks without the aid of architects.

Turn left back onto Bedford Street, and walk one block further north past **102 Bedford Street***, a bizarre, vaguely Tudor building with half-timbering and futuristic scooped-out windows.*

An exact replica of a house in Nuremberg, the building contains bricks from White's Madison Square Garden, a 2nd Avenue slum flat, and a West End apartment house, and is nicknamed the 'Twin Peaks' or the 'Hansel and Gretel Building'. In 1925 it was renovated for Otto Kahn, the banker, by Clifford Daily, a local architect who planned to turn the house over to local artists and writers. At the opening ceremony an actress and a princess were perched, swigging champagne, on the two peaks. Daily was highly pleased with his efforts, calling the house an oasis of taste growing in a desert of mediocrity.

Continue walking along Bedford Street and turn right onto Christopher Street. Walk north, crossing Bleecker Street, which at this point has a mass of very expensive antique shops, culminating incongruously in **Bird Jungle** *(at 401 Bleecker and West 11th Streets), where gangs of toucans, mynah birds and green parrots roam free.*

Walk another block along Christopher Street and cross 7th Avenue South.

Bursting with leather shops, back-room bars, and an interesting 'erotic' bakery, Christopher Street is the main artery of gay Greenwich Village. At night it is swamped by a crowd of wide-eyed tourists as the residents swagger down the street in leather jackets and caps, and tight jeans.

Christopher Street became a citadel for Manhattan's gay caucus after the Stonewall Riot of 1969, when police blitzed the Stonewall Inn, a gay bar on the Street, and tried to evict 200 patrons, provoking a riot which lasted for two days. The upshot was the formation of New York's first Gay Lib movement, and every June the riot is commemmorated in a Gay Pride march through the Village to Christopher Street.

Past 7th Avenue, on the left at 59 Christopher Street, are steps leading down to the sleazy gloom of the **Lion's Head**, *and its clientele of sports writers and journalists from the tabloid press.*

In the 1970s, Norman Mailer and his running mate Jimmy Breslin used the bar as a makeshift campaign headquarters while he ran for Mayor of New York. Mailer launched quite a serious campaign for New York City to secede and become the 51st State.

Have a beer, and then continue walking up Christopher Street to the next block where the road meets an island filled by the **Northern Dispensary**, *another building squashed into a triangle by the eccentricities of New York's grid.*

One of the city's first free hospitals, it was built in 1831 when it stood in the northern outskirts of the city. Edgar Allen Poe was treated for a cold here in 1837, and the clinic remained open until 1988 when it was fined for refusing to treat two men infected with the AIDS virus and finally ran out of funds. It has now been taken on by the Roman Catholic Archdiocese, who have converted it into a nursing home for AIDS patients.

The building is infamous for having two sides on one street—Waverly Place, and one side on two streets—Christopher Street and Grove Street. Take the righthand fork and walk up Waverly Place to **Gay Street**, *and then turn left.*

Gay Street was gay before the rest of the Village. Originally a well-to-do residential street, in the 1920s it was invaded by a boisterous Prohibition nightclub—the Pirate's Den. The 46-year-old Jimmy Walker regularly used to descend on the street to visit his 23-year-old mistress, a showgirl called Betty Compton, and in the 1930s, Ruth McKenney and her sister lived in Bohemian style in a basement flat at number 14, where she wrote *My Sister Eileen*.

All pink-painted jalousies and baskets of geraniums, the street is respectable again. Only 200 ft long, it is also the third shortest in the city.

Walk round the crook of Gay Street and turn right, back onto Christopher Street.

On the corner, at 15 Christopher Street, is the first gay bookshop in the world, the **Oscar Wilde Memorial Bookshop**. A few doors away, at 10 Christopher Street, an Eerie-Sound Chime opens the door to a superb novelty shop called **Abracadabra** which sells a comprehensive selection of squirting flowers, rubber roaches, custard-pie foam and Doggy Doo.

Make your way to the foot of Christopher Street, which ends in the Village Square where Greenwich Avenue, 6th Avenue and West 8th Street all collide. Cross the triangle to the east side of the junction. A block further up on 9th Street and 6th Avenue, is **Balducci's**, *a heavenly delicatessen where scavengers cruise round the free samples and consume entire meals without buying anything.*

Leave Balducci's and walk a block north to the **Jefferson Market Courthouse**, *an extraordinary medieval castle standing on the lefthand side of 6th Avenue, opposite 10th Street.*

Voted the nation's fifth most beautiful building in the 1880s, it is the kind of daring and spirited version of Victorian Gothic you rarely find in England, dolled up with all sorts of turrets, pinnacles, gargoyles and fancy iron- and brick-work. It was designed in 1877 by Frederick Withers and Calvert Vaux, Olmsted's partner in Central Park. Striped red and white like streaky bacon, the tower originally served as a fire lookout, and stood in a complex containing the city gaol and the sheds of a large food market. In 1967 the building was restored as a library.

Turn left onto West 10th Street and then sharp right to **Patchin Place**, *a hidden mews which faces the Jefferson Courthouse between 6th and Greenwich Avenues.*

Originally built in 1848 for Basque waiters working in the village, the mews gradually evolved into a writers' warren. Theodore Dreiser, John Reed and John Dos Passos all moved in at various times, and for 40 years e. e. cummings lived in number 4 opposite Djuna Barnes, the reclusive author of *Nightwood*. Occasionally, the story goes, cummings stuck his head out of his study window and shouted, 'Are ya still alive, Djuna?'.

The walk finishes here, unless you want to carry on to the **Gansevoort Meat Market**, *up on 14th and Gansevoort Streets.*

Deserted by day, the strip of cobbled streets, greasy sidewalks and rusting warehouses comes to life at night as an eerie but fascinating place. Refrigerated lorries exhale blasts of freezing air while the meat men swing carcasses, some still furred, onto a conveyor belt of hooks. Taxis glide in and out, unloading their own batches to the clubs and tough gay bars in the area, and in the early hours of the morning the meatmen take themselves off to the Homestead or Howley's where they consume mountains of steak sandwiches.

The nearest subways for going home are the **A** *and* **C** *at West 4th Street and 6th Avenue, or the* **4, 5** *and* **6** *and the* **N** *and* **R** *at Union Square and 4th Avenue. Anyone feeling adventurous, however, could board the PATH train from 9th Street and 6th Avenue to* **Hoboken** *in New Jersey.*

It costs a dollar and takes 13 minutes to get to Hoboken. Though it gets teased (affectionately) as Ho-Ho-Hoboken, the old shipbuilding city is currently enjoying a modest Renaissance as independent spirits move in to convert its factories and townhouses. Most New Yorkers know it as the birthplace of Frank Sinatra, and as the place where Elia Kazan, protected from the toughs by a fleet of bodyguards, shot *On the Waterfront* using real dockworkers as well as actors.

From the beautiful old Erie Lackawanna ferry terminal, (a verdigris palace of 1907 that looks so grand it gets hired out for balls), there is a magnificent view of the west side of Manhattan laid out in front of you like a fantastical pincushion; a view which Cartier-Bresson snapped, encrusted in icicles, when he visited the city in 1946.

Walk V
Vertical City

Prometheus

Empire State Building—Garment District—Times Square—Sin Street—New York Public Library—5th Avenue—Diamond Row—Rockefeller Center—Radio City—MoMA

Midtown is quintessential, clichéd New York: exhilaration, bustle, vertigo, glamor, concentrated exuberence—and noise, confusion, and anxiety; objects plummeting from heights, lunatic bicycle messengers, and demented traffic; the most expensive restaurants and real estate, the worst theaters and the best skyscrapers in the world.

The walk starts at the city's pre-eminent scraper, the Empire State, takes in the sleaze of Times Square, the breathtaking elegance of Rockefeller Center, and finishes up in that encapsulation of high culture and chic, the Museum of Modern Art (or MoMA, as it is endearingly known). It is a good walk for an afternoon: start with lunch in the most boisterous area of all, the Garment District, move on to tea in the Royalton Hotel, then to a cocktail at the Rainbow Room and finally, to an evening at MoMA which is free and open late until 9pm on Thursdays, the fashionable day to go.

Start: by subway, take the **N** or **R** train to 34th Street and 6th Avenue, or the **4** to 33rd Street and Park Avenue. By bus, take the **M3** or **M2** to 34th

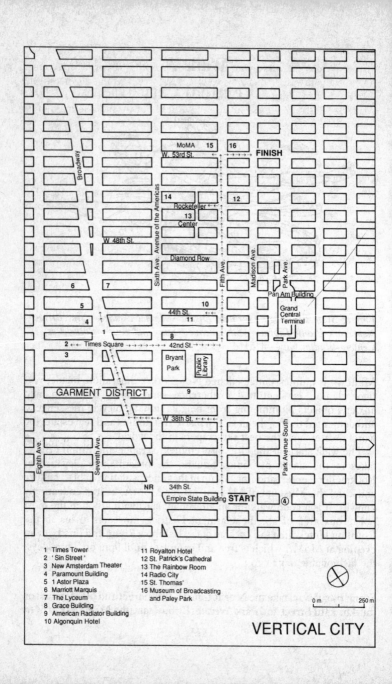

MoMA 15   16   **FINISH**
W. 53rd St.

14
Rockefeller
13
Center

Diamond Row

6   7

5   10
                44th St.
4   11
1
2 ← Times Square →→→→→→ 42nd St. →→→→→→
3   8

Broadway

Avenue of the Americas

Sixth Ave.

W 48th St.

Fifth Ave.

Madison Ave.

Park Ave.

Pan Am Building

Grand
Central
Terminal

12

Bryant

Park

Public
Library

GARMENT DISTRICT   9

←←←←←← W. 38th St. ←←←←←←

Eighth Ave.

Seventh Ave.

Park Avenue South

NR   34th St.

Empire State Building **START**   ④

1 Times Tower
2 ' Sin Street '
3 New Amsterdam Theater
4 Paramount Building
5 1 Astor Plaza
6 Marriott Marquis
7 The Lyceum
8 Grace Building
9 American Radiator Building
10 Algonquin Hotel

11 Royalton Hotel
12 St. Patrick's Cathedral
13 The Rainbow Room
14 Radio City
15 St. Thomas'
16 Museum of Broadcasting
   and Paley Park

0 m   250 m

VERTICAL CITY

Street and Park Avenue South, or the **M5** to 34th Street and 5th Avenue. From the subway or bus stop walk east or west to the entrance to the Empire State on 5th Avenue between 33rd and 34th Streets.

Walking Time: 2 hours, but allow another hour for the fascinating tour round Radio City Music Hall, and then as much time as you need for MoMA.

LUNCH/CAFÉS

Cabana Carioca, 123 West 45th St., near Broadway. Fried eggs on top of a steak or a pork chop, and *feijoada* or black bean stew (the Brazilian national dish). One of the jolliest restaurants in New York, no doubt partly due to the *caipirinha*, the Cabana's knock-you-sideways-and-senseless lime juice and rum cocktail.

Sapporo, 152 West 49th St., near 7th Ave. Noodle and squid soup is a favorite. You can sit at the counter and watch short-order chefs preparing *sushi*, *teriyaki* and *tempura* at breakneck speed.

Southern Funk Cafe, 330 West 42nd St., between 8th and 9th Aves. Tortillas, *quesadillas*, gumbo and chilli served in the unlikely surroundings of the stupendous McGraw-Hill Building, Raymond Hood's blue-green palazzo that turns green-blue at the top. Although the food really is funky, there is lox omelette and bread pudding for anyone who feels daunted.

Algonquin Rose Room, 59 West 44th St., between 5th and 6th Aves. Dignified continental breakfasts.

Café Madeleine, 403 West 43rd St., near 9th Ave. There is a lovely garden patio with delicious, simple, and quite pricey Provençal food, like *moules marinière*.

Old-fashioned Mr Jennings, 12 West 55th St., between 5th and 6th Aves. Old-fashioned ice-cream parlor with banana splits and Mr Jennings.

Manganaro's Hero Boy Restaurant, 492 9th Avenue, near 38th St. If you come here with 40 friends you can order their 6 ft long hero, otherwise have a heavenly one-person-sized hero filled with your own selection of salami, parma ham, mozzarella, olives and salad.

Verve Naturelle, 157 West 57th St., between 6th and 7th Aves. Healthy Californian salads and pastas.

Audrone's, 342 West 46th St., between 8th and 9th Aves. Gourmet French cooking on the pricey side.

Rainbow Room, 30 Rockefeller Plaza, on the 65th floor of the RCA Building, between 49th and 50th Sts. You can just have a cocktail or order a meal from the bar for $25. If you want to eat in the dining room you will have to make a reservation (632 5000) and contend with incredibly elaborate Americo-French food.

> 'What a funny place New York was—all sticking
> up and full of windows'.
> —H. G. Wells, *The Shape of Things to Come.*

When most people think of New York, they imagine the skyscrapers of Midtown Manhattan. These are the archetypal symbols of the city—of America even—although just over a century ago they barely existed. The word 'skyscraper' referred to the little triangular sails on top of the rigging on 18th-century schooners, and in slang to that foremost totem of potency, the honorable John Thomas, esquire.

Another John, a certain John J. Flinn, first referred to buildings as 'sky-scrapers' in a little book about Chicago published in 1890. When the first 12-story building went up on Broadway in 1889, the architect lived on the 11th floor to prove it was safe. Less than 30 years later, however, New York had sprouted a forest of skyscrapers. They were touted as miniature cities: 'One can live in them, indefinitely, without going out for food, clothing or lodging', wrote one publicist. By 1930 H. G. Wells was predicting the death of the skyscraper: the New York of the 21st century, he divined, would go underground; people would live in excavated catacombs, and by 2055 high-rises would be cobwebby dinosaurs, like flying buttresses and Stonehenge.

But as the 20th century gives up the ghost, skyscrapers remain omni-present. There are two distinct skyscraper clumps in the city: in the Financial District and in Midtown, sometimes called the Himalayas and the Alps. Wall Street's scrapers are monolithic, staid monuments to corporate wealth; Midtown's are irresistible: flighty and mad, topped with fantastical hats, and flaunting a Promethean defiance of gravity, nature and sensible economics. Most were built by an army of spectacu-larly reckless skywalkers, the Caughnawaga Indians, who came to New York from a reservation near Montreal in the heady building boom of the twenties and currently make up 40 per cent of the construction work-force in New York. Today, skyscrapers still shoot up and down faster than anyone can keep track, and even though many companies no longer need to be based physically in New York, the extraordinary, ludicrous pincushion keeps growing.

The walk starts with the icon of skyscrapers, (and also the HQ of the US Soccer Federation), the **Empire State Building**. *To get to the*

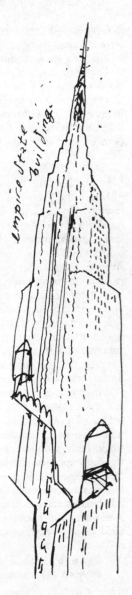

top you need a ticket from the office at the bottom. If it seems very crowded, you may prefer to come back in the evening, since the decks are open from 9.30 am until midnight.

The best time to come, in fact, is at night; during one of New York's electric storms which illuminate the city in a most dramatic fashion, with jagged forks of lightning. If the conditions are right, the *Empire State Fact Sheet* informs us, 'Static electricity build-up is so mammoth', that when you stick your fingers through the observatory fence, 'St Elmo's fire will stream from your fingertips' and blue electric sparks will fly from the quivering lips of kissing couples. In the daytime things are still lively; on the 86th story observation platform is the world's highest colony of ants, which must have evolved specially adhesive footpads to withstand the ferocious winds that occasionally thrash the skyscraper so it sways an inch and a half to one side.

After the 86th deck, visit the second observatory on the 102nd floor. This is really part of the building's 'mooring mast', a 150 ft glass and metal spire which was added at the last minute, supposedly so dirigibles could dock on the roof, but mostly to make it taller and discourage rivals.

Although one zeppelin did manage to cling on for 3 minutes, the mast was incredibly dangerous and the idea was abandoned in 1931 after a blimp keeled over, drenching pedestrians below with water from its ballast, and nearly sweeping away the celebrities who had come to watch. In 1983 a similar disaster was narrowly avoided when an 84 ft tall,

177

2000 lb, half-inflated rubber King Kong, commemorating his 50th birthday, threatened to take off in a freak gust of wind. The brute started leaking, but was dismantled just before it whizzed off like a burst balloon.

The tower has a high-tech lighting system and is lit in various color combinations according to the occasion: blue and white if the Yankees win the World Series; red and white for St Valentine's. On foggy nights in the spring and autumn the lights are turned off to prevent mesmerized migrating birds from colliding with the building—the fate of a B-25 bomber when it crashed into the 79th floor, causing $1 million worth of damage, in 1945.

Less than 200 years ago the site was a farmyard. In 1827 it was bought for about $20,000, by John Jacob Astor, and from then on it has been pivotal in the history of 5th Avenue. In 1857, the Astor sons built two mansions on the farm—these became the hub of 'Millionaire's Row', at a time when the élite 'Four Hundred' who constituted Society were limited to the number of coat-tails Mrs Astor could squeeze into her ballroom. A family feud in 1893 altered the whole character of the Avenue. To spite his overbearing aunt, William Waldorf Astor demolished his mansion, built the Waldorf Hotel, and upped sticks for Europe. Mrs Astor replied in kind. She built the Astoria next door, moved uptown, and Society followed at her heels.

Joined together, with the proviso that connecting corridors could be sealed off from each other if necessary, the Waldorf-Astoria reigned supreme until the 1920s building boom. Offices and department stores were disagreeable companions, and in 1929 the hotel moved uptown and the site was sold for a new office building—the Empire State.

A month later, the Stock Market crashed. The developer went ahead, and the architects, Shreve, Lamb & Harmon, miraculously completed the building in a year and 45 days. Spectators gathered on the sidewalk to watch the steel framework rise at the astonishing rate of $4\frac{1}{2}$ stories a week. Though building costs were cut by half, thanks to the Depression, the skyscraper was dubbed the 'Empty State Building', and it was said that money collected from tourists was all that the owners had for paying taxes on the construction. Today, it is practically fully occupied. About 500 tenants make menswear, and there is a gentleman in the basement Xerox shop who has been working in the Empire State since it opened in 1931: 'Boy oh boy', he says, wiping away a sentimental tear.

Leave the Empire State Building by the 5th Avenue entrance, and walk up 5th Avenue. On the lefthand side at 366 5th Avenue, between 34th and 35th Streets, is the **Genroku**, *an extraordinary sushi restaurant, serving* 'Japanese Express on Conveyor'.

Inside, wobbling sushi, sashimi and teriyaki circle the restaurant on a conveyor belt, and up above is a complicated system of chrome pipes and taps from which patrons help themselves to tea which is literally piping hot.

Walk three blocks more up 5th Avenue. Turn left at 38th Street and walk west towards Broadway. This is the northerly fringe of the **Garment District** *which stretches roughly between 5th and 9th Avenues, and 25th and 41st Streets, and all the shops here specialize in trimmings and ribbons. The sweatshops, workshops and show-rooms of the Lower East Side migrated to this area during World War I: the workers were mostly Jewish or Italian immigrants, although recently the labor force has been revitalized by Hispanic, black and Asian immigrants.*

On the right, between 5th and 6th Avenues, at 49–53 West 38th Street, is a treasure trove called **Sheru Enterprises**.

Inside, a civil war rages between *Max's Dept* and *Yetta's Dept*. They both sell the same things: thousands of shiny beads, costume gems, ribbons and trimmings, arranged in boxes in chaotic heaps and mounds.

Make your way down 38th Street towards **Broadway**. *Max and Yetta's combative style imparts itself to whole streets. In the mornings the traffic is always gridlocked: moving clothes-racks trundle down streets in between the cars, and pedestrians on the sidewalk are bombarded with circulars advertising cut-price treatment for corns, embarrassing warts and broken nails. Between 6th Avenue and Broadway, people wear show-biz make-up and the kind of se-quinned designer dresses, court shoes and shoulder pads sold in the shops at wholesale prices.*

The district is full of frenetic coffee shops and take-aways. For hearty Italian food, go down 38th Street as far as 7th Avenue to **Veronica's**, on the lefthand side at 240 West 38th.

From 38th Street head north up Broadway (or 7th Avenue if you have gone to Veronica's), to **Times Square**, *a short walk away of four blocks, on 42nd Street between Broadway and 7th Avenue. The*

New York equivalent of London's Leicester Square (plus more sex and violence), Times Square is roughly the area between 42nd and 48th Streets where Broadway and 7th Avenue cross over each other and make an X. This is a dangerous area at night, and not one you want to wander around too aimlessly.

In the stories of Damon Runyon, this is the 'Dream Street' where you see a motley bunch of 'burlesque dolls, and hoofers, and guys who write songs, and saxophone players, and newsboys... and midgets, and blondes with Pomeranian pooches...' Today's crowds are just as captivating. They pour into the cinemas, ostensibly to watch the film, but really to shout wisecracks at each other; or they hang around in Times Square's underground city, the **subway station**. This Piranesian labyrinth is actually an excellent busking venue. The Grand Central Shuttle has jazz, while the 7 train to Queens is more unorthodox, featuring gangs of Peruvian xylophonists, and a one-armed one-man band with a ghetto blaster.*

Above ground, Times Square is a haven for card-sharks, con-artists and Murphy men, whose real profits come from the teams of pick-pockets they have working for them while you are destracted by their games and hustling. A recent scam is 'swashbuckling': passers-by have their belts slashed and their wallets whipped away, and are left stranded, their trousers crumpled round their toes. It takes two to make a sucker, however, and if you keep your wits about you, and don't get involved in the three-card monte rugby scrums, you should be all right (see 'Crime' pp. 21–23).

Make your way to the island where Broadway, 7th Avenue, and 42nd Street collide. In the middle is **Times Tower**, *a triangular skyscraper which you can't miss because of its Motogram, a 360ft electrified band which circles the whole building relaying the news in digital letters.*

This is more or less the heart of Times Square: the spot where Runyon's ashes were secretly decanted from an aeroplane according to instructions in his will (in which he also expressed the hope that he might wake up 'dead' at a poker game with his departed pals).

---

* During rainstorms, the subway smells of elephants. It was only when the Transit Authority sent in the sensitive nose of Pat Kelly (who was usually employed sniffing out gas and water leaks) that they discovered why. A water mains burst, 'Smelly Kelly' deduced, had leaked into the basement of a former circus which contained an accumulation of half a century's elephant dung.

Times Tower is better known for its **ball**, an illuminated apple which perplexingly ushers in the New Year by descending from the top on the stroke of midnight, a gimmick dating from 1908 when a sphere was used instead of an apple. The first revellers, however, gathered in 1904, when the *New York Times* moved into Times Tower with fanfares and fireworks, and 'Longacre Square' became 'Times Square'. In the 1930s the newspaper moved a few hundred yards to 229 West 43rd, where 'All the News that's Fit to Print' is still published from a location seething with news of the most unfit sort.

Nowadays Times Tower is associated with neon extravaganzas rather than newspapers. 'The Great White Way' was coined by an ad man called O. J. Gude in 1901, and actually referred to the stretch of Broadway *below* 34th Street which was illuminated in 1880 and got its first electricity-driven advertisement (promoting Long Island beaches) in 1891. Foreigners were dumbstruck by the artificial daylight 'more blinding that a tropical day at its zenith'. In the heyday of neon you could see a man advertising Camels who puffed real smoke rings into the air, a penguin smoking Kools, a girl who endlessly blew her nose on Kleenex, and soap bubbles billowing out of a packet of Lux flakes.

Today's less vivacious signs are upstaged by an evangelist ranting Eternal Damnation down a microphone at the base of the Motogram. 'You've been brainwashed with filth and contamination, by 5th Avenue and David Letterman' he informs the pigeons, huddled a dozen abreast on the lamp posts. If you can negotiate your way past, you might like to look in at Elvis Presley's guitar pick in the **Songwriter's Hall of Fame and Museum** (open Mon–Sat 11–3; free), on the 8th floor. In 1966 Times Tower was sheathed in a façade of bathroom marble, and now developers want to tear it down.

From Times Tower, turn left and walk one block west along 42nd Street to 8th Avenue, past **'Sin Street'**, *Midtown's famed cesspit of sleaze.*

Sin Street's specialty is porn. Decked out in all the colors of the neon rainbow, it must be one of the gaudiest streets in the world. Crammed into one block are 15 cinemas, including the Harem House of Hores [sic], astrologers, 25c peep shows at the Triple XXX Video and shifty men offering to test your blood pressure. The less hard-core shops sell fake IDs and a series of books called *How To Get Even*, explaining how to pick locks and make a bomb out of urine.

Although this is not a street to linger on, do look out for the shells of some of Broadway's most glamorous theaters, whose crumbling baroque façades somehow suit the general seediness.

The best three are the **Lyric** on the north side at 213 West 42nd Avenue, with angels hovering over a rococo entrance, the **Victory**, next door at 207, with cupids and lyres, and, opposite on the south side, **New Amsterdam** at 214. This last is one of New York's few Art-Nouveau buildings; it hosted Florenz Ziegfeld's Follies as well as a rooftop nightclub and W. C. Fields' New York début.

The theaters are all that remain of the extravagance of the 1900s, when a sprucer Broadway was glitzy and elegant, rather than tacky. The theater district was created overnight: 'I found Broadway a quiet little lane of ham and eggs in 1899,' wrote the proprietor of Rector's Lobster Palace, 'and left it a full blown avenue of lobsters, champagne and morning-afters'. The transformation was largely due to two impresarios, Charles Frohman and Oscar Hammerstein I. The latter started with the Olympia, an amusement complex containing a concert hall, a roof garden and twinkling lights, and went on to open several theaters.

Now the tattiest part of Times Square, this area is one of the principal targets of the **42nd Street Redevelopment Project**, which aims to clean it up over a 10-year period. Progress has been slow, and the projected Times Square Center, a complex comprising a hotel and four skyscrapers by John Burgee with Philip Johnson (they worked together on the AT&T Building), is still a battlefield of cranes and scaffolding on 42nd Street between 7th Avenue and Broadway.

*Make your way back to 42nd Street and Broadway and then walk a block north to 43rd Street. Immediately to your left on Broadway is the **Paramount Building**, practically the only building which has survived Times Square demolition fever.*

The Paramount has 14 setbacks piled on top of each other like a nest of Russian dolls and, right at the top, a globe that used to be illuminated. It opened as one of Broadway's most sumptuous theaters in 1927, with three black-marble lobbies and a baroque staircase. It was here that Frank Sinatra launched his career, supposedly with a bogus audience of teenagers paid to whoop and faint at appropriate moments.

Next door to the Paramount, between 44th and 45th Streets is **One Astor Plaza**, a gangling seventies skyscraper with a science-fiction crown of stream-lined concrete fins.

*Walk a block north to 45th and 46th Streets to the **Marriott***

Marquis Hotel at 1531 Broadway. A camp blend of Star Wars and showbiz, the Marriott is the Zsa Zsa Gabor of outer-space skyscrapers. Pop inside to ride the glass elevators which are decorated in a frill of rhinestone lights. They plunge thrillingly up and down through a false 1st-floor ceiling, although recently the management slowed them down after complaints from petrified guests.

*Now go back to 42nd Street, via Broadway. On the way, you pass the **I. Miller Building**, now a Sbarro pizza joint, immediately on your left at 46th Street, on the north side.*

The cornice is inscribed with the woeful epitaph *Show-Folks' Shoes Dedicated to Beauty in Footwear*, proclaiming a more glorious past. Underneath there are sickly-sweet statues wearing I. Miller shoes: Ethel Barrymore as Ophelia and Mary Pickford as Little Lord Fauntleroy, by the sculptor A. Stirling Calder, the father of the inventor of Mobiles and Stabiles, Alexander Calder. A block down on the left at 45th Street is one of the prettiest legitimate theaters on Broadway, the **Lyceum**, all neo-Baroque trims, with a verandah-style porch. The impresario Daniel Frohman had his apartment on the second floor with a secret window in the drawing room so he could peep onto the stage.

*As soon as you get to 42nd Street turn left, and walk up 42nd to 5th Avenue, a short walk of two blocks, towards the New York Public Library. The library occupies two city blocks between 6th and 5th Avenues and 42nd and 40th Streets, with **Bryant Park** behind it.*

Until recently the biggest drugs 'supermarket' in Midtown, the park is currently being landscaped and refurbished, and is scarred by scaffolding. It was named for the poet and editor William Cullen Bryant (1794–1878) and in 1853, before it was a park, a Crystal Palace stood here for the first American World's Fair. Although the engineer of the London Crystal Palace, Joseph Paxton, offered a design, it was rejected, and a bloated version by two Germans was used instead. It was 'much more beautiful as an architectural work', claimed handbooks of the time—and just as great a fire hazard, for it stood only five years before it was razed to the ground. It contained 6000 exhibits, including the new Otis elevator which eventually made skyscrapers viable.

Opposite the Crystal Palace stood the Latting Observatory, a 350 ft wood and iron tower, only 150 ft shorter than the Great Pyramid of Cheops to which it was modestly compared. This embryonic skyscraper was the prototype for the Empire State Building. Visitors bought ice-creams from the shops at the bottom and took a steam elevator to the telescopes at the top, from where they observed the city, which had spread as far as 42nd Street. In 1856 tragedy struck: the tower went up in flames, creating a space which was filled eight decades later by the **Grace Building**, a distinctly ungraceful building resembling a pair of bell-bottoms, at 41 West 42nd Street.

Bryant Park is the best place to see the **American Radiator Building** to the south on 40 West 40th Street. The charcoal-black skyscraper resembles an elongated lump of glowing coal, with a neo-Gothic black-brick body and a craggy gold crown. Built in 1924, it was the first New York skyscraper by Raymood Hood, the architect responsible for some of New York's best Art-Deco scrapers, including the *Daily News* Building and much of Rockefeller Center. The idea of the blackened façade, created by dipping the bricks in manganese, was to disguise the monotony of the windows. The entrance has a fine bas-relief of dragons, dolphins and raucous ladies.

> *Walk to the corner of 42nd Street and 5th Avenue and turn right. In Manhattan, beaux-arts buildings resort to shock tactics: you turn a corner unsuspectingly, and suddenly they pounce. Either the architect, you conclude, was experimenting with the art of surprise, or else he was stricken with amnesia and forgot that beaux-arts styles depend on a view, and that buildings in New York's grid are arranged like groceries in a supermarket, without vistas. Carrère and Hastings'* **New York Public Library** *is a prime culprit: its back and sides are so utilitarian that the grand 5th Avenue temple façade, with E. C. Potter's famous bouffoned lions, is quite devastating.*

Libraries are not generally exciting, unless you smuggle in a snake or something, but this one is an exception. The entrance hall is covered from ceiling to floor with white Vermont marble, and has a sweeping Paris Opéra staircase with dangling candlestick chandeliers. The real action goes on at the top of the staircase in Rm 315: the **Reading and Catalogue Room**. It is worth ordering a book just to observe the Luddite ritual that ensues: dispatchers stuff the request into a glass baton which is sucked up by pnuematic tubes into the library's bowels. Twenty minutes later its number lights up on an illuminated bingo board and the book is delivered by a shaking dumb waiter. Quaintly antique, the system is six times faster than that at the British Library.

At 11 am and 2 pm, there are excellent guided tours. The twinkly guide is full of recherché facts, informing you that the Polaroid camera and the Xerox were invented in the science department; that the army, apparently owning no atlases of their own, resorted to the Map Room to plan the American invasion of North Africa; and finally that the library contains 25,000 menus, and has 90 miles of shelving, with 50 more being added under Bryant Park.

No one minds if you explore on your own, for the library styles itself 'The People's Library'; it was practically the only place Trotsky approved of when he came to New York in 1917. On the ground floor, look out for the **DeWitt Wallace Periodical Room**, named after the founder of *Readers Digest* who came here to abridge articles. It has recently been painted with 13 murals by Richard Haas, best known for his illusionist mural of a warehouse in SoHo.

When you have had enough, you can join the cheerful crowd eating hot-dogs and reading between the lions on the steps outside; a prime spot for strange and fascinating conversations. On the lefthand side of the entrance is the **Caffè Strada** selling coffee and homemade cakes.

Have a rest and then start on **5th Avenue**.

Though everyone equates the name with fancy stores, this part of 5th Avenue has been taken over by shops called Al Falfa's Casbah, selling Persian carpets, luggage and telephones; permanently 'going out of business,' they are practically the only places in the world which sell electric nose-hair clippers. The smart shops—Saks, Bergdorf Goodman and Tiffany's—lie just a few blocks ahead, and one of the nice things about 5th Avenue is that everyone dresses to the nines. 5th Avenue chic is a matter of mascara and D-cups; 40-year-olds dress as teenagers, teenagers as 40-year-olds, and everyone smells of powder compacts and damp putty.

> *From the library walk two blocks north on the lefthand side of 5th Avenue until you reach 44th Street. On the way you pass* **500 5th Avenue**, *quite a dull white skyscraper but oddly familiar, because it was designed by the same architects in the same year as the Empire State Building.*
>
> *When you reach the shopper's clock at 44th Street, turn left. Opposite you at 27 West 44th Street is the* **Harvard Club**, *by New York's brilliant team of neo-classical architects, McKim, Mead and White.*

The hoi-polloi aren't really allowed in, but if you sweep through the

185

doors with sufficient *hauteur* to paralyse the doorman, you can snoop round the baronial halls inside. The walls are studded with trophies of startled elephants. Below them, terminally sunk in leather armchairs, Harvardites contribute pachydermic grunts and snores against the eerie distant groan of ladies playing bridge.

> *Right next door, at 37 West 44th Street, is the* **New York Yacht Club***; 1890 beaux-arts, and until recently home to the America's Cup.*

The club is by Wetmore & Warren, architects of the infinitely more sane façade of Grand Central, and wins first prize as New York's crankiest building. Poseidon slobbers over the entrance, while three 17th-century ships' sterns, petrified in stone and gushing limestone water, are wedged into the window frames. New Yorkers are thoroughly used to the building, in the way one gets accustomed to a dotty uncle lurking on the stairs.

> *On the other side of the Yacht Club at 59 West 44th is the* **Algonquin Hotel***.*

Ever since a traveling salesman called Douglas Fairbanks sold it some soap in 1902, the Algonquin has maintained a symbiotic partnership with hundreds of biographers, most of whom remember it as the rendezvous used by the literary club known as the Round Table. The club started in 1919, and revolved around boozey lunches and Algonquin angel cake. Anita Loos called the Round Table 'a boring set of exhibitionists' and even Dorothy Parker described it as 'just a lot of people telling each other how good they were'. Even so, their witticisms were recorded every week by 'FPA', Franklin Pierce Adams, in the *New York World*.

The Algonquin has recently been bought by a Japanese corporation, who are doing it up with the assurance that they will preserve the old-fashioned mustiness which has attracted sorts like Graham Greene, Peter Ustinov and William Faulkner, who keeled over and burnt himself on a steam pipe during a drinking bout here in the 1950s. The Rose Room bar, all distressed chintz and grubby carpets like a seaside hotel, is a soothing place to stop for a drink.

A Round Table fixture, the actor and writer Robert Benchley, was a permanent resident just across the street in the **Royalton Hotel** at 44 West 44th Street. He lived in a hammed-up Victorian suite, with a library of books chosen for their titles alone, including *Forty Thousand Sublime and Beautiful Thoughts* and *Talks on Manure*.

A few years ago the dowdy hotel was revamped by Steve Rubell of Studio 54 fame. You can tell what you are in for as soon as you see the doormen—ladies in black trouser suits and chaps wearing eyeliner—whose job is simply to stand mysteriously. There is no accounting for taste in New York, and you are almost duty bound to say you like the chairs and ottomans shrouded in dust sheets or the strange mahogany tusks poking out of the walls. At any rate, it is an interesting place to stop for a game of chess and tea, even though the idiotic menu details calories per mouthful.

> *Make your way back to 5th Avenue and walk north as far as West 47th Street. On the right you pass **535 5th Avenue** between 44th and 45th Streets and the **Fred French Building** on the next block up. Craning your neck a bit, you can see a lovely frieze in red and lime-green tiles on the roof of the Fred French, which is actually a disguise for the water tower. The rising sun surrounded by bees and griffins symbolizes progress, thrift and integrity.*

Resembling Mayan pyramids, both scrapers are copybook examples of the 'setbacks' which came in after the Zoning Laws of 1916 (see p. 83). Soon after it was built in 1926 *The New Yorker* grumbled that 535 5th Avenue had 'the grace of an overgrown grain elevator', so enraging the litigious architect, Craig Severance, that he sued for a formal retraction.

> *On the left at 47th Street, between 5th and 6th Avenues, is **Diamond Row**.*

Like the diamond trade in Antwerp, the dealers and cutters on 47th Street are nearly all Hasidic Jews, wearing 17th-century frock coats, with ringlets for sideburns and wide-brimmed hats. The real business of the district has little to do with the displays of monstrous jewelry. Every day, from Monday to noon on Friday, $400 million changes hands. Diamonds are bought and sold at skyhigh prices by the Diamond Dealers Club; deals are made in the name of 'Mazel' and 'Brooch', Yiddish for good luck and disaster, and gems are exchanged in tiny parcels of folded paper.

> *'Wise Men Fish Here', says a small sign hanging in the midst of the jewelery shops, at 41 West 47th Street. This signifies the street's unobtrusive black sheep, the **Gotham Book Mart**, New York's tiniest, most chaotic and nicest bookshop, not least because it has been befriended by the illustrator and writer Edward Gorey, and sells most of his books, which are hard to get hold of outside America.*

187

The bookshop was opened in 1923 by Frances Steloff, and became an institution after the founding of her Writers' Emergency Fund, which rescued people like Henry Miller, who sent in SOSs for food, John Dos Passos and Theodor Dreiser, who once came into the store and inscribed all the books as well as the Bible 'with the compliments of the author'. Frances Steloff died recently, but the bookshop still prides itself on its stock of works by new and unknown writers.

Now go back to 5th Avenue and walk up to 49th Street. On your right is **Saks Fifth Avenue**—*haute couture, but* very *stuffy. A block up, on the same side of the street, are the mackintosh-grey Gothic spires of* **St Patrick's Cathedral**, *the seat of the Roman Catholic Archdiocese, and a culmination of all the hopes and efforts of New York's Irish Catholic immigrants.*

Opposite, between 49th and 50th Streets, you stumble on **Rockefeller Center** *and the view down the* **Channel Gardens** *of the RCA Building that Gertrude Stein described in 1935 as 'the most beautiful thing I have ever seen'.*

Usually when you look from one end to the other of New York's vertiginous skyscraper gorges, you see nothing except wedges of sky. The gully between 49th and 50th Streets is one of the city's few vistas of a skyscraper rather than sky, and it is an exhilarating, memorable one, best seen at night when the needle-slim limestone slab of the RCA Building, nicknamed Thirty Rock, is illuminated in white. Seventy stories high, the vertical avenue of light seems even higher, framed as it is on either side of the narrow Channel Gardens by two squat buildings, the **British Empire Building** and the **Maison Française**. Even though it has no decoration except the vertical stripes made by its spandrels, the RCA is easily the most elegant skyscraper in the city.

Walk straight down the Channel Gardens, a 60-ft walkway with ponds in the center, and six nubile nereids and tritons riding dolphins (symbolizing human progress) by the sculptor René Chambellan. They point to Paul Manship's golden Prometheus *and the sunken Plaza, with its clanking flags, at the end.*

The nicest time to come here is at Christmas, when the sunken plaza is flooded and turned into a skating rink. The place smells of roasted chestnuts, and the decorations are famously tasteful.

This is the heart of Rockefeller Center. The city within a city comprises 21 buildings on six city blocks, related to each other aesthetically as well as physically by a subterranean network of truck ramps, shop concourses, shipping rooms and car parks (originally supervised by 725 attendants who slid between floors on firemens' poles). By squeezing offices, shops, apartments, theaters and cinemas into a tiny area without altering the grid plan, the Rockefeller Center really does succeed in mixing residents, office-workers and visitors. Like the Roman forum, it makes a virtue out of congestion, absorbing 250,000 people every day.

In fact the Center is a model of the American Way rather than Roman democracy. The brainchild of John D. Rockefeller, it was a perfect synthesis of private enterprise and the public interest, an embodiment of the unselfish face of making money. Rockefeller's personal credo, 'I believe in the supreme worth of the individual . . .', is inscribed in marble, like Moses' tablets, on a plaque above the ice rink. It came as rather a shock, therefore, in 1989, when it was bought by a Japanese corporation, only to be dubbed 'Wokafeller Center' by the press.

Until 1985, when they sold it for a whopping $400 million, it was owned by Columbia University. The land became their principal source of income when Rockefeller teamed up with the Metropolitan Opera in 1929 and leased it, like a miniature Hong Kong, for $3.8 million a year. The development was announced on the same day as Black Tuesday, 1929, and three months later the Met pulled out. Rockefeller went ahead without them, negotiated the largest building loan ever of $65 million and employed a think-tank of architects, Hood & Fouilhoux, Reinhard & Hofmeister and Corbett, Harrison & MacMurray. Between 1931 and 1940, during the worst ravages of the Depression, they built 13 of the Center's skyscrapers, or 'tombstones of capitalism with windows', as one visitor described the the dismally empty offices in 1934.

From the Gardens, walk to the entrance to the **RCA Building** *directly behind Prometheus and the Center's private street, Rockefeller Plaza.*

One of the joys of Rockefeller Center is the medieval way in which the architecture is integrated with murals, sculptures and mosaics: nearly a hundred artists and craftsmen were employed to work on the project. Over the entrance to the RCA Building is one of the best examples: Lee Lawrie's green and gold bas-relief of *Genius*, a bearded giant brandishing a pair of calipers. The figure was inspired, if not, as was rumored, actually snitched from the frontispiece to Blake's *Europe* which shows *Urizen*, the creator of the material world. Urizen ('your reason') also

189

created the first artist, *Los*, a blacksmith of dubious morals who bound his maker in chains of iron, and you cannot help wondering whether Lawrie intended the erudite reference as an incredibly cryptic swipe at Rockefeller.

Diego Rivera's mural in the RCA lobby, on the other hand, was so blatantly cheeky that even the Rockefellers couldn't help noticing. The vaguest of briefs—'Man at the Crossroads Looking with Uncertainty but with Hope . . . to a New and Better Future'—was a gift horse for a Marxist painter like Rivera. He immediately embarked on a depiction of the proletariat seizing the means of production. Along with scenes of police brutality, the mural showed sturdy Soviet women playing sports outside the Kremlin, and ugly capitalist tarts exuding a venereal miasma all over a card game. But it was only when Rivera painted in a portrait of Lenin that the Rockefellers objected.

The 'Battle of Rockefeller Center', as Rivera recounted the affair with barely concealed relish, ensued. At the opening ceremonies, Rockefeller sent in 'sappers' who covered the mural in a tarpaulin, while mounted police patrolled the streets and the skies 'roared with airplanes flying round the skyscraper menaced by Lenin'. When Rivera refused to capitulate, the painting was destroyed and replaced with José María Sert's bland mural of *American Progress*. Rivera got his revenge in the *Billionaires' Banquet*, showing J. D. Rockefeller, Henry Ford and J. P. Morgan dining on tickertape. This is now in the National Palace in Mexico, along with a version of the destroyed mural.

*By now you will need a drink and a break. You can get a view as well from the **Rainbow Room** on the 65th floor of the RCA, but you will need a jacket and tie. The lovely Art-Deco bar and restaurant re-opened at the end of 1987 after it was restored by 30 artists. It has a revolving dance floor, a house cabaret wearing red tuxedos, and some of the campest waiters in the city. The view is quite something. Look out especially for the Center's secret roof gardens, with pools and sloping lawns, on top of the Maison Française and the British Empire Building.*

If you have time, you can take one of the **NBC Studios** tours which leave every 15 minutes from the lobby of the RCA (Mon–Sat 9.30–4.30, Sun 10–4, adm $5.50), or pick up free tickets for television recordings from the information desk which also has standbys for *Saturday Night Live* and the *David Letterman Show*. NBC was the RCA Building's first tenant: they began broadcasting from their RCA studios in 1935 with two shows a week, including televised cookery which was restricted to salads because the heat of the studio lights melted everything else.

Before you leave the Center, definitely squeeze in a visit to **Radio City Music Hall**. *From the entrance to the RCA building, turn left and walk past the* **Associated Press Building** *(which has a superb steel relief over the entrance by the Japanese sculptor Isamu Noguchi) to 50th Street and 6th Avenue. Radio City is on the northeast corner of 50th Street, and to see the interior you must take one of the excellent tours of the auditorium. They leave every 15 minutes (adm $6).*

Art-Deco at its most bizarre, Radio City makes the rest of Rockefeller Center look neo-classically austere. The creation of the Jupiter of cinema impresarios, Samuel Rothapfel, or 'Roxy', and the architect/designer Donald Deskey, it was built in 1932 as the largest, most theatrical theater in the world.

The auditorium is astonishing. Roxy claimed he got the idea sailing on an ocean liner at dawn, and the proscenium arch, the width of a city block, is meant to resemble a sun rising out of an ocean of 6000 red-velvet seats and a carpet of Art Deco fish. The design is sometimes compared to the work of the German Expressionists, in particular the *Grosses Schauspielhaus*, a circus built in Berlin in 1919. Roxy's theater was kitted out with the latest technology, so that whole landscapes could be recreated on stage, thanks to artificial raincurtains, 20-ft high walls of city steam, and four elevators which lifted scenery and orchestras 13 ft above the audience and 27 ft below. If you are lucky you will see it when the stage lights are turned on and someone is practising on the Mighty Wurlitzer, which is so loud it can be heard in the subway.

The opening show was a flop of appropriately histrionic proportions. The five-hour marathon included a 'Symphony of the Curtain', in which the curtain performed motorized acrobatics while the orchestra played a 'Hymn to the Sun'. When people asked whether the horses on stage were mice, Roxy was carried out on a stretcher. He lost $180,000 in a fortnight and eventually the format was changed to the old Roxy formula of cinema shows accompanied by live acts.

The tour goes backstage as well, past rehearsals of the Rockettes, Roxy's can-can girls, looking forlorn inspite of their long legs, and even into the famous lavatories decorated with Deskey's murals depicting the history of cosmetics starting with Eve and ending with a flapper. In 1978, hamstrung by a new era of videos and mass releases, Radio City was

191

saved from demolition and restored. Now the theater makes a profit with a variety of shows, ranging from famous illusionists to Madonna.

From Radio City, walk back to 5th Avenue, turn left and walk three blocks north to 53rd Street. To the left, on the righthand side of 53rd Street, are the flapping banners of the **Museum of Modern Art** *at 11 West 53rd Street. (Open Mon–Sat 11–6; Sun 12–6; Thurs 11–9; free Thurs 5–9.)*

MoMa is a place to strut, and on Thursday evenings fashionable students with arty haircuts descend in droves.

Before you go in, pause outside and look at the museum building itself, with its sleek white-marble façade and mock cornice of portholes. Designed in 1939 by Edward Durrell Stone and Philip Goodwin, apostles of the International Style in New York (see p. 84), it immediately became a flagship of modernism. It was founded, at a time when Van Gogh and Cézanne were too avant-garde for any of the other Manhattan museums, by 'the ladies': Mrs John D. Rockefeller Jnr (who got her husband to donate the site even though he hated modern art), Mrs Sullivan and Lillie Bliss. The enormous tower on the west side of the museum is its most recent addition, built in 1985 by the Italian designer Cesar Pelli as apartments to generate revenue for the museum.

Inside, start on the 2nd and 3rd floors where the core of the collection, most of which dates from the first half of the century, is arranged chronologically.

There are a mass of paintings which are so familiar they need no introduction; like Matisse's dancers and their gravity-defying bosoms and, the most famous, Picasso's *Les Demoiselles D'Avignon*. There are also several less well-known gems: Bonnard's *The Breakfast Room*, and Malevich's wonderful Suprematist Composition *Airplane Flying*, abstract boxes zooming in space, supressed when Stalin made constructivism a state crime. Despite its avant-garde origins, the museum did not appreciate the latest Dada-inspired gesture of the Hungarian founder of 'Neoism', Monty Cantsin. In 1988 he spattered the walls and, incidentally, Picasso's $4 million *Interior With Girl*, with six vials of his own blood in the shape of an X, and then read out a manifesto denouncing the gentrification of the Lower East Side. In 1990 he was sentenced to 60 days in the slammer, and is presently selling paintings to try and pay off the $1000 he owes in fines.

If the main galleries now seem daunting, head off either to **Drawings**, a darkened gallery on the 3rd floor, or to the excellent—and small— **Architecture and Design** section on the 4th floor. Here, you can try to work out how Marianne Brandt's teapot and chairs by Charles Rennie Mackintosh and Frank Lloyd Wright evolved into the 'Trimline' telephone designed by Henry Dreyfuss in 1965. The collection spans all media, and apart from these two havens, the museum has three cinemas for screening films from an archive of 10,000.

On a sunny day, the best place to end up is the sculpture garden by Philip Johnson (who coined the term International Style, and is now a Pilgrim Father of Post Modernism). You can get a coffee or a whole meal from the **Garden Café**, and sit down next to Rodin's *Balzac*.

> *Before you return to 5th Avenue and go home, you should certainly visit MoMA's new* **Design Store**, *opposite the main museum. If consumer art ever had an apotheosis, this is it. Even if you don't have enough money for a Suprematist tea cup or a Bauhaus coffee pot, you can probably afford the Italian-designed lavatory brush.*
>
> *Saunter back to 5th Avenue and* **St Thomas Church** *which is on the lefthand corner of 53rd Street and 5th Avenue. St Thomas has one of the best choirs in New York and evensong is at 5.30 pm.*

St Thomas' is an urbanely Gothic Revival church. Bertram Goodhue and Ralph Adams Cram, the architects insisted on stylistic integrity. So much so that, rather than a steel skeleton, they used structural flying buttresses, although today the walls are supported with steel beams, to cope with the cataclysmic vibrations of the New York subway. The design is much cleverer than a mere imitation: the church is completely asymmetrical with a massive 15-story tower on the corner of 53rd Street, and carved figures which are deliberately out of proportion, parody the drunkenly overcrowded doors of Gothic cathedrals like Chartres.

Its extraordinary *pièce de résistance* is the 80 ft high reredos carved with 60 saints, from a design by Lee Lawrie, the Rockefeller sculptor, and Bertram Goodhue. It glows with a weird blueish light, because it is sculpted out of a mixture of limestone and sandstone which reflects the deep blue of the stained-glass windows.

> *If you have missed evensong, you can go and watch TV instead in the brilliant* **Museum of Broadcasting**, *just across 5th Avenue at 1 East 53rd Street, (open Wed–Sat, 12–5, Tues 12–8, suggested*

donation). The museum has a collection of nearly 40,000 television and radio programmes which visitors watch at private viewing consoles, or in two video theaters.

Otherwise, there is the more spiritual alternative of **Paley Park***, two doors away at 5 East 53rd Street.*

Under the shadow of 12 honey locust trees, everyone turns white plastic chairs to contemplate its altar, 'the waterwall'. The clattering water, which mysteriously comes from nowhere and goes nowhere, obliterates the sound of everything else.

As you leave, look east to the end of 53rd Street, filled by the crowstepped silhouette of the **Citicorp Building** in Queens. A solitary 663 ft, 48 stories high, it is not just the tallest, but practically the only New York skyscraper outside Manhattan.

Walk VI
The Upper East Side

Metropolitan Museum—Guggenheim—Cooper Hewitt—Central Park Reservoir—Conservatory Garden—Carl Schurz Park—Municipal Asphalt Plant—Temple Emanu-El—Central Park Zoo—Plaza—Tiffany's—Trump Tower

The Upper East Side means money and museums, in unthinkable quantities. There is nowhere else in Manhattan quite so polite or sedate. Make the most of it, take as much time as you like, and use buses rather than feet. The traffic is not so bad here, and all sorts of people go by bus, as well as the usual coterie of hardened stoics. Don't come on a Monday, when the museums are closed.

The walk starts on Museum Mile with the New York's Goliath among museums, the Metropolitan, where you can be as selective or comprehensive as you like, bearing in mind that it takes approximately 2¹/₂ hours to walk round all the exhibits without even looking at them. 'Museum Mile' is in fact a mile and a half and there are another 49 museums nearby. For health reasons this walk takes in only two more; the Guggenheim and the Cooper-Hewitt, neither of which take long to see (consult the Museums Checklist if you want to see the rest, pp. 254–61). Then we head off to the Conservatory Garden, with a picnic if it's good weather, and from there, by bus, to Central Park Zoo and the toy shop, F. A. O. Schwarz, finishing up at the Plaza Hotel for a drink.

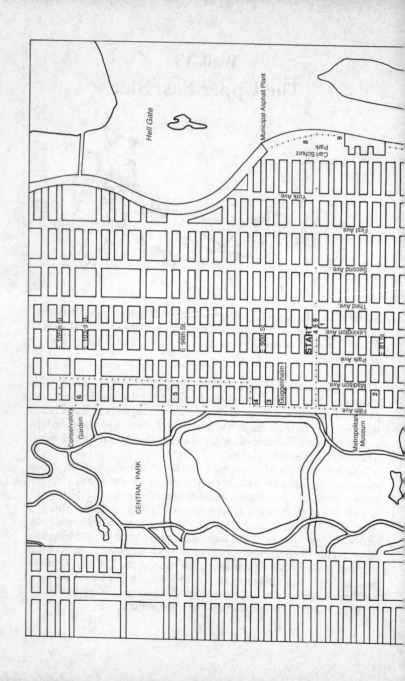

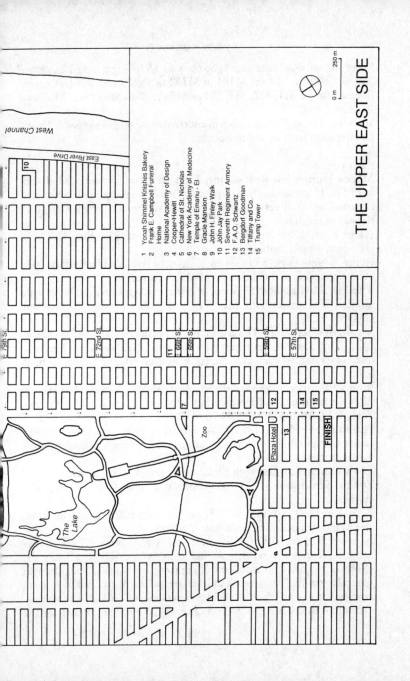

THE UPPER EAST SIDE

1 Yonah Shimmel Knishes Bakery
2 Frank E. Campbell Funeral Home
3 National Academy of Design
4 Cooper-Hewitt
5 Cathedral of St. Nicholas
6 New York Academy of Medecine
7 Temple of Emanu - El
8 Gracie Mansion
9 John H. Finley Walk
10 John Jay Park
11 Seventh Regiment Armory
12 F.A.O. Schwartz
13 Bergdorf Goodman
14 Tiffany and Co.
15 Trump Tower

0 m   250 m

Start: by subway, take the **4**, **5**, or **6** to 86th Street and Lexington Avenue. By bus, take the **M101** or **M102** to 86th Street and Lexington Avenue, or the **M1**, **M2**, **M3**, **M4** or **M86** to 86th Street and Madison Avenue.

Walking Time: 3¹/₂ hours, but of course you are bound to spend at least an afternoon tackling the museums.

LUNCH/CAFÉS

Mocca Hungarian Restaurant, 1588 2nd Ave., between 82nd and 83rd Sts. Homemade chicken paprika, smoked sausage called *Kolbasz*, chopped liver (all served with a plate of rye bread), and poppy-seed strudel to finish up.

H&H East, 1551 2nd Ave., between 80th and 81st Sts. The best take-away bagels in the city.

Benny's New York, 359 East 68th St., at 1st Ave. Middle Eastern café, plus cappuccino and delicious vegetable lasagna.

The Pie, 340 East 86th St. Russian *kasha*, chicken Kiev, and blinis with salmon. The eponymous Pie is a layer cake of blini, chicken and mushrooms.

Sarabeth's Kitchen, 47 East 92nd St., between Park and Madison Aves. The closest Upper East Siders get to neighborliness. The best thing is scrambled eggs with chunks of smoked salmon. Lunch is about $20.

John's Pizzeria, 408 East 64th St., near 1st Ave. A mixture of Woody Allen's patronage, and the fact that John's do the best pizzas in New York, led to the opening of a second branch on the Upper East Side.

Patisserie Frédéric, 1431 York Ave. near 76th St. Croissants and cookies, although it's worth a visit just to see Frédéric's curious handle-bar mustache.

Leo's Diner, 128 East 86th St. Cheerful Jewish delicatessen.

Yonah Schimmel, 1275 Lexington Ave. near 86th St. Superior knishes.

Ecco-La, 1660 3rd Ave., at 93rd St. Nineteen pastas to choose from, and as many sauces, in frantic surroundings.

Istanbul Kebap, 303 80th St., near 2nd Ave. Miniscule Turkish restaurant decorated in what looks like children's scribbles, actually the efforts of patrons who are allowed to draw on the paper tablecloths with specially provided crayons. As well as 'kebaps', there are stuffed peppers and 'mussaka', and *piyaz*, a delicious concoction of Turkish white beans.

Ottomanelli's Café, 1626 York Ave., near 86th St. Branch of the

Greenwich Village butchers serving Upper East Siders with steak sandwiches and burgers.

Golden's Delicatessen. 1175 Madison Ave., off 86th St. Exuberent
Jewish delicatessen.

El Pollo, 1746 1st Ave., near 91st St. Tiny Peruvian take-away and
restaurant for chicken fanatics.

New Wave Coffee Shop, 937 Madison Ave., near 74th St. In the
shadow of the Whitney Museum, grilled cheese sandwiches and fried
eggs.

The rich live on the Upper East Side in particularly splendid isolation.
North of its frontier on 59th Street is an Eldorado of fantastic rents,
fabulously expensive florists, chichi boutiques, psychiatrists richer than
Croesus, and so-called thrift shops, stuffed with furs and *objets d'art*. At
96th Street the desmesne comes to an end and an invisible barrier
divides the palatial apartments of Carnegie Hill from the low-rise tenements, bodegas and street markets of Spanish Harlem.

The eclecticism of Upper East Side architecture is fairly staggering:
Renaissance palazzi sit alongside Gothic castles and every possible
permutation of a château. Even so, upper class Upper East Side is a
recent phenomenon, dating from the end of the 19th century, and the
mansions and palaces are relative parvenus. Before Central Park opened
in 1863, pigs, goats and squatters resided on the stretch of 5th Avenue
north of 59th Street, and wooden tin-can shanties, farms and a few
colonial homesteads were the only landmarks in open countryside. The
great money influx began in the 1890s when businesses began encroach-
ing on the midtown mansions of the affluent, and Mrs Astor and her
crew beat a retreat to Millionaire's Row, the stretch of 5th Avenue
bordering on the newly built Central Park.

Fifth Avenue's 'Gold Coast' was the hub of the fashionable Upper
East Side until the 1920s, when the railroad tracks under Park Avenue
between 96th Street and Grand Central were covered over. Suddenly,
thanks to a combination of income tax and the Depression, it became
practical as well as acceptable for the well-to-do to live in apartments
rather than mansions. A mixture of apartment houses and hotels migrated eastwards until they merged with Yorkville, a neighborhood of
German, Czechoslovakian, and Hungarian immigrants near the East
River, reeking with the sickly-sweet smell of breweries such as Ringlers
and Rupperts.

Nowadays, only a few traces of the old Yorkville remain: shops selling

Stern and German newspapers on 86th Street and a smattering of family-run cafés and food stores like the jolly Café Geiger at 206 86th Street, and the Hungarian Meat Market at 1560 2nd Avenue and 81st Street, stuffed with a rainforest of sausages, *plockwurst, mettwurst, streichwurst* and the odd pig's trotter. Today, a nice little brownstone on the Upper East Side is a snip at two million, and you will be doing rather well if the maintenance on your million-dollar pié-à-terre costs only four times as much as the rent for an apartment on the Lower East Side.

> *You could invest your money instead in a copy of the* New York Times *and a knish from Yonah Schimmel's at 1275 Lexington Avenue, just round the corner from the 4, 5, and 6 subway exits where this walk starts. A ball of deep-fried mashed potatoes, the knish is a superior East European version of the Cornish pasty, and will keep you going all the way to the Metropolitan Museum of Art, three blocks away on 5th Avenue.*
>
> *Walk west on 86th Street, once Yorkville's* Hauptstrasse, *or high street, past* **Toy Park**, *an excellent toy shop on the left at 110 86th Street, until you reach 5th Avenue and Central Park.*

If you get here early enough you should look out for an intimidating sight: the professional dog-walkers who stride up and down 5th Avenue every morning with up to 10 pedigree beasts abreast.

> *At 5th Avenue turn left and walk down to the entrance to the* **Metropolitan Museum** *on Central Park opposite 82nd Street. (Open Fri–Sat 10–8.45; Tues–Thurs 10–4.45, Sun 11–4.45. Suggested admission fee, which means you can pay as much or as little as you like.)*

The Metropolitan is New York's Palace of Culture. It means business, and the stupendously grand neo-Baroque façade promises everything except moderation. The museum has been expanding concertina-style ever since 1880, and ultimately threatens to engulf the whole of Central Park. Just as a stately home has its gardens and meadows, so the Metropolitan has Central Park. After it went up in 1880, Frederick Law Olmsted, who landscaped the park, admitted he bore a grudge against the museum for trampling on his creation; a place where, as another person complained, 'one sometimes goes to get rid of art'.

The original Metropolitan building by Vaux and Mould, who both assisted Olmsted with the landscaping of Central Park, has long since been swallowed up inside a wing of the museum, and the present aristocratic front of 1902 is by Richard Morris Hunt, who designed the monumental plinth under the feet of the Statue of Liberty. It is flanked to the north and south by two wings, added in 1911 by McKim, Mead and White, the Manhattan's Holy Trinity of neo-classicism. Although you hardly notice, Hunt's middle section is still unfinished; the great blocks of stone over the columns were originally meant to be carved with allegorical sculptures before the curators ran out of money.

Once inside, have a brisk look round the **Great Hall**, *one of New York's grandest foyers, pick up a floor plan of the museum, and make straight for the* **Temple of Dendur**, *on the far righthand side of the museum.*

On the way you walk through the **Egyptian Galleries**, *a really colossal haul, most of which was collected by the Met's own archaeologists at a time when Egyptian policy allowed foreigners to keep half their discoveries.*

The galleries are arranged chronologically and span 36 centuries from 3000 BC to AD 641, although some of the objects, in particular the bed linen and a mummified falcon-god, are so well preserved, they look unconvincing. The most interesting room is Gallery 4 which contains models from a tomb in Thebes, discovered in a hidden chamber in 1920 in pristine condition. The models are disconcertingly naturalistic; an ox is trying to stand up and failing because it is too fat, and a rather gruesome slaughter-house is spattered with blood. Nearby, in Gallery 8, is a fragment showing the face of Senwosret III dating from the 1800s BC, said to be the world's first portrait.

Once you get to the Temple of Dendur, you can sit down and read your New York Times *in peace.*

The temple was actually a gift to the United States and was transported lock, stock and barrel to a room of its own in the Metropolitan just before the flooding of the Aswan High Dam in 1960. It was built in the first place to honour two brothers, Pedesi and Pihor, who drowned in a campaign against Ethiopia in 25 BC. The walls have several portraits of the Roman Emperor, Augustus, who commissioned the temple as part of a publicity campaign to soften his image and ingratiate himself with the recently conquered Egyptians, who were understandably cross.

The gallery itself is theatrical, and almost upstages the temple. Roche and Dinkeloo, (best known for the Ford Foundation Building on 42nd Street), have been in charge of the most recent additions to the Met and the stylishness is typical of their work. The Met itself has always been stubbornly up to date. It was one of the first museums to introduce air-conditioning in 1907, five years after it was invented, and the general slickness of the place is bound to come as a shock to anyone used to old-fashioned, ramshackle museums. New Yorkers use the Met like a club: they drop in for lectures, concerts and rendezvous, or just to eat in the restaurant and do their Christmas shopping in the Museum Shop, practically an institution in itself.

> *From the temple, you can plan your assault on the rest of the galleries. As you only have a few hours you will probably want to set off for the stars of the museum, the American Wing and the tremendous Michael C. Rockefeller Collection of Primitive Art.*
>
> *The best place in the* **American Wing***, on the northwest side of the museum, is the airy Garden Room and its trees and ponds.*

The room is famous for its Tiffany glass, some of which Tiffany designed for his own house in Long Island. There are surprises, as well, like some incorrigibly cheery stained glass windows designed by Frank Lloyd Wright for a kindergarten, and Louis Sullivan's fantastically delicate cast-iron staircase from the Chicago Stock Exchange, of 1893. Sullivan only received one commission in New York (the Bayard-Condict Building in SoHo), perhaps because his style was too functional for conservative New York. In the middle of the courtyard you can have a good look at a replica of Augustus Saint-Gaudens' golden *Diana* who used to shoot her darts from the top of Madison Square Garden. (When people complained about her brazen pose, Saint-Gaudens was forced to cast a smaller statue so the shocking details would be less immediately offensive.)

You will need a floor plan to negotiate your way round the rest of the American Wing, which contains a series of period rooms and paintings from the 18th century to early 20th-century: including works by Georgia O'Keefe, Mary Cassatt, John Singer Sargent and Edward Hopper.

The collection of **Primitive Art** has a wing to itself on the other side of the museum. The galleries span Africa and the Americas, and their scope alone, covering 3000 years, makes them fascinating. The immense differences between cultures are striking. The nomadic Fang people of Gabon, for example, thought of the head as the center of action and the stomach as the seat of thought. In the second African gallery, there is an exquisite reliquary head, blackened and gleaming with palm oil, which was used as a container for ancestral skulls. At one point it was owned by the sculptor Jacob Epstein, and similar reliquary masks inspired Cubists like Gris and Braque in the 1920s.

Round the corner in the gallery dealing with the Pacific Islands are the extraordinary carved Asmat Mbis poles collected by Nelson Rockefeller's son, Michael, who drowned in 1961 on an anthropological expedition in New Guinea. Housed in a two-story gallery (Roche & Dinkeloo again), they are illuminated with such strong lights that you can see a glistening cosmopolis of cobwebs which industrious Metropolitan spiders have woven at the top. The poles look harmless enough, but the tops originally held impaled heads which were subsequently left to fester in the jungle. Revenge was a way of life for the Asmat, who on the other hand did not believe that death was natural. Whenever someone died, even of old age or illness, they blamed their enemies or a sorceress, and went after the perpetrator on a bloody headhunt.

> *By this time you will need a breather. The Met doesn't show it on its floor plan, but if you take the elevator on the 1st floor outside the Lila Acheson Wallace Wing of 20th Century Art (Bonnard, Matisse, Soutine et al.) you end up in a secret* **Sculpture Garden** *on the roof. From here, you get the finest view in the city of Central Park, along with the Plaza Hotel 30 blocks to the south, an aristocratic Edwardian doll's house. The elevator man, who is very matey, has developed his own Beaufort Scale for sunsets; he rates them out of 10 and will do prognoses up to seven hours in advance.*

If you have any energy left, there are 30 more galleries of European Paintings containing 17 Rembrandts and a whole room of Rodin, as well as practically every European artist you ever heard of (including three astonishing landscapes: Cézanne's sinister *Rocks in the Forest*, Van Gogh's *Cypresses* and El Greco's *View of Toledo*). At some point, however, you will have to accept that it's impossible to see everything—the sections on Islamic, Asian, Chinese, Greek, Roman and 20th-century art, including the new Lila Acheson wing, all constitute museums in themselves and to see them you will have to come back. When you do, don't neglect the erotic wine cups in the section on European Decorative Arts, and Todini's baroque fantasy, a harpsichord attached to a golden mountain concealing bagpipes, in Musical Instruments. The best time to return is a Friday or Saturday evening, when the museum stays open until 9; the candlelit restaurant has someone playing a grand piano, there are free classical and jazz concerts on the balcony of the Great Hall, and the whole place becomes absurdly festive.

> *The steps outside the museum are the closest thing in the city to Rome's Spanish Steps. To the right of them are a number of benches, used on Sunday mornings for rallies of old ladies and their pugs.*
>
> *After lunch they disappear into the tea rooms of the Stanhope Hotel. They know what they are about, and anyone can join them for a good spread of sandwiches and scones, costing an astronomical $18 a head. The hotel is directly opposite the museum, at 997 5th Avenue and 81st Street.*
>
> *The same block between 81st and 82nd Street contains a peculiar sandwich of buildings. On the north side is one of the Upper East Side's disgustingly rich and handsome beaux-arts mansions, 1009 5th Avenue, and on the south side is 998 5th Avenue, one of its first apartment houses, built in 1910 when they were still thought outré, and disguised as palazzi (some of the apartments contain up to 25 rooms). In the middle of the group is Philip Johnson and John Burgee's post-modern 1979 façade for 1001 5th Avenue; a respectful parody of its neighbors, with a pastiche mansard roof tilted at the same angle as the one on the mansion next door.*

Before they go to meet their maker, most of the Upper East Side's rich and famous pass through **Frank E. Campbell's Funeral Home**, behind Johnson's building on Madison Avenue. The list of distinguished names includes Gertrude Lawrence, Montgomery Clift, Joan Crawford, James Cagney and Judy Garland, (in a glass-topped coffin lined with blue velvet).

> *Now walk up 5th Avenue towards 89th Street. On the way you pass a miniature prototype of Rockefeller Center, at 3 East 84th Street, on the north side of the street. Raymond Hood designed this narrow limestone townhouse in 1928, three years before the RCA Building, and it has the same pressed-metal spandrels between the windows, as well as a lovely silver metal door with leafy fronds.*
>
> *Go back to 5th Avenue, and walk five blocks north to Frank Lloyd Wright's extraordinary organic white snail, the Guggenheim*

Museum, on East 89th Street (open Tues 11–7.45; Wed–Sun 11–4.45, adm $4.50; free Tues 5–7.45).

The Guggenheim is actually an antidote to museums, and an especially therapeutic contrast to the vastness of the Met. Navigating it is child's play. You take the elevator to the top, scamper down the helter-skelter to the bottom, and then you leave.

'The physician can bury his mistakes,' Frank Lloyd Wright informed the *New York Times Magazine* in 1953, 'but the architect can only advise his client to plant vines'. Vine leaves, like fig leaves, would simply make the Guggenheim more prominent, and half the wit of Wright's madcap creation has to do with its setting amongst the stuffy mansions of 5th Avenue, in the heart of the conservative Upper East Side.

Solomon Guggenheim, a silver and copper mine magnate, started his collection in suitably Upper East Side style, with a group of Old Masters which he exhibited in his rooms in the Plaza Hotel. The revolution came in 1927, when he commissioned a portrait from the impossibly named Baroness Hilla Rebay von Ehrenwiesen. Enthusing him with her passion for abstract art, which she believed was mystical, she introduced him to Kandinsky, Léger, Klee, Delaunay and her lover, Rudolph Bauer. Finally, in 1943, it was the baroness who suggested Frank Lloyd Wright as a suitable architect to design a new home for what was then the Solomon R. Guggenheim Museum of Non-Objective Painting.

Wright suffered the same fate as his mentor Louis Sullivan: the Guggenheim was his only New York contract, apart from an uninspiring Jaguar showroom on Park Avenue and a house on Staten Island. He was 74 when he got the commission and it took 16 years to build, what with endless squabbles between the trustees and New York City planning authorities, and between Rebay, Guggenheim's son, and Wright himself. By the time it was completed both Solomon Guggenheim and Wright were dead.

Wright believed that architecture was superior to all the arts, and even though the pious motto 'Let each man exercise the art he knows' is inscribed in bronze on the floor, the museum upstages its own exhibits with a vengence. You can't help turning away from the gallery walls to look at the empty rotunda in the middle, or up, at the geometric skylight in the roof, which fills the centre with natural light; or across, at the people staring at you on the other side of the spiral.

The body of the museum is used for changing exhibitions of modern artists, but you should not miss the two galleries off the ramp itself, on the 4th and 2nd levels. These contain selections from the permanent collection of over four thousand paintings and sculptures which is particularly strong on pioneers like Klee, Mondrian, Picasso, Chagall and Modigliani. Eventually it will be possible to see the whole collection in a controversial annex of 10 stories which will open in a few years' time.

Before you leave, you might like to visit the shop and the Museum Café which has an outdoor terrace, frequented by a chic crowd, with several shaven heads wearing expensive black clothes and strange jewelry. Notice the way that the large bronze circles which are inlaid into the museum floor continue onto the sidewalk between 88th and 89th Streets; and the green lichen which has grown onto the concrete walls outside, making the building more literally organic than Wright intended.

Next, walk to the **National Academy of Design** *on the corner of the block next door to the Guggenheim between 89th and 90th Streets, at 1083 5th Avenue (open Tues 12–8; Wed–Sun 12–5; free Tues 5–8).*

Founded in 1825 by Samuel Morse, the painter and inventor of the telegraph, and Ithiel Town, who did the houses on Washington Square, the Academy has traditionally been a rather staid affair. But nowadays it has a knack of putting on extremely imaginative exhibitions, and could well be worth a quick investigation. A recent show of Fantasy Furniture featured a Siège d'Amour, a sleigh contraption used by Edward VII for visiting Le Chabanais, Mme Kelly's infamous Paris bordello.

On the corner of 90th Street on the same block is a beguiling Gothic Art-Deco chapel, the **Church of the Heavenly Rest**. *It is by Hardie Philip, part of the same firm of architects who did the Temple Emanu-El, which we visit later on. It has a sleek medieval portal with streamlined Art-Deco angels, and inside it is candlelit, with a lovely limestone reredos high on the wall and English stained glass. People always seem to be getting married here.*

Directly opposite the church on the lefthand side of 5th Avenue is the entrance to the **Reservoir** *in Central Park.*

It is worth going up the steps to get a look at a billion gallons of stagnant green water, diverted from the Catskills via the Delaware River. New Yorkers consume the equivalent of a whole reservoir every day, glugging down or, more likely, showering under roughly four times as much water per capita as Londoners. The reservoir is landscaped so adroitly into the park that it would look just like a lake if it weren't for the 10 ft fence that stops people from diving in. Anyway, from here you get a breath-taking view of the west and south sides of Central Park, flattened by a strange distortion of perspective. If you are clever, you will be able to pinpoint the twin towers of the Eldorado, the San Remo, the Beresford and the Majestic on the toothy Central Park West mountain range. Circuiting the reservoir is a running track where countless joggers puff their lungs out, emulating Dustin Hoffmann who ran here in *Marathon Man*.

> *Go back to 5th Avenue and 90th Street. Before they divorced, Sinclair Lewis, the novelist, and Dorothy Thompson, the* New York Herald Tribune's *'intellectual Valkyrie' and foreign correspondent, lived just down the road at 21 East 90th Street. They had a sitting room each so they could entertain their friends separately—on an 8 ft sofa in Dorothy Thompson's case.*
>
> *A block to the north, on the south corner of 91st Street, is the* **Cooper-Hewitt Museum**, *New York's equivalent of the Victoria and Albert in London (open Tues 10–9; Wed–Sat 10–5; Sun 12–5; adm free Tues 5–9).*

The collection is housed in one of the Upper East Side's most splendid châteaux, built in 1901 for steel tycoon Andrew Carnegie, who asked for 'the most modest, plainest and most roomy house in New York City'. Room he did have, because at that time 91st Street was more an idea than a reality, and the only residences on the invisible grid were squatters' hovels. Although Babb, Cook & Willard were more used to designing industrial buildings, they provided him with a 64-room Georgian mansion of imperial magnificence.

Carnegie got married at 51, having promised his redoubtable mother that he would never tie the knot while she lived. His widow, Louise, lived here until her death in 1946, when the mansion was handed on to the Smithsonian who used it for the decorative arts collection amassed by the granddaughters of Peter Cooper, the founder of New York's Cooper Union science and architecture school. Inspired by their visit to the V&A in 1897, the Hewitt granddaughters collected an amazing panoply of artefacts, ranging from textiles, architectural drawings and, bizarrely, pornography, to wallpaper, locks and keys and jewelry—wobbling diamond sprays on springs, chains of woven hair, and earrings made out of hummingbirds.

Instead of a permanent display, the Cooper-Hewitt has revolving exhibitions, which are nearly always fascinating, as well as free summer concerts of jazz and classical music on Tuesday evenings in the garden, and one of the best shops on Museum Mile, selling hand-carved Noah's arks, tin wind-up toys and a superb selection of children's books. An additional bonus is the chance to see the innards of Carnegie's palace, which are still in good nick.

The real gem is the Victorian glass conservatory on the ground floor, with its lovely Tiffany windows and mosaic walls, and a small jungle of plants. The Music Room, with its ceiling mouldings of bagpipes, and the Library, panelled in Scottish oak, reflect Carnegie's passion for his native Scotland, where he owned a castle for summer holidays and was woken by a bagpipe *reveille* every morning.

Carnegie was 5 ft 2 in tall and fat, so the doors in his library and office are correspondingly short and wide. In 1900 he published his *Gospel of Wealth*, which announced that 'the man who dies rich, dies disgraced', and the 19 years he spent in the Carnegie mansion were mostly devoted to his distinctly idiosyncratic style of philanthropy. As well as founding 2000 libraries, he set up an Endowment for International Peace, and a Hero's Fund which rewarded courageous souls, who rescued people from accidents with medals and cash. Carnegie was most famous, however, for buying and closing down a bar near Carnegie Hall where the men who were building his concert hall kept getting drunk.

After the Cooper-Hewitt, you will probably be hungry. If it's nice weather, you might like to buy a gourmet picnic from one of the innumerable delicatessens for epicureans on Madison Avenue. Closest to the Cooper-Hewitt is Canard & Co, at 1272 Madison Avenue and 92nd Street. You may get distracted, since this stretch of the avenue has an orgy of chic shops, with hideously expensive boutiques, like Commes des Garçons, competing with swish antique and jewellery shops, managed by such upper-crust Upper East Siders as Zsa Zsa Gabor's legendary mother, Jolie Gabor.

Absolutely the best place to eat your picnic is the **Conservatory Garden**, *a formal garden in Central Park, just off 5th Avenue on 105th Street. (Take the* **M1**, **2**, **3**, *or* **4** *bus up Madison Avenue if you're worn out).*

On the way up Madison Avenue to 105th Street, you pass three Upper East Side curiosities. First, an exquisite Palladian palace, on 93rd Street between Madison and Park Avenues, built in the depths of the Depression for the stockbroker and cinema moghul, William Loew. Second, the façade of a castle on Madison Avenue between 94th and 95th Streets, which was built as an armory for Squadron A of the National Guard, and is now a high school playground. Lastly, if you turn left at 97th Street and walk back to 5th Avenue, you will see the five onion-domes and red, yellow and blue majolica tiles of the Russian Orthodox **Cathedral of St Nicholas** at 15 East 97th Street.

*The entrance to the **Conservatory Garden** is a 10-minute walk away at 105th Street, seven blocks up 5th Avenue on the lefthand side.*

The secret garden is prettiest in the spring, when maniacal gardeners have a field day with 20,000 tulips, rows of miniature and giant daffodils, and a great froth of quince and crabapple blossom, white on one side of the path, and pink on the other. After lunch, you could look in at the most recherché library in the city, a collection of 4000 cookery books including a rare manuscript on roast boar in the **New York Academy of Medicine** at 2 East 103rd Street (open Mon 12.30–5; Tues–Fri 9–5).

*The **M1**, **2**, **3**, and **4** buses all go down 5th Avenue, and after lunch you can catch any one of them to 65th Street and the Temple Emanu-El. (See p. 210.) The buses run very frequently and the trip won't take more than 15 minutes.*

*Anyone who likes industrial architecture, meanwhile, can make a special pilgrimage, which takes about an hour, to New York's apotheosis of exposed concrete, the **Municipal Asphalt Plant** near Carl Schurz Park and Gracie Mansion. The park and promenade are very pleasant too. Get off the **M1**, **2**, **3**, or **4** at 86th Street and transfer to the **M86** at 86th Street which drops you a block away from the park at 86th Street and York Avenue.*

From York Avenue walk a block further east to Carl Schurz Park at the end of 86th Street.

In the middle of the park, standing on the site of a Dutch house razed by the British in 1776, is **Gracie Mansion**. The country house has been used by the city's mayors ever since Fiorello LaGuardia moved in, in 1932. If you peep through a thick knot of leaves and fence, you can see a copybook example of Federal architecture: clapboarded walls, shuttered sash windows and an elegant verandah all dating from 1799.

Walk down to the esplanade by the river, and then north for about 5

*minutes to the end of the promenade, which is parallel with East
90th Street. From here you can't possibly miss the silver letters on the
supremely elegant concrete parabola of the **Municipal Asphalt
Plant**, across the road on York Avenue.*

The plant was built in 1944 by Kahn & Jacobs (who did the American
Airlines building at JFK), under the heady influence of Corbusier and
the dictum that form should follow function. Squeezed within the
minimum geometric space possible, a parabola, it used to contain machinery for making city-street asphalt, which is mixed with glass so it
sparkles; now it is being converted to a sports complex.

The end of the promenade is unnaturally peaceful; it is a popular spot
for city fishermen, and if you are lucky you may see one of them hoisting a
sludge-colored fish from the East River. From here anyway you get a
splendid view to the north of the treacherous, sloshing waters of **Hell
Gate**, which Washington Irving claimed, in his *Knickerbocker's History of
New York*, contained a vortex of spectres and hobgoblins. Spanning it are
two bridges, Hell Gate Bridge, with its bowstring trusses, and the
Triborough, which connects Manhattan, Queens and the Bronx. You
also see Wards Island and Randalls Island, which are connected by
landfill, and contain the city's psychiatric hospitals; as well as a soccer
stadium, and a firemen's training centre where firemen set on fire and
extinguish a model Manhattan during training exercises.

Stroll back down the esplanade as far as 79th Street.

The brainchild of Robert Moses (who abhorred the Municipal Asphalt
Plant), the walkway was built on top of the FDR highway in 1938. At 84th
Street it turns into **John H. Finley Walk**, named after an editor of the
New York Times who apparently enjoyed hiking the 32 miles around
Manhattan.

> *At 79th Street take the **M79** back to 5th Avenue, unless you want to
> go for a swim in the outdoor pool in John Jay Park between 77th and
> 78th Streets.*
> *Back on 5th Avenue and 65th Street, is **Temple Emanu-El**,
> New York's oldest and largest Reformed synagogue. (Open Sun–
> Thurs 10–5; Fri 10–4; Sat 12–5; organ recital Fri at 5).*

The temple was built in 1929, replacing Mrs Astor's twin-towered
château designed by Richard Morris Hunt in 1898 and equipped with an
immense marble bath weighing two tons.

While the limestone 5th Avenue front of Temple Emanu-El is austere and Romanesque, the interior is probably more magnificent than Mrs Astor's fabled ballroom. The hall is 7 ft wide, 150 ft long and 103 ft tall, with seating for 2000, although it is so Byzantinely dark inside that practically the only thing you can see is the huge rose window. Once your eyes get adjusted, you can make out the gleaming gold-and-blue sanctuary mosaics by Hildreth Meiere, and the handsome bronze grille of the Ark. If you come in the autumn, during Sukkoth, you will see a wonderful four-poster-bed affair of fruit, leaves and cornucopias, constructed in the sanctuary to celebrate the harvest.

After the Temple Emanu-El, you can make a little detour to the **Seventh Regiment Armory**, *a short walk away, two blocks to the east of the synagogue, on Park Avenue between 66th and 67th Streets. Every January the Armory has its annual antiques fair in the vast steel-skeletoned drill hall on Lexington Avenue. The building itself is worth a look, not just for the curious sight of a red-brick Victorian fortress sitting equably on Park Avenue, but also for its interior, which was designed with High-Victorian exuberence by Louis Tiffany in 1880, with stained glass, immense 7 ft tile fireplaces and axe-head light fittings.*

Go back to the Temple Emanu-El and walk a block down 5th Avenue to 64th Street. On the righthand side in Central Park is the city's old Arsenal, throttled by ivy, with an eagle and its cache of cannon balls over the doorway. The building dates from 1848, before the park was landscaped, and is now the headquarters of the Parks Department. Exactly behind it is the entrance to **Central Park Zoo**. *(Open April–Oct, Mon–Fri 10–5; Sat–Sun 10–5.30; Tues 10–8, and Nov–March Mon–Sun 10–4.30, adm $1).*

Zoos are generally depressing, and for years Central Park Zoo was only really popular with people who came to throw themselves to the polar bears. In 1988, however, it was completely refurbished by Kevin Roche, and $35 million was spent on the project, provoking an outcry amongst those who believed the money should have been spent otherwise.

The new zoo is wonderfully cheerful; there is hardly a cage in sight, and nearly all the 450 or so animals are the right size for its small scale. In the centre, an artificial Californian rocky outcrop is home to barking sea-lions, who obviously relish an audience. The rest of the zoo is divided into three regions, the Polar Circle, the Temperate Territory

211

and the Tropic Zone. The Polar Circle is the most innovative, with enormous glass walls so you can watch the polar bears and two flocks of gentoo and chinstrap penguins skimming underwater, less than an inch away from your nose. In the Tropic Zone, you walk along catwalks through a steamy fibreglass rainforest of poison-arrow frogs and Indian fruit bats. Special heating pads have apparently been installed under the beach to keep the crocs and piranhas in good humor.

> *From the zoo, walk down 5th Avenue to East 60th Street, past the Strand Bookshop's second-hand kiosk on the Central Park side of the road.*
>
> *This stretch of the Gold Coast is New York's equivalent of Pall Mall and on the way to 60th Street you brush past a clutch of gentlemen's clubs and one for ladies, the Colony. Facing each other at 1 and 4 East 60th Street are two of the most famous, the **Metropolitan** and the **Harmonie Club**, housed in Florentine palazzi.*

The Metropolitan was formed in 1880, when the Wall Street kingpins, J. P. Morgan and Commodore Vanderbilt, broke away from the Union Club, and formed their own *Millionaire's Club* where they could exercise complete control over the membership. Despite the demure façades, the baroque interiors of the clubs are apparently extremely lavish. They are both by Stanford White, the most flamboyant member of McKim, Mead & White, who died in such dramatic style (see p. 79) that he doomed his colleagues to relative obscurity.

A very different kettle of fish, just down the road, at 10 East 60th Street, is the **Copacabana Club**, which has been immortalized in Barry Manilow's song *Lola*. The club is less glamorous than in its heyday in the 1950s, when Ella Fitzgerald and Nat King Cole sang there. Now a disco, the place comes to life on the first Thursday of each month, when body-builders and drag queens with basketball nets hanging from their cleavages are hired to dance on podiums on the dance floor.

> *Go back to 5th Avenue. To the right, the square off 5th Avenue between 58th and 60th Streets is known as **Grand Army Plaza**. In the middle is the **Pulitzer Fountain** which was paid for with $50,000 from the will of newspaper proprietor, Joseph Pulitzer, a reclusive Upper East Sider who was buried with a copy of the New York World tucked under his arm.*
>
> *Walk down 5th Avenue to 59th Street. On the left is the fantastically expensive toy shop, **F. A. O. Schwarz**, housed on the bottom*

*floor of the 50 white-marble stories of the General Motors Building,
at 767 5th Avenue, between 58th and 59th Streets.*

Children are seldom seen in F. A. O. Schwartz; they are constantly
heard, singing the shop's unbearably syrupy anthem, *Welcome to our
World of Toys.* The shop is always full of grown-ups captivated, for the
most part, by the prominently displayed price tags on all the toys—
especially a scaled-down Ferrari which cruises at 30 mph and costs
$12,500.

*Now cross 5th Avenue to the **Plaza**, a French hotel of white glazed
bricks on the west side of 5th, between 58th and 59th Streets.*

This really is one of the most charming buildings in the city, elegant and
festive at the same time; the alter ego of the sinister Dakota apartments
on the Upper West Side, which were also designed by Henry Hardenburgh, but two decades previously in 1887.

Do pop inside, just to look at the enormous bunches of lillies and roses
in the lobby and the **Palm Court**, where you can have tea—if you can
stand it, for what with the Chopin and cucumber sandwiches, the place
has all the potential horror of a headmistresses' party. The Plaza's almost
funereal **Oak Bar**, on the other hand, is a nice place for a drink, and has
been unaltered since Zelda and F. Scott Fitzgerald drank there in the
1920s. The rest of the hotel has undergone endless renovations. Most
recently the 800 or so bedrooms have been refurbished in mawkish pinks
and blues with baroque swags on the curtains, by Ivana Trump, the
sometime-wife of Donald, who currently owns the hotel.

*As you leave the Plaza, look up at the fantastical gothic spikes and
finials on top of the Sherry-Netherland Hotel, which was built in
1929 almost exactly opposite, on the corner of 5th Avenue and 59th
Street.*

*Make your way down 5th Avenue to 57th Street. This two-block
stretch has some of the avenue's most shockingly expensive shops.*

On the right, between 57th and 58th Street is **Bergdorf Goodman**,
with its agonizingly elegant and expensive clothes for women. A block
south again, between 56th and 57th Streets, at 727 5th Avenue, on the
other side of the street, is **Tiffany & Co.**. Here, as Holly Golightly said
in *Breakfast at Tiffany's*, 'Nothing bad can ever happen to you . . .'

When you leave Tiffany's, stand on the corner of 5th Avenue and

57th Street, look west down 5th Avenue, and up. *The water tower on the building to the west of the glass ski-slope style skyscraper at 9 West 57th Street is the most endearing in the city. It is decorated with a portrait of Napolean III gazing out of a giant replica of the Imperial Cross of the Legion d'Honneur. The medal was given to the Chickering Piano Company, who proudly emblazoned it on the top of their showroom in the Ampico Building when it was built in 1923. Although Chickering pianos are still made, the bottom of the building on 29 West 57th Street is now home to the* haute couture *bookshop,* **Rizzoli's**, *which has foreign magazines, and excellent calendars, as well as books.*

The walk ends with the most catastrophically ugly building in the whole world, **Trump Tower**, *next door to Tiffany's at 725 5th Avenue.*

The shopping atrium inside is a really hideous combination of cascading waterfalls, red ashtray-marble, gleaming bronze, moving staircases and piped music. Incarcerated somewhere in this shrine of tack are Donald Trump, the owner, Johnny Carson and Stephen Spielberg, who live in three of the tower's 263 condominiums.

It is only natural to feel violent urges in such surroundings, and anyone who does would do well to recall the arrest of Salvador Dali in a pool of water, blood and broken glass on the same spot in 1939. Dali had been invited to dress a window for Bonwit Teller, the expensive clothes store, which moved round the corner when the shop was demolished for the construction of Trump Tower in 1983. Of course Dali obliged, producing a grisly tableau of aged mannequins bathing in an astrakhan bath and sleeping on charred sheets stained with trickling pigeon's blood. Bonwit Teller were appalled and began dismantling the display, so incensing the Surrealist that he got into the window and overturned the bath, which slid across the floor, and smashed into the window and out onto the sidewalk, taking Dali in its wake. The performance won him more glory, Dali said afterwards, than if he had devoured the whole of 5th Avenue.

Walk VII

The Civic Center, Chinatown and SoHo

Woolworth Building—City Hall—Foley Square Courthouses and Night Courts—First Shearith Cemetery—Chatham Square—Mott Street—Bowery—Little Italy—Canal Street Casbah—Greene Street—Broadway—Bayard-Condict Building—West Broadway

Getting from the Civic Center to Chinatown and SoHo takes less than 15 minutes, and yet the neighborhoods are so radically unalike that walking from one to the other is like crossing the frontier between two countries.

We start with a brisk tour through the Civic Center, a gruff place visitors sometimes omit, not realizing that its courts and municipal monoliths contain some of the most fascinating spectacles in the city. There is also the Clocktower Gallery, from where you get an eagle's-eye view of sprawling Chinatown. Chinatown itself is practically next door, and you can eat your way through it. The stalls of king prawns and cree; apothecaries of hairy seaweed; litter-strewn, jam-packed betting parlors; gaudy red-and-gold temples and, above all, the astonishing crush of people, all but blot out the buildings from view.

After lunch, the walk finishes in SoHo, (the rectangle *South* of *Hous*ton Street), where apart from the glamor of its galleries, shops, cafés, and the most dauntingly dressed people in New York, there is the excitement

W. Houston

Prince St.

FINISH

N R

Broadway

6

18

Watts St.

Broome St.

1 19

West Broadway

Wooster St.

Greene St.

Mercer St.

Grand St.

15

LITTLE ITALY

17

Mulberry St.

Hester St.

Bowery

TriBeCa

Varick St.

Canal St.

16

Lafayette St.

Centre St.

11

Bayard St.

Broadway

10

Mott St.

Pell St.

Elizabeth St.

Chatham
Square

Division St.

East Broadway

Manhattan Bridge

Worth St.

9

14

Henry St.

8

FOLEY
SQUARE

7

2
14

12

Madison St.

13

Catherine St.

St. James' Place

START

5

6

6

CITY HALL
PARK

4

NR

Park Place

23 3

Barclay
St.

Brooklyn Bridge

1 Cupping Room	11 The Tombs
2 Little Szechuan	12 Spanish and Portuguese Cemetery
3 Woolworth Building	13 St. James' Church
4 City Hall	14 Buddhist Temple
5 Tweed Court House	15 Bowery Savings Bank
6 Municipal Building	16 Approach to Manhattan Bridge
7 U.S. Courthouse	17 Canal Street Casbah
8 County Courthouse	18 Haughwout Building
9 New York State Office Building	19 Museum of Colored Glass
10 Clocktower Gallery	

0 m   250 m

THE CIVIC CENTER, CHINATOWN and SoHo

backdrop of cast-iron industrial palazzi—the greatest concentration of such buildings anywhere in the world. The façades are iron disguised as stone, and so are the sidewalks, and you clank on them as you walk. Some buildings, however, are stone, and sometimes even experts can only tell the difference with a magnet.

Come on a weekday, when the Civic Center's rackety bureaucratic machine is in full swing, Chinatown is less cramped than on the weekend, when the Chinese who live in satellite communities in Brooklyn and Queens flood in to do the next week's shop.

Start: by subway take the **N** or **R**, or the **2** or **3** train to Park Place and Broadway, or the **6** to Brooklyn Bridge–City Hall. (On the 6, if you get in the last carriage and stay on the train at the end of the line at Brooklyn Bridge, you see the astonishing Victorian tiles and mosaics of an architectural Miss Haversham—the abandoned City Hall subway station—as the train loops around to go north.) By bus, take the **M101**, **M102** or the **M6** to City Hall.
Walking Time: 4 hours.

LUNCH/CAFÉS
Civic Center:
Exterminator Chille, 305 Church St., south of Canal St. Industrial-strength exterminator chille, in a restaurant sporting knobbly walls of cacti, stetsons and chilli-shaped fairy lights.
Delphi Restaurant, 109 West Broadway, at Reade St. Delicious pitta sandwiches and shishkebab.
Chinatown and Little Italy
Little Szechuan, 31 Oliver St. Tiny, but one of the best in Chinatown. Shredded beef with bean curd and diced scallions is especially good.
Petite Szechuan, 10 East Broadway, near Chatham Sq. Almost as good, although it is no relation. The noodle soup is an excellent cure for a hangover.
Lan Hong Kok Seafood House, 31 Division St., near Chatham Sq. Birds'-nest soup, and Maryland blue crabs sautéed with black beans and ginger, in spartan surroundings.
Nom Wah Tea Parlor, 13 Doyers St. Excellent *dim sum* brunch.
Kuan Sing Dumpling House, 9 Pell Street, near Chatham Sq. Dumplings from 10 to 10.
Wong Kee Steak House. 113 Mott St., near Hester St. Such a favorite,

there is often a queue to get in. Still, everything is served at breakneck speed.

Benito I, 174 Mulberry St., between Grand and Broome Sts. Cheap, unfancified pasta. Cash only.

SoHo:

The Cupping Room, 359 West Broadway at Broome St. 'Waffle orgy' menu plus jazz from Thursdays to Mondays.

Lupe's. 110 6th Ave., and Watts St. Especially good for Mexican brunch in an eccentric dining room.

Patisserie Lanciani, 177 Prince St., near Sullivan St. Stylish pastry shop, with 42 pastries, breakfast, lunch and tea.

New York is a Jekyll and Hyde city, and nowhere more blatantly than in these three neighborhoods. First, there is the **Civic Center**, where New Yorkers get married and divorced, pay parking fines and death duties, and where municipal workers do battle with mounds of paper. The buildings here range from the windowless AT&T skyscraper, which is downright sinister, to an unlikely City Hall—a gem-like Frenchified palace—and the sublime Woolworth Building, the King of Gothic sky-scrapers. At its heart is Foley Square's jumble of courthouses, where New Yorkers, who are fascinated by crime, drop in to listen to contro-versial cases during their lunch hours.

While the bureaucracy of the Civic Center is curiously antidiluvian, **Chinatown** is changing faster than anywhere else in Manhattan. Before 1965, when immigration quotas were still limited by exclusion acts passed in the 1880s, it was the size of a handkerchief. Since then, it has enveloped Little Italy and continues to grow by leaps and bounds. There could be a million Chinese in New York City by the year 2000, and Manhattan's Chinatown may have stretched as far north as Houston Street.

Today it is home to 100,000 people and, to them, and especially to the 50,000 who have arrived in the last five years, America is a land of opportunity: *Gam San*, the Mountain of Gold. Now the lease on Hong Kong is about to expire, financiers are siphoning more than $400 million into Chinatown.

And yet, while $37 million is being spent on the Mandarin Plaza, a Hong Kong-financed, 25-story luxury condominium on White Street, most residents are poverty stricken. Cutters and seamstresses working long hours in factories and sweatshops earn wages on a par with the Third World. And their isolation from the rest of the city is not just economical, but political and cultural; although the labor unions are strong, many are wary of the polls, not least because 55 per cent don't speak English.

SoHo, like Chinatown, went through a massive upheaval in the sixties. Most of the millinery, textile and other light industries abandoned it for the suburbs, and there were so many fires in the warehouses that still operated, it was dubbed 'Hell's Hundred Acres'. In the end, New York's omnipotent Parks Commissioner, Robert Moses, designated the district the 'wastelands of New York City' and attempted to raze it to the ground to make way for the Lower Manhattan Expressway.

At the same time, artists drifted in, attracted by cheap rents and light-filled lofts. The artists illegally renovated the lofts into living quarters and studios, then banded together with conservationists and lobbied for landmark status. New Yorkers suddenly had their eyes opened to the beauty of cast-iron, and, phoenix-like, fashionable SoHo was born.

After the artists came the galleries, launching the careers of Julian Schnabel, Rauschenberg and Jasper Johns. As always, in the rear of the avant garde came gentrification: real estate rocketed; SoHo became chic, and the artists fled for places like New Jersey or Brooklyn. Some went to TriBeCa, the *Tri*angle of industrial warehouses *Be*low *Ca*nal Street, which real estate brokers tried to create as an appendage to SoHo, but which never quite took off in the same way.

Now SoHo has come full circle, back to the pre-industrial years of the early 19th century when it was a fashionable district of hotels and brothels. The only difference today is that it looks industrial. Shabbiness is somehow integral to the glamor: advertisements for yarn and cardboard boxes are left to flake off the walls, iron rusts, paint peels off façades, and the garbage that inspired artists in the sixties to make works of art out of ephemera still piles up in mountains on the sidewalk.

> *The **4**, **5** and **6** take you to the east side of City Hall Park, and the **2**, **3**, **N**, and **R** to the west side. Which ever side you start on, make your way to Broadway (on the east side) and then walk up towards Chambers Street, at the north end of the park.*
>
> *At 270 Broadway, just south of Chambers, is **Ellen's Luncheonette**, where a little discreet eavesdropping over breakfast gives you an insight into the preoccupations of the archetypal Civic Center civil servant.*

Ellen Hart Storm was Miss Subways 1959, and her diner is plastered with photographs of Miss Subways past and present. Look out for the demure Rosemary Wilson, of 1963: 'Ultimate ambition: Happy marriage and home in California: Recently mastered the art of making Argyll socks for a favorite beau'.

After breakfast walk three blocks south down Broadway and straight through the revolving doors of the Gothic **Woolworth Building**, *between Park Place and Barclay Street at 233 Broadway.*

The interior is one of New York's most spectacular surprises—an astonishing Ravenna mosaic, glinting greens, blues and golds like a grotto, although in fact it is no more than a lobby, complete with mail chutes, barbers and Harry's Diner.

Under the cornices are gargoyles; caricatures of the men involved in the construction. One shows the architect Cass Gilbert, clutching a model of the building, and another shows Frank Winfield Woolworth paying for his scraper with a saucer-sized nickel bearing Gilbert's profile. (He actually coughed up $13.5 million in cash.) Woolworth himself began as a salesmen on $8 a week and ended his life in 'Winfield,' a 62-room mansion in Long Island, with a dining-room ceiling coated in 14-carat gold, and a suite of bedrooms where his wife used Marie Antoinette's dressing table and he slept in Napoleon's bed.

Built as headquarters for Woolworth's 2000 five and dime stores, the skyscraper was a suitably imperial enterprise. Gilbert was a master plagiarist of historical styles, but he also used the most sophisticated steel-framing techniques available for its construction. When completed, the skyscraper was briefly the tallest in the world. At the opening ceremony in 1913, Wilson pressed a button in the White House and, to the strains of the 'Star Spangled Banner', it was illuminated by 80,000 lights. Later the charismatic American radio preacher the Rev. Parkes Cadman, dubbed it the 'Cathedral of Commerce', and the nickname has stuck.

The scraper really does soar, an effect Gilbert achieved by letting the tower rise sheer off Broadway for the whole of its 792 ft. From the 27th story upwards, the panels under the lacework façade change to a dark green bronze, making it all seem taller and more soaring than it is. Gilbert described the flamboyant Gothic tracery as 'tongues of flame', and either side of the Broadway entrance he put two salamanders, symbolizing the transmutation of clay into terracotta and iron into steel, since alchemists believed salamanders withstood fire. They are coiled up beneath two empty niches, originally meant for statues of Woolworth, and possibly Napoleon.

For years the Woolworth Building had an observation deck on the 58th floor with 'the most wondrous view in all the world'. Now it is closed, but anyone who feels so inclined can sneak a view.

Take the elevator to the 47th floor. This part of the building is colonized by lawyers' offices with names resembling Latin conjugations. Cross the lobby and take another elevator to the 54th floor, where there is one solitary lawyer's office and a spiral staircase. At the top of this is a set of miniature wooden steps leading to a window surrounded by gargoyles of frogs, bats and pelicans, from where you get a superb view up Broadway.

After you have seen the Woolworth, cross Broadway to **City Hall Park**.

Originally cow pasture, the park dates from 1730 and is best in the spring when it turns into a pink cloud of magnolia. In 1817 it was used for Vanderlyn's Rotunda, a miniature replica of the Pantheon in Rome. Inside was a superior 19th-century version of 'Son et Lumières', where visitors could see painted panoramas of places like Versailles and the Grand Canyon, with realistic sound effects of winds, storms and avalanches.

Plumb in the middle is **City Hall**, *one of Manhattan's exceptionally elegant buildings. (Open Mon–Fri 10–3, adm free).*

When it was completed in 1812, City Hall stood at the city's northernmost edge, and the idea of New York expanding beyond this frontier was so preposterous that the City Fathers saved $15,000 by facing the back in brownstone. The design was by Joseph Mangin, a Frenchman, and John McComb, a Scotsman—and the two nationalities are both reflected in the slightly fey mixture of French Renaissance and Georgian Colonial styles.

Inside, the central hall is really exquisite. The 'look no hands' marble staircase, which has no visible supports, and the coffered dome overhead have the lightness of McComb's mentor, Robert Adams.

The Mayor's office is on the ground floor. At the top of the stairs is the **Governor's Room** where you can see John Trumbull's portraits, contemporary with the building, of Washington on Evacuation Day in 1783, and Stuyvesant, New York's Dutch governor, looking uncharacteristically rakish.

Also on the 2nd floor is a chamber used until recently by the **Board of Estimate**, a committee of the Mayor and the borough presidents, and the real fiscal power in city until it was abolished in 1989. Across the landing is the **City Council Chamber**, a hefty 1898 addition. Both bodies are being restructured so the system of voting between the boroughs is more fair.

> *Directly behind City Hall is the **Tweed Courthouse**, a dingy, blackened pile that makes City Hall look positively virginal.*

In 1858, the city agreed to spend $250,000 on a new criminal courthouse; in 1871 this building was finished at an outrageous cost of between $12 and $13 million. At the bottom of the heist was New York's grafter *par excellence*, William Marcy 'Boss' Tweed. Under his direction enough carpet was purchased to cover City Hall Park three times; a carpenter got $360,747 for a month's work, and the 'Prince of Plasterers' earned $3 million. Which was nothing compared to the total of $160 million pocketed by Tweed and his crew during their reign. They met their nemesis in the year the courthouse was completed, after their book-keeper was killed in a sleighing accident and documents were leaked to the press. The 'Boss' was tried in his own courthouse, and although he was never convicted, died in his own prison on Ludlow Street. Ironically, the courthouse itself is actually quite handsome: inside is a truly grand rotunda modelled on the Reform Club in London.

> *Walk round to the front of the courthouse on Chambers Street. To the left, on the other side of the street, is a modest seven-story palazzo dating from 1846.*

'Stewart's Folly' was America's first department store, the brainchild of Alexander Stewart who guessed that the gentility preferred fixed prices to haggling. When Mary Lincoln and Julia Grant came to shop here, the sceptics were silenced, and Stewart became the richest man in America. Eventually the *New York Sun* moved into the building, which explains the legend on the cheerful clock outside: 'The Sun It Shines For All'.

> *Now turn left and walk along Chambers Street to the next junction at Centre Street. Directly in front of you is the **Municipal Building**, whose wedding-cake tower, topped by a statue of 'Civic Virtue', acts as a lighthouse for the Civic Center, which lacks anything more central.*

The wedding cake is a replica of the Choragic Monument of Lysicrates in Athens, first reproduced in New York on top of St Paul's Church. By the end of the 19th century, it had become so vogueish that it mush-roomed all over the city as a disguise for water towers.

Stranger still, the tower has influenced Stalinist architecture. In the 1920s it was copied for Cleveland's Terminal Tower, then the tallest outside New York. This so impressed the Soviets that it, in turn, was copied for the Moscow University tower and then the 800 ft tall Palace of Culture in Warsaw.

Close to, you see that the Municipal Building is actually a latter-day Triumphal Arch. It was built in 1914 by McKim, Mead and Stanford White (who designed the arch in Washington Square). Inside, 648,000 sq ft housed the quantities of paperwork generated by the incorporation of the Bronx, Staten Island, Queens, and Brooklyn into New York City in 1898. New Yorkers come here to get married and pay their parking fines.

From the Municipal Building walk north two blocks up Centre Street to Foley Square and its nest of federal and municipal courthouses.

For years this area was notorious for its crime, slums and filth, and it was only in the last century that halls of justice rose out of the quagmire. In Dutch times the square lay under the Collect Pond, New Amsterdam's main source of fresh water. In the 18th century, however, tanners moved in and the water went putrid. New York lived off foul-tasting pond water, so polluted it spawned a series of epidemics. When the city started filling in the pond, New Yorkers obligingly pitched in, and by 1807 a 15 ft evil-smelling mountain of garbage had risen in the middle.

Foley Square is nowadays a grand euphemism for a maze of honking cars and lorries. On the right are two Corinthian temples, their steps beseiged by armies of cameras and journalists. Cass Gilbert's US Courthouse of 1936 is nearest, with a 32-story tower crowned by a golden pyramid. Next door is the County Courthouse dating from 1926.

You might think of going inside to watch a trial. American lawyers wear suits and chew gum, and some cases have been going on for so long that volumes of paper have to be trundled down the corridors on trolleys. Once inside, the doorman will probably advise you where to go. Imelda

Marcos and Leona Helmsley were recently tried in the US Courthouse, but the interior of the County Courthouse is more interesting architecturally. Inside is a mosque-like rotunda covered in Works Progress Administration (WPA) frescoes from 1939, somehow reminiscent of childrens' atlases. Along with the steps outside, it was used for shooting Sidney Lumet's brilliant film *Twelve Angry Men*.

> *Keep walking north on Centre Street as far as the* **New York State Office Building** *on the northeast corner.*

The charming Art-Deco shell houses New York's **Vehicle Registration and Sales Tax Offices**. Inside is a scene of Kafkaesque bureaucratic misery: dirty walls, dimmed lights and wheezing elevators. There are snaking queues, the air hangs thick and humid in spite of giant whirring fans, and a cheerful sign reminds you to 'Please put brain in gear before engaging mouth: strong language is the sign of a weak mind'.

> *From here, walk north one block up Centre Street, turn left and walk two blocks west to the* **Clocktower Gallery**, *between Lafayette Street and Broadway at 108 Leonard Street on the* 13th *floor.*

The avant garde gallery is housed in a Victorian pile remodelled in 1896 by McKim, Mead and White. Apart from looking round the exhibition, you can climb up a spiral staircase, past the 5000 lb clock, to the roof which is decorated with a parapet of crusty stone eagles, and has a tremendous view of downtown Manhattan.

> *Next, walk east along Leonard Street to Centre Street. On the right at 100 Centre Street, occupying the whole block between Leonard and White Streets, is New York's most gruesome building, the* **'Tombs'**, *its criminal courts and prison.*

Although it suits this mouldering iceberg, the macabre nickname actually refers to its grandfather, a replica of an Egyptian mausoleum built opposite in 1838. 'This dismal-fronted pile of bastard Egyptian', as Dickens called it, was sunk in a pit, and it was decorated with trapezoid-shaped windows and lotus columns. It was here that Melville's Bartleby the Scrivener stood with his face to the wall and said 'I prefer not to dine to-day', before he finally lay down on the floor with his knees huddled up against him.

In 1893 the Tombs was replaced by another prison, and in 1939 with the present building, built by Harvey Corbett, who was part of the consortium which built Rockefeller Center in the same year. Both are of white limestone, but the Tombs are terrifying. The inscription *'Only the Just Man Enjoys Peace of Mind'*, is engineered to make you feel guilty, and there is a sinister green low-tide mark round the base of the first two stories. Room 218, inside, is used for the horrid **Night Courts** (also open to the public). These go on round the clock to cope with the weight of arrests in the city, although most of the people who go up have been waiting for two days or more.

Continue east on Leonard Street for another block to Baxter Street, turn right, and walk a block south to Worth Street.

This intersection was once the most infamous in the city. Known as the Five Points, the slum was inhabited by freed slaves and desperately poor immigrants. By 1840 New York's first gangs began forming in the area. There were the 'Forty Thieves' and the 'Plug Uglies' who rallied together as the 'Dead Rabbits' and boasted 'Hell-Cat Maggie', a virago who filed her teeth to points and wore brass fingernails. In 1842 Dickens visited the Old Brewery, which stood nearby. 'All that is loathsome, drooping and decayed is here', he wrote of the 'leprous' lodging house for a thousand down-and-outs presided over by a 'buxom fat mulatto'. (Dickens' trip was a disaster: he was lambasted in the press for his 'cockney' looks and the 'rowdyism in his manner'. He longed to go home, and finally got his revenge in the first half of *Martin Chuzzlewit*, a savage satire on New York.)

Now walk two blocks east on Worth Street to St James' Place. The junction is part of Chatham Square, a disingenuous name for a harum-scarum collision of 10 streets at Chinatown's southern frontier. Make a sharp right down St James' Place. Marooned on an island on the east side of the road at 55 St James' Place, is the **First Cemetery of the Spanish and Portuguese Synagogue.** *Dating from 1682, it is one of three burial grounds belonging to New York's first Jewish congregation, Shearith Israel, or 'Remnant of Israel'.*

Raised at man's height above the street, the cemetery is hard to see and harder to get into. If you chat to Ignatio, the gardener, he will probably let you in, or you can phone ahead (tel 873 0300). Inside, the stones are bleached and worn like old bones and the inscriptions are in Hebrew,

Ladino (a mix of Spanish and Hebrew), and English. The earliest graves are raised on stone stilts, like sarcophagi, since the original settlers came to New York via the West Indies, where the water table is high and burials are above ground. The sole decoration is an ominous angel of destruction, who holds a flaming sword over the city while an axe appearing from a cloud above hacks down the tree of life.

> *Walk a little way south and turn left down James Street, a tiny alley linking St James' Place to Madison Street. On the left is* **St James**, *a pretty Greek Revival church built in 1827 for a staunchly Irish Roman Catholic congregation. New York's Nicely Nicely Johnson governor, the paunchy, cigar-puffing Al Smith, was an altar-boy, who grew up in considerable poverty round the corner on Oliver Street.*
>
> *Turn left onto Madison Street, and then immediately left again onto Oliver Street. At the top of the street is the* **Mariner's Temple***, St James' doppelganger, built 18 years later. Turn right onto* **Henry Street***, noisy with caged birds chattering on window sills and balconies, and then left again onto* **Catherine Street***.*

Catherine Street is Chinatown's meat and fish high street. It is lined as far as the East River with stalls selling shark's fin, fresh squid, flounders, and tanks full of monstrous carp and turtles. The fish are delivered to the tanks through a vacuum pipe, although occasionally it comes loose and all the carps slither back to the East River at the end of the street.

> *Now walk a block west on Catherine Street to East Broadway and turn left. A block to the south is Chatham Square, and just before it, at 9 East Broadway, on the 2nd floor, a* **Buddhist temple** *dedicated to Wong Tai Sin.*

Inside are nuns, ottomans and the altar, a colorful affair of flashing fairy lights, bottles of Mazola oil, prayer-papers and ripe fruit. The hairy wig in the middle is part of an image of Wong Tai Sin, who stands, broom in hand, ready to sweep things new. To the right is an oven for burning up petitions and to the left booths for telling fortunes. The questioner shakes a batch of a hundred sticks until one falls out. The number on the stick is matched with one of the messages hanging from a row of hooks on the wall and taken off to the booth for interpretation.

The northern end of East Broadway has a mass of Chinese grocers and **medicine shops**. The one at 150 East Broadway has an antiquated system of drawers stuffed with herbs and sliced antelope horn, ginseng and sea horses. Customers stick out their tongue, the assistant makes an on-the-spot diagnosis, and a concoction is weighed on a pair of scales and wrapped in a beautiful tissue-paper parcel.

Walk to the southern end of East Broadway and make a sharp right turn onto **Chatham Square***. A block north, on the lefthand side, is Doyers Street, opposite an exotic branch of the* **Manhattan Savings Bank** *decked out as a mock-Chinese temple in a sickly orange. It stands on the site of the old studio belonging to Rocks Grillo, a thirties artist who made his living out of literal* trompe l'oeils, *which he painted over the black eyes of victims of fights on the Bowery.*

The **Doyers Street** *side of Chatham Square is always particularly crushed, thanks to fruit and vegetable stalls, and an Off-Track Betting parlor, strewn with betting slips and permanently crowded. Have a look inside and then walk round the dog-leg bend of Doyers to Pell Street.*

For years Doyers Street was relished by the press as the city's pit of iniquity, chock-a-block with opium dens, criminals and henchmen. In the Tong Wars, it was a prime spot for assassinations, since killers could make speedy exits through a covered arcade to Mott Street. The corner of Pell and Doyers Streets, now the Yun Lucke Rice Shoppe, was the headquarters of the Hip Sing Tong, whose leader, Mock Duck, took on the On Leongs for control of the gambling and opium rackets. The bend of Doyers Street was dubbed 'Bloody Angle' after Mock Duck deflected a flying bullet from his silver dollar belt-buckle. Today, although Chinatown has the least violent crime in the city, drug trafficking via Hong Kong and local gangs like the Ghost Shadows are still rife.

In the 1930s, the street was the meeting place of the Chatham Club, where Irving Berlin, then Isadore Baline, worked as a singing waiter. Berlin returned years later, so the story goes, and settled down at the piano for a solitary rendition of *Oh, How I Hate to Get Up in the Morning*, while a guide ushered in a party of tourists. 'Fella, if Oiving Boilin could hear the way you're moiderin one of his greatest songs', the guide said, 'he'd toin over in his grave.'

Turn left onto **Pell Street***, almost entirely composed of neon signs for restaurants, and walk a block south to Mott Street. On the way you can pick up a curry patty, a lotus-seed moon cake, or a Coke*

flavored with lemon ginger, from the **May May Chinese Gourmet Bakery** *at 35 Pell Street.* **Mott Street**, *round the corner, is
Chinatown's spinal cord, an amorphous conglomeration of neon,
jostling bodies and souvenir shops.*

*Walk north as far as Bayard Street. Just to the right at 65 Bayard
Street is the* **Chinatown Ice Cream Factory**, *which sells green
tea and red bean-flavor ice cream in competition with Häagen-Dazs
across the street.*

On the next block of Mott Street, between Bayard and Canal Streets,
look out for the bedraggled **Golden Dragon neon sign**, which is
famous for lighting up on both sides at once. On the right, at 62 Mott
Street, is the Chinese Consolidated Benevolent Association, the oldest
of Chinatown's community associations for new and old immigrants.
Next door at 64 Mott Street is the **Eastern States Buddhist Temple of
America**, aimed rather specifically at tourists, with a barrel of fortune
cookies costing a dollar a piece, and a souvenir shop at the back more
than twice the size of the temple.

*Walk up Mott Street as far as Canal Street. On the corner is a
branch of* **Maria's**, *a Mcdonald's-style chain of bakeries which
Westernizes Chinese cakes by decorating them with pink and blue
icing.*

*Round the corner, on the stretch of Canal Street between Mott and
Mulberry Streets, is a clutch of Chinese supermarkets, in particular*
Kam Man *and the* **Chinese-American Trading Com-
pany**.

These are mesmerizing. The stalls are arranged aesthetically, according
to color. On one side are the white and green root vegetables—bean
sprouts, white chestnuts and snow peas, and on the other, the gaudier
fruits. In the windows behind are laquered octopusses, squids, and
ducks, and inside, baskets of cree and slimy tripe which is eaten hot on
the street. Alongside the curiosities are specially imported English 'delicasies'—Smarties, Marmite and Horlicks.

*At this point Canal Street becomes an obstacle course of stalls, whose
owners pay higher rents per square foot than Tiffany's. Look out for*
'The Good Luck Newsstand', *which is red and gold (Chinese
lucky colors), and sells all of the ten Chinese dailies.*

Walk east up Canal Street as far as the Bowery. From here you can see the beaux-arts **Approach to the Manhattan Bridge**, *which is wonderfully inappropriate in relation to the more hum-drum buildings round about and the modest bridge behind it.*

Dating from 1912 it is by Carrère and Hastings, who designed the even grander New York Public Library on 42nd Street. They were inspired by the City Beautiful movement, a Utopian vision of neo-Classical cities with vistas, boulevards and pomp that took America by storm after the Chicago World's Fair of 1893. Here, their work is a cross between St Peter's Colonnade in Rome and a triumphal arch based on Porte St Denis in Paris. At the top is a frieze, inspired by the Parthenon, of Indians hunting buffalo on winged horses. It faces Chinatown's largest restaurant, the football-pitch sized **Silver Palace**, and another beaux-arts anomaly, the **Manhattan Savings Bank**, which is topped by a dome, with pineapples at each corner. Inside, however, you are back in China again: there are Chinese lamps and pictures, and a safe disguised as a temple.

Turn left onto the Bowery and walk two blocks north to Grand Street, past a stretch of jewelry shops and pawnbrokers left over from the 19th century when this was New York's Diamond District. On the corner of Grand Street at 130 Bowery you stumble on the Lower East Side's third City Beautiful remnant, the **Bowery Savings Bank** *designed in 1894 by the McKim, Mead & White trium-virate.*

The outside is magnificent enough: a pedimented Renaissance temple with viciously spiked lamps. If you are here during banking hours, however, have a quick look inside at one of the grandest interiors in the city. Set up specifically for Lower East Side immigrants, the bank stayed open in the evenings and on Saturdays.

Walk three blocks west down Grand Street as far as Mulberry Street and the banner welcoming you to **Little Italy**.

Between 1880 and 1924, Little Italy stretched from Five Points to Houston Street, as a stream of immigrants arrived escaping the terrible poverty of southern Italy and Sicily. By 1900 the population had swelled to 145,000, and Italian visitors found little to choose between the squalor here and their homeland. Today, Chinatown has spilled in, and Italian Little Italy has retreated to three blocks on Mulberry and Grand Streets. The place is now a tourist attraction, about as Italian as tinned ravioli, while New York's real Italian enclaves are Arthur Avenue in the Bronx and *Saturday Night Fever* land—Carroll Gardens and Bensonhurst in Brooklyn.

Still, along with the novelty shops there are some food havens, especially **Parisi**, a bakery selling semolina breads, and **Di Palo's** cheese shop, filled with footballs of homemade mozzarella. If you want a sandwich, the **Italian Food Center** at 186 Grand Street sells truck-drivers' heroes stuffed with hot veal, mozzarella balls and olives for less than $5. Otherwise you could sit down over a cappuccino and Italian pastries at the **Caffè Roma**, a block north from Grand and Mulberry Streets, at 385 Broome Street.

> *On the corner of Grand and Mulberry Streets, you can still get a bowl of seafood from* **Umberto's Clam House**, *where in 1972 Joey Gallo was rubbed out on his birthday by hitmen while he was eating* scungili *(a bowl of seafood) with his wife and daughter. Gallo was himself credited with the shooting of Albert Anastasia, the director of Murder Inc., in the Park Sheraton Hotel barber shop a few years previously. Turn left and walk south down Mulberry Street.*

A few doors away at 142 Mulberry Street, on the lefthand side of the street, is the **Glass Workshop**. Inside is an excellent gallery where in cold weather you can warm yourself unobtrusively in front of the furnaces and watch the glass-blowers at work.

> *Make another left turn onto Hester Street, and walk a block west to Mott Street. On the corner at 176 Hester Street is a Chinese shoeshop selling Reeboks—this is actually a front for* **Aquaworld**.

The distant gurgling sounds give it away. Behind the till is a door to an enormous back-room aquarium where you can buy bat, panther, and squirrel fish, elephant noses, gobies and albino frogs. Every Chinese New Year there is a rush on goldfish which are given to children as New Year's presents.

> *Retrace your steps to Mulberry Street, walk a block south and then turn right onto* **Canal Street**.

In 1799, New York was so smelly that travelers came armed with pomanders and nose-gays. Well-to-do residents hired slaves to deliver their 'nastinesses' to the river, and the city council employed two men who patrolled with a cart collecting rubbish. Finally, by 1805, there was such an accumulation of 'Street Dirt and Manure' that the street commissioner planned an open drain for raw sewage. A ditch was dug, and Canal Street was born.

The sewer has long since been covered, and today's Canal Street is not so whiffy. But lorries and trucks hurtle down it to the entrance of the Holland Tunnel at its west end, and some of the street vendors wear cloth yashmaks to protect themselves from the fumes.

Walk west down Canal Street as far as Greene Street. At this point Chinatown fades into SoHo, and the stretch of Canal Street between Broadway and Wooster Street is a kind of no-man's land; a fascinating one, filled with a 20th-century **casbah**.

The stalls sell tack, while the shops are mostly industrial, specializing in anything from disco balls to industrial fans and rubber. **Pearl Paint**, at 308, has the cheapest art supplies in Manhattan, and **Uncle Steve's** opposite has the cheapest hifi and computers. But the king of the casbah is **Canal Surplus**, at 363. This sells industrial junk: dentist's tool kits, jerking motors, (including the 'erotimotor'), cauterizers and compasses. It is always crammed with curious scavengers.

Now walk north up Greene Street into **SoHo** *which fills the self-contained four by five grid of streets above Canal Street and below Houston Street (pronounced 'Howston').*

West Broadway has the swishest galleries, while the smart clothes shops and restaurants are on Prince and Spring Streets. Mercer Street is more industrialized, like all of SoHo was before gentrification. Finally, there is Broadway: grimy, crowded and down-to-earth, a mixture of secondhand boutiques and wholesalers like **Al Kay's Buttons Buckles and Novelties**, which has every button that has been made since 1951. If your main interest is art, head straight off to the nearest gallery and pick up one of the 'Gallery Guides' which are published free every month.

Greene Street *is SoHo's Grand Canal of cast-iron. On the right, 28 Greene Street is the 'Queen of Greene Street', a tremendous Second Empire château.*

This part of Greene Street still has its original Belgian Block cobbles: chunks of granite able to withstand the wear of iron-rimmed carriage wheels. Most of the street dates from the 1870s and 80s when a rash of cast-iron hit SoHo. It was the cheapest building material on the market, and miraculously quick to assemble. Parts were pre-fabricated, numbered, and then assembled in the street, sometimes in less than a week. Often, if you peer closely, you can see where the decorations were simply bolted on.

The buildings are an eclectic mix of European styles, since clients chose designs from catalogues which ranged from French and Italian Renaissance, to Second Empire, and neo-Grecian. Typically, a cast-iron warehouse had a ground floor window display of fabrics and trimmings, and top floors used for goods, paperwork, and sometimes for sweatshops. Outside, you can still see the old loading platforms, waist-high off the ground so horses could back up into them.

> *Walk up Greene Street to the next junction with Grand Street. To the right on the south side at **91 and 93 Grand Street** are a couple of oddities. These two buildings are actually constructed out of common brick, but John Snook, one of SoHo's most prolific architects, disguised the façades with sheets of cast-iron tacked onto the front with prongs and grooved to resemble mortared blocks.*
>
> *Carry on to Broome Street. On the southwest corner is one of SoHo's most elegant buildings, the **Gunther Building** at 469 Broome Street.*

Designed by an Englishman, Griffith Thomas, in 1871, its lovely bay windows remind you of seaside hotels in a Victorian resort. This is the time to get out your pocket magnet, since the Gunther Building is one of SoHo's best stone simulations, partly thanks to a coat of off-white paint, which was often used in the 19th century. (Sometimes a textured look was achieved by mixing the paint with ground marble.) Today, it houses two galleries, **SoHo 20** and **Katzen Brown**, and if you pop inside you will see one of SoHo's typical pressed tin ceilings, which are still made in a factory on Houston Street.

> *On the opposite side of the street, at **472 Broome Street**, is an amusing basement-window display of motorized automatons by an artist called Steve Gerberich.*
>
> *Now walk east along Broome until you get to Broadway. As you pass Mercer Street, look north: in the distance you can see the spectral shapes of the Chrysler Building and the Citicorp skyscraper in Midtown. In the 1850s, when SoHo was still relatively un-indus-*

trialized, this section was famous for its brothels. The 1859 Directory to the Seraglios in New York by 'Free Loveyer' particularly recommended Madame Kant's House of the Germanic Order on Mercer Street.

On the northeast corner, at 488 Broadway, is the **Haughwout Building***, SoHo's oldest surviving cast-iron palazzo.*

Dating from 1857 it is based on the Sansovino Library in Venice, although in many ways it anticipates the skyscraper to a greater extent than the more whimsical cast-iron buildings that followed. Two factors made skyscrapers feasible: cast-iron frames to support their weight, and elevators. The Haughwout had both, and a third: rhythm; produced by a single element repeated over and over again, in this case thick and thin Corinthian columns. It was the first equipped with Elisha Otis' safety elevator. In a dramatic demonstration at the 1852 World's Fair, Otis was presented with a red velvet cushion and a silver dagger which he used to slash the cable, a demonstration worthy of Victorian melodrama. The elevator is still in use, and the rusty palazzo is now a linen outlet.

Before the 1870s, this stretch was the most fashionable in the city, and at 521 Broadway you can just see the remnants of the deluxe **St Nicholas Hotel** which accommodated 30 miles of pipes, a thousand guests and 600 rooms furnished with chandeliers and gold-framed mirrors from Haughwout's department store.

Continue up Broadway, passing the **'Little' Singer Building** *at Prince Street, unusually elegant for a cast-iron building. It has a light, Art-Nouveau touch reminiscent of Guimard's Castel Béranger flats in Paris and the open metal arches of the Métro.*

From the corner of Broadway and Prince Street, turn right and walk a block east to Crosby Street. If you look north up Crosby Street to Bleecker Street at the end, you suddenly see its thrilling full-stop, the **Bayard-Condict Building***.*

As one architecture critic put it, 'Who would expect an aesthetic experience on Bleecker Street?'. Built in 1898, it was designed by Chicago's master-builder, Louis Sullivan. It was his only New York commission, (perhaps because it was too radical for New York's more conservative tastes). From this distance you can see how the skeleton is exposed on the outside, according to Sullivan's dictum that form should express function. Closer to, you see Sullivan-style terracotta leaves, tendrils and lacework; intricate decorations that do not disguise the interior structure. Under the cornice are six, magnificent, bosomy angels, supposedly added against Sullivan's wishes.

> *Walk back to Broadway and then two blocks west along Prince Street to Greene Street. On the Greene Street side of the corner is a* trompe l'oeil *of a cast-iron warehouse painted on the brick sidewall of a real cast-iron façade facing Prince Street. Richard Haas, the artist, is famous for his* trompe l'oeils *in Galveston, Boston, Milwaukee, Munich, and Times Square.*
>
> *Turn left and walk south down Greene Street. On the lefthand side is another curiosity,* **'Subway Map Floating on a New York Sidewalk'** *a topological map of the New York subway system in reverse, and inlaid into the pavement with subway stops made out of glass basement lights. (Patented by Thaddeus Hyatt in 1845, they were used all over SoHo to light up dingy basements).*
>
> *Walk all the way down Greene Street to Broome Street, turn right and walk a block west to Wooster Street. At 70 Wooster Street, on the lefthand side, is the* **Museum of Colored Glass and Light**.

This is an unusual museum, in that it displays the work of only one man, Raphael Nemeth, also its founder and custodian. The pictures range from illustrations of the *Divine Comedy* to a portrait of J. F. Kennedy. They are mostly kiln-fired, and lit from the back by electric light. Be warned: Nemeth expects you to look at each one of the 150 or so pictures on display, and he has a short Hungarian temper. 'CHAGALL MAKES ME SICK', he says, with a face the color of raw steak, and then launches into a thunderous tirade in Latin, the 'language of scholars'. He believes in the intrinsic spirituality of light, since the whole world is perceived by reflected light.

> *Walk back to Broome Street and Wooster and turn right. On the righthand side is* **484 Broome Street**, *an eccentric red-brick industrial castle covered with griffins, gargoyles and dragons.*

This was designed in 1890 for a dry goods firm by Alfred Zucker, who was responsible for an equally festive Venetian Gothic skyscraper on Union Square. Until recently, this building was used for avant-garde performances.

> *Now walk a block west to West Broadway and Broome Street. Directly opposite on the triangle between Watts and Broome Streets is an unconventional sculpture by Robert Bolles, whose nickname is Bob*

Steel. It is constructed out of rusty iron and doubles as a parking space used by local bikers in black leather jackets.

*You will probably want to finish off with a stroll up **West Broadway**, SoHo's main shopping street, where people strut, as well as merely stroll.*

There are galleries all along the street, and the two most famous, both at 420 West Broadway, are **Mary Boone**, which spearheaded the migration of galleries to the East Village in the 1980s, and **Leo Castelli**. Just off West Broadway, on Prince Street, is a clutch of cafés and shops left over from the time when the area was annexed to Little Italy. Near an encyclopedic postcard shop at 160 Prince Street, is the **Cafe Borgia II**, and further on, at 177 Prince, the **Patisserie Lanciani**, which is excellent for tea. Opposite, the **Vesuvio Bakery** has a pretty lime-green front with gold lettering which has been left untouched since the 19th century.

*At one point West Broadway was called Fifth Avenue South, and if you keep going north you hit Greenwich Village and the bottom of 5th Avenue proper. The nearest subway stops to West Broadway are the **N** and **R** on Prince Street and Broadway, the **6** on Spring Street and Lafayette, and the **1** on Houston and Varick Streets.*

Walk VIII
Midtown East

Roosevelt Island Cable Car—Bloomingdale's—57th Street—Park Avenue—Waldorf-Astoria—Grand Central Terminal—Chrysler—Automat—Tudor City—United Nations—East River Heliport—Beekman Tower—Sutton Place

This walk along Park Avenue and East 42nd Street is nice and short. Yet it covers an architectural battlefield, taking in some of New York's pre-eminent Art-Deco skyscrapers, (including the Chrysler, the only scraper with a cult following), some of the best and worst glass boxes from the sixties and seventies, as well as the most controversial recent additions to the skyline. It begins with a trip across the Roosevelt Island Aerial Tramway, from where you get an eagle's-eye view of the scrimmage, and ends with a cocktail and a terrifying helicopter ride, which gives you the most exciting view of all.

At the heart of the walk is Grand Central Station, at once the endearing grand old man of Midtown and an extraordinary feat of engineering. If you can possibly arrange it, do the walk on a Wednesday, and get to Grand Central for the Municipal Arts Society's weekly tour. It is conducted by various eccentrics, including one enthusiast who believes that the 21st century will see the renaissance of high-speed railway travel, and the concomitant death of the automobile. The tours, which last an

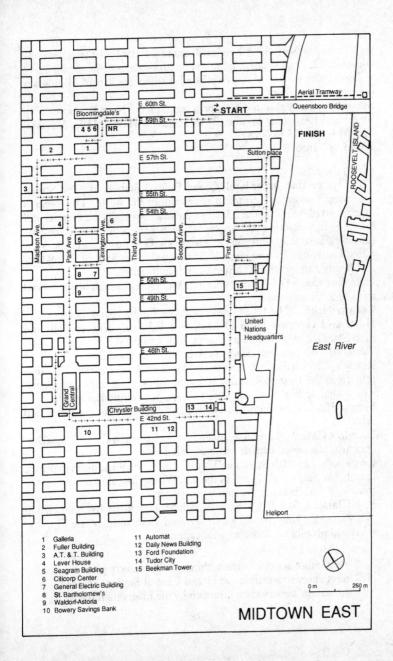

E 60th St.

Bloomingdale's

← START

Aerial Tramway

Queensboro Bridge

FINISH

E 59th St.

4 5 6   NR

Sutton place

2   1

E 57th St.

3

E 55th St.

E 54th St.

Madison Ave.

Park Ave.

Lexington Ave.

Third Ave.

Second Ave.

First Ave.

ROOSEVELT ISLAND

4   6

5

8 7

9

E 50th St.

E 49th St.

15

United Nations Headquarters

East River

E 46th St.

Grand Central

Chrysler Building

13   14

E 42nd St.

10

11   12

Heliport

1 Galleria
2 Fuller Building
3 A.T. & T. Building
4 Lever House
5 Seagram Building
6 Citicorp Center
7 General Electric Building
8 St. Bartholomew's
9 Waldorf-Astoria
10 Bowery Savings Bank
11 Automat
12 Daily News Building
13 Ford Foundation
14 Tudor City
15 Beekman Tower

0 m   250 m

MIDTOWN EAST

hour, meet outside the Chemical Commuter Bank in the main concourse at 12.30 and cannot be too highly recommended.

Don't come on a Saturday or a Sunday when this part of Midtown is deserted and boring.

Start: by subway take the **4, 5**, or **6** train, or the **N** or **R** train to 59th Street and Lexington Avenue. By bus take the **M101, M102, M1, M2, M3, M4**, or **M15** to 60th Street.

Walking Time: 3 hours.

LUNCH/CAFÉS

The Oyster Bar, lower level, Grand Central Station, at 42nd Street. The most famous subterranean restaurant in the world. The menu is overpriced (dinner is about $38), but the fish, especially the snapper and Dover Sole, is always good—none of which matters because the restaurant itself is so jolly, and you can always go there just for a drink.

Chez Laurence Patisserie, 245 Madison Ave., at 38th St. Breakfasts and lunches of croissants, brioches and sandwiches.

Café Europa, 347 54th St., near 1st Ave. Quiet French bistro tucked away in a brownstone.

Country Life, 244 51st St., near 2nd Ave. Filling vegetarian spread.

Horn and Hardart Dine-O-Mat, 942 3rd Ave., between 56th and 57th Sts. Delicious stodge in a mock-fifties automat.

Taro, 20 47th St., near Madison Ave. Japanese noodles.

Reidy's, 22 54th St., between 5th and Madison Aves. Irish steakhouse, a relic from the forties. Recently it fought off demolition by developers, who ended up having to wrap their skyscraper around it instead.

Seto's, 356 51st St., between 1st and 2nd Aves. Seaweed, *sashimi*, and *sake*.

Harglo's Café, 974 2nd Ave., near 51st St. Excellent Cajun Jambalaya, crawfish, blackened catfish and barbecued ribs.

Costello's, 225 44th St. James Thurber once took 90 minutes to draw a mural, *The Battle of the Sexes*, in the bar. When Costello's moved up the road from 3rd Avenue, the mural moved too.

P. J. Clarke's, 913 3rd Ave., near 55th St. Legendary bar recreated in Hollywood for Billy Wilder's *Lost Weekend*. (The noise of the El tracks overhead prohibited shooting on location.)

'As a bullet seeks its target, shining rails in every part of our great country are aimed at Grand Central Station, heart of the nation's greatest city. Drawn by the magnetic force of the fantastic metropolis, day and night great trains rush towards the Hudson River ... dive with a roar into the 2½-mile tunnel which burrows beneath the glitter and swank of Park Avenue and then ... Grand Central Station! Crossroads of a million private lives! Gigantic stage on which are played a thousand dramas daily.'

Grand Central Station, NBC radio serial, 1937

In 1913, the railroad tracks of Grand Central were electrified, sunk nine levels underground, and covered over with an 18-inch skin of asphalt called Park Avenue. The new boulevard sparked off a building boom of truly spectacular proportions, and since the twenties it has been a sort of real estate battleground between the offices and shops of Midtown and the residences of the East Side.

After a slump during the Depression and the War, the area was hit by another tidal wave of building, and the first of Park Avenue's glass boxes, starting with Lever House, shot up. This time the area became a new theater of war: a confrontation between the American Old and New, most obviously between the flighty, whimsical, aerodynamic Art Deco of the twenties, and the drab realism of the down-to-earth corporate slabs of the fifties and sixties.

In 1963 the Pan Am Building, an ugly glass monolith and just co-incidentally the headquarters of a massive airline, was built and blotted out the New York Central Building, the once-glorious symbol of the biggest railroad in the country and of the beginnings of America's industrial pre-eminence. During the same period, New York Central railroad merged with Pennsylvania, and almost immediately went bust. Completing the ghastly irony, the building was renamed when it became the eyrie of Leona Helmsley.

*The walk starts with the **Roosevelt Island Aerial Tramway**, a couple of blocks away from the **N, R, 4, 5,** and **6** subway stops, at 60th Street and 2nd Avenue.*

The trip costs $1.25 one way. Once you have got over the faintly ridiculous feeling of swinging silently over 1st Avenue in a Swiss-made cable car, you can enjoy the superb view of Midtown East's forest of skyscrapers. The ride takes 3½ minutes, and when you arrive there is nothing much to do except go back again. Formerly known as 'Welfare Island', the island was used as a base for the city's gaols, asylums, workhouses and almshouses. In the 1970s, however, it was seized by

239

developers who created an instant suburb of nearly 10,000 residences, many of which have yet to be filled. Cars are banned, making the island eerily silent, and the subway connection to Manhattan is only just being completed. If you want to explore, there is a free electric bus service running up and down the whole length of the narrow 2½-mile sliver of land. (See Day Trips, pp. 410–11).

> *Take the cable car back to Manhattan, and from 60th Street walk a block south to 59th Street. Turn right and walk another block west. On the corner, at 3rd Avenue and 59th Street, is the* **Papaya King***, which has frankfurters which are 'Tastier than Filet Mignon'. The hot dogs are smeared in emerald-green relish, and come with a polystyrene cup of frothy papaya juice.*
>
> *Walk a block east from the Papaya King to Lexington Avenue and the good-looking Art-Deco entrance, on the right, to* **Bloomingdale's***.*

Bloomingdale's is the New York equivalent of Harrods, but even more glittery. At Bloomingdale's, you must brave asphyxiation by battalions of aggressive perfume-sprayers stationed at the top of every escalator. New Yorkers generally scorn the shop's pretensions, but it's well worth going in, just to admire the lavish displays which range from the simply excessive to the hi-tech and downright bizarre. Shoppers match the displays to a tee—the most fascinating department for observing them is Interior Design, an extraordinary series of rooms resembling sets from *Dallas*.

North of Bloomingdale's, Midtown East merges into the well-off residential Upper East Side, with Lexington Avenue as the frontier between old-money and new-money. At 140 East 63rd Street is the **Barbizon Hotel**, where Sylvia Plath spent a month in 1953 as a guest editor of *Mademoiselle* magazine. In her novel *The Bell Jar*, the hotel became the Amazon, a mainstay for wealthy parents 'who wanted to be sure their daughters would be living where men couldn't get at them and deceive them'. The real Barbizon was recently renovated for both sexes, but in its heyday Grace Kelly, Lisa Minelli and Joan Crawford all stayed behind its chaste doors.

> *We'll continue south, however, down Lexington to 58th Street. Turn right and then left into the faintly apocalyptical entrance to the* **Galleria***, on the lefthand side of the street at 122 East 58th Steet. A slick atrium of glass roofs and granite floors, it was built in 1975 and*

*filled with smart shops. Walk through it and turn right onto **57th** **Street**.*

This part of 57th Street almost upstages the shops on 5th Avenue. Between Madison and 5th Avenues are Chanel, Burberry, Hermes and Laura Ashley. Further east, at 145 East 57th Street, there is **Hammacher & Schlemmer**, which sells an idiotic selection of gadgets ranging from a machine for mixing an egg before it is broken to a walkman/hearing-aid for eavesdropping on conversations up to 20 yards away.

*Cross Park Avenue and walk a block west along 57th Street to Madison Avenue. On the northeast corner, at 41 East 57th Street, is the **Fuller Building**, (Walker & Gilette, 1929), a dapper black-and-white Art-Deco tower, now home to a number of art galleries, including Robert Miller, which always has excellent shows.*

Above the entrance is a group of particularly fine sculptured figures against a background of abstracted skyscrapers, by Elie Nadelman. The mosaic tile floors of the lobby are definitely worth a look. One shows the Tacomen Building, the first steel structure ever built in New York, and another, the Flatiron, the Fuller Company's old home.

*Turn left onto Madison Avenue and then walk a block south to 56th Street and the **AT&T Building**, a hulking pile of dove-pink granite on the righthand side of the street with an enormous 60ft glass atrium, or 'galleria', inside.*

According to Philip Johnson, who designed the building in 1984 with John Burgee, AT&T's timorous request was 'Please don't give us a flat top'. Johnson's cheeky reply was a neo-Classical broken pediment snitched directly from a Chippendale chest-of-drawers. The roof provoked flurries of controversy, and the impudent building immediately became a totem pole of post-Modernism. Although the Chippendale plagiarism is the wittiest joke, the best part of the building is the windy Roman atrium down below. There are historical allusions to Gothic, Renaissance and neo-Classical styles, but everything is ludicrously out of scale except for a statue in the center illustrating the 'Spirit of Communication' moved here from the roof of the old AT&T headquarters on Broadway.

Madison Avenue is associated with two phenomena: stuffy mens' clothes shops and the advertising industry. Even though most of the agencies are actually based elsewhere, the image persists, partly because for some strange reason the Madison ad-man was the focus of many films and sitcoms made in the fifties and sixties. During the same period, some of the avenue's best clients—among them Lever Bros, (soap and detergent), Colgate, Seagrams (distillers whose headquarters are tinted the same color as their bottles of rye whiskey), Union Carbide and Philip Morris (Marlboros)—moved in force onto Park Avenue, supplanting its grand apartment houses and turning this area into New York's nerve center of consumption. The connection still thrives, and even the most recent skyscrapers like the AT&T Building and the Citicorp Building (with its distinctive roof angled at 45 degrees) have become inseparable parts of their corporate images.

From the AT&T Building, walk a block east along 55th Street, turn right onto **Park Avenue**, *and then walk a block south.*

The avenue is actually a hollow skin, braced together with metal planks and rivets, and it judders and clanks as an endless stream of cars whizzes down to 42nd Street. The buildings either side stand on stilts wedged between nine levels of railway tracks leading to Grand Central, and if you listen hard you can just hear station announcements below.

On the right at 54th Street is **Lever House**, *which the company were so pleased with when it was built in 1952, that they put a little picture of it on all their detergent boxes.*

Lever House is Manhattan's protypical glass box, 'as fecund as the shad', as Tom Wolfe put it in *From Bauhaus to Our House*. It has been so influential that it is now almost impossible to imagine how revolutionary it seemed when it was first built. The architect, Gordon Bunshaft, a partner in America's largest practice, Skidmore, Owings & Merrill, simply cut a swathe of light, air and space into Park Avenue's solid wall of classical masonry apartments. The skyscraper itself is transparent, and its curtain wall of turquoise and black spandrels (the spaces between the windows) started a craze which eventually spread all over the world. From a distance, you see how Bunshaft created an architectural *trompe l'oeil* by balancing a tall vertical slab on top of a long horizontal slab supported by stilts.

The illusion of weightlessness had even more of an impact when Park Avenue was packed with stone buildings, although ironically the success of Lever House led to their demolition. Today, diagonally across from Lever House is Manhattan's handsomest and sleekest *glass skyscraper: the **Seagram Building**, between 53rd and 52nd Streets.*

It was designed in 1958 by Mies van der Rohe, (the director of the Bauhaus until the school was closed by the Nazis in 1933), and Philip Johnson, who did the interiors. (Johnson, a lapsed disciple and biographer of Mies van der Rohe, still has an office in the building, even though his own work, in particular the AT&T Building, now blasphemes the Miesian manifesto.)

The inscrutable bronze-glassed tower is most admired for its proportions, set back 90 ft from Park Avenue, and poised in front of a plaza of ponds, ginkgo trees and munching office-workers. Mies was so fastidious that he installed blinds which were specially adapted so they could only stay in three positions—completely rolled up, completely rolled down, or exactly half-way up the window. The bronze skin, moreover, has to be oiled every year to stop it turning a nauseating green. Although Mies was adamant that buildings should be utterly unequivocal, critics have quibbled about the Seagram's purity, calling it 'a beautiful lady with hidden corsets', because the curtain skin is in fact held up by invisible supports.

At any rate, the Seagram was not so pure that it shunned publicity. Apparently, while it was being constructed six sets of Plexiglass portholes were set into the grey fencing surrounding the site. Each was a different height—tall, medium, or short, and each was equipped with a loudspeaker, so itinerant salesmen could stop off and plug their wares (and incidentally the Seagram Building itself) to the crowds on Park Avenue.

Through the lobby, a staircase leads to **The Four Seasons**, one of the most expensive restaurants in New York (see pp. 292–3). You can peer through the windows at *Le Tricorne*, an enormous stage backdrop of a gory bullfight painted by Picasso in 1919.

*From the Seagram walk a block east down 53rd Street to Lexington Avenue. On the northeast corner of Lexington, between 53rd and 54th Streets, is the **Citicorp Center**, whose toothy slanted profile, which shot up in 1978 as the fourth highest in the city, is now as familiar a silhouette on the skyline as the Chrysler's silver dunce's hat and the Empire State's dirigible mast.*

The futuristic 45-degree slant faces south, and originally the idea was to cover the slope with solar panels which would generate electricity for the whole building. Citicorp were so taken with the shape that they kept it, even when it became clear that the solar panels were impractical. So impractical, in fact, that even without panels the slope becomes a hazard in heavy snowfalls, and the area around the base of the skyscraper has to be fenced off to prevent unwitting pedestrians getting flattened by an avalanche.

The bottom, with its four hefty columns set in the middle of each side (rather than at the corners), is just as dramatic as the top. Close to, you see that what makes the building look white from a distance, is actually sunlight catching its aluminum skin. Crouching meekly in its shadow is the wedge-shape of the diminutive **St Peter's Church**, built here in 1977 after Citicorp bought its old headquarters on the understanding that a new church would be erected in its stead.

In the last decade, commercial office buildings have been migrating eastwards, colonizing Lexington and 3rd Avenues. Behind the Citicorp, is the most recent (pink-and-beige) addition, **885 Third Avenue**, another Johnson and Burgee creation, dating from 1986 and since dubbed 'The Lipstick' because of its curious elliptical shape and three-wedding cake tiers.

Next, walk a block south down Lexington to between 52nd and 51st Streets.

On the righthand side of the street is the world's only famous **subway grating**, the one which billowed a great puff of hot air up the skirts of Marilyn Monroe as she left a showing of *Creature from the Black Lagoon* at the (now demolished) Lexington Avenue Trans Lux Theater. Shooting the scene for *The Seven Year Itch*, Billy Wilder turned the occasion into a publicity stunt. 'Do you feel the breeze from the subway? Isn't it delicious?', chirruped Monroe, to the delight of a rowdy crowd who clapped, bellowed and chanted 'Higher, higher!'.

Walk down Lexington for half a block and turn right onto 51st Street. Beside you, on the southwest corner of Lexington and 51st, is one of the most fantastic survivors from old Midtown Manhattan, the **General Electric Building***, by Cross and Cross, whose specialty was Gothic Art Deco.*

Built for the Radio Corporation of America in 1931, its extravagant terracotta top is a crown of filigree lightning bolts—symbolizing radio waves, electrical energy and power. In between the lacework, and illuminated at night, are mysterious figures, a blend of African masks and Egyptian mummies. Pop inside the lobby, which is even more fanciful, with an aluminum ceiling of silver sunrays, and silver torches for lights.

Now walk back to Park Avenue via 51st Street and look back at the General Electric. It is a futuristic illusion: the 570 ft needle-point of the General Electric rises out of the squat Byzantine dome of St Bartholomew's in front. The strange juxtaposition was entirely intentional, engineered by Cross & Cross, who chose a salmon-colored brick to match the orange-pink tones of the church.

Described as 'the swaggerest church in town' when it was built on Park Avenue in 1902, St Bartholomew's has a lovely interior gleaming with mosaics—of the Creation, in the narthex, and the Transfiguration in the apse. Only the portico dates from 1902, since the rest of the church was remodeled in 1919 by Bertram Goodhue, who did St Thomas's a few blocks away on 5th Avenue.

*Walk a block further down to 50th Street and Park Avenue's Art-Deco masterpiece, the enormous **Waldorf-Astoria Hotel**, with its two chrome-capped, jelly-mould towers.*

In 1931 the hotel, which was originally based on 34th Street, upped sticks for the more fashionable surroundings of Park Avenue. The new Waldorf-Astoria set itself up as the tallest, largest, flashiest hotel in the world: 2200 rooms, 2700 telephones, with a switchboard said to be 'large enough for a good-sized city'; and 16 elevators, one of which was large enough to take a limousine for the annual automobile exhibition in the ballroom.

The most glamorous parts of the hotel are the very bottom and the very top. Its entire weight, some 27,000 tons of steel, is supported on stilts wedged between the tracks of Grand Central, (the wine cellars are on the 5th floor to avoid the vibrations of trains below). Originally guests arrived in private trains shunted into a spur in the basement from where they took an elevator straight to the lobby. In the sixties Andy Warhol sent out disingenuous invitations to a party at '101–121 East 49th Street', actually a sidedoor to a 100 ft staircase connecting the siding to the street. He installed a rock group in the storage yards at the bottom, and served supper from abandoned dining cars.

At the top of the hotel is the Waldorf Towers, made up of 113 apartments for permanent tenants such as the Duke and Duchess of Windsor, President Hoover, Marilyn Monroe, Nixon and Kissinger. When the big-nosed comedian, Jimmy 'Schnozzola' Durante, stepped into a crowded elevator bound for the Towers, he was so smothered with compliments, he held his hands in the air and begged, 'Folks, folks—save them adjectives—we got thoity floors to go!'

In its palmiest days, before the War, the Waldorf was full of 'men puffing fat cigars and telephoning', and residents went in for extravagant parties. The gossip columnist, Elsa Maxwell, once challenged the management to transport a whole farmyard—apple trees, chickens, donkeys, cows, hayricks and all, to the Starlight Room on the 18th floor.

If you look unobtrusive enough you can take an elevator to the 18th floor, and sneak a look round the Starlight's electrically retractable roof and its engraved mirrors illuminated with green lights. Even the urinals are Art Deco. Downstairs, the hotel has lost some of its original splendor since it was covered in gold during the sixties, in an attempt to make it look Edwardian.

*As you leave the Waldorf, look south down to 46th Street where the New York Central Building, now the **Helmsley Building**, straddles Park Avenue and guzzles cars through two arches at the bottom.*

From here, you get a good view of the cheerful little pyramid at the top, punched with little eyelets and porthole windows, and crowned by a pseudo gazebo. This was the roost of Leona Helmsley, New York's own Imelda Marcos, twice married to aging hotel baron, Harry, and currently doing time in Danbury women's slammer for a few million-dollars' worth of tax evasion. Leona's trial in 1989 revealed, among other things, that she once slaughtered a flock of sheep grazing on her lawn in a flash of anger and fed them to the servants. Her own contribution to Park Avenue was the gilding and theatrical night-time illumination of the pyramid at the top of the Helmsley Building.

Built in 1929 as headquarters for the New York Central's railway executives, the tower stood as a glorious symbol of the biggest railroad in the country and of the beginnings of America's industrial pre-eminence. In 1963, just as the railroad was bankrupting itself, a galumphing airline headquarters, designed by a consortium of architects including the founder of the Bauhaus, Walter Gropius, suddenly loomed up and blotted out the vista down Park Avenue. Today, the **Pan Am Building** is probably New York's most universally hated skyscraper. It was the scene in 1977 of one of the most dreadful accidents in the city's history: a helicopter landed on the roof during the rush hour, its undercarriage gave way, and debris from the accident drifted as far as Madison Avenue, killing five people and injuring seven.

Cross the road from the Waldorf, walk south down Park Avenue,
turn right onto 46th Street and then left onto Vanderbilt Avenue.
There are several entrances to **Grand Central Terminal***, but the*
most exciting one is on Vanderbilt Avenue, opposite 43rd Street.

Walking through the entrance, you find yourself at the top of an operatic flight of stairs opening out onto a marble cathedral vault, an immense 375 by 125 ft. On the lefthand side of the staircase is a **bar**, where you can order a gin and tonic and lunch, and observe the action. Below you, there is the mesmerizing drama of people endlessly threading and zigzagging across the concourse. Above, filling the gigantic windows, are nine levels of vertigo-inducing glass catwalks, which pedestrians use for crossing the building without setting foot on the concourse below, and for throwing the occasional water bomb.

In the thirties and forties, Grand Central was stylish: passengers boarded trains grandly named the *Empire State Express* and the *Super Chief*, and every evening a red carpet was rolled out for the *Twentieth Century Ltd* to Chicago. There was a newsreel theater inside the station, and CBS broadcast from studios in the Long Gallery, parallel to the main concourse. Now the space houses tennis courts and a health club.

Nowadays, Americans travel by plane, and a shabbier Grand Central is mostly used by commuters, subway passengers and the homeless. Even so, the concourse is still thrilling. On sunny days Jacob's ladders pierce the skylights, throwing theatrical spotlights of sun across the concourse. Overhead, the ceiling is painted cerulean blue and decorated with a firmament of illuminated constellations. For some reason Orion is excluded and the constellations are reversed, so the sun sets in the east—the designer, a French artist called Paul Helleu, followed an illuminated medieval manuscript which commonly showed the Heavens viewed from the godly viewpoint.

Underneath you is a Dantesque world of 27 miles of tracks. To save space they loop around each other and are arranged on a double-decker, with express trains running on the top tiers, and commuter trains underneath. Below the main hall is another subterranean concourse for commuters, and a whole lower level, vaulted with guastavino tiles, of shops and restaurants. These include the delightful **Hoffritz'**, which sells cutlery, razors and scissors, and the **Oyster Bar**, which entertains three million oyster-eaters a year, and has such booming accoustics that speculators are supposed to lurk in the whispering gallery outside to eavesdrop on the latest financial gossip.

There is a labyrinth of seven more stories under the Oyster Bar, filled with tunnels containing mains, sewers, water pipes, a colossal generator, and grimy machine shops serviced by motorized carts. Air is forced down funnels from the columns in the concourse down to the bowels, and it is possible to walk in steamy rat-infested tunnels, used as shelters by tramps, from 43rd to 49th Streets and from Lexington to Madison Avenues. Lex Luther's underground empire in *Superman* was set deep in the bowels of Grand Central, though the film was actually shot in Pinewood Studios outside London.

Although the trimmings are by the beaux-arts architects Warren & Wetmore, the overall design, dating from 1913, was the combined inspiration of the station's chief engineer, William Wilgus, and Reed & Stem, an architectural practice from Minnesota. Reed was responsible for the magical way in which pedestrians, passengers, subway travellers and cars are sifted through ramps inside the station, and for the endearingly named 'Elevated Circumferential Plaza', the viaduct circling the station outside.

Before you leave, make sure you explore the extraordinary glass catwalks, which can be reached via the elevators on either side of the main concourse.

> *Make your way back to Vanderbilt Avenue, walk a block south and turn left onto 42nd Street. Grand Central's grandiose beaux-arts façade with a 2000-ton sculpture depicting the* Spirit of Commerce *faces 42nd Street. You can hardly see it, however, because of the ramp which connects the south end of Park Avenue to the viaduct circling the station, and sticks out of the middle like a great tongue.*
>
> *Directly opposite, on the southwest corner of 42nd and 120 Park Avenue, is the* **Philip Morris Building***. Inside is a branch of the Whitney Museum of American Art which has about five exhibitions a year. They are generally excellent, although space is limited.*
>
> *Now walk east down 42nd Street. On the righthand side of the next block, between Park Avenue and Lexington at 110 42nd Street, is the* **Bowery Savings Bank***, by York & Sawyer, who did a mass of banks in New York during the 1920s, including the vast* **Federal Reserve** *palazzo on Liberty Street.*

This bank is the best of the lot. It has a tremendous Romanesque interior, with a mosaic floor, and imperial arches and columns with animals on their capitals: the bull and bear, symbolizing Wall Street, and squirrels for thrift. Next door is the even more handsome Art-Deco scraper, the **Chanin Building**, commissioned in 1929 by the real estate developers, the Chanin Brothers. It has a mass of eccentric details, such as flying buttresses on the 4th floor and a floral bas-relief of fronds and curls on the 3rd floor.

*At Lexington Avenue, cross over to the north side of 42nd Street. Diagonally across from the Chanin Building is the unmistakable church-like entrance to the **Chrysler Building**. New York's barmiest building, it is also everyone's favorite.*

The bravely modern skyscraper was the first to be dressed in exposed steel. It shot up during the Depression, in 1931, as a talisman of that other American Dream, the automobile. In fact, in the same year Chrysler built a line of cars to go with the scraper—'Airflow' models which were streamlined and also covered in steel. They were a miserable flop, while the skyscraper was an unprecedented success. Streamlined and aerodynamic, it was decked from head to toe in tokens and totems of the automobile: from actual hub caps stuccoed to the walls and bas-reliefs of abstracted cars carved in the brickwork, to the famous eagle gargoyles, which are actually hugely oversized hood ornaments.

Having begun his career in humble style (designing rollerskates) Walter Chrysler set his heart on building the tallest skyscraper in the world. A secret race ensued between the architect William Van Alen and his old partner, H. Craig Severance, who was working on the Bank of Manhattan on 40 Wall Street. When the Chrysler's dome reached 925 ft and looked as though it was finished, Craig Severance tacked a flagpole onto 40 Wall Street, increasing its height to 927 ft. In retaliation, Van Alen suddenly whipped out a Nirosta metal spire he had assembled on the sly, hoisted it through a hole in the roof and bolted it onto the Chrysler in 90 minutes.

The Chrysler was the first building to beat the Eiffel Tower but a year later, to Van Alen's chagrin, the 1250 ft Empire State Building towered above them both. Undaunted, Van Alen attended the year's beaux-arts ball dressed as the Chrysler, in a silver coat with patent leather attachments and eagle shoulder pads, in the company of several other buildings including the Empire State, the Daily News and an unnamed subway station. The theme was *Fête Moderne* and guests drank silver liquid and roasted marshmallows, or Miniature Meteorites.

Inside is the city's most sumptuous lobby. It has red-veined African marble walls, a chrome clock and amazingly exotic elevators, inlaid with rich mahogany-colored laminated woods arranged in a jagged pattern.

Originally Chrysler used the lobby as a showroom for a revolving motor car, and the ceiling still has a mural of cars and the Chrysler Building under construction, symbolizing 'transportation and human endeavor'. Unfortunately the old Cloud Club, an observation room and restaurant on the 66th floor filled with budgies, canaries and industrial executives, has been closed, although it is supposed to be re-opening at some point.

Cross 42nd Street again and walk past Woolworth's to the next block between 3rd and 2nd Avenues. On the nearest corner is Horn & Hardart's **Automat**, *at 200 East 42nd Street.*

Although it seems to crop up in every single Doris Day film, the Automatic Food Dispensing System was invented in Germany, and imported to the States in 1902. Inside, invisible hands place portions of beans, franks and wobbling green jello into a wall of tiny glass doors which open with a coin or a token. In 1935, with 36 Automats dotted all over the city, a delegation of bemused Soviet journalists investigated the restaurants. 'The sausages and cutlets, deprived of liberty, somehow produce a strange impression,' they reported back. 'One pities them, like cats at a show.'

Today, the Automat on 42nd Street is the last in the world, and Horn & Hardart, who own the local Burger King franchise, have converted their other restaurants into fast-food joints. A lot of people come and eat here on their own, and even if you bury your nose in a book, it is practically impossible to avoid a conversation. 'If you ask me,' somebody inevitably announces, without being asked, 'it's all going to pot.'

Leaving the Automat, walk east to the **Daily News Building**, *which is more or less next door at 220 East 42nd Street.*

New York's great populist newspaper, the *Daily News*, has one of the largest circulations in the country as well as the most talented headline-writers (everyone remembers *'Ford to New York: Drop Dead'* after the city went bankrupt in 1975). The skyscraper itself was built in the same year as the Chrysler, but it has hardly any Art-Deco trims and frills. Raymond Hood, the architect, treated it quite daringly as a pure slab, using its windows to stress all the verticals. Much the same technique was used for the Rockefeller Center, which Hood spent the next eight years working on with a consortium of architects.

Inside the Daily News is another shadowy lobby, filled with an 8 ft high globe, which is lit from a well underneath and rotates under a black glass canopy. When it was unveiled it was spinning the wrong way, and had to be adjusted. The newspaper keeps it updated, and round the edge there are various pompous statistics, such as the fairly mind-bending thought that, 'If the *Sun* were the Size of this *Globe* and Placed here then Comparatively the *Earth* would be the Size of a *Walnut* and located at the Main Entrance of *Grand Central Terminal*'.

> *Cross 2nd Avenue, and walk a block east along 42nd Street. 2nd Avenue was one of the main arteries of the Elevated Railroad, or the El, as it was usually known, which choked the city with grime and soot until the first subways arrived around the turn of the century. The 2nd Avenue El was finally removed in World War II, when the industrialist Henry J. Kaiser bought all the trains and all the tracks to carry war workers to the Alameda shipyards in California.*
>
> *On the lefthand side of the block, at 320 East 42nd Street, is the* **Ford Foundation***, whose workers apparently go to work in a jungle installed in the atrium. Built in 1967 by Roche & Dinkeloo, the Ford Foundation is one of the most urbane recent skyscrapers.*
>
> *A few steps east are some steps up to* **Tudor City***, which fills the area between 1st and 2nd Avenues and 40th and 43rd Streets.*

The elevated complex of 13 apartment towers and one hotel was funded and built in 1928 by the private developer Fred French, at a time when the district was mostly slums and factories—breweries, glue-makers and power plants that showered the area with heavy soot fall-out. The apartments all face inwards, and hardly any windows look onto 1st Avenue and the East River, where there was the enormous Abattoir Center which fed the whole city, and where sickly immigrants used to buy blood at 5c a glass, rather than face the exorbitant costs of going to hospital.

From the top of the stairs, there are magnificent **views** up and down 42nd and 43rd Streets (which rather surprisingly look lumpy rather than flat) and to the east, of the East River and the Pepsi-Cola neon sign in Queens. The apartments themselves are all a bizarre pseudo-Tudor, with the odd heraldic shield, gargoyle or latticed window.

> *Walk along the elevated pathway as far north as 43rd Street, and take another stairway down to First Avenue. Then walk north up 1st Avenue to the entrance to the* **United Nations Headquarters***, which is just off 46th Street.*

In 1823 the site was used by George Youle for making cannon balls. He built a protypical skyscraper, and poured in molten lead from the top which turned into perfectly formed balls by the time it landed in a pool of water at the bottom. In 1946, the 18 acres surrounding the site were bought by J. D. Rockefeller Jr, who donated it to the United Nations. As you walk in you are officially stepping out of the United States and onto international territory—like the Vatican, the United Nations has its own post office and prints its own stamps. By now you will probably be utterly exhausted, in which case you should go and recover in the soothing **rose gardens** on the riverside promenade.

The initial scheme was devised in the early fifties by Le Corbusier, although he dropped out and the project was designed by a committee of international architects. Osbert Lancaster described the end result as 'the ultimate in boredom'. Corbusier was responsible for its separation into three elements: the Secretariat, a vertical 39-story green glass slab; the Conference Building, a low, horizontal, practical slab: and lastly the solid and grandiose General Assembly slab. The Secretariat houses offices for the UN's bureaucratic machinery, and so completely dominates the area that the critic Lewis Mumford reflected that it showed that bureaucracy, rather than political authority, 'rules the world'.

To see inside the buildings you must take one of the hour-long guided tours (daily, every 20 minutes, from 9.15–4.45, adm $4.50). Most interesting are the various works of art, of varying quality, donated by all the major nations, including a 21-ft high sculpture by Barbara Hepworth and a disappointing stained-glass window by Marc Chagall. The guides whisk you through all three Council Chambers, eulogize over the uninspiring red, green and blue seats, and thoroughly explain the history of the UN.

To finish off, there are two options. The first is to take a helicopter flight from the **Heliport** *on the East River at 34th Street. Prices range from $30 for 16 miles, or 15 minutes, to $139 for 100 miles (tel 683 4575 for information). Although the rides are very thrilling, it's advisable to take one of the shorter rides as the noise of the choppers can be quite deafening.*

Alternatively, you can go for a peaceful cocktail at **Beekman Tower**, *which is at the north end of the UN, on the corner of East 49th Street and Mitchell Place. Built in 1929, the top of the lovely rust-coloured Art-Deco tower has the nicest and snazziest cocktail bar in the city, with wonderful views to the north and south.*

*From Beekman Tower, you can walk along the string of tranquil private parks and smart townhouses on **Beekman Place**, between 49th and 51st Streets. A little further north is one of the prettiest and most tranquil spots in the city, **Sutton Place**, which runs between 53rd and 59th Streets, one block to the east of 1st Avenue.*

Once slums and gangland, the area became an enclave of glamor after it was reclaimed by the well-to-do in the thirties. Nowadays residents are all diplomats and celebrities, including Katherine Hepburn, who lived here fictionally as well, with Spencer Tracy in *Woman of the Year*.

In the center is **Sutton Square**, a group of houses sharing a common park on the block between 57th and 58th Streets. It is overshadowed by the **Queensboro Bridge**, a great hulk of 50,000 tons of steel, whose architect is supposed to have exclaimed 'My God—it's a blacksmith's shop', after it was finished in 1909. The park is practically the only genuinely secluded retreat in New York: Woody Allen and Diane Keaton came here on their first date in *Manhattan*, and in the middle, less romantically, is a replica of 'Il Porcellino', copied from the boar standing in the Straw Market in Florence.

*The nearest transport home is the **M15** bus which runs up and down 1st and 2nd Avenues, or the **M57** across 57th Street. By subway, you can take the **4** from 59th Street and Lexington, or the **N** or **R** from 60th Street and Lexington.*

Museums

New Yorkers love going to museums, and on 'free' days, unless you arrive early, the big institutions will be ridiculously crowded (the exception is the Frick which has a policy of only admitting 200 people at a time). Most museums charge admission fees (between $2.50 and $5), with concessions for students and senior citizens. Where there is a 'suggested admission' charge (usually around $5 for adults) you can give as little or as much as you like, as long as you give something. Museums are generally closed on Mondays, and open late on Tuesdays when admission is free. The exceptions are the Museum of Modern Art, which is open late on Thursdays and closed on Wednesdays, and the American Museum of Natural History and the Metropolitan Museum of Art which open late on Fridays and Saturdays and close at normal times on Tuesdays.

The city is crammed with a bewildering variety of cultural institutions, but fortunately for the visitor nearly all of them are lined up in one place along a riviera on 5th Avenue, between 82nd and 105th Streets, known as 'Museum Mile'. (On the first Tuesday of June the stretch is closed to traffic, and 10 of the museums are open free of charge.)

The museums below start with the heavyweight institutions and finish up with smaller, idiosyncratic museums which are scattered all over the city (unfortunately the Dog Museum of America has recently departed for St Louis, Missouri). For further reading, Robert Garrett's *New York's*

Great Art Museums (Chelsea Green, 1988), is an intrepid tour through seven of the big museums, and Fred McDarrah's *Museums in New York* (Frommers, 1983), is a brisk but comprehensive guide to every single museum in the city. Where a more detailed description of a museum has been provided in one of the walks in this book, there is a page reference.

The Big Museums and Collections

Ellis Island Immigration Museum: Ellis Island, tel 883 1986. Transport by ferry from Battery Park, adm prices and opening times not available at time of going to press. Opened in September 1990, the new museum is housed in the abandoned immigration station which received 17 million people between 1892 and 1954. It is a disconcertingly ghostly place, especially the cavernous Great Hall. This vast, empty barn-like structure is being restored, with no exhibits, as it was in 1907, the peak year when 1,004,756 immigrants passed through. So far the museum has cost $150 million, some of which was raised from a Wall of Honor inscribed with ancestors' names at the cost of $100 a throw.

American Museum of Natural History and Hayden Planetarium: Central Park West at West 79th St., tel 769 5100/5920. Natural History Museum open Sun–Tues and Thurs 10–5.45; Wed, Fri and Sat 10–9, planetarium Mon–Fri 12.30–5. Suggested adm, and free adm on Friday and Saturday evenings, Sat–Sun noon–5. New York's enthralling, ghoulish shrine to natural history, most spectacular and theatrical at night after the youngsters have gone. Inside are fascinating displays of stuffed and fake animals frozen in lifelike poses in front of superbly painted dioramas. The highlight is the 10-ton steel and fiberglass blue whale, suspended over the Hall of Ocean Life. There is also entrance through the museum to the Hayden Planetarium where Burt Lancaster's spectral voice relates the seven wonders of the universe, and there is laser dancing to U2 on Friday and Saturday nights.

Brooklyn Museum: 188 Eastern Parkway, Prospect Park, Brooklyn, tel (718) 638 5000. Open Wed–Mon 10–5. Built in 1895 as the largest museum in the world, it is now the most underrated. Money ran out when only a sixth of the design had been completed, but even so the museum is vast. The Egyptian collection is the best outside London and Cairo, the whole top floor is devoted to an excellent collection of American and European art, and the Museum Shop is the best in New York. (See pp. 395–6.)

The Cloisters: Fort Tryon Park, tel 923 3700. Open Tues–Sun 9.30–

5.15. Suggested adm. Cloisters from five medieval monasteries bizarrely reconstructed in one building on a hilltop at the northern tip of Manhattan. It seems oddly fake, but the collection of treasures is astounding, especially the extraordinary Hunt of the Unicorn tapestries. The whole thing is perched picturesquely on a promontory in Fort Tryon Park, one of the most beautiful open spaces in Manhattan, and ideal for picnics. (See p. 277.)

Cooper-Hewitt Museum: 2 East 91st St., on 5th Ave., tel 860 6898. Open Tues 10–9, Wed–Sat 10–5, Sun noon– 5. Free Tuesday evenings. The Smithsonian's collection of decorative arts (including the largest collection of architectural drawings in the world), housed in splendid style in Andrew Carnegie's mansion on 5th Avenue. Only a fraction of the collection is on show at one time, but the revolving exhibitions are nearly always fascinating. The museum shop is one of the best in the city for books about the decorative arts and toys. (See pp. 207–208.)

Frick Collection: 1 East 70th St., at 5th Ave., tel 288 0700. Open Tues–Sat 10–6, Sun 1–6. Stupendous collection of European old-masters (two Rembrandts, two Goyas, two El Grecos and three Vermeers), in one of the most beautiful galleries in the world. (See pp. 128–9.)

Guggenheim Museum: 1083 5th Ave., at 89th St., tel 360 3500. Open Tues 11–7.45, Wed–Sun 11–4.45, adm $4.50, $2.50 students and senior citizens, free Tues 5–7.45. Frank Lloyd Wright's inscrutable white shell. It upstages everything else on 5th Avenue, including some its own more vulnerable exhibits. Inside paintings are arranged on the outside wall of a spiralling ramp, and shows range from temporary exhibitions to selections from the permanent collection (of abstract 20th-century artists including 200 Kandinskys, Klee, Picasso and Delaunay) displayed in the new gallery building designed by Siegel in 1990. The café is very sophisticated, as is the museum shop. (See pp. 204–206.)

International Center of Photography: 1130 5th Ave., at 94th St., tel 860 1777. Open Tues 12–8, Wed–Fri 12–5, Sat–Sun 12–6. Free Tuesday evenings. Fascinating exhibitions of single photographers and groups like Magnum—and the grandest lavatory in the whole city—all housed in an elegant 5th Avenue townhouse.

Metropolitan Museum of Art: 5th Ave., at 82nd St., tel 535 1710. Open Tues–Thurs and Sun 9.30–5.15, Fri–Sat 9.30–8.45. Suggested adm. The biggest of them all. The sheer scope of the collection can be overwhelming. Make sure you find your way to the sculpture garden on the roof and its view of Central Park. The Egyptian rooms and the American Wing are the most impressive of all. (See pp. 200–204.)

Museum of Modern Art (MoMA): 11 West 53rd St., between 5th and 6th Aves., tel 708 9400. Open Fri–Tues 11–6, Thurs 11–9, adm $6, or pay what you want on Thursday evenings. 20th-century painting, design and sculpture from the Post-Impressionists to now. There is also an extensive film collection, a soothing sculpture garden, and drawing and print galleries which always get unfairly neglected. A fashionable crowd, dressed for a cocktail party, cuts a dash through the museum on Thursday evenings and the café is hideously expensive. (See pp. 192–3.)

Museum of the City of New York: 1220 5th Ave., at 103rd St., tel 534 1672. Open Tues–Sat, 10–5, Sun and holidays 1–5. Suggested adm. Staid exhibitions describing the history of the city, and whole galleries devoted to dolls houses, teddy bears and fire engines. The 'Big Apple' multi-visual extravaganza can be traumatic.

National Academy of Design: 1083 5th Ave., at 89th St., tel 369 4880. Open Tues 12–8, Wed–Sun 12–5. Adm free Tues 5–8. Fey but generally enthralling temporary exhibitions. In the past shows have ranged from grotesque furniture to Edward Lear and the London Transport graphic designer, E. McKnight Kauffer. (See p. 206.)

New Museum of Contemporary Art: 583 Broadway, between Houston and Prince Sts., tel 219 1355. Open Wed, Thurs, and Sun 12–6; Fri and Sat 12–8. Suggested adm. Exhibitions, performance pieces and experimental installations of contemporary art in a conceited museum in SoHo.

New-York Historical Society: 170 Central Park West, tel 873 3400. Open Tues–Sun 10–5. Audobon watercolours, Tiffany lamps and works by early American painters, including a self-portrait and a series of loony end-of-the-world architectural fantasies by Thomas Cole called 'The Course of Empire'. The museum building itself is particularly handsome.

The Studio Museum in Harlem: 144 West 125th St., tel 864 4500. Open Wed–Fri 10–5, weekends 1–6. Adm $5. Paintings, sculpture and photographs by contemporary black artists, and exhibitions on black culture.

Whitney Museum of American Art: 945 Madison Ave., at 75th St., tel 570 3676. Open Tues 1–8, Wed–Sat 11–5, Sun 12–6. Free Tues 6–8.

Whitney Downtown: 33 Maiden Lane, tel 943 5655. Open Mon–Fri 9–5. More than 6000 20th-century American paintings and sculptures, stored inside the most sinister building in New York: a brutal granite block with a shadowy eye and distressing overhangs designed by Marcel Breuer in 1966.

Just inside the entrance, is the best exhibit of all: a case containing Alexander Calder's circus; a curious collection of animals and performers made out of scraps and junk: tin, lead, paper clips, rags, springs and clockwork movements. Next to the case is a terribly funny video of Calder-the-Ringmaster giving one of his 'performances' (sometimes considered the first example of performance art). A spring releases a flying rider who leaps onto a circus horse propelled by an egg beater, paper pigeons flutter down spindly wires onto a big-bosomed lady, and a wire lion gets shot by the ringmaster.

Small, Quirky or Specialist Museums

Abigail Adams Smith Museum: 421 East 61st St., tel 838 6878. Open weekdays 10–4, Sun 1–5. 18th-century carriage-house, tended by the doughty Colonial Dames of America, and clearly holding its own in the midst of midtown's skyscrapers.

Afro Arts Cultural Center: 2191 Adam Clayton Powell Jr. Blvd., tel 996 3333. Open weekdays 9–4.30. Artefacts from all over Africa.

American Craft Museum: 40 West 53rd St., tel 956 3535. Open Tues 10–8; Wed–Sun 10–5. Well-meaning but antiseptic museum showing crafts from 1900 to the present day (pottery, patchwork, textiles, furniture, etc).

American Museum of the Moving Image: 34–12 36th St., Astoria, Queens, tel (718) 784 0077. Open Wed–Thurs, 1–5, Fri 1–7.30, Sat 11–7.30, Sun 11–6. Adm $5. Supposedly a complete history of the cinema, but unfortunately the museum pales in comparison to the infinitely more imaginative MoMI in London. (The kiddies, however, clearly enjoy creating their own commercials, and the collection of fanzines is interesting.) Two screening rooms, showing an esoteric and fascinating selection of films you won't get a chance to see anywhere else, make up for the inadequecies of the rest. Phone ahead to find about the current program, or look at the listings and reviews in the *Village Voice*. (See pp. 409–10.)

Black Fashion Museum: 155 West 126th St., tel 666 1320. Open weekdays 12–8 **by appointment only**. Work by contemporary black fashion designers, as well as clothes from the 19th century worn and made by black slaves. Though the collection includes 5000 items of clothing, less than a score seem to be on display at any one time.

Bronx River Gallery: 1087 Tremont Ave., Bronx, tel 589 5819. Open Wed–Sat 1–5. Contemporary photography and a sculpture garden in a rough part of the South Bronx.

Clocktower Gallery: 13th floor, 108 Leonard St., tel 233 1096. Open Thurs–Sun 12–6. Voluntary adm. Avant-garde gallery situated in the clocktower of the old New York Life Insurance building which often has exciting exhibitions of contemporary architectural drawings, as well as paintings and sculpture. There is an astonishing rooftop view of the whole of downtown Manhattan. (See p. 224.)

Dezerland's Dream Car Collection: 270 11th Ave., tel 564 4590. Open Tues–Fri 6–midnight, weekends midday–midnight. Adm $5. A batty collection of 1950s convertibles, and an indoor drive-in movie theater filled with vintage automobiles.

El Museo del Barrio: 1230 5th Ave., at 104th St., tel 831 7272. Suggested adm. Open Wed–Sun 11–5. Contemporary Puerto Rican and Latin American art in a neighborhood center with spirited exhibitions of painting and sculpture by local artists. A fascinating collection of *santos de Palo*, or carved votive figures, is on permanent display.

Forbes Magazine Galleries: 62 5th Ave., tel 206 5548. Open Tues–Wed and Fri–Sat 10–4. Adm free. Malcolm Forbes' extraordinary collection of Fabergé eggs, plus armies of toy soldiers and boats.

Garibaldi Meucci Museum: 420 Tompkins Ave., Staten Island, tel 442 1608. Open Tues–Fri 9–5, Sat–Sun 1–5. Adm free. Relics, including 17 candles made by Garibaldi while he lived in exile on Staten Island with his friend Anotonio Meucci and worked as a candlemaker.

Hispanic Society of America: Broadway at 155th St., tel 926 2234. Open Tues–Sat 10–4.30; Sun 1–4. Adm free. One of the city's most neglected museums: an opulent Spanish Renaissance courtyard in the middle of Harlem. Exquisite lustre-ware and tiles, and paintings by Goya, Velásquez and El Greco. (See p. 272.)

Isamu Noguchi Garden Museum: 32–37 Vernon Blvd., Long Island City, Queens, tel (718) 204 7088. Open April–Nov, Wed–Sat 11–6. An hourly bus service to the museum leaves at 30 minutes past the hour from the Asia Society, Park Avenue, fare $5. Indoor and outdoor sculpture gardens in Noguchi's old studios, originally a lamp factory, well worth a special expedition. (See p. 411.)

Jacques Marchais Center of Tibetan Art: 338 Lighthouse Ave., Staten Island, tel (718) 987 3478. Open April–Nov Wed–Sun 1–5. In the Himalayas of Staten Island, the largest collection of Tibetan art in the West. Jacques Marchais was an arts dealer.

Lower East Side Tenement Museum: 97 Orchard St., tel 431 0233. Open Tues–Fri 11–4. Voluntary adm. Tiny museum in the middle of the Orchard Street market devoted to tenements and immigrant cultures. Admittedly there isn't a great deal to see, but the gallery of 19th- and early 20th-century photographs of the area is illuminating.

Museum of Broadcasting: 23 West 53rd St., tel 752 7684. Open Tues 12–8, Wed–Sat 12–5. Suggested adm. Here you can watch telly to your heart's content, and not feel guilty. Not really a museum, but a library-cum-archive of 30,000 television programs and 10,000 radio shows which visitors can request and then watch on video consoles. (The two most popular are an hour of vintage television commercials and the Beatles' live debut on television.) There are also two excellent small video theaters which the museum uses for retrospectives (Monty Python, the Three Stooges, Watergate, etc). (See pp. 193–4.)

Museum of the American Indian: Broadway at 155th St., tel 283 2420. Open Tues–Sat 10–5, Sun 1–5. Largest collection in America of Indian artefacts—beautiful feathered costumes, tomahawks and some rather chilling shrunken heads. The collection is superb, but it doesn't get many visitors and sadly it is soon going to be split up and moved to the Smithsonian and the Customs House downtown. (See pp. 271–2.)

New York City Fire Museum: 278 Spring St., tel 691 1303. Open Tues–Sat 10–4. Fire apparatus, in all its incarnations.

New York City Transit Exhibit: Boerum Place, at Schermerhorn, Brooklyn, tel (718) 330 3060. Open Mon–Fri 10–4, Sat 11–4. Subway token as adm. Ancient trains and carriages housed underground in an enormous abandoned subway station in Brooklyn.

New York Hall of Science: Flushing Meadows Park, 47–01 48th Ave., and 111th St., tel (718) 699 0005. Open Wed–Sun 10–5. A marvelous relic from that apogee of the American Tasteless Movement, the 1964 World's Fair. Fascinating exhibits on display inside a corrugated blue brain deposited in a Space Park filled with three rockets, including parts of an Apollo spacecraft. Nearby, you can explore the kitsch remaining ruins of the 1964 World's Fair. (See p. 406.)

North Wind Undersea Museum: 610 City Island Ave., Bronx, tel 885 0701. Open Mon–Fri 10–5, Sat–Sun 12–5. A 9 ft wide whale's jaw, and three seals trained by the police to retrieve drugs and people from under the sea. (See pp. 417–8.)

Pierpont Morgan Library: 33 East 36th St., tel 685 0610. Open Tues–Sat 10.30–5; Sun 1–5. A sumptuous marble library and Italianate palazzo used for several recondite but interesting exhibitions a year ('Orientalism' and '18th-century prints of Venice').

Police Academy Museum: 235 East 20th St., tel 477 9753. Open Mon–Tues, Thurs–Fri 9–3. Adm free. The quirkiest museum in Manhattan, worth a special trip to see a fascinating history of organized crime and display cases of 'recently acquired contraband weapons' including saw-tooth knuckledusters and a mace. Schoolchildren are especially impressed by the exhibits. (See p. 159.)

Queens Museum: Flushing Meadows Park, tel (718) 592 2405. Open Tues–Fri 10–5; Sat–Sun 12–5.30. Suggested adm. Another underrated museum, worth a trip on its own to see the famous Panorama – an 18,000 square-foot model of the city built for the World's Fair of 1939. It is updated regularly. Also a superb and extensive collection of 1939 and 1964 World's Fair memorabilia. (See p. 406.)

Ukrainian Museum: 203 2nd Ave., between 12th and 13th Sts., tel 228 0110. Open Wed–Sun, 1–5, adm $1. Photographs of Ukrainian life and the inevitable painted Easter eggs, situated near Manhattan's 'Little Ukraine' on 7th Street.

The Heights and the Harlems

El Barrio and La Marqueta—Central Harlem—North Harlem and Hamilton Heights—Morningside Heights and Columbia—Washington Heights, Fort Tryon Park and the Cloisters

Above 110th Street the city gets a landscape, and sheer bluffs and precipices divide the Heights (Washington, Hamilton and Morningside) from the Harlems (North, Central, and El Barrio and La Marqueta). To many New Yorkers, the north end of the island is a disorientating place, where wild-looking forest and craggy rocks devour the grid; where a white face stands out; and where a summer mansion housing Napoleon's bed sits absurdly in the middle of some of the most tense and impoverished streets on the island.

Accompanying the unexpected and shocking, however, are some nice surprises: the most chaotic soul-food restaurants in Manhattan, the steamiest, smelliest and most disorganized market, the grandest views, and two exceptional museums—the Smithsonian's American Indian collection in North Harlem; and the 'Cloisters', the Metropolitan's vast and eccentric collection of medieval art, on a wooded hilltop in Morningside Heights.

The Heights and the Harlems couldn't be more dissimilar: one is wealthy, narrow and high-up; the other is poor, broad and low-lying. Both, however, possess some of the finest Gothic, Romanesque, Art-

Deco and even Medieval churches in the city (including St John the Divine, the largest Gothic-hybrid cathedral in the world, and the authentic 12th-century French and Spanish monastic buildings of the Cloisters Museum). So, come on a Sunday if you can, when outsiders are generally made welcome at Gospel services in Harlem. (For a more formal visit, the black-owned Harlem Spirituals, tel 718 275 1408, and Harlem Gospel Tours, tel 691 7866, both organize tours to Gospel churches).

The north end of Manhattan stretches nearly 6 miles from 220th Street at the top to 110th Street at the bottom, and because distances are great you won't be able to see everything in one go. The trips below divide the area into two, with a few bus journeys to save your feet. If you're really nifty, however, you could easily combine a trip to Harlem with an afternoon visit to the Cloisters, finishing up with a picnic in Fort Tryon Park—one of the few good picnicking spots in Manhattan, with the notable exception of Central Park.

Walking Time: for each of the two trips, allow a morning and an afternoon, or about 5 hours.

Harlem
El Barrio—La Marqueta—Canaan Baptist Church of Christ—
St Martin's Episcopal Church—Marcus Garvey Park—125th Street—
Studio Museum of Harlem—Apollo Theater—Striver's Row—
Morris-Jumel Mansion—Audubon Terrace—Church of the Intercession—
Trinity Cemetery

> Harlem is today the Negro metropolis and as such is everywhere known.
>
> James Weldon Johnson, *Black Manhattan*, 1930.

Harlem is now a notoriously troubled district, suffering from years of underfunding and unemployment; but it is still the spiritual center of Black America. Walking around, the visitor immediately becomes conscious that Harlem is a symbol as well as a place. White sightseers, especially, won't be able to turn a blind eye to its past, whether they meet with the coolest brush-off, or, as is much more likely, the friendliest welcome.

Today Harlem looks scruffy, rather than decimated in the manner of the South Bronx and East Brooklyn. It is a neat neighborhood of broad

263

boulevards bustling with activity, and quieter wide streets. Typically the streets contain a mixture of proud-looking row houses with high stoops, tenements and Victorian churches (which have all survived thanks to years of hardship), alongside more recent red-brick housing projects and vacant lots.

Harlem only became a black neighborhood in 1904, after a proposal for a new subway in the area sparked off a speculative building boom which backfired: so many desirable houses and apartment buildings shot up that the market collapsed. A black realtor, Philip A. Payton, negotiated deals with the Harlem landlords, filling the empty buildings with black tenants, often at higher rents than whites. At that time a number of black neighborhoods in the rest of the city were being demolished, and the uprooted inhabitants were being excluded from established white communities. Blacks naturally gravitated toward Harlem, and they were soon joined by laborers drifting north, away from the devastated American South and the West Indies.

In the twenties, while its population swelled to over 200,000, Harlem basked under what became known as the Harlem Renaissance—a tremendous flowering of black talent and (for whites) a new, exotic social life. Manhattan looked to Harlem as a nightclub fantasy-land, bursting with jazz, clubs, casinos and cabarets—Small's Paradise, the Lafayette, the Savoy, the Cotton Club and the Harlem Casino. Some of these clubs were whites-only and most were white-owned, though ironically black musicians like Duke Ellington and Cab Calloway were welcomed.

For black intellectuals, writers and artists, on the other hand, Harlem became a cultural home, and a laboratory for new ideas and the raising of black consiousness. At its core were the writers W.E.B. Du Bois and James Weldon Johnson, the poet Langston Hughes; and Marcus Garvey, the militant leader of the Back-to-Africa movement, who emigrated to Harlem from the West Indies in 1916.

The Depression exposed the extent of the poverty hidden beneath the glamor, with an unemployment rate of 50 per cent—twice as bad as the rest of the city. In the post-War years Harlem became increasingly overcrowded: more than a million blacks moved north from the rural south, and Puerto Ricans and other Hispanics from the Caribbean area moved into El Barrio, or Spanish Harlem.

By the sixties Harlem was a key center of black political consciousness, thanks to figures like Malcolm X, H. Rap Brown and Stokely Carmichael. After the riots and protests of 1968, funds started trickling in, but still Harlem was desperate for investment. Recently, however, hopes have been raised for a second renaissance, as new money has revitalized places like 135th Street and the Apollo, and Harlem now boasts institutions like the Dance Theater of Harlem and the Schomburg Center of Research in Black Culture, with the largest collection of its kind anywhere. On the minus side, there are still complex underlying tensions, and problems which need to be solved before the community will be able to compete economically with the rest of Manhattan.

Start: you can start the trip either in East Harlem ('El Barrio'), or, if you are visiting on a Sunday when the market in East Harlem is closed, in Central Harlem. For East Harlem take the **M102** bus to Lexington Avenue and East 116th Street, or the **M1** bus to Madison Avenue and East 116th Street, or take the **6** subway to 116th Street and Lexington Avenue. For Central Harlem, take the **2** or the **3** subway to 116th Street and Lenox Avenue, and start the walk at the **Canaan Baptist Church** (see p. 267).

Lunch/Cafés: In **East Harlem** the best place for lunch is **Patsy's Pizzeria**, on 2287 1st Avenue and 117th Street. A bastion of the old Italian Harlem, Patsy's has been going since 1932, and has one of the last coal-fired ovens in the city. In Central Harlem there are two main choices: **Sylvia's Restaurant**, at 327 Lenox Avenue between 125th and 126th Streets, and **La Famille**, at 2017 5th Avenue, between 124th and 125th Streets. The latter is one of the oldest and cheapest restaurants in Harlem, with a jazz bar downstairs and a family restaurant upstairs serving a delicious and filling continental and soul-food lunch for under $5. It is closed for lunch on Saturdays and Sundays, when you should head off for Sylvia's, which serves vast, hearty breakfasts, lunches and suppers. In North Harlem there is **Wilson's Bakery and Restaurant**, 1980 Amsterdam Avenue at 158th Street, a hectic café which serves soul-food breakfasts and lunches of spicy sausages and grits, ribs and fried chicken.

The trip starts on the east side of the district in Spanish Harlem, or *El Barrio* ('the neighborhood'). At first glance the area seems more lively than so-called Black Harlem: it throbs with salsa; and a jumble of graffiti, neon signs and brightly painted riot gates and murals assault the eye. The streets are a hive of activity: clogged with 'Productos Tropicales', tarot-card readers and astrologers, bakeries filled with 10-tier wedding-cake towers, and cut-price clothes, electronics and toys which spill out onto the pavement and pile up on cardboard boxes or swing from racks on wheels.

Even so, El Barrio is the most economically battered district in Harlem: all tenements and housing projects, and no parks; and with some of the worst pockets of poverty and unemployment in Manhattan. As far as architecture goes, moreover, this part of Harlem has never been distinguished: it began as a slum in 1879 after the building of the 'El' along 3rd and 2nd Avenue, was settled by German, Italians, Irish and even Finnish workers, and today it is still an impoverished district with a hopeless unemployment rate of 40 per cent.

*From the bus stop on 116th Street and Lexington Avenue, walk a block west to the Puerto Rican fruit, meat, vegetable and houseware market—**La Marqueta**—on 116th to Park Avenue.*

Stretching under a covered arcade on Park Avenue between 116th and 112th Streets, the market is concentrated Spanish Harlem: thudding salsa and utter chaos. It was opened in 1936 by Mayor Fiorello LaGuardia, an East Harlem resident, and a reformer whose sometimes overzealous crusades began with the banning of street peddlers and organ-grinders from the streets. The market sits in four arcades under the dour stone-vaulted commuter railroad which trains hurtle down before diving underground at 96th Street. This is the dramatic Great Divide which all too visibly marks the border between the monstrous eldorado of wealth of the Upper East Side, where residents are protected from undesirables such as dirt and belching trains, and El Barrio, where, by force of circumstance, inhabitants are inured to the ugliness of a stone wall darkening the whole length of Park Avenue.

In the market itself, expect to have beef tripe, cows' feet, incense and banana palms wafted under your nose; and if you are female, to be bamboozled in the nicest possible way by a barrage of 'darlings', 'dolls' and 'honeybunches'. The market boys are so persistent that unless you shake your head with real determination you will probably come away laden with hundreds of soggy parcels wrapped in brown paper and banana leaves. Which is fine, because as long as you bargain, La Marqueta is the cheapest market in the city.

The top end of the market near 116th Street is the wettest, dirtiest and smelliest, and sells conches, catfish, snappers and prawns. Hurry past the pong to the next arcades, which are the most colorful and sell an extraordinary variety of Latino and Caribbean meats, fruits and vegetables—dry *baccalao* (salt cod), sugar cane, rotten bananas, yams, coriander, papaya, and every part of a pig imaginable—including spine-chilling gallon-bottles of blood.

266

A stall in the third arcade sells a fascinating range of religious paraphernalia. It belongs to **Otto Chicas Rendon**, *whose two other shops, just round the corner from the top of the market, on 56 and 60 116th Street between Park and Madison Avenues, are worth a special trip.*

Rendons are the Harrods of the *botánicas*, the religious shops that are a fixture in the Hispanic areas of New York. Their products, which can cure practically any ailment—physical or mental—range from joblots of horseshoes, crystal balls, evil eyes, apothecary's herbs and incense, to aerosal Money sprays, Run-Devil-Run syrup, Mr Wippler's Latin American Love Potion and dried-up frogs. At the front of the main shop on 56 116th Street is a wishing-well equipped with a parrot which speaks Spanish, and a huge billboard saying 'Rendons Renders Results'.

Have a look round this enthralling shop, and then walk two and a half blocks along 116th Street to Lenox Avenue. (The walk takes about 7 minutes, but you can catch the **M102** *from outside Rendon's, and jump off at Lenox Avenue). Here, on the southwest corner, you will see the aluminum turnip-shaped dome topped by an eternally revolving golden crescent of the* **Malcolm Shabazz Mosque**.

Originally the Lenox Casino, it was converted into a 20th-century-style Arab Emirates mosque in 1965 by Elijah Muhammed. Muhammed was also known as the Last Messenger, the chief disciple of the virulently anti-white separatist movement called the Black Muslims, which was founded in Detroit in 1930 by an Arabian door-to-door salesman known as Mr Farrad. Shortly before his great break with the Black Muslims and Muhammed, Macolm X preached inside the mosque.

Around the shops are a number of Muslim stops and stores, and a little way further down at 132 West 116th Street is the **Canaan Baptist Church of Christ**, where visitors are given a really effusive welcome by the pastor, Wyatt Tee Walker, at gospel services on Sundays (services begin at 10.45 am).

Further along still, on the southwest corner of 7th Avenue and 116th Street is one of the strangest sights in Harlem: a flash replica of the Doge's Palace in Venice, covered in tiles, oriental confections and spindly columns. Now home to the **First Corinthian Baptist Church**, it was built in 1913 as the city's first motion picture theater. The cinema launched the career of the impresario Samuel L. Rothapfel, latterly the 'Roxy' of Radio City (see pp. 191–2), who rescued the cinema from being an utter flop with a number of innovations, most notably programed music which fitted the action of the film.

Now retrace your steps back to the corner of Lenox Avenue and 116th Street, turn left and walk six short blocks north to 122nd Street. On the southeast corner is **St Martin's Episcopal Church**, *one of the finest Victorian-Romanesque churches in the city with a bulky brownstone tower housing a big carillon of 40 bells. Turn right and walk down 122nd Street, past a row of some of the best-preserved late-Victorian townhouses in Harlem, to* **Marcus Garvey Park** *at the end.*

Filled entirely by an steep hunk of rock resembling a volcano, Marcus Garvey Park qualifies as the most peculiar park in Manhattan. The rock-mountain was too massive to dynamite, so in 1839 the city resorted to turning it into a park. It is not advisable to go exploring in the park on your own, but from the street you can catch a glimpse of the extraordinary pylon at the top of the craggy summit—made of cast-iron with an elegant spiral staircase and a bell, it served for years as a watchtower.

The park was originally known as Mount Morris Square, and renamed in 1973 in honor of Marcus Garvey, the magniloquent and charismatic West Indian leader of the Back-to-Africa movement and self-styled Sir Provisional President of Africa. Lying along the west flank of the park is the **Mount Morris Historic District**, which was landmarked in the sixties to preserve the area's splendid collection of late-19th century Victorian houses. One of the best is the enormous neo-Renaissance mansion built in 1890 on the corner of Mount Morris Park West at 1 West 123rd Street. Now the **Ethiopian Hebrew Congregation**, it is presently home to a congregation of black Jews belonging to the Ethiopian Hebrew Movement, founded in 1920s. The Saturday service combines the Jewish liturgy and gospel singing. As in an Orthodox synagogue, the women sit separately from the men.

By now you will probably be peckish. You can get a huge soul-food/Continental lunch at **La Famille**, *just north of the square between 124th and 125th Streets at 2017 5th Avenue; or, round the corner from La Famille, there are fattening pies, cakes and banana pudding at* **De de's Bakery** *at 69 125th Street. (See Lunch/ Cafés, above: La Famille is closed for lunch on weekends,* *but you can get a delicious meal at Sylvia's Restaurant, just north of 125th Street at 328 Lenox Avenue.)*

Even if you aren't hungry, walk up 5th Avenue for one block from Marcus Garvey Park, and turn left onto 125th Street, one of Harlem's most hectic shopping streets and thoroughfares. Make your way down 125th Street, past Lenox Avenue and the small outdoor market selling clothes, bags and hats made out of African textiles. A little way on is the **Studio Museum in Harlem**, *on the lefthand side of the street between Lenox and 7th Avenues at 144 West 125th Street, (open Wed–Fri, 10–5, Sat–Sun, 1–6, adm $5).*

Inside this amazingly slick art gallery, as well as excellent temporary exhibitions of painting, photography and sculpture relevant to black culture, there is a permanent collection of old photographs of Harlem, and work by James Van DerZee who lived on Lenox Avenue from the 1920s until the 1960s.

Facing the museum is the **New York State Office Building**, a rather grim tower block built as a token of state support for Harlem in 1973, after the upheavals and unrest of the sixties.

Carry on along 125th Street to 7th Avenue. Here, on the southwest corner, is **Theresa Towers**, *Harlem's smartest and largest hotel before it was made into offices in 1971. Its most famous guest was Fidel Castro, who flounced out of an East Side hotel and moved into the Theresa in 1960. Khrushchev came to visit him in his suite, as did Malcolm X, who set up offices in the hotel shortly before his assassination in 1965.*

A few steps along from the hotel, look in at **Mart 1-2-5**, *a large indoor market which exists mostly for the benefit of tourists, and sells an impressive array of African carpets, clothes and sculptures. It stands opposite the canopy of the* **Apollo Theater**, *at 253 125th Street.*

Launching pad for a string of black musicians and performers, the Apollo was a whites-only vaudeville theater until 1934. Bessie Smith, 'Empress of the Blues', appeared there in the late-thirties; and Billy Holiday, Duke Ellington, Charlie Parker, Aretha Franklin, the Supremes and the Jackson Five followed in her footsteps. By the seventies, however, the theater was visibly mouldering, and in 1976 it was finally forced to close down.

After several attempts, it re-opened properly in 1985, and the gold-and-white auditorium inside was refurbished from top to toe. The famous Wednesday Amateur Nights—astonishingly raucous affairs—were also revived (tel 749 5838 for performance schedules). In the day time it is often used for radio broadcasts before a live audience, and it is worth asking the ushers, who are extremely amenable, if they will let you look round.

Walk back to Lenox Avenue, and board the M2 bus which takes you north up the Avenue. If you have time, you can hop off 14 blocks north at **Striver's Row**, *an extraordinary block of housing built for white occupants in the 1890s on 138th and 139th Streets.*

Striver's Row is the most distinguished enclave of 19th-century row-housing in Harlem, situated in the middle of an otherwise tattered district of vacant lots and dingy stores. During the real estate boom of 1891, three architectural firms were commissioned to design the houses by David King, the developer responsible for the old Madison Square Garden and the base of the Statue of Liberty.

All the buildings on 138th Street are neo-Georgian with beautiful limestone and terracotta trims. The northernmost row on 139th Street, designed by the architects of New York's *beau monde* McKim, Mead & White, are neo-Italian in style, with Renaissance medallions and balconies, and no stoops. All have rear allies for garbage—a conspicuous waste of valuable real estate that is virtually unheard of in New York.

As Harlem became black, Striver's Row retained its cachet: in the thirties the musicians W. C. Handy and Eubie Blake became residents, and since then prominent Harlemites, including black lawyers, doctors and civic leaders, have always lived on the block.

Nearby, on 138th Street, between Lenox and 7th Avenues, is the **Abyssinian Baptist Church**. Architecturally undistinguished, it was adopted by the charismatic preacher Adam Clayton Powell, who turned it into the richest and most powerful black church in America. A potent speaker and politician with a flamboyant temper, Powell battled for black civil rights in Congress until he was expelled on charges of misusing government funds. Nowadays the impossibly named Rev. Calvin Butts presides over proceedings, and welcomes strangers to gospel services on Sundays.

Jump on the M2 once more, and take it all the way to the end of Lenox Avenue, and then two blocks west and six north to 160th

Street and Edgecombe Avenue. Here on 160th Street, in stark contrast to the urban devastation surrounding it, is the **Morris-Jumel Mansion**, *a pre-Revolutionary Georgian summer house which is the nearest thing New York has to a stately home (open Tues–Sun, 10–4).*

The place is in considerable disrepair, and the peeling paint on the clapboard outside gives it the appearance of an abandoned house. The custodians skulk round it, pretending it is empty, but if you give the front door a good bash they eventually reveal themselves. It is worth being persistent, because the interior is quite fascinating. Upstairs, as well as the office Washington occupied during the disastrous Battle of Harlem Heights, is Eliza Jumel's boudoir. Done up in all the trappings of a Loire château, the room contains a tiny French Empire bed, a pair of silk stockings and a garter embroidered with *Amore*. According to the curators, the bed originally belonged to Napoleon and was bought after his fall by Madame Jumel, who spent the next few years trying to persuade him to emigrate to the States. A doughty, business-minded lady, Jumel scandalized New York with her love affairs and reputedly left her husband to bleed to death in the attic in 1832.

Wander through the rather romantically disheveled backyard, and then walk two blocks west along 160th Street past Sylvan Terrace, a row of pretty wooden cottages built for workers in the 1880s, to Amsterdam Avenue. Two blocks east of here, at 158th Street and 1980 Amsterdam Avenue, is **Wilson's**, *where you can stop off for a tea of biscuits and rolls, or peach cobbler with vanilla ice cream, in an extremely popular neighborhood bakery and café (those who are more hungry can also get a full-blown soul-food lunch with pudding).*

From Wilson's walk a block west to Broadway, and then two blocks south to the complex of museums on **Audubon Terrace** *between 156th and 155th Streets. Situated on the estate of the naturalist and painter John James Audubon, the neo-Classical terrace has been turned into a home for four museums, probably the least-visited in Manhattan due to their remote location. This is unfortunate, because the* **Museum of the American Indian** *is also one of most interesting (open Tues–Sat, 10–5, Sun 1–5).*

Start on the 3rd floor (Central and South American Indians) where there is an extremely colorful display of Inca feather-costumes—some resembling fifties bathing hats—and a fascinating case of Amazonian blowguns and *tsantsa*: (shrunken heads and figures). The heads were shrunken by the Jivaro Indians, and used in various religious ceremonies to render their enemies powerless. The skull was removed, the eyes and lips sewn shut to prevent the soul escaping, and the head boiled in glue for hours and then dried on hot stones, after which it was rubbed with charcoal and polished. Downstairs, the museum includes a vast diorama of life in Indian Manhattan, and an interesting show of tomahawks and scalps captured by Government bounty hunters.

Next door to the Indian Museum is another superb and unjustly neglected museum belonging to the **Hispanic Society of America** (open Tues–Sun, 10–4.30, Sun 1–4.30). Simone de Beauvoir caught the particular charm of the building when she visited New York in 1947: 'I was amazed on going through a door,' she wrote, 'to find myself in the very heart of Spain; the quiet rooms smelt of Spain; they are decorated with majolica, carved panelling and fine stamped leather; hanging from the walls of the gallery which runs round the central hall are Goyas, Grecos and Zurbarans: some of them look of doubtful origin . . . Americans, no doubt, are too avid for Old Masters to be over-particular.'

Opposite Audubon Terrace, in an otherwise ragged stretch of Broadway and 155th Street, is a really exceptional Gothic-Revival building, the **Church of the Intercession**.

It was designed in 1914 by Bertram Goodhue, the eclectic architect of St Thomas' Church and St Bartholomew's in midtown, and sits reassuringly on high ground overlooking Broadway like a heftily-massed country church. Inside, Goodhue lies in a flamboyant wall-tomb below an effigy and a golden frieze of his own buildings. Surrounding the church is **Trinity Cemetery** (open 9–4.30 daily, entrance on 155th Street near Riverside Drive). A strangely rural place, it was established by Trinity Church in 1846, as land downtown began to get swallowed up. Now surrounded by shabbiness, it contains the graves of Eliza Jumel, John James Audubon, and New York's crooked Tammany mayor and double-dealer, Fernando Wood.

The 1 subway train, which is just up the road on 157th Street and Broadway, will whisk you back to central Manhattan. Anyone who wants to carry on to the Cloisters, containing the Metropolitan Museum of Art's medieval collection, could catch the **M4** *from*

Broadway which drops passengers on its doorstep in Fort Tryon Park (see below, p. 277).

Morningside Heights and the Cloisters

Amsterdam Avenue—Cathedral of St John the Divine—Église de Notre Dame—Columbia University—Riverside Church—Fort Tryon Park—the Cloisters

Start: take the 1 subway train to 110th Street and Broadway.
Lunch/Cafés: In good weather, bring a picnic lunch to eat in Fort Tryon Park, and stop off for breakfast and tea in the various cafés and restaurants along the way. On Amsterdam Avenue one of the best is the Latino **Elsa Café**, at 886 Amsterdam Avenue between 104th and 105th Streets. Here a juke box blithely booms out salsa despite a sign saying 'The music is controlled so it don't sound too loud'. Patrons drink beer and *clamato* mixed, and eat Diplomatic Pudding—a kind of rusty crème caramel—and goat stew. Otherwise there is the excellent Mexican **Mi Tierra**, at 668 Amsterdam Avenue and 93rd Street, or the Haitian **Caribbean Creole Cuisine Restaurant**, one of only two Haitian restaurants in New York at 852 Amsterdam Avenue and 102nd Street. Also at 665 Amsterdam and 92nd Street you can pick up a take-away breakfast from the **Patisserie Les Friandises**, at 665 Amsterdam and 92nd Street. Opposite the Cathedral of St John the Divine are two favorite neighborhood restaurants, the **Hungarian Pastry Shop** at 1030 Amsterdam Avenue, a heavenly coffee-house which smells of *sachertorte* and strudel, and the less hectic **Green Tree Hungarian Restaurant** next door.

The subway lands you in Morningside Heights, a rocky island of wealth surrounded by downtrodden areas to the north, east and the south. Most of the money here is in the hands of big institutions like Columbia University (the wealthiest landlord), the Union and Jewish Theological Seminaries, St John the Divine, and Riverside Church. The area around the subway stop itself is a lively part of Broadway, surrounded by bars, restaurants and grocers, and miles of extremely cheap secondhand books laid out on plastic sheets on the sidewalk.

From the subway stop walk a block east to **Amsterdam Avenue**.

To the south, between 92nd and 110th Streets, lies a lively Latino, West Indian and Haitian stretch of Amsterdam Avenue which retains the kind of raw vitality which used to be typical of the whole of the Upper West Side before gentrification. Local residents stroll up and down the avenue, or take chairs out into the street and sit in the open air and chat. There are supermarkets selling all manner of tropical fruits and vegetables, and curious places like the shop at 672 Amsterdam Avenue between 92nd and 93rd Streets, which is hidden under heaps of loose sweets.

If you want to search out a Latino or a Mexican lunch before going to the Cathedral of St John the Divine, walk south down Amsterdam Avenue to one of the restaurants mentioned in the lunch and café section above. Otherwise walk up to 112th Street and the **Cathedral of St John the Divine***, on the righthand side of the street.*

This extraordinary, elephantine hybrid has been evolving for over a century, and now, towerless and still unfinished, it looms over everything on Morningside Heights. It is already the largest Gothic cathedral in the world—and, if it ever is finished, it will be *the* largest cathedral in the world.

Work began on the project in 1887, after the competition for an Episcopalian cathedral was won by the Heins & LaFarge partnership, which specialized in Victorian interiors and kiosks for the subway as well as buildings. A quarter of a century later, however, only the four arches and the choir were complete, and Heins and Lafarge were both dead. Tastes change, and in 1916 the original Romanesque-Byzantine plan was jettisoned for a French-Gothic design by Ralph Adams Cram which incorporated the original apse, choir and crossing. Construction proceded at a snail's pace, and after several financial hiccups, by 1942 only the nave and the west front were complete. Then the War brought building to a complete halt.

After the War, minor construction dribbled on. After a plan to construct a contemporary-style campanile nearly as tall as the Eiffel Tower was rejected in the sixties, work ceased altogether, and was only resumed in 1978. This time a major fund-raising campaign was launched, and stonemasons were imported from England to apprentice local people in the art of stonecutting. (On weekdays you can see teams chiseling away in the yards and workshops adjacent to the church.)

From the outside the towerless façade looks medieval, if rather more like a massive block of Gothic flats than a church. The immense gully inside, however, is a rather more impressive space—narrow and dark,

274

with a strangely oppressive atmosphere. At the uncompleted **Crossing** where the delicate Cram-Gothic meets the more rough-and-ready Romanesque of Heins & Lafarge, the visitor gets a fascinating glimpse into the cathedral's anatomy: its massive granite piers, its unfinished arches; and its vast temporary dome of red Italian tiles, which was put up in a hurry in 1909 to save money. From here you get a good view of the extraordinary rose window, 40 ft in diameter, and containing 10,000 pieces of glass.

Scattered throughout the cathedral are various priceless bits and pieces of art—in the Crossing, the Barberini Tapestries woven on papal looms in the 17th century; in the Ambulatory a diptych of the *Annunciation* attributed to Simone Martini, and some glazed terracotta by Luca della Robbia; and, best of all, in the bays of the north aisle the Mortlake Tapestries woven from a series of cartoons by Raphael. Before leaving, it is also worth investigating a small museum in the North Transept which describes the construction of the cathedral; and the temporary exhibitions in the Museum of Religious Art in the South Ambulatory.

> *Leave the cathedral and stop off for tea at the* **Hungarian Pastry Shop***. Then walk round the side of the cathedral to an exquisite little church on 114th Street and Morningside Drive, the* **Église de Notre Dame***.*

One of the prettiest classical churches in the city, it easily holds its own against the monstrous hulk of St John. Outside is a fine Corinthian portico, and inside the immaculately kept church is laid out on a Greek cross-plan. At the very back is a fuzz of green ivy, a replica of the grotto at Lourdes which was donated by a parishioner who promised it in her prayers in return for the recovery of a son. Recently it was dusted and pruned, to the great dismay of the French Catholic congregation.

> *Now walk two blocks north to 114th Street, turn left and then walk a block west to Amsterdam Avenue and the entrance to the* **Columbia University** *campus.*

A McKim, Mead & White creation of the 1890s, the campus is rather disappointing except for the grand space in the center which serves as a kind of forum for the university. At the north end is McKim's impressive domed **Low Library**, with its three magisterial tiers of steps leading up to the entrance.

> *Make your way west across the campus to Broadway, turn right, and walk four blocks to 120th Street. A block further west, on Riverside*

Drive between 120th and 122nd Streets, is the Gothic **Riverside Church**.

Though its Gothic trims, carvings and stained glass are borrowed from Chartres, the church is actually a skyscraper, with a steel-framed tower that shoots into the air for 392 ft and 22 stories. Inside is a chapel based on the Romanesque Church of St Nazaire at Carcassone in France, with an exquisitely carved reredos showing the Last Supper and the Transfiguration.

From the narthex, visitors can take an elevator and a flight of 147 steps to the tower's windswept observation deck. At the top is a 74-bell carillon, the largest in the world, and a 20-ton bass bell, the largest ever cast (the observation deck is best avoided on Saturday at noon and Sunday at 3 when the carillonneur plays deafening recitals).

From the deck, you get as near a view as you could wish for of **Grant's Tomb**, which commemorates Ulysses S. Grant, the Civil War general, and is famous for being the most boring and pompous monument in the city. 'The only perfect architectural structure in the world,' goes the familiar quip, 'you couldn't alter one detail without improving it'. All the more humiliating for the Victorian architect, John Duncan, is the fact that it was a copy of one of the Seven Wonders of the Ancient World, the tomb of Mausoleus at Halicarnassus.

Take the elevator down, leave the church, and then make your way back to Broadway, where you can catch the northbound **M4** *which takes you all the way to the front door of the Cloisters Museum at the very northern tip of Manhattan. The bus journey is diverting: on the way, at 165th Street and Broadway, the route passes an enormous old movie theater, the* **Audubon Ballroom**, *where Malcolm X was shot at point-blank range during a rally in 1965 after he fell out with Elijah Muhammed. And 10 blocks further up, in an otherwise depressing district, the bus passes another, excessively exotic cinema, the* **United Church** *on the east side at 175th Street and Broadway. Apparently a Syrian mosque, with a fantastical terracotta façade and an oriental mosaic tower topped by a neon star, it was actually built as a Loew's movie palace in 1930. In recent years, it has been taken over for services (backed up by the old 'Wonder Organ') commandeered by the preacher, shaman and media personality Frederick Eikerenkoetter, who is known more simply as the Rev. Ike.*

About 5 or 10 minutes later, when the bus starts climbing through the breathtaking terraces and bluffs of **Fort Tryon Park** *on the* *edge of the Hudson, you will know that the **Cloisters Museum** is only a short distance away (open March–Oct, Tues–Sun, 9.30–5.15; and Nov–Feb 9.30–4.45, suggested adm $5).*

The Cloisters building is Manhattan's most engaging *trompe l'oeil*, an utterly convincing mock-up of a medieval monastery, perched high up in the grounds of a landscaped park that on sunny days resembles the south of France or Tuscany. The turret that you see popping up over the trees is a 1938 replica of the towers of the 12th-century St Michel de Cuxa in France, made out of granite blocks specially cut to the dimensions of those used in Romanesque churches of the same period. The rest of the building somehow incorporates four Gothic and Romanesque French and Spanish cloisters, as well as a 12th-century chapter house and a French Romanesque chapel, nearly all of which was assembled before World War I by George Grey Barnard, the eccentric founder of the collection.

A self-schooled medievalist and sculptor, Barnard lived in France for years, foraging through the countryside for remnants of medieval architecture and art. Frequently he stumbled on priceless odds and ends mouldering away in barns, outhouses and pigpens, or used by villagers as garden ornaments (one find was a Romanesque torso of Christ used as a scarecrow). In 1925 John D. Rockefeller Jr bought the entire collection, and commissioned Charles Collens, the architect behind Riverside Church, to design a suitable building to house it.

Inside, the collection is arranged in a roughly chronological sequence, starting with Romanesque and finishing with Late-Gothic. Upstaging everything else, is the museum's most prized possession, the 16th-century Unicorn Tapestries which were salvaged from the La Rochefoucauld estate in Verteuil (where they were used to keep frost off the vegetables), and reluctantly donated by Rockefeller in 1938. They alone make the laborious trip to Washington Heights worthwhile.

The museum has pretty grounds landscaped with apples and crab-apples, as well as a herb garden which destroys all medieval illusions with the creepy sound of medieval chants and monks' voices booming out of invisible loud-speakers.

*At this point, you should leave the museum and head off for a picnic in the flower gardens of Fort Tryon Park, beautifully maintained and a tranquil spot. The nearest subway home is the **A** train, a short walk away at the south end of park on 190th Street and Fort Washington Avenue.*

Food and Drink

In New York consumption is conspicuous. Everywhere you go, you see New Yorkers eating; as they walk down the sidewalk, in elevators, as they run to catch a bus. Mobile food-stalls clutter up the streets, and eating goes on round the clock. Half-way through the afternoon, New Yorkers get bored and hurry off to a four-star restaurant for a five-course supper. In the middle of the night, they leap out of bed and rush off to a 24-hour café for a midnight breakfast.

The reason for all this eating is simple—New Yorkers never, ever, cook at home. Rather than make something themselves, they will sit for half an hour and twiddle their toes while they wait for a take-away or home delivery. Their fridges are full to bursting with stuff like tofu, camera film, lemons, flour, sugar and vitamins, year-old muesli, and endless plastic bottles: steak sauce, catsup, relish and Thousand Island dressing. Turn in desperation to the freezer, and you find a packet of half-finished frozen cigarettes, an empty box of ice cream, a bottle containing a finger of gin, and a small glacier of ice.

Yet New Yorkers are fanatical about food. And you can find out more about New York by spending a day sitting in a diner than by seeing any number of tourist attractions. New Yorkers spend most of their meals talking because they eat at incredible speeds, pushing food around the plate so it is all mixed up into a mulch before it enters their mouths, and then munching it up like lawn mowers. They discuss food with the relish of a hypochondriac describing his illness, and restaurant critics devote whole essays and disquisitions to a single restaurant. Every May, there is a food fair on 9th Avenue attended by nearly a million New Yorkers. Stall-holders of every ethnic extraction crowd onto the avenue, alongside 9th Avenue's mass of different food shops and stores known as Paddy's Market.

There are presently something like 15,000 restaurants in New York serving practically every dish under the sun, and eating out is one of the supreme pleasures of being in the city.

The best meal of all is **breakfast**. Portions come in incapacitating sizes and there is no distinction between sweet and savory—French toast comes doused in maple syrup and sweet pancakes on the same plate as a mound of bacon. Ordering can take a long time unless you know the code: the trick is to say 'Can I get a . . .', 'I'll have a . . .', or 'Gimme a . . .'. Eggs come 'any style', and you must specify which:

sunny side up—fried on one side only
over—fried on both sides
over-easy—fried on both sides, but quickly so the yolk is runny
over-hard—fried so the yolk is hard

Just as Americans don't have kettles, they don't have egg cups, and if you ask for a boiled egg you will get it in a bowl. Toast and sandwiches are just as complicated as eggs, and you must identify exactly which kind of bread you want:

wholewheat—brown bread with grains
rye—black rye bread
light rye—brown rye bread
white—white bread, which like brown bread is usually mixed with honey or sugar so it tastes sweet
pumpernickel
challah—Jewish braided egg bread pronounced 'halla'
sour bread—served with vinegar and tasting like rye bread

Sometimes orders get incredibly cryptic, viz:

whicky down—egg fried on both sides on a slice of dark rye bread
Adam and Eve on a raft and wreck 'em—scrambled eggs on toast
a corn muffin 'high and dry'—toasted with no butter
wadder—all restaurants serve customers iced water as a matter of course, but if you want more, remember to ask for wadder or you will get blank looks
budder—(see above)

279

Other confusions will be:

grape jelly—a purple glue-like substance tasting of bubblegum which invariably accompanies toast
pancakes—thick, sweet and perfectly round
corn/bran muffins—cakes filled with blueberries and raisins or nuts
English muffin—unsweetened, like a crumpet
hushpuppies—potato croquettes
hash browns—fried potatoes with onions
egg cream—not egg nog nor eggs with cream, but a dementingly delicious froth of iced milk, a squirt of chocolate or vanilla syrup and a blast of seltzer in a tall glass with a spoon
OJ—orange juice
regular coffee—can mean anything: usually white coffee with sugar but sometimes black coffee with no sugar
light coffee—white, and often it comes with a packet of 'half and half'—a mixture of milk and cream. The best thing about drinking coffee, and Americans drink it by the gallon, is that if you sit around for long enough, most restaurants refill your cup for free
tea—comes iced (and often heavily sweetened) or as a do-it-yourself mug of boiling water with a bag of Lipton's and a lemon
the check—the bill

New Yorkers eat their midday meals on the run, so **lunch** in an expensive restaurant is always an excellent bargain. If you have lost your appetite because of a big breakfast, you can do as the New Yorkers do and grab a hot-dog, a *gyro* (spit-roasted meat in a soggy pitta bread envelope), a *hero* (a sandwich in French bread), a carton of frozen yoghurt, or a salad sold by weight from one of the city's Korean delicatessens. For pudding there are 'dove bars' (vanilla bars dipped in chocolate) and enormous ice-creams loaded with as many toppings as you dare (including crunched-up Oreo cookies, chocolate flakes, and crushed pecans—pronounced *pa-kahns* in snooty joints, rather than 'pee-cans'). Ben & Jerry's and Häagen Dazs are the two main rivals on the ice-cream front. On the weekends most people take themselves off to **brunch**—a midday meal combining breakfast, lunch and alcohol.

A Brief Glossary of Unfamiliar Terms

à la mode—with ice cream
baccalao—dried, salted cod (Carribean/Portuguese)

bagel—chewy doughnut-shaped bread, plain or with cinammon and raisins, poppy or sesame seeds (Jewish)

batido—milkshake with tropical fruit (Latin American)

bialy—onion-roll (Jewish)

biscuit—hot bread-roll

blintz—pancake filled with cheese or fruit

broiled—grilled

burrito—rolled up flour tortilla with a filling (Mexican)

Caesar's salad—cos lettuce with anchovy paste, olives and lemon

café con leche—expresso with warm milk (Latin American)

chips—crisps

club sandwich—skyscraper-high sandwich with two fillings, three slices of bread and a cocktail stick holding the whole thing together

collard greens—boiled spiced greens (Afro American)

cuchifrutos—fried pork-parts (Puerto Rican)

empanada—meat or vegetable pasty (Latin American)

feojada—Brazilian national dish of black beans and meats

frijoles—refried beans (Latin American)

gefilte fish—fish balls made of white fish meat (Jewish)

grits—crushed maize served with butter

gumbo—thick tomato soup often made with shellfish (Cajun-Southern)

jello—viscid jelly

jerk—hot barbecued chicken or pork (Jamaican)

kasha—buckwheat crushed oats served with gravy (Eastern European and Jewish)

kielbasa—spicy pork sausage (Polish)

knish—savory dough envelope filled with cheese or potato (Jewish)

kugel—sweet potato pudding (Jewish)

lox—smoked salmon, best eaten with cream cheese on a bagel (Jewish)

mauby—Jamaican drink made of bark

mahi mahi—Hawaiian fish, very tasty

mole poblano—savory sauce of bitter chocolate, chilli and spices, served with meat or *enchiladas* (Mexican)

mondongo—tripe soup (Colombian)

plantain—green, banana-like fruit, fried and served as a side-dish (Latin American)

polenta—cornmeal porridge (Italian)

red snapper—carnivorous fish, delicious grilled

reuben—sandwich of corned beef, melted Swiss cheese and *sauerkraut*

scrod—young cod or haddock

seafood—all kinds of fish, not just shellfish
seltzer—fizzy or soda water
shashlik—skewered meat (Russian)
shrimp—prawns
soda—soft drinks
soft-shell crabs—delicious, recently-molted blue crabs which you crunch down whole
spanakopita—spinach pie (Greek)
squash—a kind of marrow
tabouli— cracked wheat salad (Middle Eastern)
teriyaki—marinade for meat, poultry and fish (Japanese)
zucchini—courgettes.

Below is a select choice of favorite restaurants in the city. Bear in mind that as restaurants get more popular prices go up, and vice versa, so phone ahead to doublecheck prices and opening times. Reservations are always a good idea, and if you go to a top-notch restaurant, you may need to reserve a few days in advance (Rao's in East Harlem has a *three-month* waiting list). Some restaurants are closed on Sundays and even Mondays.

In the smartest restaurants make sure you have a jacket and tie if you are a man, and at least a token gesture to establishment tastes (like a scarf or a tweed jacket) if you are female. If you turn up wearing shorts you will be ignominiously turfed out. In general New Yorkers dress to the nines when they go out (even if it's just to go shopping) and wearing glitzy clothes is part of the fun of eating in restaurants.

In fancy restaurants, waiters divide into two species: the cringeing and pandering, who tell you their name and constantly interrupt the meal to ask if everything is all right, and the haughty and despising, who try to make customers feel guilty for ever stepping into the restaurant in the first place. Remember to ask for the 'check' when you want the bill.

The prices below are for an evening meal, excluding drinks, service (15–20 per cent) and sales tax (8¼ per cent). Tipping is a matter of course in America, (see Tipping, p. 35) and the easiest way to calculate the right amount is to double the sales tax, giving you 16½ per cent, and to add or subtract from the resulting figure depending on service. Waiters, busboys and bartenders generally pool their tips, so unless you specially want to, it is not necessary to separate out the 16½ per cent. The *maître d'* likes to get up to $10 for showing you to your table, but as a rule he will not be too offended if he gets nothing at all.

LUXURY	over $60	CREDIT CARDS:		
EXPENSIVE	$35–$60	AE	=	AMERICAN EXPRESS
MODERATE	$15–$35	DC	=	DINER'S CLUB
INEXPENSIVE	under $15	MC	=	MASTERCARD
CHEAP	under $10	V	=	VISA

Lower Manhattan and TriBeCa

LUXURY

Chanterelle, 2 Harrison St., near Hudson St., tel 966 6960; French (AE, DC, MC, V; reservations requested). Elegant, refined, and astronomically priced gourmet eating. The menu changes every fortnight and the cheeseboard is said to be the best in the city.

EXPENSIVE

Windows on the World, 107th floor, 1 World Trade Center, tel 938 1111; Continental (AE, DC, MC, V; reservations requested). The highest restaurant in Manhattan; so high that in certain weather conditions the city dissolves into pea soup and you can't see anything at all. The food is first-rate, and there are 800 offerings on the exhaustive wine list. The bar and Sunday brunch are infinitely cheaper alternatives, and the best way of seeing the World Trade Center without the tourists (see p. 108).

Duane Park Café, 157 Duane St., between West Broadway and Hudson St., tel 732 5555; American (AE, DC, MC, V; reservations suggested). New TriBeCa restaurant highly praised for pasta and fish.

Ecco, 124 Chambers St., between West Broadway and Church St., tel 227 7074; Northern Italian (AE; reservations suggested). Straightforward and reasonably priced.

The Odeon, 145 West Broadway, at Thomas St., tel 233 0507; American (AE, DC, MC, V; reservations suggested). Several years ago the Odeon was hot stuff, and now it is only just recovering from the craze. Meat is the best choice—particularly the roast lamb, the steak, or calf's liver—and the puddings are delicious,

Bridge Café, 279 Water St., near Dover St., tel 227 3344. American (AE, DC). The food is not up to much, but the location, under the Brooklyn Bridge, is lovely. The place is jollier and cheaper at lunchtime when it fills up with businessmen and civil servants from Wall Street and the Civic Center.

Tommy Tang's, 323 Greenwich St., between Duane and Reade Sts., tel 334 9190; Thai (AE, DC, MC, V; reservations suggested). Los

Angeles-style restaurant filled with brassy Hollywood types golloping down won tons and talking in booming voices.

INEXPENSIVE

Exterminator Chilli, 305 Church St., south of Canal St., tel 219 3070; Mexican (no credit cards; no reservations). Chillis graded by ferocity—domestic, commercial, industrial and exterminator—in a palace of kitsch illuminated with jalapeno-shaped fairy lights.

SoHo and TriBeCa

EXPENSIVE

150 Wooster, 150 Wooster St., between Houston and Prince Sts., tel 995 1010; American (AE, DC, MC, V; reservations requested). Presently the hottest restaurant in the city; and the one with the most unimaginative name. Limos and cadillacs line up in the parking lot next to the restaurant and getting a table is notoriously difficult.

MODERATE

Raoul's, 180 Prince St., between Sullivan and Thompson Sts., tel 966 3518; French (AE, MC, V; reservations suggested). It tries to look French, but instead is an archetypical and charming New York establishment with tin ceilings, bar, booths, blackboard menu and a goldfish tank. The style, as well as the food, is very tempting and well worth the expense.

Omen, 113 Thompson St., between Prince and Spring Sts., tel 925 8923; Japanese (AE, DC; reservations suggested). Big gangs of good-humored eaters keep the restaurant crowded. The menu is full of unusual offerings, and the vegetable and seaweed dishes are particularly good.

Abyssinia, 35 Grand St., near Thompson St., tel 226 5959; Ethiopian (AE). Fiery meat and fish dishes. Straw tables, wooden stools and, instead of cutlery, *injera*, or white pancakes, to mop up the food. Try the *kefa-fal*, curried plantain stew.

Greene Street Café, 101 Greene St., between Prince and Spring Sts., tel 925 2415; American (AE, DC, MC, V; reservations suggested). Popular and always crowded, a SoHo mainstay.

SoHo Kitchen and Bar, 103 Greene St., between Prince and Spring Sts., tel 925 1866; American (AE, DC, MC, V; reservations suggested).

The bar, with 110 items on the list, is generally thought superior to the kitchen. Noisy and crowded, implying that everyone is having a good time.

INEXPENSIVE

Arturo's, 106 West Houston St., at Thompson St., tel 677 3820; Italian pizzeria (AM, DC, MC). Lots of bustle and cheer, a jazz band (making the place feel almost like a club) and delicious, crusty oven-baked pizzas.

Lupe's East LA Kitchen, 110 6th Ave., at Watts St., tel 966 1326; Mexican (no credit cards). This is a neighborhood dive, with basic decor, fly-blown waiters and scrumptious *tortillas* and *burritos*.

Broome Street Bar and Restaurant, 363 West Broadway, near Broome St., tel 925 2086; American (AE, DC, MC, V). Noisy, hectic and cheap; burgers and beer.

CHEAP

Patisserie Lanciani, 177 Prince St., between Sullivan and Thompson Sts., tel 477 2788: (AE). Heavenly pastries, brioches and tarts; cappuccino, expresso and homemade lemonade.

Lower East Side and East Village

EXPENSIVE

Delia's, 197 East 3rd St., between Aves. A and B, tel 254 9184; American (AE, DC, MC, V). Pub-food restaurant and club which has enormous cachet with the young suit-and-tie set, partly because of its unlikely location in Alphabet City and its late opening hours.

Sammy's Famous Romanian, 157 Chrystie St., near Delancey St., tel 673 0330; Continental/Romanian-Jewish (AE, DC; reservations suggested). Huge portions of potato pancakes, beef sausages, sliced brains, and all the equipment to make your own egg creams. Come prepared to be jollied up with a blast of songs round the piano, and large parties of boisterous eaters with big appetites.

MODERATE

Bernard, 145 Ave. C, at East 9th St., tel 529 3800; Provençal (no credit cards; reservations suggested). One of the nicest and simplest French restaurants, located in a rough part of Alphabet City (the launderette opposite has bullet-proof glass to screen the management from the customers, and a special glass window for posting clothes). The menu is all organic: fish is always absolutely fresh and very tasty—especially the swordfish and the moules marinière. Bring your own wine.

Pedro Páramo, 430 East 14th St., between 1st Ave., and Ave. A, tel 475 4581; Mexican (no credit cards). Neighborhood restaurants like this are dying out in Manhattan, and Pedro Páramo, painted pink from roof to sidewalk, is one of the nicest. The appetizers are especially good: crispy deep-fried *taquitos*, homemade *tortillas* and a potent *ceviche*, fish marinated in lime.

Everybody's, 31 2nd Ave., between 1st and 2nd Sts., French (AE, DC, MC, V). Tiny bistro with checked tablecloths and the smiliest waitress in the East Village. Delicious, delicate food, especially the hot goat's cheese salad. Though the menu veers to the pricey side, you can share one serving between two.

Sugar Reef, 93 2nd Ave., between 5th and 6th Sts., tel 427 8427; Dominican (no credit cards). Rum cocktails to cheer you up, and loopy waiters.

Roettelle A.G., 126 East 7th St., between 1st Ave., and Ave. A, tel 674 4140; German/Swiss/Italian/French (AE, DC, MC, V). Foods from the Common Market. The tiny restaurant is squeezed into a corridor, with a pretty garden at the back, just big enough for one table and lit with fairy lights. If you don't reserve in advance someone will have got there before you.

SoHo Star, 330 Lafayette St., near Bleecker St., tel 925 0070; Chinese/macro/TexMex (AE, DC, MC, V). The mixture sounds revolting, but tofu *burritos* with soy sauce are quite nice.

Time Café, 380 Lafayette St., at Great Jones, tel 533 7000; Organic (AE, MC, V; no reservations). Full of well-dressed hip-looking people who seem to clash with the cafés muesli aspirations. The cooking, though fairly basic, is good, but service can be awfully haphazard.

INEXPENSIVE

Dandi's Garden Café, 153 1st Ave., near 10th St., tel 979 1655; Balkan (no credit cards). Balkan food seems to mean lots of yoghurt and spicy sausages. The garden is actually a narrow strip of gravel, but even so, it's quite pretty and a splendid place for brunch or breakfast in the summer.

Veselka, 144 2nd Ave., and 9th St., tel 228 9682; Polish-Ukrainian (no credit cards). A 10 ft by 5 ft mural outside says 'We serve soup to nuts'. Inside the eaters are a well-behaved East Village cross-section, and though you might see the occasional nutter, you won't find any crazies. The soups are filling and hearty: red Ukrainian borscht and delicious sludge-thick pea soup with hunks of challah bread. The *pirogis* (hefty Polish dumplings filled with meat and cheese) are good too, and regulars claim the vanilla milkshakes taste like 'Mother's milk'. It takes a millenium for food to get to your plate, but the restaurant doubles as a newsagent, so you can happily wile away an afternoon or a morning reading the papers.

Marion's, 354 Bowery, between 4th and Great Jones Sts., tel 475 7621; French (no credit cards). Spoof restaurant, oozing 1950s glamor and glitz, dedicated to the memory of the legendary hostess 'Marion Nagy'. The food—steak au poivre, bouillabaisse, roasted monkfish and the inevitable onion soup—is ridiculously cheap.

El Sombrero, 108 Stanton St., between Ludlow and Houston Sts., tel 254 4188; Mexican (no credit cards). Nicknamed 'The Hat', the place looks appealingly disreputable. Excellent cooking, disheveled clientele and potent frozen margheritas.

KK's, 192–4 1st Ave., between 11th and 12th Sts., tel 777 4433; Polish 'Cooking like Mama Made it' (no credit cards). A family business, KK's has one of the prettiest outdoor gardens in New York, lit by more fairy lights than Blackpool and bombarded by kamakaze caterpillars. The cold *borscht*—a lurid pink with a white boiled egg bobbing about on top—is heavenly on a hot day.

Katz's Delicatessen, 205 East Houston St., near Orchard St., tel 254 2246 (cash only). Quintessential Lower East Side deli: fatty pastrami and corned beef piled up high with a pickle and Dr Brown's celery soda. You get a ticket as you enter which the countermen mark off, and you pay as you leave.

Moisha's Luncheonette, 239 Grand St., at Bowery, tel 226 0780; Jewish (no credit cards). Plain Jewish cooking, and egg creams, lime rickeys and invincible waiters.

Two Boots, 37 Ave. A, betwen 2nd and 3rd Sts., tel 505 5450; Cajun/Italian (no credit cards). Cuisine based on the premise that Louisiana and Italy have the same geographical shapes. Apparently the mixture is not so strange down in New Orleans, and at the Two Boots the fiersomely spiced combination somehow comes off.

Cucina di Pesce, 87 East 4th St., between 2nd and 3rd Aves., tel 260 6800; seafood (no credit cards). Frantically crowded. Sometimes so full that you can nip into the bar as you are passing by, help yourself to the free *moules marinières* and leave. On the other hand, if you leave you'd miss an excellent meal.

Mingala Burmese Restaurant, 21–3 East 7th St., near 1st Ave., tel 529 3656; (AE). Try the Rangoon Night Market Noodles with tender strips of duck and scallions, or the extraordinary thousand-layered butter pancake with a chicken curry.

Princess Pamela's Southern Touch Restaurant, 78 East 1st St., near 1st Ave., tel 477 4460; Southern cooking (no credit cards; reservations suggested). In spite of the 'live entertainment', the star of the place is Princess Pamela, the uncontainable manageress. She sings and booms, or chivvies on her eaters like a demented general leading troops into battle. A really delicious meal, not recommended for the easily intimidated.

2nd Avenue Deli, 156 2nd Ave., at East 10th St., tel 677 0606; Jewish (no credit cards). Classic deli fare: *kasha*, potato knishes, boiled beef flanken, strudel and *kugel*, (noodle pudding).

The Hole in the Wall, 345 East 10th St., corner of Ave. B; American (no credit cards; no reservations). A curious combination of nightmarish decorations, charred walls, curly vinyl and a churned-up backyard. The burgers and fries are outstanding, and the waiters are quite charming.

Mary Ann's, 300 East 5th St., and 2nd Ave., tel 505 7834; Mexican (no credit cards). A branch of the excellent Mary Ann's in Chelsea. All the portions are dauntingly generous, even so the gallon jugs of *margheritas* are surprisingly good value.

Around the Clock, 8 Stuyvesant St., near 3rd Ave., 598 0402; (AE; open 24 hours). Big-portions of eggs, bacon and chips swiftly delivered to the rescue of anyone who has started to flag at 5 in the morning.

Odessa, 117 Ave. A, between 7th and 8th Sts., tel 473 8916; Ukrainian (no credit cards). The biggest meal in New York at the cheapest prices, patronized by a friendly crowd of Ukrainians and punky Lower East Siders.

6th Street Little India, 6th St. between 1st and 2nd Ave's. Fifteen Bengali restaurants on one side of one block, all serving outstanding Indian food at staggeringly cheap prices. **Panna**, **Kismoth** and **Sonali** are three of the best (and cheapest). Bring your own beer, unless you are going to one of the more upmarket establishments with a license, like Mitali.

Leshko Coffee Shop, 111 Ave. A, and 6th St., tel 473 9208; Eastern European (no credit cards). The best place for watching and eavesdropping on the bizarre to-ing and fro-ing of Tompkins Square. The soups are stodgy, but the fried egg sandwiches (the cheapest in the city), are very tasty indeed. Fat policemen file in and out for quantities of thick coffee.

The Cloister Café, 238 East 9th St., tel 674 9302; American (no credit cards). Pleasant cobblestoned garden and fish pond, and an easy atmosphere. Good for brunch or tea.

Chinatown, Little Italy and the Civic Center

MODERATE

Il Cortile, 125 Mulberry St., near Hester St., tel 226 6060; Italian (AE, DC, MC, V; reservations suggested). Proud of its sleek and expensive interior, with a beautiful garden room at the back. The cooking is the best in Little Italy.

Phoenix Garden, 46 Bowery, in arcade near Elizabeth St., tel 962 8934; Cantonese (no credit cards). Expensive for Chinatown, but still excellent value.

20 Mott Street, 20 Mott St., between Bowery and Pell St., tel 964 0380; Cantonese (no credit cards). Dim sum, trundled round between 8 am and 3 pm makes an excellent brunch.

CHEAP

Mon Bo, 65 Mott St., tel 964 6480; Cantonese (no credit cards). Furiously hectic inside, but the noodle soups soothe hangovers.

Wong Kee, 113 Mott St., near Hester St., tel 966 1160; Chinese (no credit cards; reservations requested). Renowned as one of the best in Chinatown: service is at breakneck speed, but the food is superb and is cheaper than cooking at home.

Little Szechuan: 31 Oliver St., between Madison and Henry Sts., tel 965 4598. Szechuan (no credit cards). Four tables and a Coke machine only just squeeze into one of the tiniest restaurants in Chinatown. A trifle cramped, but no matter. The delicate Szechuan cooking is exquisite; the peppered shrimp and shredded beef with bean curd and diced scallions are especially good.

Petite Szechuan, 10 East Broadway, near Chatham Square, tel 966 2839; Szechuan (no credit cards). No relation, but almost as good.

Lan Hong Kok Seafood House, 31 Division St., Chatham Square end, tel 964 9832; seafood (no credit cards). Real bird's-nest soup, and Maryland blue crabs sautéed with black beans and ginger, in spartan surroundings.

Nom Wah Tea Parlor, 13 Doyers St., tel 962 8650; (no credit cards). Perfect for a *dim sum* brunch on a Sunday.

Kuan Sing Dumpling House, 9 Pell St., near Chatham Square, tel 349 0503 (no credit cards). Dumplings from 10am to 10pm.

Vietnam Restaurant, 11 Doyers St., near Chatham Square, tel 893 0725; (no credit cards). One of the few exclusively Vietnamese restaurants in Chinatown.

West Village

EXPENSIVE

Gotham Bar and Grill, 12 East 12th St., near 5th Ave., tel 620 4020; Northern Italian (AE, DC, MC, V; reservations requested). 'Post-Modern' (slickly tasteful) decor, sleek and fashionable clientele and incredibly sophisticated five-star food: quail salad with *shiitake* mushrooms, and rabbit ravioli. Come here when you're fed up with burgers.

Frank's Restaurant, 431 West 14th St., between 9th and 10th Aves., tel 243 1349; American steakhouse with sawdust floors (AM, DC, V). Big steaks, key-lime tart, pecan pies and hefty waiters. In the meat-packing district.

One Fifth, 2 East 8th St., at 5th Ave., tel 260 3434; (AE, DC, MC, V; reservations suggested). A fancy interior decorated with relics from a wrecked ocean-liner and full of smart eaters. If the prices quell your appetite, stick to cocktails.

MODERATE

Florent, 69 Gansevoort St., between Greenwich and Washington Sts., tel 989 5779; French (no credit cards; reservations suggested). Trendified meat-packing-district diner, open 24 hours and a big rendezvous for the pallid crowd emerging from clubs in the small hours. Fierce air-conditioning sometimes makes it as chilly as a refrigerated lorry.

Gulf Coast, 489 West St., at West 12th St., tel 206 8790; Southern/Cajun (no credit cards). Fried alligator, whole fried catfish with hushpuppies (potato croquettes). Tasty but weird.

Rio Mar, 7 9th Ave., near Little West 12th St., tel 243 9014; Spanish (no credit cards). Charmingly degraded-looking with delicious food, especially the steaks and *paella* washed down with a jug of Sangria.

Mitali West, 296 Bleecker St., between Barrow and Grove Sts., tel 989 1367. Indian (AE, MC). Reliable Northern Indian cooking.

Tortilla Flats, 767 Washington St., near West 12th St., tel 243 1053;

Tex/Mex (no credit cards). Wild interior, where neighborhood eaters down their tofu *enchiladas* with gusto. Very jolly indeed.

Jane Street Seafood Café, 31 8th Ave., at Jane St., tel 242 0003; (AE, MC, V). Staunchly unpretentious. Best for sole—grilled and fried.

INEXPENSIVE

Cucina Stagionale, 275 Bleecker St., between 6th and 7th Aves., tel 924 2707. Italian (no credit cards). Superior and very reasonably priced pastas and salads. Be prepared for queues, or come for lunch.

John's Pizzeria, 278 Bleecker St., between 6th and 7th Aves., tel 243 1680; (no credit cards). Famously delicious pizzas, with nearly as many varieties as Heinz.

Ray's Pizza, 456 6th Ave., at 11th St., tel 243 2253; (no credit cards). Pizza slices swimming in enough oil for an axle. Aficionados swear Ray's makes the best and greasiest in New York.

Caribe, 117 Perry St., at Greenwich St., tel 255 9191; Caribbean-Creole-West-Indian (no credit cards). Powerful cocktails in an exotic setting—a tropical rain forest—encourage rowdiness, but the cooking is excellent.

White Horse Tavern, 567 Hudson St., at 11th St., tel 243 9260; saloon (no credit cards). Delicious hard-boiled eggs, cheeseburgers and watery beer, in honour of Dylan Thomas who famously drank himself to death here.

Carmella's Village Garden, 49 Charles St., at West 4th St., tel 242 2155; Italian (no credit cards; no liquor licence). Lasagne, meatballs and ravioli in a packed basement at incredibly reasonable prices.

CHEAP

Benny's Burritos, 113 Greenwich Ave., at Jane St., tel 633 9210; Mexican (no credit cards, no reservations). Simple Mexican meals in a store-front restaurant.

The Pink Teacup, 42 Grove St., between Bleecker and Bedford Sts., tel 807 6755; soul food (cash only, no liquor licence). Venerable and miniscule Village institution serving homely sausage patties, pancakes and bacon, macaroni and cheese, fried pork chops, salmon croquettes, cheeseburgers and fries as well as pig's feet.

Flatiron District, Gramercy, Murray Hill and Chelsea

EXPENSIVE

An American Place, 2 Park Ave., at 32nd St., tel 684 2122; American

(AE, DC, MC, V; reservations suggested). American cooking at a pinnacle of elegance: smoked sturgeon, trout and salmon, warm oysters in buttered sauce, New Orleans blackened fish, roast salmon coated with cracked wheat, and banana betty to finish off.

Sofi, 102 5th Ave., between 15th and 16th Sts., tel 463 8888; American (AE, DC, MC, V; reservations suggested). Glamorous new restaurant with lots of fake-marble columns. The cooking is good, but verges on the showy.

MODERATE

Union Square Café, 21 East 16th St., near Broadway, tel 243 4020; Northern Californian (AE, DC, MC, V; reservations suggested). Currently one of New York's favorite restaurants, with an innovative menu. Try the brown rice pancakes covered with caviar and sour cream, and the tuna steaks.

Harvey's Chelsea Restaurant, 108 West 18th St., near 6th Ave., tel 243 5644; American (AE). Ancient Chelsea 'tavern', famous for shepherd's and pecan pies, steaks and seafood.

Empire Diner, 210 10th Ave., at West 22nd St., tel 243 2736; (AE, MC, V; open 24 hours). Revamped as a shrine to the classic 1940s diner. Gleaming with stainless steel, chrome, and a fashionable crowd. Someone plays nostalgic tunes on a piano, and though the sandwiches, soups and french toast are a little overpriced, they are welcome at 4 in the morning.

Meriken, 189 7th Ave., at 21st St., tel 620 6174; Japanese (AE, DC). Looks potentially intimidating, but the waiters are easy-going, the prices are surprisingly reasonable and the *sushi* is excellent.

INEXPENSIVE

Mary Ann's, 116 8th Ave., at 16th St., tel 633 0877; Mexican (no credit cards). Cheapest, fastest and most reliable Mexican in the city.

Old Town Bar, 45 East 18th St., between Broadway and Park Avenue South, tel 473 8874; (no credit cards). A crowded 19th-century bar with avuncular barmen and a bunch of regulars who like their lunchtime beers. Good bar food with delicious burgers and crunchy fries.

Curry in a Hurry, 130 East 29th St., at Lexington Ave., tel 889 1159; Indian (cash only). The best-named restaurant in Manhattan.

Midtown

LUXURY

The Four Seasons, 99 East 52nd St., near 5th Ave., tel 688 6525;

American (AE, DC, MC, V; reservations requested). Given its reputation as New York's restaurant *par-excellence*, The Four Seasons breezes along with extraordinary panache. Designed by Philip Johnson in the sixties, the restaurant sits sleekly at the bottom of the Seagram Building, Mies van der Rohe's only New York commission. By day an indomitable business crowd stumps past an enormous Picasso mural to gnaw through lunch in the grill room, and at night the glittery people come to eat in the more elaborate pool room, with its plashing fountain in the center. The pudding trolley is still hallowed, and the rest of the menu, while not *quite* so stupendous as Lutèce (see below), still holds it own, changing every season, along with the uniforms of the doormen.

Lutèce, 249 East 50th St., near 2nd Ave., tel 752 2225; French (AE, DC; reservations are requested and you should make them days in advance). Lauded by some as the best and most unassuming restaurant in the city, swiped at by others as smug and drab—the debate about Lutèce continues to land food critics in bloody scrimmages. Meanwhile the restaurant coolly cruises on, dishing out unpretentious Alsatian delicacies (*foie gras en brioche*, snails *à l'alsacienne* and salmon and bass *en croûte*) behind a modest brownstone front. It's cheaper at lunchtime. In fact lunch at Lutèce is one of the great bargains in the city, with a *prix fixe* presently of $38.

The Rainbow Room, 30 Rockefeller Plaza, near 48th St., tel 632 5000; American (AE, DC, MC, V; reservations requested). Perhaps the campest restaurant in New York, and everyone loves it. Perched at the top of the RCA Building, the flamboyant Art-Moderne dining room was recently renovated at a cost of $25 million. In the middle is a revolving dance floor and a tacky cabaret. Round the edge there are the picture-book views. The nightclub food is unabashedly excessive (lobster, salmon, quail and caviar in one feverish mouthful) but what you eat is secondary to everything else (see p. 190).

Le Bernadin, 155 West 51st St., between 6th and 7th Aves., tel 489 1515; seafood (AE, DC, MC, V; reservations requested). Fancy seafood: baked sea urchins in butter, black bass, halibut in warmed vinaigrette, and so on. For pudding, a heavenly *mille-feuille* of green apples and raisins.

La Caravelle, 33 West 55th St., between 5th and 6th Aves., tel 586 4252; French (AE, DC, MC, V; reservations requested). *Haute cuisine*, once considered the best in the city, and now making a comeback. Critics are particularly admiring at the way the meat is carved at the table with a dexterous flourish.

La Grenouille, 3 East 52nd St., between 5th and Madison Aves., tel 752 1495; French (AE, DC, MC, V; reservations requested). Gallic opulence teetering on the prissy: brace yourself for *quenelles*, frogs' legs, quails, ducklings and banquettes of flowers.

Russian Tea Room, 150 West 57th St., near 7th Ave., tel 265 0947; Russian (AE, DC, MC, V; reservations requested). The management can be impossibly stuck-up, but the old-fashioned Russian menu is outstanding, and blinis and caviar (with a choice of 20 vodkas) are heavenly. Don't have anything to do with the inferior puddings.

Grand Central Oyster Bar and Restaurant, Grand Central Terminal, tel 490 6650; fish (AE, DC, MC, V; reservations suggested). Deep in the bowels of Grand Central Station in a cavernous vaulted room, the subterranean oyster bar is one of the most amusing restaurants in the city. The fish is always as fresh as can be; snapper, sole, shellfish and smoked fish are excellent. There are up to 10 varieties of oyster; you can order them one by one, very cheaply, or in an assorted dozen.

Le Perigord, 405 East 52nd St., near 1st Ave., tel 755 6244; French (AE, DC, MC, V; reservations requested). Again, immaculate *haute cuisine*.

Sparks Steak House, 210 East 46th St., near 3rd Ave., tel 687 4855; (AE, DC, MC, V; reservations requested). Fame as the place where mafia mobster Paul Castellano was rubbed out has ensured the popularity of this midtown steakhouse. You will have a memorable meal: grotesquely big lobsters, and hefty steaks oozing blood and juice.

Bice, 7 East 54th St., between 5th and Madison Aves, tel 684 0215; Northern Italian (AE, DC, MC, V). Old-world service and impeccable food.

Nirvana on Rooftop, 30 Central Park South, between 5th and 6th Aves., tel 486 5700; Indian (AE, DC, MC, V; reservations suggested). Unfashionable because touristy, but the food is really excellent and the panoramic view from the window is splendid.

Tang's Chariot, 236 East 53rd St., between 2nd and 3rd Aves., tel 355 5096; Chinese (AE, DC, MC, V; reservations suggested). Outstanding cooking by Hunan master-chefs: according to some, the best Chinese in New York.

Brasserie, 1016 2nd Ave., near 54th St., tel 751 4840; American-French (AE, DC, MC, V; reservations suggested, one of the few places in midtown open 24 hours). In the small hours there's a touchingly end-of-the-world atmosphere about the place: the customers have a bleached, morning-after look, the waiters look grimly philosophical and even the bus boys look jaded. The delicious, thick onion soup, however, will set you right in no time. In normal eating hours the Brasserie returns to its cheerful self, and the waiters bustle about with good-humor.

Hatsuhana. 237 Park Ave., on 46th St., tel 661 3400; 17 East 48th St., between 5th and Madison Aves., tel 355 3345; Japanese (AE, DC, MC, V; reservations requested). First class *sushi*—some say the best in New York—but frantic at lunchtime.

Chez Josephine, 414 West 42nd St., near 9th Ave., tel 594 1925; (AE, MC, V; reservations suggested). Delightful and welcoming French bistro in the theater district.

Dawat, 210 East 58th St., near 3rd Ave., tel 355 7555; Northern Indian (AE, DC, MC, V; reservations suggested). An amiable, laid-back style and fantastically good cooking. The menu, developed by the actress and cookery writer Madhur Jaffrey, is as imaginative as you would expect.

Jezebel, 630 9th Ave., at West 45th St., tel 582 1045; Southern and soul food (AE; reservations suggested). One of the best and most amusing soul food restaurants in the city. A theatrical place decked out like a Louisiana bordello and tended by exuberent waitresses dressed in all manner of outfits. Deep-fried porgies (a kind of fish), spare ribs, grits, fried chicken, sweet-potato pie and bread pudding to eat.

Mme Romaine de Lyon, 29 East 61st St., between Madison and Park Aves., tel 758 2422; (AE, DC). 560 different omelettes.

Pearl's, 38 West 48th St., near 6th Ave., Chinese (AE). First-class Chinese, famous for its lemon chicken.

INEXPENSIVE

Manganaro's Hero-Boy, 492 9th Ave., between 37th and 38th Sts., tel 947 7325; Italian (no credit cards). The sandwich reaches its apogee at Manganaro's in the form of a 6 ft-long hero. For the merely mortal appetite there are the standard-sized proscuitto and provolone heroes which are scrumptious with strong mustard and a bottle of Italian beer.

Café Madeleine, 403 West 43rd St., at 9th Ave., tel 246 2993; French (AE, MC, V). Homemade *moules marinères*, salads, soups and patés gobbled up in great quantities by journalists from the *New York Times* who work round the corner. It is all incredibly cheap and there is a tiny garden for eating outside in the summer.

P. J. Clarke's, 915 3rd Ave., at 55th St., tel 759 1650; (AE, DC;

reservations suggested). Definitive New York bar, recreated as Nat's Bar in Hollywood for the shooting of Billy Wilder's *The Lost Weekend*. Investigate the urinals at the back.

Carnegie Delicatessen & Restaurant, 854 7th Ave., near West 54th St., tel 757 2245; (no credit cards). Legendary pastrami on rye in jaw-breaking portions. The waiters are some of the funniest in the city, though cavillers say the coleslaw has lost its crunch since the loss of the late Leo Steiner.

Sapporo, 152 West 49th St., near 7th Ave., tel 869 8972; Japanese (no credit cards; no reservations). Superb *teriyaki*, *sukiyaki* and *tempura*.

Genroku Sushi, 366 5th Ave., between 34th and 35th Sts., tel 947 7940; Japanese (no credit cards). A bizarre development for fast food: *sushi* shudders round the restaurant on what the management calls an express conveyor belt. A continuous supply of tea hisses out of a plumbing system of nickel-plated pipes and taps suspended above the customer.

The New York Delicatessen, 104 West 57th St., between 6th and 7th Aves., tel 541 8320; (AE, DC, MC, V). Housed in an Art-Deco dome, once a Horn & Huddart Automat. Its pumpernickel sandwich stuffed with Norwegian nova scotia salmon, red onions and cucumber was voted the best sandwich of 1989 by Hellman's Mayonnaise.

CHEAP

Cabana Carioca, 123 West 45th St., near 7th Ave., tel 581 8088; Brazilian (AE, DC, MC, V; reservations suggested). Enormously popular, hence crowded; huge steaks, big pork chops topped with fried eggs, piles of fried potatoes and *feijoada*, a stew of black beans and meats. You will undoubtedly stagger out of the restaurant feeling very well-fed indeed.

Market Diner, 572 11th Ave., at West 43rd St., tel 244 6033; (AE, MC, V). A classic diner, refurbished and chromed, full of an unlikely selection of outcasts, cab-drivers and chic clubbers.

Christine's, 344 Lexington Ave., between East 39th and East 40th Sts., tel 953 1920; Polish-American (AE). Delicious and cheap blintzes, *pierogis*, (Polish stuffed dumplings, boiled or fried), french toast, *babka*, etc., part of an excellent Polish-American chain.

Burger Heaven, 20 East 49th St., between 5th and Madison Aves., tel 755 2166. (no credit cards). Another good chain offering the best fast-food burgers in the city.

Dosanko, 135 East 45th St., between 3rd and Lexington Aves., tel 697 2967; (no credit cards). Superbly prepared Japanese fast food.

Chez Laurence Patisserie, 245 Madison Ave., at 38th St., tel 683 0284; (no credit cards). Parisian pastry house, with dainty but filling lunches of soups and omelettes as well.

Upper East Side

LUXURY

Parioli Romanissimo, 24 East 81st St., off 5th Ave., tel 288 2391; Italian (AE, DC; reservations requested). Staggeringly expensive, but by all accounts staggeringly good. Excellent pasta, sausages and rack of lamb, and an enormous cheese trolley.

Le Cirque, 58 East 65th St., near Park Ave., tel 794 9292; French (AE, DC; reservations requested). Sometimes everything else gets swamped by the chichi crowd that eats here, but the menu, prepared by prize-winning chefs from France, is one of the most interesting you will find in the city.

EXPENSIVE

Rosa Mexicano, 1063 1st Ave., at East 58th St., tel 753 7407; Mexican (AE, DC, MC, V; reservations suggested). Authentic Mexican cooking, of unerringly high quality, but pricey.

Island, 1305 Madison Ave., between 92nd and 93rd Sts., tel 996 1200; Eclectic (AE, DC, MC, V; reservations suggested). Smart food from everywhere (pasta, grilled goat's cheese salad, fish and *crème brûlée*). Mostly first-class, but the restaurant can get uncomfortably hectic.

Le Bilboquet, 25 East 63rd St., between Madison and Park Aves., tel 751 3036; French (no credit cards; reservations suggested). Gallic waiters as snappily dressed as their clientele, and lots of bonhomie and conviviality. On the pricey side though.

Paola's, 347 East 85th St., between 1st and 2nd Aves., tel 794 1890; Northern Italian (AE; reservations suggested). Small Italian restaurant—occasionally a little cramped—serving exotic pasta.

L'ecco-la, 1660 3rd Ave., at 93rd St., tel 860 5609; Italian (AE). Flash decorations and lots of neon lights, considered 'Euro-chic'. Nevertheless the main course pasta dishes are excellent and the helpings excessive.

Fu's, 1395 2nd Ave., between 72nd and 73rd Sts., tel 517 9670; Chinese (AE, DC, MC, V; reservations suggested). Delicately cooked Peking duck, shredded beef and dumplings, none of it greasy.

Ideal Lunch and Bar, 238 East 86th St., tel 535 0950; German (no credit cards). Yankee pot-roasts, meatball sandwiches and Jupiter-sized omelettes served in a ramshackle restaurant.

Mocca Hungarian Restaurant, 1588 2nd Ave., near 83rd St., 734 6470; (no credit cards; reservations suggested). Delicious, but requires a lusty appetite for cheese pancakes, *wiener schnitzel*, goulash, sauerkraut and strudel. Outstanding value.

Istanbul Cuisine, 303 East 80th St., between 1st and 2nd Aves., tel 744 6903; Turkish (no credit cards). Tiny café. Exceptional value.

John's Pizza, 408 East 64th St., near York Ave., tel 935 2895; (no credit cards). Uptown annex to the downtown John's, and just as good.

Café Bonjour, 801 Lexington Ave., at 62nd St., tel 223 2270; French (AE, DC). French café with extremely good onion soup and Dijon chicken. Very cheap.

Rathbones, 1702 2nd Ave., near East 88th St., tel 369 7361; American steaks and burgers (AE, MC, V; no reservations). Sawdust on the floor, steakburgers, beer, sole, chicken cutlets, in pub-like surroundings.

Chef Ho's Hunan House, 1546 3rd Ave., at 87th St., tel 348 9444; Chinese (AE, MC, V). Chinese steak with oyster sauce, *dim sum*, and lunch specials.

Café Geiger, 206 East 86th St., near 3rd Ave., tel 734 4428; German (no credit cards). Ancient German café, with pastries and *eisbein*— steamed pigs' feet—which brave souls say are splendid.

Papaya King, East 59th St., on 3rd Ave., and East 86th St., and 3rd Ave., tel 753 2014; (no credit cards). Papaya juice, frankfurters and luminous green relish. Delicious.

Upper West Side

Café Luxembourg, 200 West 70th St., near Amsterdam Ave., tel 873 7411; American/French (AE, DC, MC, V; reservations suggested). One of the snazziest restaurants on the Upper West Side with a stylish clientele to match. The food is excellent and good value (around $45 a head).

Café des Artistes, 1 West 67th St., near Central Park West, tel 877

3500; (AE, DC, MC, V; reservations requested). Famous for its naughty murals and the pearl-bedecked dowagers who frequent it. Expensive but reliably good.

Tavern on the Green, Central Park West, at 67th St., tel 873 3200. American (AE, DC, MC, V; reservations requested). People come for the glitteringly tacky setting—chandeliers, 'rococo ceiling' and 350,000 lightbulbs. The cooking is suitably flamboyant. Lunch is a reasonable $30.

The Terrace, 400 West 119th St., near Amsterdam Ave., tel 666 9490; French (AE, DC, MC, V; reservations requested). Perched on top of a Columbia University dorm, with a romantic view of the city to the east and west and first-rate cooking.

MODERATE

Sarabeth's Kitchen, 423 Amsterdam Ave., between 80th and 81st Sts., tel 496 6280; (AE, DC, MC, V). An excellent place for brunch in spite of the twee decor. Try the scrambled eggs with smoked salmon and toast.

Sakura, 2298 Broadway, near 83rd St., tel 769 1003; Japanese (AE, DC, MC, V). Reasonably priced *sushi* served in a flash.

INEXPENSIVE

Ollie's, 2957 Broadway, at 116th St., tel 932 3300; Chinese American (AE). Cheap Chinese and American fast food mostly catering to students from Columbia.

Ottomanelli's Café, 50 West 72nd St., at Columbus Ave., tel 787 9493; (no credit cards). Pizza and juicy, meaty burgers.

V&T Restaurant, 1024 Amsterdam Ave., between 110th and 111th Sts., tel 663 1708; pizzeria (no credit cards). Morningside Heights' mecca for perfectly cooked pizza.

Popover Café; 551 Amsterdam Ave., between 86th and 87th Sts., tel 595 8555; (no credit cards). Popovers are hot little parcels of unsweetened buttery pastry delivered in baskets with jam and butter. Delicious at breakfast or anytime, along with sandwich extravaganzas and swoonmaking puddings.

CHEAP

Gray's Papaya, 2090 Broadway, at West 76th St., tel 799 0243; (no credit cards). Frothy batter-colored Papaya juice (which the check-out boys say is an aphrodisiac) and floppy frankfurters at Grand Prix speeds.

East and Central Harlem

MODERATE

Rao's, 455 East 114th St., near Pleasant Ave., tel 534 9626; (no credit cards; reservations requested). Deep in the old Italian East Harlem, this is the restaurant with the longest waiting list in Manhattan, and you will have to book as much as three months in advance to be absolutely sure of getting one of the three tables and four booths. The lure, justifiably, is the cooking: the best simply-prepared pasta, veal and chicken entrées you will eat in Manhattan. The Rao family has been running the restaurant in an old Dutch saloon since 1896.

INEXPENSIVE

La Famille, 2017 5th Ave., between 124th and 125th Sts., tel 289 6899; Southern (MC, V). Outstanding Southern cooking and generous portions in one of Harlem's friendliest restaurants—staggeringly good value.

Sylvia's, 328 Lenox Ave., between 126th and 127th Sts., tel 996 0660; Soul food (no credit cards). A breakfast feast prepared by Harlem's self-proclaimed Queen of soul food: eggs any style, sausage patties, grits, pork chops, smothered chicken, collard greens, candied yams, home fries, black-eyed beans, short ribs and sweet-potato pie.

Jamaican Hot Pot Restaurant, 2260 7th Ave., at 133rd St., tel 491 5270. Jamaican (no credit cards). Pot roasts, curried goat stews and oxtails served with corn bread, collard greens and fried plaintains or macaroni and cheese.

Floridita, Broadway and 129th St., tel 662 0090; Puerto Rican (no credit cards, no reservations). For wonderful *mofongo*, a delicious broth of plantains and fried pork.

Brooklyn

EXPENSIVE

Peter Luger's, 178 Broadway, Williamsburg, tel (718) 387 7400; (no credit cards; reservations suggested). Plate-size steaks at the best steak-house in the universe, according to Hitchcock.

The River Café, 1 Water St., under the Brooklyn Bridge, tel (718) 522 5200; American (AE, DC, MC, V; reservations requested). The restaurant with the best view in the city and impeccable cooking.

CHEAP

Nathan's Famous, corner of Surf and Stillwell Aves., Coney Island,

Brooklyn, tel (718) 946 2202; (no credit cards; open 24 hours). The birthplace of the hot-dog (and ultimately of fast food), which was first known as the Coney, swaddled in bread, and delivered to the general public here at the turn of the century by Nathan Hardwerker.

Bars

New York has millions of bars. There are four main categories: the cheerfully fleabitten and down-to-earth neighborhood bar (mostly in the West and East Villages, Chelsea and midtown), the gay and lesbian bars (mostly in the East and West Villages and Chelsea), the rowdy Upper East and West Side preppy and singles bars, and the chichi cocktail bars (mostly in midtown and the West Village).

Serious drinkers sit at the bar, watch the television, and lay their dollars on the counter in front of them as a kind of bank from which the barman helps himself. It's politic to tip the barman a dollar or so each time you order a round.

Whether you like it or not, spirits and soft drinks always come with masses of ice, which Americans crunch up like bones. In the fleabitten establishments nearly everyone drinks beer which you can order by the glass or, more cheaply (although you end up drinking more quickly), by quart or half-gallon pitchers. There are thousands of different brands, but they are all much of a muchness. 'Dark' beer is stronger than 'light' beer, and Mexican and Canadian beers are usually better than American beers.

Below is a brief list of favorite bars, beginning with the cheerful but ordinary and finishing with the fancy. The former, patronized by a rough and ready crew of friendly beer-guts, punks, gays, drunks, youthful slummers and Irish, are usually located in the East and West Villages, Chelsea, Gramercy Park and Columbia. On the Upper West and East Sides, louts and hoydens make up the clientele of the standard singles bars. A rather more high-stepping, glittering crowd frequents the cocktail bars in midtown, the Upper West and East Sides, the Flatiron District and the West Village. Remember that many of New York's smartest restaurants, like Windows on the World, the Rainbow Room and the Four Seasons (see above), have good-humored cocktail bars where you can go and take in the atmosphere without breaking the bank. (You must don a jacket and tie, however, and women won't get a foot in the door unless they are wearing a skirt). Liquor laws allow bars to stay open until 4 am, and most do so until at least 1 or 2 am.

East Village

The Holiday Inn, St Mark's Place, between 1st and 2nd Aves. East Village regulars call it the most fashionable bar in the world. The management is Ukrainian, kindly and put up with enormous crowds on Friday and Saturday nights. Best to go during the week.

Mona's, Avenue B, near East 13th St. Fashionable new bar patronized by local sophisticates who drink Guinness and cider on tap.

The Bar, 68 2nd Ave., at East 4th St. Well-established gay bar filled with young men from the neighborhood.

Blanche's, Ave. A, between 7th and 8th Sts. Proper drinker's bar lit with bright supermarket lights.

Blue & Gold, 79 East 7th St. Ukrainian bar also known as the 'Loser's Bar' because of its clientele of loners: a good bolthole from the more popular bars.

Boybar, 15¹/₂ St Mark's Place, between 3rd and 4th Aves. Extremely fashionable gay bar, crammed with a youthful and maverick crowd, with the notorious Boybar Beauties drag shows on Thursdays and Fridays.

Tunnel Bar, 116 1st Ave., at East 7th St. Small gay neighborhood bar, with pool and billiards, and porno films all day on Tuesdays and Thursdays (the bar has a special licence to show them).

The Horseshoe Bar, 108 Ave. B, at East 7th St. With its horseshoe-shaped counter, the bar was used for the filming of *Crocodile Dundee* and *The Victim*. It can get impossibly crowded on the weekends when Columbia students migrate from Washington Heights and fight over the pinball machine.

The Gas Station, Ave. B, between 2nd and 3rd Sts. Housed in an abandoned petrol station with a studiously weird interior decorated to resemble a scrap yard, and furniture made out of car-junk. It is frequented by a well-behaved mix of artistic types and East Village gentry. Often used for avant-garde poetry readings and performance art events. Open after hours.

The Baroque Bar, Ave. B, at East 10th St. New club/bar with a rather snooty policy of only admitting people who conform to the East Village hipster mould.

The Dug Out, 3rd Ave., between 13th and 14th Sts. Crusty dipsomaniacs, dog-eared barmen, and hazes of cigarette smoke.

The Aztec Lounge, East 9th St., between Ave. A and 1st Ave. A pitch-black cave illuminated by a faintly flickering stroboscopic light and adopted by East Village punks.

Joe's Bar, East 5th St., between Aves. A and B. More easy-going than most East Village establishments, with a good pool table and a Country music jukebox.

Sophie's, East 5th St., betwen Aves. A and B. Madly crowded on the weekends, but filled with fewer die-hard regulars on weekday lunch-times.

Save the Robots, Ave., B at 2nd St. Opens at 4 am so describes itself as a private club rather than a bar. Membership only, but you can usually find members outside who will take you in. Inside there is a disco on a sawdust floor and exhausted, human robots who have somehow got themselves here from the clubs.

McSorley's Old Ale House, 15 East 7th St., between 2nd and 3rd Aves. One of the oldest bars in the city with Irish barmen and ancient furnishings. It's a good lunchtime place, but not so congenial in the evening when it fills up with student-rowdies. It became internationally famous when it went (unsuccessfully) all the way to the Supreme Court to keep women out.

Bandito's, 153 2nd Ave., between 10th and 11th Sts. Mexican food and good *margheritas*, and a cheerful crowd, though the music in the bar inside sometimes gets unbearably loud.

Cave Canem, 24 1st Ave., near 2nd St., tel 529 9665. Decadent club-cum-bar in a former Turkish baths. There is a disco and a tiled pool in the basement, and sofas and a bar upstairs.

Telephone Bar & Grill, 149 2nd Ave., between 9th and 10th Sts. Cider and fish and chips wrapped in fake newspaper in the East Village's idea of an English pub.

Downtown Beirut II, 157 East Houston St., near Ludlow St. Tough venue for hard rock bands with a bar.

West Village
The White Horse Tavern, 560 Hudson St., at West 11th St. All the English Literature majors in the country make a pilgrimage to the bar where Dylan Thomas drank himself to death. The pub is very amiable, though the beer is surprisingly watery.

Badlands, 388 West St., between Christopher and West Sts. Leather and Western gay bar with pool table and disco, and screenings of Hollywood movies on Thursday nights.

Peculier Pub, 182 West 4th St. Over 200 brands of beer from 45 countries with their labels stuck to the walls.

Chumley's, 86 Bedford St., between Barrow and Grove Sts. An old speakeasy in the West Village; still unmarked, with two entrances on

Barrow and Grove Streets. Headquarters of the US Chess Federation.
Bowlmor Lanes, 110 University Place, at 12th St. Congenial bar in one of the city's last few bowling alleys.
Keller's, 384 West St., at Christopher and Varick Sts. Oldest gay bar in the West Village, with a mostly black clientele
Kelly's Bar, 46 Bedford St., at 7th Ave. Lesbian and gay bar, with straights as well, and a good piano player from Wednesday to Saturday.
The Lion's Head, 59 Christopher St. Typically shady journalists' bar in a basement, used as a campaign headquarters by Norman Mailer when he ran for mayor. Running mate was Jimmy Breslin.
Marie's Crisis Café, 59 Grove St., at 7th Ave. Jolly gay piano bar with an enthusiastic singing clientele.
No Name Bar, 621 Hudson St. Friendly West Village bar with a good jukebox and all kinds of drinkers.
Uncle Charlie's, 56 Greenwich Ave., between Perry St., and 7th Ave. Packed-out gay video bar with a mixed bunch of college students, preppy Wall Street executives and stockbrokers, and Madison Ave. advertising men. Women are also allowed in.

SoHo
Fanelli, 94 Prince St., at Mercer St. Old-fashioned SoHo dive with a jolly clientele and good pub food.

Chelsea and Flatiron District
Angry Squire, 216 7th Ave. Chelsea pub with highly acclaimed live jazz.
Old Town, 18th St., between Park Ave. South and Broadway. Ancient pub full of beer-gut regulars.
The Eagle's Nest, 142 11th Ave., at West 21st St. Established in 1960, the oldest gay bar in the city, with a relaxed denim and leather crowd, wrestling videos and a lively disco.
The Spike, 120 11th Ave., at West 20th St. Less hardcore than it used to be, a packed, rough and tumble denim and leather bar near the Eagle's Nest in Chelsea.
Rawhide, 212 8th Ave., at West 21st St. Leather, Western and S&M in a friendly neighborhood gay bar.

Midtown Cocktail Bars
Beekman Tower, 3 Mitchell Place, between 1st Ave. and 49th St. A

swish piano bar at the top of a beautiful Art-Deco skyscraper, with a breathtaking outdoor view of midtown.

Top of the Sixes, 666 5th Ave., 39th floor. Another view. Drinks veer on the pricey side but there are huge quantities of free *hors d'oeuvres*, practically a meal in themselves.

Trader Vic's, 59th St., and 5th Ave. A bizarre concept: tropical cocktails in mud huts in a basement inside the Plaza hotel.

Top of the Park, Gulf and Western Plaza, Columbus Circle. Again a thrilling midtown view—this time of Central Park—and a rather showy crowd of cocktail-drinkers.

Algonquin Hotel, 59 West 44th St. Old Round Table hang-out and still elegantly fuddy-duddy with a suave clientele propping up the bar.

Elaine's, 1703 2nd Ave. A much-loved restaurant, though in fact the drinks are rather better than the cooking.

Gotham Bar and Grill, 12 East 12th St., off 5th Ave. Snappy drinkers in an elegant West Village restaurant.

Café Luxembourg, 200 West 70th St., between Amsterdam and West End Aves. Glamorous, preening drinkers propping up the bar in an extremely stylish restaurant. Sometimes a trifle too cramped and noisy for comfort.

Upper East Side
Swell's, 1429 York Ave., at 76th St. Full of boundlessly cheerful Upper East Side rowdys—advertising executives, stockbrokers and merchant bankers. Striped shirts, pictures of race horses lining the walls, and backgammon.

Uzie's, 1444 3rd Ave., at 82nd St. Glamorous Upper East Side sophisti-cates and a shadowy, elegant bar.

Jim McMullen, 1341 3rd Ave., between 76th and 77th Sts. Models and football players, and a palpable sexual undertow.

Useful Publications
Daniel Young's *The Under $15 Good Eating Guide* is an unerring and witty guide to the inexpensive restaurants of New York; Sylvia Carter's *Eats* is nearly as good. Myra Alperson and Mark Clifford's *The Food Lover's Guide to the Real New York* is a fascinating account of New York's ethnic restaurants and markets, particularly those in the outer boroughs.

Seymour Britchky's *The Restaurants of New York* proclaims itself as the bible of fancy restaurants with microscopic essays and blow by blow accounts of Britchky's encounters with butter knifes and banquettes. Gault Millau's *The Best of New York* also has a large section devoted to restaurant reviews, though they tend to err on the side of the eulogistic and hyperbolic. Zagat's *New York City Restaurant Survey* compiled from the reviews of 4700 New Yorkers is disappointingly clichéd and sketchy.

Where To Stay

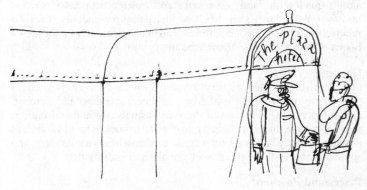

Finding a suitable place to stay is a headache. With a permanent shortage of space in the city, prices are inflated, if not astronomical. If you don't mind a little discomfort and have a friend in New York, ask if you can stay on their floor; or whether they know anyone who is going away and wants to rent their apartment for a couple of weeks. (Sometimes it's possible to find short rents listed in the *Village Voice*, but it's always best to find out by word of mouth.)

Hotels in the city range from a stratosphere of luxury—a penthouse in the Waldorf Towers, for example—to utterly miserable dumps filled with strange muttering old men. Even if you don't mind slumming it, it's worth taking into account the location of the hotel, and inquiring before-hand about safety in the area, and noise. Whatever you do, don't expect anywhere to be charmingly spartan, elegantly faded or appealingly shabby—just expect it to be spartan, faded, shabby, and sometimes depressing. Do not be alarmed, either, if you stumble on a gang of mean-looking cockroaches—they make their nests in the swankiest hotels as well, only there they maintain a lower profile. If you see a rat, however, you should start to worry.

In general, hotels in the Upper East Side are the most expensive, and hotels on the quieter east side of Midtown are the best value. The west side of Midtown has the really cheapo hotels, mostly used by package groups and conventions; 9th Avenue, Times Square and the area round

Penn Station are all fairly unsavory at night. Hotels in unusual areas like Gramercy Square, the Flatiron District, the Upper West Side, the far north end of the Upper East Side, Chelsea and the West Village, are always good value, and often safer and quieter than most parts of midtown. Youth hostels are excellent alternatives for students. B & Bs, a relatively new phenomenon in the city, are more pleasant, with the added bonus of getting to know the inhabitants.

Booking

Not surprisingly, hotels get very crowded during those seasons when it's nicest to be in New York (April, May and June, September and October, and at Christmas). The rest of the year businessmen and conventions move about like flocks of starlings, so it's *vital* to book as far in advance as possible. Usually hotels ask for a credit card number as a guarantee, and some exact a penalty if you cancel a booking at short notice.

Prices and Payment

All hotels add $8^1/_4$ per cent sales tax to their bills, and an occupancy tax of 5 per cent, plus $2. Most take all major credit cards, but some ask for an American Express card as a guarantee of payment. It's always a good idea to enquire about weekend packages, when many hotels reduce their rates by as much as 40 per cent. For more information, write to the New York Visitors and Conventions Bureau, 2 Columbus Circle, New York, NY 10019, (tel 212 397 8222).

The prices below are for double rooms, excluding $13^1/_4$ per cent city and state sales tax and $2 occupancy tax. For single rooms, take off 10–15 per cent, and for 1992 onwards, add 5–10 per cent. If you have children, you may be able to have a bed moved into a double room. All the hotels have private baths and air-conditioning, unless otherwise stated.

****	LUXURY	over $260
***	EXPENSIVE	$200–$260
**	MODERATE	$160–$200
*	INEXPENSIVE	under $160

Upper East Side

****The Carlyle, 35 East 76th St., at Madison Ave., New York NY 10021, tel (212) 744 1600. John F. Kennedy's favorite, the Carlyle still maintains an absolute reign over all the other hotels in Manhattan. The

308

building itself is lovely: dating from 1929, it is shaped into an Art-Deco rocket with a verdigris pyramid and a nozzle on top. At 38 stories high, it is the only proper skyscraper on the Upper East Side. Inside the pianist Bobby Short presides over the famous Café Carlyle. There is also the less expensive, slightly noisier Bemelmans' Bar decorated with peculiar animal murals by the illustrator and author of the 'Madeleine' children's books, Ludwig Bemelmans who painted them while he worked as a waiter ($220–275).

****Plaza Athénée**, 37 East 64th St., between Madison and Park Aves., New York NY 10021, tel (212) 734 9100. Elegant, but a bit pompous: every room has is own kitchen and a trouser press; staff are suitably peremptory ($275–315).

****The Lowell**, 28 East 63rd St., New York NY 10021, tel (212) 838 1400 or (1–800) 345 3457. Civilized and grand, with old-fashioned charm and a library. Wood-burning fireplaces and kitchenettes in the bedrooms ($220–290).

****The Mayfair Regent**, 610 Park Ave., at 65th St., New York NY 10021, tel (212) 288 0800 or (1–800) 545 4000. An antidote to the glittery luxury hotels, the Mayfair Regent is quiet, welcoming and discreetly decorated; one of the nicest, most subdued hotels of its class in the city, with tasteful rooms, an excellent tea room and the fashionable restaurant, Le Cirque (see p. 297) ($230–270).

****The Pierre**, 5th Ave., at 61st St., New York NY 10021, tel (212) 838 8000 or (1–800) 332 3442. An Art-Deco palace looking onto Central Park, disconcertingly magnificent, with gargantuan bedrooms and bathrooms ($265–355).

****The Stanhope**, 995 5th Ave., at 81st St., New York NY 10028, tel (212) 288 5800 or (1–800) 828 1123. Snooty enough for ties and jackets to be required at all times, and tricked out in Second Empire chandeliers and sofas. It is in a superb location overlooking the Metropolitan Museum with an outdoor café that is very jolly ($250–325).

***The Regency**, 540 Park Ave., near East 60th St., New York NY 10021, tel (212) 759 4100 or (1–800) 243 1166. Modern hotel dignified with lots of French antiques. Rooms are big and look nice, service is good, and there is a lively bar downstairs, popular with bourbon-swigging ladies and businessmen ($195–255).

***The Mark**, 25 East 77th St., near Madison Ave., New York NY 10021, tel (212) 744 4300 or (1–800) 847 8483. New, neo-Classical Upper East Side establishment boasting such mod cons as VCRs, a jacuzzi in every bathroom and a sneaky location, in the shadow of the

Carlyle Hotel. Service is snappy, and rates are extremely good for a hotel that ought to be in the four star category ($210–260).

***The Westbury**, 69th St., at Madison Ave., New York NY 10021, tel (212) 535 2000. Comfortable and friendly, the Westbury is one of the best-liked hotels on the Upper East Side. The rooms are understated (what the management calls 'French Provençal'), and guests have a reputation for panache ($210–250).

***Sherry Netherland**, 781 5th Ave., at 59th St., New York NY 10021, tel (212) 355 2800. One of two Art-Deco châteaux looking onto Central Park by Schultze & Weaver, who were responsible for the Pierre next door as well as the Waldorf-Astoria. Like the Pierre, it retains an antiquated elegance and swank ($175–250).

Wales, 1295 Madison Ave. at 92nd St., New York NY 10028, tel (212) 876 6000. Really excellent value due to its location in a quiet area near the Museum Mile and the northern end of the Upper East Side. (It takes about five minutes on the Lexington Avenue Express to get to midtown Manhattan and there are frequent, reasonably fast, buses running down 5th Avenue.) Built in 1900, the hotel itself is old-fashioned and staid in a nice way thanks to charming if stuffy furnishings. The bathrooms, in particular, are especially nice ($65–70).

Midtown East

***Morgans**, 237 Madison Ave., at 38th St., New York NY 10016, tel (212) 686 0300. Started by the disco entrepreneurs Ian Schrager and the late Steve Rubell—the partnership responsible for Studio 54, the Palladium and, now, three Manhattan hotels. As expected, it oozes minimalist chic and pop stars ($170–205).

***The Waldorf-Astoria**, 301 Park Ave., New York NY 10022, tel (212) 355 3000 or (1–800) HILTONS. Occupying a whole city block with 1692 rooms and its own underground railway spur, the Waldorf was the swishest hotel of thirties New York. It is comparatively shabby nowadays, but its Art-Deco interior is being spruced up and with luck the old hotel will get a new lease of life ($175–280). (See pp. 245–6).

***United Nations Plaza**, 1 United Nations Plaza, New York NY 10017, tel (212) 355 3400 or (1–800) 228 9000. Flash skyscraper by Kevin LaRoche opposite the UN, with a rooftop pool and tennis courts, and a clientele of businessmen and diplomats. By all accounts service is unbeatable ($200–235).

***The Drake**, 440 Park Ave., at 56th St., New York NY 10022, tel

(212) 421 0900 or (1–800) 63-SWISS. Jet-set hotel with civilized rooms which have been prettified with European touches. Each room has a fridge and the hotel is very proud of its gourmet dining room, the Restaurant Lafayette ($205–235).

***The Inter-Continental New York**, 111 East 48th St., near Park Ave., New York NY 10017, tel (212) 755 5900 or (1–800) 33-AGAIN. Despite its name, the hotel has so far resisted modernization. Pleasantly faded, with old Persian carpets and a gilded aviary in the lobby, and slightly cranky but impeccable service ($205–245).

***The Omni Berkshire Place**, 21 East 52nd St., near 5th Ave., New York NY 10022, tel (212) 753 5800 or (1–800) THE-OMNI. An imposing lobby: comfortable, spacious rooms and an off-premises health club ($205–265).

The Doral Inn, 541 Lexington Ave., at 49th St., New York NY 10022, tel (212) 755 1200 or (1–800) 223 5823. Low key, but good value, in an excellent location opposite the Waldorf. A new fitness center, with squash courts, saunas and a laundry ($116–134).

The Helmsley Middletowne, 148 East 48th St., between Lexington and 3rd Aves., New York NY 10017, tel (212) 755 3000 or (1–800) 221 4982. Pleasantly laid-back hotel in an old apartment house. The staff are helpful instead of cringing ($125–135).

The Hotel Elysée, 60 East 54th St., between Madison and Park Aves., New York NY 10022, tel (212) 753 1066. It looks slightly eccentric to Americans; appealingly fuddy-duddy to the English. Used by Tennessee Williams and Harold Robbins, the rooms all have names (e.g. 'The Sunset') rather than numbers, and also video machines. The hotel is conveniently tucked away in a nice part of the center of midtown ($140–190).

Manhattan Suites East, Sales office, 505 East 75th St., New York NY 10001, tel (212) 772 2900 or (1–800) ME-SUITE. Excellent-value apartment hotels in nine different locations in midtown, including the handsome Art-Deco Beekman Tower at 3 Mitchell Place near the UN ($160–200).

The Roger Smith Winthrop, 501 Lexington Ave., near East 46th St., New York NY 10017, tel (212) 755 1400 or (1–800) 241 3848. Rather fusty, but in a good location. Comfortable, clean bedrooms, some surprisingly lavish ($160–200).

The San Carlos, 150 East 50th St., near Lexington Ave., New York NY 10022, tel (212) 755 1800 or (1–800) 722 2012. Friendly residential hotel with clean bedrooms, and suites with kitchens (from $159).

**Halloran House, 525 Lexington Ave., at East 49th St., New York NY 10017, tel (212) 755 4000. Handsome 1920s building painted many times by Georgia O'Keefe. Comfortable, traditionally-decorated rooms (from $175).

**Barbizon Hotel, 140 East 63rd St., on Lexington Ave., New York NY 10017, tel (212) 838 5700. Formerly a buttoned-up women-only hotel which figured in Sylvia Plath's *The Bell Jar* as the Amazon. It has recently been smartened up for both sexes, and is extremely well thought of ($160–195).

**Tudor, 304 East 42nd St., New York NY 10017, tel (212) 986 8800. A modest but convivial hotel in Tudor City—an unnaturally quiet enclave slapbang in the middle of a noisy part of midtown. Small but pleasant rooms and good views (from $165).

*The Pickwick Arms, 230 East 51st St., between 3rd and 2nd Aves., New York NY 10022, tel (212) 355 0300 or (1–800) PICKWICK. Absolutely the best deal in Manhattan, especially for anyone new to the city: the location is good, the rooms are clean and comfortable, the staff are extremely helpful, and there is a garden on the roof. Reports are unanimously good. ($75, or as low as $37 for a single with shared bath.)

*Vanderbilt YMCA, 224 East 47th St., between 3rd and 2nd Aves., New York NY 10017, tel (212) 755 2410. The best Y in New York with clean, cupboard-sized rooms for one, two or four. Write at least two weeks in advance enclosing a deposit for the first night ($38, singles from $27).

Midtown West

***The Paramount, 235 West 46th St., New York NY 10021, tel (212) 764 5500. Steve Rubell's newest venture (see Morgan's above) with the French designer Phillippe Starck. The entrance, manned by bouncers garbed in Jean-Paul Gaultier outfits, looks forbiddingly like a funeral parlor, thanks to the dozen red roses stuck in individual holes in the doorway. The interior is a joke on a 1930s club, with black telephones sitting on low tables, a skew-wiff staircase and elevators colored in orange, violet and green neon. People are most impressed, however, by the bathrooms—in particular the conical stainless steel basins. Sleeping quarters are more commodious than the Royalton (see below), though the restaurant is a great disappointment (from $230).

***The Royalton, 44 West 44th St., near 5th Ave., New York NY 10036, tel (212) 869 4400 or (1–800) 635 9013. Another fashionable

Rubell/Starck curio (see above and Morgan's). The furniture is covered in dust covers, the walls and light-fittings with rhinoceros horns, and the staff wear black and try to look mysterious. Bedrooms are a trifle pokey: the slate bathrooms are much admired (from $215).

****The Ritz-Carlton, 112 Central Park South., New York NY 10019, tel (212) 757 1800 or (1–800) 223 7990. Recently kitted out as a pretty English country house, with lashings of chintz, by the redoubtable interior designer Mrs Henry 'Sister' Parish the Second ($225–325).

****The Plaza, 768 5th Ave., at 59th St., New York NY 10019, tel (212) 750 3000 or (1–800) 228 3000. The grand old man of New York hotels, home to Frank Lloyd Wright and Marlene Dietrich, a vast white Victorian château perched on the edge of Central Park. Trump snaffled it up in 1988 and passed it on to Ivana for re-upholstery. The result is a pleasant enough motel-floral. Bedrooms are immense and bathrooms palatial, though the latter's slippery marble floors are potential killers ($225–410).

***Le Parker Meridien, 118 West 57th St., near 6th Ave., New York NY 10019, tel (212) 245 5000 or (1–800) 543 4300. Plush, showy and modern. All the glamor and extravagance, however, somehow lacks an edge and can seem bland. Slick service and glitzy guests. Swimming pool on the roof, workout center in the basement ($205–260).

**The Algonquin, 59 West 44th St., between 5th and 6th Aves., New York NY 10036, tel (212) 840 6800 or (1–800) 548 0345. Doggedly traditional, the small and friendly hotel still has considerable charm. Renovations and a new Japanese management have preserved the reassuringly old world atmosphere ($150). (See pp. 186–7).

*The Wyndham, 42 West 48th St., near 5th Ave., New York NY 10019, tel (212) 753 3500. Unassuming but stylish, with pretty rooms and superb service. Excellent value ($120).

*Hotel Wentworth, 59 West 46th St., near 6th Ave., New York NY 10036, tel (212) 719 2300 or (1–800) 223 1900. Old Art-Deco hotel with clean, rudimentary bedrooms in a good position between 5th Avenue and a safe part of Times Square ($80–110).

*Gorham, 136 West 55th St., between 6th and 7th Aves., New York NY 10019, tel (212) 245 1800. Small, well-looked after and in an excellent location on West 55th Street. Many of the rooms have been recently renovated (from $95).

*Hotel Edison, 228 West 47th St., near 8th Ave., New York NY 10036, tel (212) 840 5000. Modest and clean, air-conditioned hotel in a scruffy part of the Times Square area (from $90).

*Hotel Iroquois, 49 West 44th St., between 5th and 6th Aves., New York NY 10036, tel (212) 840 3080. Grimy but not seedy; well-placed next to the Algonquin on 44th Street, (from $85).

*Mansfield, 12 West 44th St., near 5th Ave., New York NY 10036, tel (212) 944 6050. A bit down-at-heel, but cheap for its excellent midtown location opposite the Algonquin (from $75).

*Remington, 129 West 46th St., near Broadway, New York NY 10036, tel (212) 221 2600. Budget prices for a hotel in Times Square which is proud of its private baths in every room (from $70).

*Ramada Inn, 48th St., and 8th Ave., New York NY 10019, tel (212) 581 7000 (1–800) 2-RAMADA. Part of a no-frills hotel chain. Outdoor swimming pool on the roof, but in a bad area near Times Square, ($115–137).

*Sloane House YMCA, 356 West 34th St., near 9th Ave., New York NY 10001, tel (212) 760 5860. A real dive, in a dodgy neighborhood, but the prices are good (from $47.50).

*Wellington Hotel, 871 7th Ave., at 55th St., New York NY 10019, tel (212) 247 3900 or (1–800) 652 1212. Basic and very big, often used by tour groups (from $104).

*Westpark Hotel, 308 West 58th St., near Columbus Circle, New York NY 10019, tel (212) 246 6440. An exceptionally good deal in this bracket: small, modest and tastefully decorated (from $75).

*Milford Plaza, 270 West 45th St., at 8th Ave., New York NY 10036, tel (212) 869 3600 or (1–800) 221 2690. Even more basic and even bigger, with chaos reigning in the lobby and uninspiring rooms. A cheap option if you can't find anything else (from $105).

Upper West Side

*Hotel Empire, Broadway, at 63rd St., New York NY 10023, tel (212) 265 7400 or (1–800) 221 6509. Unlovely, but clean, well-maintained and well-placed near Lincoln Center. One of the best alternatives to the budget hotels located in the more flyblown setting of Times Square (from $110).

*New York International Youth Hostel, 891 Amsterdam Ave., near 103rd St., New York NY 10025, tel (212) 932 2300. Largest hostel in the country with rooms for two, four, six or eight people. Good value and helpful staff ($19, no credit cards).

*West Side Y, 5 West 63rd St., near Central Park West, New York NY 10023, tel (212) 787 4400. A good location, plus a swimming pool and a gym (singles from $30, doubles $40, book in advance).

Flatiron District and Gramercy Park

**Gramercy Park, 2 Lexington Ave., at 21st St., New York NY, tel (212) 475 4320. Popular with Europeans and one of the best choices for a medium-priced hotel: away from the noise and mania of the center, but within walking distance of midtown and the Villages, and in one of the prettiest squares in New York. The rooms are handsome and the staff are generally friendly. Guests have access to Gramercy Park, the private park facing the hotel (from $130).

*Carlton Arms, 160 East 25th St., near 3rd Ave., New York NY 10010, tel (212) 679 0680. Another excellent deal, and one of the most fashionable and idiosyncratic—each room is covered from ceiling to floor (including baths, door handles and cupboards) with murals by artists who have lived there. A good location, close to the East and West Villages. The staff go out of their way to be helpful (from $49).

West Village

*Washington Square, 103 Waverly Place, New York NY 10011, tel (212) 777 9515. A bit shabby, and full of students, but in a good and safe location in the cheerful West Village, a few steps away from bars, cafés and clubs and near NYU (from $60).

*Riverview, 113 Jane St., near West St., New York NY 10014, tel (212) 929 0060. Decidedly fleabitten, (be prepared for pokey rooms and encounters with grime, smells and permanent residents) but in a good location, and exceptionally cheap (singles from $20, doubles $40).

Chelsea

**Chelsea, 222 West 23rd St., between 7th and 8th Aves., New York NY 10011, tel (212) 243 3700. Mark Twain, Sarah Bernhardt, Jackson

Pollock, Vladimir Nabokov, Virgil Thompson, and, of course, Sid Vicious, all made the Chelsea their headquarters, and the grimy, ramshackle hotel, complete with sixties artefacts, still retains a bohemian edge (from $85).

Wall Street/TriBeCa

***Vista International**, 3 World Trade Center, New York NY 10048, tel (212) 938 9100. Huge and antiseptic, but for businessmen working long hours it is conveniently close to Wall Street and the restaurants are quite good ($195–260).

Alternative Accommodation

Students
*International House of New York**, 500 Riverside Drive, at West 122nd St., New York NY 10027, tel (212) 316 8400. Open from June–mid-August. Written applications only (from $55, full-time students $25).
*International Student Center**, 38 West 88th St., between Columbus Ave. and Central Park West, New York NY 10024, tel (212) 787 7706. Dormitories, but the cheapest prices in the city and an excellent location ($10).
(See listings for each area, above, for details of youth hostels. There is **Sloane House** in Midtown West; the **West Side YMCA** (probably the best of the bunch), and the **New York International Youth Hostel** both on the Upper West Side; and the **Vanderbilt** in Midtown East.

Women Only
As a rule safety for women depends more on the area you are staying in than the hotel (the area round Times Square is not recommended), though if you are broke a women-only hotel might be a more palatable alternative. (Even the fantastically smart hotels can be problematic for women. Managements—who automatically assume that anyone who hangs about in lobbies is a call-girl—will collar even the most innocently single lady.)
*Allerton House**, 130 East 57th St., New York NY 10022, tel (212) 753 8841. Old-fashioned hotel (singles from $45).

***Martha Washington**, 30 East 30th St., between Park and Madison Aves., New York NY 10016, tel (212) 689 1900. A bit spartan, but cheap (single room from $47).

***Eych-Troughton Memorial Residence**, 145 East 39th St., New York NY 10016, tel (212) 490 5990. A week in residence for $100, two meals a day included.

Bed and Breakfast

Sometimes you can stay in a good hotel for similar rates, but you will probably have a much more interesting time in a B&B. On the minus side, many of the B&B's are out in the boroughs, and traveling in and out of Manhattan is a bore.

Bed and Breakfast Network of New York, 134 West 32nd St., Suite 602, New York NY 10001, tel (212) 645 8134. Hosted rooms from $70–90, unhosted apartments for $80–200.

City Lights Bed and Breakfast Ltd., Box 20355, Cherokee Station, New York NY 10028, tel (212) 737 7049. Hosted doubles from $60, unhosted apartments for $85–200.

New World Bed and Breakfast, 150 5th Ave., Suite 711, New York NY 10011, tel (212) 675 5600 or (1–800) 443 3800. Call during office hours, hosted doubles from about $70.

Urban Ventures, PO Box 46, Planetarium Station, New York NY 10024, tel (212) 594 5650. Hosted double from $70, unhosted studios from $68.

Hosts and Guests Inc., PO Box 6798, FDR Station, New York NY 10150, tel (212) 874 4308. Call Mon–Sat 9–7 only, hosted doubles from about $75.

Home Exchange

Make sure you know what kind of neighborhood the exchange is situated in, and ask for precise details about the apartment.

Vacation Exchange Club, tel (602) 972 2186. Part of a worldwide network listing people with homes to exchange (fee $24.70).

Residential Hotels

To qualify, you need to be staying in the city for at least a month or so.

Webster Apartments, 419 West 34th St., New York NY 10011, tel (212) 594 3950. Rooms for working women only (prices calculated according to salary).

John and Mary Markle Memorial Residency, 123 West 13th St., New York NY 10011, tel (212) 242 2400. For young businesswomen and senior citizens, on application only ($80–100 a week).

YM-YWHA, 1395 Lexington Ave., New York NY 10028, at 92nd St. On written application ($76–96 a week).

Renting/Sharing an Apartment

See Living and Working in New York, p. 379.

318

Arts, Entertainment and Nightlife

The city's cinemas, galleries, off-Broadway theaters and nightclubs seethe with activity; and, as for jazz and dance, New York is without compare. Yet, in the evenings, most New Yorkers prefer to stay in and watch television. With so much going on, however, it would be a shame to follow their example.

Fashions breeze in and fizzle out at such alarming speeds that keeping abreast with what's new requires considerable stamina and dedication. To get a good overview of what's on, you will have to invest in some magazines and newspapers. Friday's Metropolitan and Sunday's Arts & Leisure sections in the *New York Times* have reviews, discriminating listings and week-ahead surveys; the weekly *Village Voice* has comprehensive listings (especially good for films and 'cheap thrills'—a listing of the week's free–$2.50 events). Its reviews are rather more spirited than those in the *Times* (particularly on rock and pop). *New York Magazine* and the *New Yorker* have detailed listings; and both the monthly *Paper Magazine* and *Details* are good on current trends in nightclubs and as well as film, theater and dance.

Film

Even New Yorkers stir themselves to go to the movies. There are battalions of cinemas in the city, and enthusiastic audiences usually clap at the end of a film, even if it's a load of old cobblers. Of the commercial cinemas, Cineplex Odeon (which owns dozens of cinemas including a massive nine-theater complex in Chelsea) and Loews are the most expensive; the cinemas around Times Square are the rowdiest (worth visiting, to witness audience participation alone). 'Revival Houses', showing a mixture of nostalgia, Hollywood classics and cult movies, can become an addiction. Most are cheaper than the commercial cinemas and show double bills, with the added bonus that managements seldom clear the house in between films, so you can happily spend the whole day in the cinema. Unfortunately many are going out of business because of high rents. 'Art houses' are cinemas showing foreign and the kind of serious films which do not go down well with mass audiences. There are particularly good listings and reviews on the art and revival houses in the *Village Voice*. The *New York Post* movie clock is strong on commercial films.

At the end of September there is the prestigious **New York Film Festival** at Alice Tully Hall in Lincoln Center, which premieres 25 new American and European films. To be sure of getting tickets you should apply about five weeks in advance (call 877 1800 ext 489 for details), but it is possible to get returns on the day of the performance. In the spring the **Museum of Modern Art** has a special festival devoted to **New Directors/New Films**, and throughout the year it has at least 25 screenings a week (free with general admission) of films from its enormous archives. The Donnell branch of the **New York Public Library**, at 20 West 53rd St, has a continuous programme of films, which they show free, and the **Museum of Broadcasting**, also on 53rd Street, has a unique collection of over 30,000 television and radio programmes. (See p. 260).

Revival and Art Houses
Angelika Film Center, corner of Houston and Mercer Sts, tel 995 2000. Six screens showing a mixture of art-house and revival films, and a coffee-and-cake counter managed by the gourmet food shop Dean and Deluca.

Biograph, 57th St., near Broadway, tel 582 4582. Thirties, forties and fifties revivals on 35mm prints.

Cinema Village, 22 East 12th St., tel 924 3363. The programme of double features is a spirited mix of recent movies like *Withnail and I* and *Diva*, and classics by Bertolucci, Truffaut and Fellini.

Film Forum, 209 West Houston St., near Varick St., tel 727 0110.

Three screens: FF1 for independent American and foreign films; FF2 for repertorial profiles of film-makers; and FF3 for extended runs of films that had successes in the first two theaters. A wonderful concession stand sells cappuccino, brownies, expresso and popcorn.

The Kitchen, 512 West 19th St., at 10th and 11th Aves. Video screening room for experimental work.

Millenium Film Workshop, 66 East 4th St., tel 673 0090. Formed in the 1960s, this is one of the oldest experimental and avant-garde film houses in the city.

The Paris, West 58th St., tel 688 2013. Swish auditorium next to the Plaza showing mainstream films from abroad.

Public Theater 425 Lafayette St., tel 598 7150. An offshoot of Joseph Papp's Shakespeare Theater, this small cinema shows a daring, often esoteric selection of films.

Theater 80, 80 St Mark's Place, between 1st and 2nd Aves. Films from the 1930s–60s are screened in a camp shrine to moving pictures, with blue lighting, autographed stills, and a jungly café decorated with pyramids made out of candy bars.

Classical Music

New York pulls all the big names, of course, and standards are consistently outstanding. The critics complain that the repertoire veers from conservative mainstream to the wildly adventurous, with nothing in between. If you scrutinize programs carefully, however, you can usually find something for everyone, especially in the smaller venues. The best places to look are the Sunday *New York Times* Arts & Leisure section, *7 Days Magazine* and *New York Magazine*. The last two have the most organized listings.

The two most important venues are Carnegie Hall and Lincoln Center, which has four separate auditoriums (two for opera and two for concerts). For the latter you can usually get half-price tickets from the Bryant Park Ticket Booth on the day of orchestral performances (see below), and 'Rush' tickets for students from the venue itself (ring ahead to ask about availability).

Concert Halls
Lincoln Center
62nd to 66th Streets, between Amsterdam and Columbus Aves, tel 877 2011, tickets 362 6000. The Center comprises:

Avery Fisher Hall, tel 874 2424. When it first opened in 1962 the acoustics were such a disaster that the then Philharmonic Hall turned in desperation to the electronics moghul, Avery Fisher, who renovated it and added oak panelling. Since then the hall has been home to the 150-year-old New York Philharmonic and its principal conductor, Zubin Mehta, and also the American Philharmonic. In the summer there is the immensely popular six-week **Mostly Mozart Festival**, in which every seat is reduced to the same low price. During the season (Sept–May) the public can usually attend rehearsals at massively cut rates at 9.45 on Thursday mornings (phone ahead to check).

Alice Tully Hall, tel 362 1911. Recitals, string quartets, lieder and chamber music. Considered acoustically perfect.

Metropolitan Opera House, tel 362 6000. Home to the Metropolitan grand-opera machine and (unofficially) the American Ballet, this is the most lavish Lincoln Center auditorium—-the one with the showy interior: garish red and gold décor, clinking Austrian crystal chandeliers which mysteriously waft up into the ceiling as performances start, and two large Chagall murals which are visible hundreds of yards away, from the street. Critics complain that the opera productions lack innovation but, nevertheless, top international stars fill the line-up, and the New York upper-crust puts in a suitably glittery appearance. Tickets are expensive, and reductions are scarce.

New York State Theater, tel 870 5770, box office 870 5630. Home to the New York City Opera and the New York City Ballet. The Met's plebian neighbor, the State Theater has cheaper seats, and a policy of employing American performers only. Productions are usually much more imaginative than the Met. The theater takes chances with unfamiliar ballet and opera works (like the 1990 run of Schoenberg's *Moses und Aaron*, which even the composer doubted could be staged), and stages musical comedies as well as old favorites like *La Bohème* and *Swan Lake*. 'Supertitles' are used for foreign-language operas.

Carnegie Hall, 154 West 57th St., at 7th Ave., tel 247 7800. One of the top three concert halls in the world, although its acoustics have never been quite as good as those at the Boston Symphony Hall and the Vienna Musikverein. Now celebrating its hundredth anniversary, in its time Carnegie Hall has been *the* venue for virtually every star of the classical, jazz and pop music worlds (Isaac Stern, Sir Thomas Beecham, Arnold Toscanini, Itzhak Perlman, Pinchas Zukerman, Leornard Bernstein, Jack Benny and even the Beatles).

After refurbishment in 1986, audiences complained of a treble steeliness, but after some tinkering with fiber screens and chemical coatings some of the harshness has been erased. There is no resident orchestra, but the Boston, Chicago and Philadelphia Symphonies, and the Vienna Philharmonic put in regular appearances, and the programme is always fit to burst. Beware the performances coded with colored blobs, which distinguish those occasions when the main auditorium or the smaller Weill Recital Hall are hired out by amateurs for so-called 'vanity recitals'. Cheap seats in the front half of the top balcony can be very good value—the only problem being the impossibly steep rake of the auditorium, which can bring on mild attacks of vertigo. Tours on Tuesdays and Thursdays (tel 247 7800 for information).

Merkin Concert Hall, Abraham Goodman House, 129 West 67th St., at Broadway and Amsterdam Ave., tel 362 8719. Small, and more intimate than the big halls—often used for professional debuts and chamber music. Progammes are meaty and inventive.

Town Hall, 123 West 43rd St., at 6th Ave. and Broadway, tel 840 2824. An enormously wide-ranging programme, including New Music, World Beat, New Jazz and Afro-pop as well as an intrepid Classical programme (in 1990, the Manhattan String Quartet and a Steve Reich premiere). Unfortunately the handsome 1500-seat auditorium, in a building designed by McKim, Mead & White, is much neglected, though some people swear its acoustics are as good as Carnegie Hall.

Brooklyn Academy of Music (BAM), 30 Lafayette St., Brooklyn, tel (718) 636 4100. Four auditoriums, including the 2085-seat Opera House, and space for the Brooklyn Symphony, new music and dance as well. Currently the BAM is a rather lone figure waving the banner for alternative and avant-garde composers (John Cage, Lou Harrison, Steve Reich and Philip Glass). Every autumn it mounts the blockbuster Next Wave Festival of American and foreign contemporary work. And in 1991, with the support of the Metropolitan Opera, it is launching a campaign to put on lesser-known productions as well as to commission new work.

Smaller Venues

Bargemusic, Fulton Ferry Landing, Brooklyn, tel (718) 624 4061. Jazz and string quartets inside a barge moored under the Brooklyn Bridge.

Cathedral of St John the Divine, 1047 Amsterdam Ave., at 112th St., tel 316 7540. All kinds of free lunchtime and evening concerts, often by distinguished touring groups from abroad. Concerts take place in St John's cavernous vault, two football fields long, a century old and still unfinished. A dramatic setting if ever there was one, though sound tends to wobble, as though the cathedral were a swimming pool.

The Damrosch Park Guggenheim Bandshell, southwest corner of Lincoln Center, tel 870 1630. Free outdoor concerts in the summer, including the excellent Serious Fun (contemporary and avant-garde) and Classical Jazz Festivals.

The Donnell Library, 20 West 53rd St., off 5th Ave., tel 621 0618. All kinds of concerts for free in a branch of the New York Public Library. There are also concerts in other libraries throughout the city (see listings in the *Voice*).

Frick Collection, 1 East 70th St., on 5th Ave., tel 288 0700. Splendid monthly afternoon concerts by top performers which are kept deadly secret and attended by the Upper East Side aristocracy. If you ring the number above you may be able to extract some dates. If you arrive at least half an hour before you have a pretty good chance of getting in, but you can't be sure. Tickets are free.

The Julliard School, Michael Paul Hall, Lincoln Center, tel 874 7515. Free or fantastically low admission to recitals, master-classes and full-blown operas put on by students and faculty members. Standards can be outstanding.

Manhattan School of Music, 601 West 122nd St., at Broadway, tel 749 2802. Free student concerts during the academic year.

Metropolitan Museum of Art, Grace Rainey Rogers Auditorium, 5th Ave. and 82nd St., tel 570 3949. Particularly good on string quartets, chamber music and early music. First-class performers like the Lindsay and Guarini Quartets are imported from abroad, so tickets can be pricey. In the evenings various performers are stationed all round the hall—on galleries in the main hall, in the Temple of Dendur and the Spanish Patio.

Museum of Modern Art, 11 West 53rd St., between 5th and 6th Aves, tel 708 9480. Late-summer concerts outdoors in the elegant sculpture garden. A generally high-brow selection of 20th-century composers.

92nd Street Y Kaufmann Concert Hall, 1395 Lexington Ave., at 92nd St., tel 427 4410. The Y has its own symphony orchestra and a varied and imaginative programme. Also recitals by visiting string quartets and top soloists (Dietrich Fischer-Dieskau and Elly Ameling), and poetry readings by contemporary writers.

Summer Parks Concerts, tel 362 6000. Starting in June, an extraordinary programme of free music events takes place in parks throughout the five boroughs. The most exceptional being the productions and concerts mounted by the Metropolitan Opera and the New York Philharmonic in Central Park. Thousands of people gather on the Great Lawn with beers and picnics as the sun sets. The booming loud-speaker systems warp the sound a bit, but that doesn't matter. Arrive as early as possible to get tickets, which are served on a first-come basis. The Metropolitan Opera stages two productions every summer; the Philharmonic's program is more varied.

Symphony Space, Broadway at 95th St., tel 864 5400. An immensely varied selection, from gospel to Gilbert and Sullivan.

Ticket Agencies

Bryant Park Music and Dance Half-Price Ticket Booth, 42nd St., at 6th Ave., tel 382 2323. Try to get to the booths by lunchtime on the day of the performance.

Centercharge, 874 6770. Tickets by telephone for Avery Fisher Hall and Alice Tully Hall in Lincoln Center.

New York Philharmonic Audience Services, Avery Fisher Hall, 132 West 65th St., at Broadway, tel 799 9595. Half-price tickets after 6, but phone ahead to ask about availability.

Rock, Disco, Punk

In New York, rock thrives. Venues range from massive 55,000-seat stadiums, to weird and wonderful punky East Village caverns with psychedelic interiors and bands with names like Total Annihilation String-Vest and My Papa is a Curry. The latter are generally easy enough to get into, and many won't even charge a cover fee. They are also great fun, though, sadly, as rents rise many are closing down. If you want to go to one of the big cheeses (Shea Stadium to see the Rolling Stones, say) you need to keep on your toes and act quickly: consult the listings in the *Village Voice* and then try one of the city's various ticket agencies or phone **Ticketmaster**, tel 307 7171, with your credit card number at the ready.

The Big Venues

Apollo Theater, 253 West 125th St., between Adam Clayton Powell Jr and Frederick Douglas Boulevards, tel 749 5838. This legendary Harlem theater saw the baptism by fire of performers as diverse as Ella Fitzgerald, James Brown, the Jackson Five, and Frankie Lyman and the

Teenagers. Revamped and restored in 1978, the Apollo closed again in the eighties; it was brought back to life by the Wednesday Amateur Nights organized by the octogenarian Ralph Bellamy, who managed them back in the thirties. The real show is the audience, which whoops and boos with infectious gusto. Tickets range between $5 and $30, and between $5 and $40 for the Supershow on the last Wednesday of the year, when previous winners are brought together in one performance.

Beacon Theater, 2124 Broadway, at West 75th St., 496 7070. Biggest venue on the Upper West Side for a range of mainstream and offbeat rock groups. The management is currently resisting attempts to turn it into a disco.

Madison Square Garden, 7th Ave., between West 31st and West 33rd Sts, tel 680 8300. Stadium hovering over Penn Station with room for 20,000. Various pop extravaganzas as well as boxing, basketball, wrestling.

Meadowlands, East Rutherford, New Jersey, tel (201) 935 8500. Another 20,000-seat arena, the Giants Stadium, for big-crowd pullers.

Palladium, 126 East 14th St., between 3rd and 4th Aves, tel 473 7171. Vast disco hall with a variety of gigs, from the Gypsy Kings to Neil Simon and Soul II Soul. As a club it is clapped out, but worth attending not just for the gigs but for the architecture as well. An old movie palace, it was converted in 1985 by the Japanese designer Arata Isozaki, and inside is an immense double staircase, a suspended glass-block disco floor filled with 2400 glass lights, and frescoes by Keith Haring, Kenny Scharf and Francesco Clemente.

Radio City Music Hall, 1260 6th Ave., at 50th St., tel 757 3100. The cream of all rock venues: an Art-Deco palace for a firmly established stratosphere of stars (in the past, Madonna, Billy Joel, and encampments of the Grateful Dead). From late November the Rockettes (Radio City's can-can girls) swing their legs into action for a two-month extravaganza of camp—the 'Magnificent Christmas Spectacular'. Admission to any event is a costly $20–45.

The Ritz, 254 West 54th St., near Broadway, tel 541 8900. Recently moved into the old Studio 54 premises from cramped headquarters downtown. The line-up is always quite potent: 2 Live Crew, the Pixies, G. B. H., Jane's Addiction and Dead Milkmen, Mojo Nixon and the Cave-dogs. Now 3000 fans can sit down on the balcony, while the area below remains a big dance floor.

Shea Stadium, 126th St., at Roosevelt Ave., Flushing, Queens, tel

(718) 507 8499. The biggest of all, with seating for 55,000, where the Beatles played in 1965, and the Stones in 1989.

Smaller Venues

A–7, 7th St., and Ave. A, tel 279 1980. Typical East Village shoestring-dive used as a launching pad for newly formed punky local bands.

The Black Cat, 21 Hudson St., tel; 465 3377. New rock showcase, featuring Kikapoo Joy Juice, Black Mariah, Spider Junkies and Dashboard Mary.

The Bottom Line, 15 West 4th St., near 5th Ave., tel 228 6300. Established West Village venue, not as wild and crazy as its East Village counterparts, with a mixed bag of up-and-coming bands. Bruce Springsteen, Stevie Wonder and Suzanne Vega all catapulted to fame after appearances in the Bottom Line cockpit.

Cat Club, 76 East 13th St., between 4th Ave. and Broadway, tel 505 0090. A grab-bag of heavy rock in a spacious venue, with a seventies weekend disco every Friday and Saturday, and a special swing dance-night on Sundays.

Chameleon Club, 505 East 6th St., and Ave. A, tel 777 9105. Brain-damaging neighborhood bands; mostly rock, but sometimes quieter folk as well. $3–5 cover.

Continental Divide, 25 3rd Ave., at St Mark's Place, tel 529 6924. Popular East Village Mexican café with a stuffed plesiosaur, and rock and blues every Wednesday night (featuring bands like the Blue Jays, Mumbo Gumbo and the inimitable Christy Rose). An excellent deal with no cover or minimum at the bar.

CBGB, 315 Bowery, at Bleecker St., tel 982 4052. In the 1970s, the birthplace of New York punk and the Talking Heads. At the end of a long, narrow corridor, new violent rock bands still thrash and squeal out of the gloom and grime. Among the bands you can see nowadays are the Sic F*cks, Lunachicks, Unsane, Educated Monkeys and Osgood Slaughter. CBGB actually stands for country, bluegrass and blues, though no one alive can remember hearing them here.

Downtown Beiruts I and II, 157 East Houston St., and 158 1st Ave., tel 260 4248. Two hard-core ear-flattening East Village bars, both respected venues for East Village thrash, metal and skate, heavy rock and punk (Monkey Head and Rickey Methylene Blue) softened by the odd comedy acts. Decorated with graffiti and authentically punky audiences.

Knitting Factory, 47 East Houston St., between Mott and Mulberry

Sts, tel 219 3055. Experimental jazz, rock, folk and poetry readings in a friendly neighborhood joint with a café adjoining the performance space and a restaurant (speakers eavesdrop on performances) downstairs.

Lismar Lounge, 41 1st Ave., at East 2nd St., tel 777 9477. Grotty East Village basement with punky bands like Frigger Millenium.

Pyramid, 101 Ave. A, between 6th and 7th Sts, tel 420 1590. Like CBGB's (see above) a ratty East Village mainstay for punk, drag and heavy rock, nowadays notorious enough to be touristy. The storefront exterior is decorated with weird excrescences; the interior comprises a psychedelic bar, a cellar for sitting down, and a miniscule dance floor. As well as gigs, the club has a drag night on Sundays, drag performances after midnight, and sometimes performance art.

Tramps, 45 West 21st St., tel 727 7788. Hugely varied program, from the Mekons, 'the sole remaining legacy of UK punk', to New Orleans Blues (Snooks Eaglin) and Irish folk (the Wolftones). Scrutinize listings for details.

Jazz and Blues

Since the forties, when they huddled round Harlem and the speakeasies of 52nd Street ('The Street'), most of the jazz clubs have drifted down to the Greenwich Village. They still have the authentical speakeasy look—small, dingy basement rooms, cramped bars, so-so food and doleful aficionados.

In general, there are two or three sets a night starting at 9 or 10 and finishing at 2 or 3 in the morning. All clubs except Arthur's (see below) will demand a cover charge of $15–20, unless a really big name is playing, and a minimum charge for food or drink (about the price of two vodkas). Often you can sit at the bar for a reduced cover, and weekdays and brunches on the weekends are normally less expensive. Cheapest of all is the free open-air jazz in Central and Riverside Parks, and there are remarkably good buskers in subways such as Times Square and Grand Central.

The best deal is the 10-day **Greenwich Village Jazz Festival** which takes place in early September, when you can buy a $15 pass that gets you into Village clubs for free or at massively reduced cover charges (tel 242 1785). Also, in June there is a **New York Women's Jazz Festival** with free entrance to many performances (tel 505 5660).

Which clubs you visit will depend, of course, on your predilections; and in New York you are spoilt for choice. Consult the club advertisements in the *Voice* and the reviews and listings in *Downbeat*, the city's jazz monthly and *Hot House* a monthly give-away which you can pick up in the clubs themselves. There are also well-balanced listings in the *New Yorker* and telephone listings on (718) 465 7500.

Arthur's Tavern, 57 Grove St., near 7th Ave. and Sheridan Square, tel 677 3820. Excellent value: a coal-black room and bar with a tiny raised platform, and entrance for the price of a drink. A young, tipsy and smoochy crowd and, on the whole, good jazz.

Birdland, 2745 Broadway, at 105th St., tel 749 2228. Reincarnation of the elegant forties and fifties jazz and dining club: Mark Morganelli and the All-Stars, Peggy Stern and Freddie Bryant.

Blue Note, 131 West 3rd St., between Macdougal St. and 6th Aves, tel 475 8592. It looks like a converted garage, but it still pulls all the big names—Dizzy Gillespie, Sarah Vaughan, Ray Charles and Oscar Peterson. For one of these, the cover charge can be astronomical ($35–45). The clientele includes all types, including fleets of bearded Japanese tourists.

Bradley's, 70 University Place, between 11th and 12th Sts, tel 228 6440. A suave, low-ceilinged piano bar with wood-paneling, Bradley's has been going for 20 years. Traditional high-quality jazz, mostly duos or trios, with a low cover charge. Good for brunch.

Condon's, 117 East 15th St., tel 254 0960. American trad jazz, big bands, and a good Sunday brunch from 1 to 5.

Dan Lynch, 221 2nd Ave., near 14th St., tel 677 0911. Ancient all blues night-club and neighborhood bar, still going strong, with late-night live jams.

Fat Tuesday's, 190 3rd Ave., between 17th and 18th Sts, tel 533 7902. The most easy-going and welcoming of the downtown clubs. A literal translation of 'Mardi Gras', Fat Tuesday's is home to the 'living legend', Les Paul, inventor of the electric guitar, who plays with his charming trio in the cramped little basement on Monday nights. The rest of the week sees a wide range of jazz artists.

Greene Street Café, 101 Greene St., tel 925 2415. Cavernous two-story club/restaurant in SoHo, with seating on two levels and a rather sleek-looking clientele. The food is uncharacteristically good. Piano on weekdays and trios on weekends.

The Knitting Factory, 47 East Houston St., between Mott and Mulberry Sts, tel 219 3055. Jazz crops up fairly frequently in this East Village outpost with a wildly eclectic range of programmes, usually experimental or *avant-garde*.

Manny's Car Wash, 1558 3rd Ave., tel 369 BLUE. New Upper East Side blues club.

Michael's Pub, 211 East 55th St., between 2nd and 3rd Aves, tel 758 2272. Flash Upper East Side club renowned for Woody Allen's clarinet extravaganzas on Monday nights.

Sweet Basil, 88 7th Ave., between Bleecker and Grove Sts, tel 242 1785. Traditional and mainstream jazz, in the requisite tin-ceilinged, wood-paneled room. Nailed into the tourist circuit.

Tramps, 45 West 21st St., between 5th and 6th Aves, tel 727 2288. Mostly blues but programs can be excitingly varied.

Village Gate, 160 Bleecker St., corner of Thompson and Bleecker Sts, tel 475 5120, Piano and bass duos in the terrace café, 'Salsa meets Jazz' every Monday in the large downstairs room; and comedy acts, theater and not-bad food upstairs.

Village Vanguard, 178 7th Ave. South, at Perry St., tel 255 4037. Vanguard of Manhattan jazz, 56 years old and still going strong in Max Gordon's pokey smoke-cellar in the West Village. The slightly ruffled and windswept people that come here form the old guard of serious jazz buffs. In the past Mingus, Davis and Monk have all done a stint at the Vanguard, and the basement has been used for literally hundreds of recordings. Nowadays Mel Lewis and his 17-piece jazz orchestra take over on Monday nights, and on other nights there is usually an exciting program of mainstream jazz—the great technical saxophonist, Pharoah Sanders, Kenny Barron, and the unique jazz basist, Buster Williams. Imports from Europe include such fascinating and rare combinations as the great French bassist Pierre Michelot and Christian Escoudet; alongside local Django, Hank Jones. The only Village club that doesn't serve food.

Zanzibar and Grill, 550 3rd Ave., between 36th and 37th Sts, tel 779 0606. Easy-going restaurant and jazz club, with the emphasis mostly on the high quality of the food (burgers, grilled tuna, Caesar salad).

Salsa

Originally from Cuba, salsa's mishmash of Latin and African rhythms and American jazz is an all-pervasive sound in New York: on the streets, in apartments and blaring over the radio. Every September, the city hosts the **Salsa Festival** marathon, with an impossibly large number of gigs in venues all over the city including the Village Gate, MKs, and Meadow-lands which gulps up big names like Celia Cruz, Hector La Voe, Willie Colon and Papo Lucca all in one go (call 201 935 3900 for more information). In the past two years, many Manhattan salsa clubs have closed because of cocaine raids, and have moved out to dangerous parts of Queens. A few salsa, samba and merengue bastions remain in Manhattan:

Club Broadway, 2551 Broadway, tel 864 7600. Spacious ballroom lined in blue velvet, in a solidly Hispanic part of the Upper West Side. Big bands.

Copacabana, 10 East 60th St., tel 755 6010. Latin nights on weekdays, entrance $5 before 9.30, and then $10 for women and $15 for men (see Nightclubs, below).

Corso, 205 East 86th St., tel 534 4964. New York's most famous Puerto Rican nightclub, with the best salsa dancing in Manhattan and wall-to-wall mirrors.

Palladium, 126 East 14th St., between 3rd and 4th Aves, tel 473 7171. Free salsa before 10 (see Rock, Disco, Punk, above).

Village Gate, 160 Bleecker St., at Thompson. An extremely popular 'salsa meets jazz' night every Monday from 9 to 3, with jazz and salsa musicians jamming together. Packed out, so come early.

Country, Folk and Ethnic

New York isn't exactly the folk and country center of the world, but they are well represented. Reggae and Afro-Caribbean sounds are also strong.

Eagle Tavern, 355 West 14th St., tel 924 0275. Irish pub with a back room. Here, on Saturdays and Mondays, you will find fiddles, penny whistles, harmonicas and accordions; on Fridays, bluegrass.

Lone Star Roadhouse, 240 West 52nd St., between Broadway and 8th Ave., tel 245 2950. Originally a genteel soda fountain; now a loud-mouthed Texas saloon full of cow skulls and horns. Mostly Country and Western music, but also all kinds, from Yellowman and Pure Prairie

League to James Brown, blues, western swing and R&B. Habitués are mixture of buttoned-up New Yorkers and loud ersatz Texans. Presented with the 1990 'Keeping the Blues Alive' award by the Blues Foundation.
McAnn's Country, 133 West 33rd St., tel 695 8429. New country music club plus country rock 'n' roll.
S.O.B. (Sounds of Brazil), 204 Varick St., at Houston St., tel 243 4940. Absurdly convivial supper club, with good Brazilian food (including *feojada*, the hearty Brazilian national dish of black beans and sausage), and a cheerfully drunken audience that likes to dance. Mostly Brazilian music, but also salsa, calypso, reggae, Trinidad-carnival, zydeco, and other Afro-Caribbean sounds.
Speakeasy, 107 Macdougal St., off Bleecker, tel 598 9670. Folk.
The Spiral, 244 East Houston St., at Ave. A, tel 353 1740. Rock and country—Cowboy Dick, the Smokestack Bros and the Rough Riders.
Wetlands, 161 Hudson St., near Vestry St., tel 966 4225. Popular new blues and country club, in the style of the Lone Star, with organic food. British blues band Noel Redding; Latin R&B from Los Angeles in the form of the Wildcards; funk-rockers Bootsy and his Rubber Band; reggae and Irish folk.

Theater and Performance Art

Establishment theater is in a sorry state: seats are hideously expensive, the theater area round Times Square has sunk into sleaze, and the productions that survive are 75 per cent dog-eared musicals and 20 per cent Lloyd Webber imports. Occasionally, however, something really good crops up, and it is worth skimming through the *New Yorker*, the On Stage column in the Friday Weekend section in the *New York Times*, or the *TheaterWeek*, a weekly magazine which lists every production in the city.

For the most part, you will have to pin your hopes on the more interesting and daring productions staged on the fringe. Here prices are cheaper and shows are less commercial. Standards vary tremendously, but if you do your homework you will certainly be able to dig out something exciting or shocking, if not outstanding. 'Off-Broadway' theater productions are professionally staged, and tend to lean towards contemporary political and social dramas, often by American authors. 'Off-off-Broadway' productions are generally the cheapest, most experimental and weird, and the best reviews for these can be found in the *Village Voice*.

The TKTS booth in Times Square sells half-price tickets for Broadway and off-Broadway productions on the day of the performance; between 3 and 8 for an evening performance, and between 10 and 2 for matinées, although queues for both start forming in the morning. 'Twofer' coupons, which you can pick up from shops, hotels and restaurants, and the Visitors and Conventions Bureau on Columbus Circle, entitle two people to large discounts and allow you to book ahead. Students with IDs can often get discounts or standby 'rush' tickets half an hour before the performance (phone the theater for details). At most of the agencies listed below you will be charged the full price, but you can pay over the telephone.

Ticket Agencies
Telecharge, tel 239 6200.
Keith Prowse, tel 398 1430.
Ticketmaster, tel 307 7171.
Ticket Gallery, tel 938 5545.
Miller Ticket Service, tel 757 5210.
TKTS, West 47th St., and Broadway, half-price tickets on the day of the performance (see above).

Experimental Theaters and Repertory Companies

Circle in the Square Downtown, 159 Bleecker St., between Thompson and Sullivan Sts, tel 254 6330. One of the oldest Off-Broadway theaters, with a consistently imaginative program.
Circle Repertory, 99 7th Avenue South, at Sheridan Square, tel 924 7100. New American writers, including Lanford Wilson, who was a member of the company for several years. *Burn This* and *As Is* moved from here to Broadway.
Jean Cocteau Repertory, 330 Bowery at Bond St., tel 677 0060. A clever mix of new work and obscure classics.
The Kitchen, 512 West 19th St., tel 255 5793. *The* place for performance art in Manhattan.
La MaMa ETC, 74a East 4th St., between Bowery and 2nd Ave., tel 475 7710. A bastion of off-off-Broadway experimental theater, founded in 1961 by Ellen Stewart and based in the East Village. Since then it has been the launching pad of writers like Lanford Wilson, Sam Shephard and Harvey Fierstein. For the most part productions are of a high standard, and they cover a whole range: avant-garde, experimental,

foreign playwrights and companies (*Crime and Punishment* improvised in Polish), and performance art.

Medicine Show Theater Ensemble, 353 Broadway at Worth St., tel 431 9545. Unusual establishment which specializes in twenties Broadway musicals.

P.S. 122, 150 1st Ave., at East 9th St., tel 477 2588. A whole range of exciting events taking in performance art, new music and improvisation, with work by John O'Keefe and a marathon festival in February.

Public Theater, 425 Lafayette St., tel 598 7150. Productions by Joseph Papp's New York Shakespeare Company, which can vary wildly in quality. Papp was the man who fought for the Central Park Shakespeare festival against all the odds (see below) and his work at the Public is nearly always controversial, spanning not just Shakespeare but Yiddish theater, Afro-American playwrights, and new or lesser-known plays such as the splendid recent production of Chikamatsu's *Gonza the Lancer*.

Ridiculous Theater Company, 1 Sheridan Square, tel 691 2271. Farce, parody, lampoons and revivals, including a recent production of *Turds in Hell* by the late Charles Ludlam, who founded the company in the sixties.

Shakespeare Festival in Central Park, Delacorte Theater, Central Park at West 79th St., tel 598 7100. Two productions per summer of Shakespeare in American, presented in Central Park's outdoor theater between June and September. Names like Meryl Streep, Kevin Kline and Michelle Pfeiffer draw big crowds and you should try and get into the queue (with a picnic) by the late morning. Tickets are free.

Sullivan Street Theater, 181 Sullivan St., between Houston and Bleecker Sts, tel 674 3838. New York's equivalent of London's *Mouse-Trap*, the fifties musical *The Fantasticks* has run here for over three decades.

Thirteenth Street Repertory Theater, 50 West 13th St., at 6th Ave., tel 675 6677. Two shows a night, with six productions in repertory, and a mix of classics and new work.

Writers Theater, 145 West 46th St., tel 869 9770. A pioneering platform for new writers, who are given the opportunity to work with established directors and develop their plays in front of an audience. There is an interesting audience discussion afterwards.

Comedy and Cabaret

In the seventies the cult TV show 'Saturday Night Live' spawned a clutch of new clubs, and gave New York comedy a much-needed boost. Now clubs range from dingy 'rooms' to full-blown theaters; standards plummet from outstanding to abysmal. Whether you see a bomb or a triumph depends mostly on luck and word of mouth. Check the listings in *New York Magazine* and the advertisements in the *Voice*.

Piano bars and cabarets are also a mixed bag; paradise for some, hell for others. In the downtown piano bars audiences are jollied into boisterous singalongs of Broadway jingles round the piano, and, worst of all, into silly dances during the choruses. Those who don't join in are ostracized, in a room so crowded with happy singers there is no escape.

Uptown cabarets and piano bars, on the other hand, are rather more elegant affairs, in plush drawing rooms where someone plays smoochy jazz on the piano or sings Cole Porter. The only required audience participation is to sip cocktails and talk in hushed voices.

The Ballroom, 253 West 28th St., between 7th and 8th Aves, tel 244 3005. Lavishly presented stage, cocktails, and Eartha Kitt-style performers.

Café Carlyle, Madison Ave., at East 76th St., tel 744 1600. Bobby Short, the aristocrat of New York cabaret, plays Gershwin and Cole Porter to assorted glitterati. The cover charge is $35 and you should dress swish.

Catch a Rising Star, 1487 1st Ave., between 77th and 78th Sts, tel 794 1906. Packed out but relatively comfortable: the club which launched a thousand comedians, including Robin Williams.

The Comic Strip, 1568 2nd Ave., between 81st and 82nd Sts, tel 861 0386. A bare room with a sharp audience and an open mike: anyone can get up and have a go, sometimes with disastrous consequences. About 15 comedians a night including, occasionally, Eddie Murphy, who got his first break here.

The Duplex, 61 Christopher St., at 7th Avenue South, tel 255 5438. West Village cabaret and piano bar (New York's oldest) with a kindly audience composed of gays and tourists. Established comedians and an open-mike spot for foolhardy amateurs.

Improvisation, 358 West 44th St., tel 765 8268. Over a quarter of a century old with a very funny amateur night on the first Sunday of each month.

Karaoke Night at MK, 204 5th Ave., between 24th and 25th Sts, tel 779 1340. Singalongs on Sunday nights to backing tracks of Ray Charles.

Mostly Magic, 55 Carmine St., tel 924 1472. Not so peculiar combination of comedy and magic. First-class restaurant.

National Improvisational Theater, 223 8th Ave., at West 21st St., tel 243 7224. An extremely funny ad-lib hour called *Assembly* in which the audience directs a troupe of brilliant improvisers. In another show, called *Interplay*, the audience can also take part.

Stand-Up New York, 236 West 78th St., tel 595 0850. Upper West Side comedy club with a stage and an amateur contest at midnight. Brave souls are jeered off stage by a vicious audience, and the ones who survive longest win money.

Zanzibar and Grill, 550 3rd Ave., between 36th and 37th Sts, tel 779 0606. Caribbean and Latin cabaret and supper club, with a wild and drunken audience.

Art Galleries

There are something like 90,000 artists and 500 art galleries in New York. Getting about the galleries can be a daunting and a chore unless you get hold of the *Art Now Gallery Guide*, a monthly guide to all the exhibitions which is available free in galleries and a few bookstores. You may also find it useful to read over the reviews in the *New York Times* and the magazines *Artscribe*, *Arts Magazine* and *Artnews*.

Even if you never usually go to art galleries, you may find yourself enthused in New York. In the galleries, there is an enormously wide range of work: you will stumble on a mixture of exciting lesser-known artists as well as fantastically big names—from Picasso, French Impressionists and Matisse to Julian Schnabel and Jasper Johns. And you can also have a good time, especially if you invite yourself to the various openings that are listed in the *Gallery Guide*.

Sadly, nearly all the maverick and youthful East Village and Lower East Side galleries which rocked the art world in 1981 have now closed down, or moved to SoHo. These East Village galleries were shoe-string affairs, started up in tiny storefronts and filled with furniture and lamps made by the artists themselves. Eventually they were forced out of the gradually gentrifying East Village by spiraling rents, or were lured into the more established SoHo art scene.

Today the city's art galleries divide into two camps: those on the Upper East Side and 57th Street, showing well-known and respectable artists (Julian Schnabel, Robert Rauschenberg and Louise Nevelson); and those in SoHo, showing more provocative and controversial works

(Cindy Sherman, Stephen Westfall and Eric Fischl). At opposite ends of the spectrum are the galleries on Madison Avenue in the Upper East Side (the stuffiest of all, they deal in Renoir, Magritte and Klee); and the so-called 'Alternative Spaces' established in the seventies: not-for-profit, co-operatively run institutions which show a mixture of installations, performance art, the unsaleably shocking, the way-out or the merely political.

Remember that the galleries each represent a 'stable' of artists whose work is often available for viewing in a back room. If you buy anything, you will find that most refuse credit cards, and if you pay by check they will wait for it to clear before allowing you to make off with your purchase. For the most part, galleries are open 10–5 Tuesday–Saturday, and nearly all close in July and August.

Upper East Side and 57th Street

ACA, 21 East 67th St., near 5th Ave. Specializes in 20th-century Americans: an enlightening place for seeing lesser-known work by Georgia O'Keefe, Reginald Marsh, the Ashcan School, the Stieglitz group and Judy Chicago.

André Emmerich, 41 East 57th St., between Madison and Park Aves. Contemporary American, especially the color-field school: Morris Louis, Lawrence Poons, Kenneth Noland, and also some Hockney prints and photographs.

Marion Goodman, 24 West 57th St., between 5th and 6th Aves. Emphasis on the European avant-garde, and promoting their reputations in New York.

Hireschl & Adler, 21 East 80th St., between 5th and Madison Aves. 18th- to early 20th-century painting, with an interesting annex for modern figurative artists round the corner at 851 Madison Avenue, between 70th and 71st Streets.

Sidney Janis, 110 West 57th St., between 6th and 7th Aves. Museum-like gallery with heavyweight shows of 20th-century and contemporary art: Mondrian, Gaicometti, Saul Steinberg and George Segal.

M. Knoedler & Co. Inc., 19 East 70th St., between 5th and Madison Aves. Specializes in American Abstract Expressionists, with impressive shows of Frank Stella, Alexander Calder and Adolph Gottlieb.

Robert Miller, 41 East 57th St., at Madison Ave. Grand, tall-ceilinged gallery showing American work, including the recent exhibition of Robert Mapplethorpe.

Prakapas Gallery, 19 East 71st St., near 5th Ave. Photographers from the early 20th century, and the twenties and thirties: Jacob Riis, Man Ray and Moholy-Nagy.

Holly Solomon, 724 5th Ave., between 56th and 57th Sts. A SoHo parvenu: seventies decorative European and American artists, and occasional performance pieces and installations, with some good photography shows.

SoHo

Mary Boone, 416 West Broadway, between Spring and Prince Sts. A prime mover in the past decade, Boone specializes in neo-expressionist contemporary art and introduced New York to the likes of Francesco Clemente, Julian Schnabel (who has left her for the Upper East Side), David Salle and George Baselitz.

Leo Castelli, 420 West Broadway, between Spring and Prince Sts. The Jupiter of the New York art world since the sixties, when he battled for the success of Andy Warhol and Roy Lichtenstein. Now the representative of blockbusters like Jasper Johns, Claes Oldenburg, Robert Rauschenberg and Cy Twombly. There is a graphics annex up the road at 578 Broadway.

O. K. Harris, 383 West Broadway, between Broome and Spring Sts. Solo shows of new work in a spectacular gallery space, with an impressive group show in June and July.

Phyllis Kind, 139 Spring St., near West Broadway. Figurative American art, and the Chicago School of 'Hairy Who' artists which Kind launched in the seventies.

Gracie Mansion, 532 Broadway, betweeen Spring and Prince Sts., 4th floor. The first of the East Village galleries, uprooted from home turf, but preserving its maverick style with artists like Louis Sciulla and Rodney Greenblat.

Max Protetch, 560 Broadway, at Spring St. Fascinating shows of contemporary architectural drawings and models (Louis Kahn, Aldo Rossi and Frank Lloyd Wright), as well as architecturally inspired sculpture and some ceramics and paintings.

John Weber, 142 Greene St., between Houston and Prince Sts. Conceptual and Minimal art, including Sol LeWitt.

Alternative Spaces and Not-for-profit Galleries
Alternative Museum, 17 White St., between 6th Ave and White St. Run by artists as a platform for unknowns.

338

Artists Space, 223 West Broadway, between Franklin and White Sts. Cockpit for new artists like Cindy Sherman, David Salle and Jonathan Borofsky. Stimulation exhibitions with space for video art and installations.

Dia Art Foundation, 77 Wooster St., between Spring and Broome Sts. Sponsorship for ambitious environmental projects and long-term installations, like Walter De Maria's *The New York Earth Room* at 141 Wooster, and the same artist's *The Broken Kilometer*, at 393 West Broadway.

The Drawing Center, 35 Wooster St., between Broome and Greene Sts. Anything on paper—by established and unknown artists. Open till 8 on Wednesdays.

P.S.1, 46–01 21st St., Long Island City. Enterprising exhibitions of contemporary work and the chance to see resident artists at work in a rambling Victorian public school in Queens. The institute also organizes the enterprising **Clocktower Gallery** in Manhattan (108 Leonard Street and Broadway).

Dance

For people in the know, New York is the dance capital of the world. Jerome Robbins, Twyla Tharp, Gerald Arpino, Martha Graham, Arthur Mitchell, Susan Jaffe, Paul Taylor and Merce Cunningham are all permanent residents. Dance Valhalla is to be found in Lincoln Center, the base for New York's two main companies – the unrivalled New York City Ballet (NYCB) and the American Ballet Theater (ABT). Moreover, in recent years the Brooklyn Academy of Music (BAM) has become the acknowledged center of modern dance.

During the seasons (September to January and April to June), you can see almost any kind of dance in New York: classical, ballet-based modern dance, experimental performance dance, swing, tap, be-bop, hop. For the best listings consult *The New Yorker* or *New York Magazine*.

The Established Companies
New York City Ballet (NYCB), New York State Theater, Lincoln Center, tel 870 5570 (see also Classical Music, above). The company is still smarting after the recent death of its founder and mentor, George Balanchine, though the quality of the dancing remains first-class. Usually there are tickets left over on the day of the performance, and

some returns. Two seasons, from November to February (*Nutcracker* in December), and April to June.

American Ballet Theater (ABT), Metropolitan Opera House, Lincoln Center, tel 362 6000 (see also Classical Music, above). Baryshnikov has resigned, spectacularly, but the *corps de ballet* is still exceptional. Repertoire ranges from 19th-century classical to modern, and tickets from $18–$80.

Brooklyn Academy of Music (BAM), 30 Lafayette Ave., Brooklyn, tel (718) 636 4100. One of the most important platforms for contemporary dance in the city. Three theaters, including the handsome 19th-century Opera House, used for dance premieres and encompassing both the mainstream and the completely way-out. The exciting Next Wave Festival in the autumn celebrates the international and American avant-garde.

Other Venues

Aaron Davies Hall, City College, West 135th St., at Convent Ave., tel 690 4100. A big venue for the classical Dance Theater of Harlem which always has a stimulating mix of works in repertory (tel 690 2800 for venues).

City Center, 131 West 55th St., between 6th and 7th Aves, tel 581 7907. Based under a Moorish dome, the City Center is a paradise for classical and modern dance. An impressive line-up of companies comes and goes from September until June: the Joffrey Ballet, (presenting a classical but inventive programme under Gerald Arpino); the Alvin Ailey American Dance Theater (modern, jazz and blues); the Dance Theater of Harlem; and the companies of Merce Cunningham, Paul Taylor and Trisha Brown.

Dance Theater Workshop (DTW), Bessie Schomberg Theater, 219 West 19th St., between 7th and 8th Aves, tel 924 0077. Pokey theater, for one of the country's most respected champions of unknown avant-garde companies.

Joyce Theater, 175 8th Ave., at 19th St., tel 242 0800. Contemporary and classical dance in a converted movie palace, with eight or nine top-class touring companies passing through the theater per season. A spectacular range of dance—avant-garde, jazz and Flamenco—and the classical Eliot Feld company in permanent residence.

The Kitchen, 512 West 19th St., between 10th and 11th Aves, tel 255 5793. Sometimes bizarre and sometimes innovative: avant-garde dance as well as video and performance art.

P.S. 122, 122 150 1st Ave., at 9th St., tel 477 5288. Post-modern dance, often combined with performance art, in a converted school gymnasium. **St Mark's-in-the-Bowery**, 2nd Ave., and East 10th St., tel 674 8112. Experimental dance and poetry readings in Manhattan's second oldest church.

Nightclubs

All the horrors of getting into nightclubs can be overcome in an instant, if you decide to be brave. Wearing anything in the least bit eccentric or risqué (a hat made out of banana skins or an unattractive-looking pair of flares will suffice), is guaranteed to get you past the bouncer. The only other option is to try tagging along with a group of friends who cut a dash and seem interesting. In general it is much easier to get into a club if you arrive early, if you are a woman, or if you look like one. Sometimes, if you arrive early (at about 10.30), you will get in free.

Once inside, you will be inundated with cards inviting you to other clubs at discount prices. With a wad of these, you can then start working your way round the circuit, and, if the bouncers take to you, sooner or later they will start waving you in for free. It is a good idea not to drink at the clubs as prices are ludicrously high—a glass of tap water can cost as much as $2. A lot of clubgoers rely on hipflasks and bottles of beer concealed in their clothing, though the clubs are seething with beady-eyed security guards who chuck out such offenders. Don't arrive in a voluminous coat or you will have to pay ridiculous prices to have it stored in the cloakroom.

Having a good time in a nightclub depends almost entirely on the club-going fraternity. If everyone is excited because the club is new and different, their energy and enthusiasm will be infectious; and if the club is clapped out and empty, you certainly won't enjoy yourself. Clubs in New York, like most elsewhere, have the delicate lifespans of dragonflies. Before you venture out, ask New Yorkers which are what they call 'happening', and do a little research in magazines and papers like *Paper Magazine* and *Details*.

The clubs nearly all play House, which can get tedious. The fashionable night to go out is Thursday (New Yorkers like to prove that they can dance all night, and still get themselves to work the next morning).

341

Big Haus, 179 West Broadway, between Leonard and Worth Sts, tel 941 8655. Small chic club in TriBeCa, kitted out in fake Bauhaus furnishings and very popular, though the dancing is rubbishy.

Carmelita's Lite Lounge, 150 East 14th St., near Broadway, tel 673 9015, (open Mon, Thur, Sat). The kitschest club in New York, in a venue that doubles as a reception-hall for Puerto Rican weddings on Fridays, Sundays and Wednesdays. A constellation of fairy lights, a terrible sound system, and Columbia students.

Cave Canem, 24 1st Ave., at East 2nd St., tel 529 9665. Miniature disco and bar, in a 19th-century Turkish baths with tiled walls and a number of ottomans. Attracts a boisterous clientele, who launch themselves into the marble-walled jacuzzi, displacing water all over the disco floor. Drinks are expensive.

Copacabana, 10 East 60th St., near 5th Ave., tel 755 6010. Once the kingpin of New York clubs, thanks to regular bookings of performers like Frank Sinatra and the Supremes, and strong ties with the criminal underworld and Frank Costello, the mafia boss. It closed down in 1973 after the owner's death, only to re-open again as a discothèque three years later. Now it is a big venue for Latin dancing and, on the last Thursday of each month, the scene of an orgy of camp hosted by the nightclub impresario Susanne Bartsch. Drag queens dance on podiums, while club-goers dress to the nines in a let-everything-hang-out sort of way and jive to seventies disco beats. Cheaper to get in if you're a woman.

Delia's, 197 East 3rd St., between Ave. A and B, tel 254 9184. A rather snooty supper and dance club arranged like an elegant drawing room; with American and Mediterranean cooking, well-behaved dancing, and roast beef and Yorkshire pudding prepared by the Irish manageress on Sundays.

Dezerland, 270 11th Ave., at 27th St., tel 564 4590. Hot Rod disco and club inside a batty breed of drive-in movie house, where patrons arrive on foot, sit in one of 30 convertibles, and watch a screening of *Little Shop of Horrors*.

The Island Club, 285 West Broadway, at Canal St., tel 226 7691. Hardcore reggae and Latin beats in a dance-hall decorated with fake trees.

Kilimanjaro, 513 West 19th St., at 10th Ave., tel 627 2333. Laid-back club playing mostly African beats: funky reggae, House, African and Calypso, blues, rocker and world-beat jams, and Hugh Masekela.

Larry Tee's Love Machine, The Underground, 860 Broadway, at East

17th St., tel 243 4677. Housed in Andy Warhol's old Factory, and now all the rage. Lots of drag queens and the cream of way-out club-goers
Lift Up Your Skirt and Fly, 74 Leonard St., between Broadway and Church St., tel 941 9499. Raunchy members-only club with one-night membership for visitors, though getting in can be tricky. There is an expensive French provençal restaurant where waiters and waitresses are decked out in Calvin Klein knickers, and a red velvet swing hurls a similarly attired lady from one end of the room to the other.
Limelight, 47 West 30th St., at 6th Ave., tel 807 7850. Once famous, now poxy little disco, opened, to the horror of New York's Episcopal community, in the former Church of the Holy Communion in 1984. On Tuesdays live bands and acoustic music, and free entrance on weekends.
Lotto, West 13th St., between Greenwich and 10th Aves, no telephone. The most bizarrely decorated club in the city, with truly nauseous color schemes and working automatons. In the meat-packing district near MARS (below).
MARS, 10th Ave., at West Side Highway and West 13th St., tel 691 6262. Named after the chocolate bar, six labyrinthian floors of frenetic cave-black disco in a former meat-packing plant and S&M basement. Inside it is sweaty and you can make out, through the gloom, a hint of sixties neon colors and leopard skin. There is bingo on the 5th floor on weekends and a gay night on Sunday. On the top is a postage-stamp of a rooftop garden, and a nice view over the West Village and Chelsea. In fashionable circles it's had its day, but frantic crowds and the sheer size of the place keep it amusing.
The Michael Todd Room, 126 East 14th St., between 3rd and 4th Aves, 473 7171. Preppy new club filled with glamorous Uptowners. The sound system is much admired.
MK, 204 5th Ave., between 24th and 25th Sts, tel 779 1340. The most with-it club of 1989, now past its best but still a lark, with two genuinely superior restaurants and a decent disco floor. A sitting room-cum-study is kitted out with books and occult paraphernalia, including two stuffed dobermans and hundreds of scorpions. Sunday night is *karaoke* night: a Japanese singalong hosted by clubland hostess Anita Sarko.
Nell's, 246 West 14th St., betwen 7th and 8th Aves, tel 675 1567. Sitting-room decorated pretentiously with chandeliers, velvet sofas and wood-paneling, in a former Edwardian gentlemen's club. Nell's started the trend for elegant supper clubs and salons in 1986 and is now out of date but less frantic than the new clubs, and a nice place to listen to jazz on Sundays.

343

Payday, locations vary. Floating nightclub that goes by various names (Milky Way, $100,000 Bar and Ritubirla) to avoid crippling license laws. On a Friday night it descends on various community spaces, decks them out in Bacofoil and plays hip-hop. In the clubs, word gets out as to the next venue on the Thursday. The **Love Transporter Room** is an even more enigmatic floating nightclub playing House, with locations fitfully listed in the press.

The Powerhouse, 25th St., at Broadway. Housed in an enormous powerplant, which is revamped in outré decor every week so it looks like a different club. Currently one of the most exciting in New York.

Roxy, 515 West 18th St., at 10th Ave., tel 645 5156. Feverish disco-dancing until you drop or, as several have in the past, pass out.

Red Zone, 440 West 54th St., at 10th Ave., tel 582 2222. Nightmarishly crowded: incautious dancers and clubland leafleteers scattering free invitations like seeds. The VIP room (you can go in), is like an airport lounge, but it does have an air-conditioned balcony overlooking the main disco floor.

Roseland, 239 West 52nd St., near Broadway, tel 247 0200. Wonderful chintzy fifties relic. Sambas, waltzes and fox-trots, for $9^1/_2$ hours from 2 pm on Thursdays, Saturdays and Sundays, in a football-pitch sized ballroom; and a disco with a sophisticated lighting system after midnight on Fridays and Saturdays. A Wall of Fame is inscribed with the names of 600 couples who met and married at the Roseland, and display cases contain the shoes of famous dancers.

SOS Save the Robots, corner 2nd St. and Ave. B, open Thur–Sat 1–6. Apocalyptic after-hours club for those who can't face going home. Pallid faces, staring eyes, and a disco-floor covered in sand.

Sound Factory, 535 West 27th St., between 10th and 11th Aves, tel 643 0728. Even if it goes out of fashion, go to the Sound Factory. Everything is kept very simple: there is an excellent (computerized) lighting and sound system, a free juice bar loaded with fruit, and the dancing, which is the most important thing, is very impressive.

The World, 254 East 2nd St., between Aves. B and C, tel 477 8677. Large old theater in a fantastic state of dilapidation with a vast cathedral-like dance floor, and enormous tinkling glass chandeliers. Visit for the vertiginous view of the gyrating dance-floor from the upper balcony. On Tuesdays there is the Rock 'n' Roll Fag Bar, and on Thursdays a Celebrity Club is hosted by the famously bizarre drag queens Rupaul and Larry Tee.

Zone D.K., 540 West 21st St., near 10th Ave., tel 463 8599. Dark tunnels and cubicles, the sound of flesh slapping flesh; and Vanna's Wheel of Fortune, on which men in leather jockstraps are tied up and twirled around.

Shopping

You can buy practically anything in New York, including adhesive bras. Even if you have no money, you will spend a good deal of time wandering in a mesmerized state from shop to shop. The range and quantity of goods on offer is mind-boggling. In supermarkets and drugstores, for example, there are so many different types and kinds of soap that choosing becomes impossible. To make things even more difficult, most shops are open most of the time.

Worst of all, shopping in New York is amusing. All over the city, shops have a sense of theater: their displays are mounted with sophistication and panache, while hi-tech window dressing has become an art form. Even the grottiest corner shop has an exuberantly painted sign, an eccentric window show, or a riot gate painted with a mural.

In general, you find most of the big-time department stores and clothes shops in **midtown** Manhattan, though the area also includes the shabbier, more entertaining retail mayhem of the Garment District on 7th Avenue and mid-thirties. At the weekends midtown and the Financial District are dead, and shoppers decamp for the East and West Villages. The **Upper West Side**, particularly Columbus Avenue, has natty clothes shops, gourmet delicatessens and shops specializing in idiotic trivia; and Broadway in the nineties is good for second-hand books. The **Upper East Side** has the most expensive clothes, as well as astronomically priced antiques. Downtown, the **East Village** is the place for punk designer fashions, junk shops, record shops and the offbeat. Here the shops stay open late into the night. In this part of town as well there are two havens for the New York nosher and the flea-market scavenger: the **Lower East Side**, which properly comes alive on the Jewish sabbath, and **Chinatown**, which bubbles with activity all week long. The **West Village** has gourmet food, vintage clothes, antiques, books, pets and shops specifically for gays, including gay insurance brokers and opticians.

One thing you will have to get used to is the $8^{1}/_{4}$ per cent **sales tax** which is usually not shown on the price displayed on shelves, but whacked on to everything as you pay for your purchases at the till. It comes as a shock to British visitors who are used to having their sales taxes (which are actually double) already disguised in the shelf price.

Sizes

Cuts tend to be more generous in America, so if you are a size 12 in England, you will probably find you have shrunk to a size 10 (US: size 8) in New York.

Women's clothes

UK	8	10	12	14	16	18
US	6	8	10	12	14	16
Eu	38	40	42	44	46	48

Men's shoes

UK	6	7	8	9	10	11	12
US	8	9	10	11	12	13	14
Eu	39	40	41	42	43	44	45

Women's shoes

UK	4	5	6	7	8
US	5	6	7	8	9
Eu	37	38	39	40	41

Remember that tights are called pantyhose, waistcoats are called vests, vests are called undershirts, dressing gowns are called robes and of course trousers are pants, but panties are knickers.

Weights and Measures

The US uses imperial weights and measures—inches, yards, miles, ounces and pounds (body weight is measured in pounds and not stones). American gallons/quarts/pints are five-sixths the size of Imperial gallons/quarts/pints. In cookery, a 'cup' of liquid is $1/2$ a US pint, and an English pint is $2^1/2$ US cups.

Alcohol

Liquor stores are closed on Sundays and forbidden to sell cigarettes by law. The cheapest places to get beer are supermarkets and bodegas.

Astor Wines & Spirits. Practically a department store of wines and spirits, often at discount prices.

Schapiro's, 126 Rivington St. Powerfully sweet kosher wines, made in a winery underneath the shop the size of a city block.

Sherry-Lehmann Inc., 679 Madison Ave., at 61st St. Smartest wine merchant in the city.

Antiques

Madison Avenue between the 70s and 90s has a mass of antiques shops, many specializing in English antiques, and full of objects verging on the priceless. Prices are more realistic down in the West Village, in the stretch of Bleecker and Hudson Streets north of Christopher Street, but they are still high. Some of the best bargains are to be had from the row of furniture warehouses on 4th Avenue between 10th Street and Union Square. They have auctions once a week or once a month. There are still excellent bargains to be had in the junk shops scattered around the East Village and the Lower East Side, and also from the city's flea markets and sidewalks.

10th Street Junk Shop, 10th St., between 2nd Ave. and Stuyvesant St., opposite St Mark's Church. Pretty junky junk, but good prices.

20th Century Design, 151 Ave. A, between 10th and 11th Sts. Specializes in 1970s plastic furniture and other horrors.

American Hurrah Antiques, 766 Madison Ave., at 66th St. Americana.

Backpages, 125 Greene St., between Prince and Houston Sts. Wurlitzer juke boxes, Coca-Cola vending machines, and advertising memorabilia.

Essex Street Antiques Market, Essex Street., between Rivington and Stanton Sts. Quite a trove, filled with a wide range of antiques, from sedans, wickerwork chairs and sofas, and 19th-century tables and chairs, to pre-war fans and bicycles. Good prices.

Ilene Chazanof, tel 254 5564 or 737 9668. Open by appointment only. A loft stuffed with all kinds of oddities, especially jewelry.

Leo Kaplan Ltd., 967 Madison Ave., between 75th and 76th Sts. Specializes in exceptional 18th-century English pottery and porcelain.

Lost City Arts, 275 Lafayette St., between Houston and Prince Sts, with a warehouse at 257 West 10th St., and a gallery at 339 Bleecker St. Extraordinary architectural antiques: all kinds of fascinating urban ephemera in a cavernous warehouse—urinals, juke boxes, mail boxes, barber's chairs, shop signs, etc. They don't come cheap.

Primavera, 808 Madison Ave., at 68th St. Astronomically priced Art Deco.

Rita Ford Music Boxes, 19 East 65th St., between Madison and 5th Aves. Music boxes of every possible shape and size.

Beauty Shops and Pharmacists

Body Shop, 759 Broadway, between 9th and 10th Sts. A branch of the worthy English chain.

Caswell-Massey, 518 Lexington Ave., at 48th St. Manhattan's oldest apothecary, dating from 1752, and selling stuff like snuff, pomander balls, whalebone nailfiles, rice powders and Washington's shaving cream.

Kaufman Pharmacy, 557 Lexington Ave., at East 50th St. Manhattan's only 24-hour pharmacy.

Kiehl's, 109 3rd Ave., near East 13th St. Established in 1853, and still making an absolutely superb range of homemade natural preparations and beauty treatments: henna, musk oil, botanical drugs, herbal laxatives and rejuvenating rose water.

Books

New York has a plethora of bookshops, ranging from the encyclopaedic to the abstruse. Browsing in them is addictive, and a bookshop tour can eat up a whole day in the city.

Peddling any sort of literature is legal, as it ought to be. You can pick up some of the best bargains off sidewalks in the areas around the Cooper Union and Astor Place, and Columbia University up on Broadway in the 90s.

Academy Book Store, 10 West 18th St., off 5th Ave. A superb selection of second-hand academic and art books, and also of second-hand classical and jazz CDs and records.

A Photographer's Place, 133 Mercer St., near Prince St. Photographic books and prints.

Barnes & Noble, 126 5th Ave., at 18th St. New books, all reduced. Opposite the main store is the huge Barnes & Noble Annex where you shop with supermarket trolleys for massively reduced remaindered books.

The Biography Bookshop, 400 Bleecker St., at 11th St. The only specialist bookshop of its kind in the city.

Books & Co., 939 Madison Ave., at East 75th St. A choice, rather highbrow selection of new fiction and non-fiction, and staff who go out of their way to help.

The Complete Traveler Bookstore, 199 Madison Ave., at East 35th St. Travel books and maps dealing with the whole globe.

Cooper Hewitt Museum Shop, 2 East 91st St., at 5th Ave. A brilliant stock of decorative arts books—as well as toys.

Drama Bookstore, 723 7th Ave., at West 48th St. Scripts and biographies.

Djuna Books, 154 West 10th St. Radical feminist literature.

Forbidden Planet, 821 Broadway, corner West 12th St. Two floors of books, magazines and comics devoted to science fiction, and a weird clientele in duffle coats and anoraks.

Gotham Book Mart, 41 West 47th St., near 6th Ave. Nearly half a million books, in a miniscule space signaled by a small sign announcing the shop's motto WISE MEN FISH HERE. Started in the 1920s by the late Frances Steloff, the Gotham rescued writers like Arthur Miller and D. H. Lawrence from banishment by the literary establishment. It has a particularly good poetry department, and a whole shelf devoted to books, some signed, by the writer and illustrator, Edward Gorey.

New York Bound, Associated Press Building, lobby 50, Rockefeller Plaza. A fascinating, comprehensive range of books about New York, from the extremely rare and out-of-print to recently published guidebooks.

Oscar Wilde Bookshop, 15 Christopher St., near 6th Ave. The world's first gay bookshop.

Pageant Bookstore, East 9th St., between 3rd Ave. and Stuyvesant St. Used books again, but a small shop in the East Village, and a more intimate atmosphere than the Strand.

Revolution Books, 13 East 16th St., between Union Square and 5th Ave. New York's biggest Marxist bookshop.

Rizzoli's, 31 West 57th St., between 5th and 6th Aves. *Haute couture* books (especially on art, architecture and fiction); chichi and rather intimidating. Their stock of calendars is always superb.

Sohozat, 307 West Broadway, between Canal and Grand Sts. Fan magazines, comics and second-hand clothing.

St Mark's Bookshop, 13 St Mark's Place, off 3rd Avenue. 'Alternative' books on every possible minority subject. On the sidewalk outside, between 2nd and 3rd Avenues, vendors flog coffee-table books and Rizzoli art books at massively reduced prices.

St Mark's Comics, 11 St Mark's Place. Marvels and D.C.S. Also posters and magazines.

Union Square Book Stall, west side of Union Square, between 15th and 16th Sts. A small stand of second-hand books on Union Square next to the postcard man. Fairly mainstream, but good value.

Strand Book Store, 828 Broadway, at East 12th St. A vast 8-mile long emporium, some say the largest in the US, of over 2 million second-hand books, all smelling of damp libraries and spectral readers. The store specializes in reviewers' copies and unproofed trade paperbacks, and though the sheer quantity of books can be a little overwhelming, the staff are nice and helpful.

Urban Center Books, Villard Houses, 457 Madison Ave., between 50th and 51st Sts. The Municipal Arts Society's excellent selection of books dealing with urban design and architecture.

351

Weiser's, 132 East 24th St., near Lexington Ave. Specializes in occult and metaphysical books; the largest bookstore of its kind in the country.

Botánicas

Otto Chicas Rendon, 56 and 60 East 116th St., and 177 East 115th St. There are *botánicas*, or religious shops, in most of the Hispanic parts of Manhattan, but Rendon's is the acknowledged supremo. Three branches of Rendon's are based up in Spanish Harlem, each selling enormous quantities of peculiar charms, incenses, aerosols, evil eyes, statuettes and all kinds of paraphernalia, some dedicated to *Santería*, an African/Christian faith.

Cameras, Electronics and Hi-Fi

You can get computers and hi-fi more cheaply in New York than in Europe, as long as you know exactly what you want. Ask for advice in one of the smart electronics shops, pick up the *New York Times*' Science supplement on Thursday, to get an idea of standard prices, and only then head off to one of the cheap places listed below.

47th St Photo, 67 West 47th St., near 6th Ave. Chaos reigns, but bargains are incredible.

Uncle Steve's, 343 Canal St., near West Broadway. Even cheaper than 47th St. Photo, and even more chaotic.

Willoughby's, 110 West 32nd St., between 6th and 7th Aves. Purportedly the world's largest camera and video store.

Wolff Computer, 23 West 18th St., off 5th Ave. Not the cheapest, but it has an excellent range, and assistants ready to give advice at the drop of a hat.

Clothes

With a few exceptions, New York's middle-of-the-road clothes shops, are hopelessly boring, and to find anything really exciting you will have to go to the top-notch designer shops, or second-hand shops (called 'vintage shops' in America, although hardly anything is pre-1950s). For designer clothes, New York divides into four distinct demesnes: SoHo; Madison Avenue and the Upper East Side; 5th Avenue and 57th Street; and the East Village. **SoHo** is full to the brim with preening shoppers dressed in the slickest cuts you will see in New York, and fantastically expensive but fascinating shops where fashions range from the impossibly elegant to the youthful and zany. **Madison Avenue**, from 59th Street up to 96th, is a rich, undiluted squash of tip-top designers including Armani, Lauren, St Laurent, Sonia Rykiel, Versace and Kenzo, much visited by anorexic smart-set shoppers. **Fifth Avenue**, a sad shadow of its former glory, with magnificently overdressed shoppers, has Persian carpet discount stores, and a clutch of stalwart department stores and designer shops (many on the East 57th Street annex to 5th Avenue), like Mario Valentino, Chanel, Matsuda, Jaeger and Bergdorf Goodman. The **East Village** is a mecca for the youthful spike, underwear and leather-Heavy Metal look, with tiny, fantastically good value stores run by new young designers and fashion school graduates. As gentrification encroaches, however, East Village prices are rocketing.

Designer Clothes

Banana Republic, 205 Bleecker St., near 6th Ave. Conventional, well-made clothes, supposedly for travelers but also serving for day-to-day wear.

Bomba de Clercq, 98 Thompson St. Elegant cashmere jerseys and knitwear.

Barney's, 106 7th Ave., between 16th and 17th Sts (see Department Stores, below). Six floors of exciting clothing, taking in the lesser-known designers as well as big names like Issey Miyake, Gaultier, Fendi, Calvin Klein, John Galliano, Ally Capellino, Giovanni Versace, Kenzo, Matsuda and Montana.

Bergdorf Goodman, 754 5th Ave., at 57th St. (See Department Stores, below). For Fendi, Donna Karan, Gaultier, Angela Cummings, Azzedine Alaia and Barry Kieselstein-Cord, to name just a few. Across the street is the new Bergdorf Goodman Men, which opened at the end of 1990.

Betsey Johnson, 130 Thompson St., between Houston and Prince Sts. A hipster's selection of the weird, funny and skin-tight, alongside some more conventional designs.

Bloomingdale's (see Department Stores, below), 1000 3rd Ave., at 59th St. Special rooms are set aside for Ralph Lauren, Missoni, Sonia Rykiel and Yves St Laurent. On the fourth floor is the work of more unusual designers, including the tapestry trousers of Romeo Gigli.

Brooks Bros, 346 Madison Ave., at East 44th St. Shrine of the preppy, striped stockbroker's shirt, now owned by Marks & Spencer—of all people.

Capezio, 177 Macdougal St., off West 8th St. Originally for dancewear, it now has a range of punky downtown designers, as well as people like Willi Smith and Betsey Johnson.

Chanel, 5 East 57th St. Make-up, handbags, and the trademark brass buttons and suits.

Charivari, 2307 Broadway, between 83rd and 84th Sts. Stylish, sometimes staid, sometimes bizarre, and always frighteningly expensive selection of clothes by various American and especially Japanese and European designers. The men's branch is on 85th Street and the newest branch, Charivari 5, with four floors and video screens, is on 57th Street and 5th Avenue.

The Cockpit, 595 Broadway, between Prince and Houston Sts. Mass-produced flying jackets and designer army wear.

Commes des Garçons, 116 Wooster St., between Spring and Prince Sts. Sculpturally constructed, minimalist Japanese-designed clothes in a sleek shop, by the Japanese architect Rei Kawakubo. Nearby, on 103 Grand Street, similar fare is served up by **Yohji Yamamoto**.

Dog on the Earth, 169 Ludlow St., near Stanton St. 'Vibrationally advanced' clothing with a Star Trek-look.

The Dress, 153 Ludlow St., near Stanton St. Sixties groovy pop-kitsch, designed by Amy Downs and Mary Adams; garish hats, and organza and velvet party clothes.

Emanuel Ungaro, 803 Madison Ave., between 67th and 68th Sts. Elegant, rather youthful cuts and extraordinary fabrics.

Emporio Armani, 110 5th Ave., at 16th St. Compared to the main store on Madison Avenue, the Emporio stocks younger styles—staggeringly expensive nonetheless.

Enz, 5 St Mark's Place, near 3rd Ave. Punky spikes-and-stud-wear.

Giorgio Armani, 815 Madison Ave., at 66th St. Catastrophically expensive, exquisite clothes. Cuts are immediately identifiable, and very beautiful.

Giovanni Versace, 816 Madison Ave., at 66th St. Lavish separates by the Italian designer.

Gucci, 683 5th Ave., at 54th St. Stirrups and red-and-green stripes, in a great profusion. Special customers have access to a private room at the back.

Joseph Tricot, 804 Madison Ave., near 65th St. Youthful knitwear.

Kenzo, 824 Madison Ave., near 68th St. Bright colors and elegant cuts.

Koos van den Akker, 795 Madison Ave., between 67th and 68th Sts. Zany, customized fur coats from the Netherlands designer.

Macy's, Herald Square (see Department Stores, below), 34th St. and 6th Ave. Giorgio Armani, Anna Klein, Claude Montana, Calvin Klein, etc. Macy's has recently opened the New Signatures shop, a platform for young designers including Gemma Khang and Michael Leva.

Matsuda, 854 Madison Ave., at East 70th St., and also 465 Park Ave. and 57th St. Accessible chic from Tokyo, veering on the conservative.

Missoni, 836 Madison Ave., at 69th St. Italian-designed jaquard jerseys, socks and coats.

Mud Honey, 124 East 4th St., between 1st and 2nd Aves. For the shocking, emaciated East Village look: lots of velvet, black fabrics, studs, plastic and other see-through materials.

Norma Kamali O.M.O., 113 Spring St., between Mercer and Greene Sts. Extremely elegant and beautifully cut classical linens and plaids. Also pretty underwear.

Ozey Torpe, 160 Ludlow St., near Stanton St. Well-cut, flowing silks by Ozey Torpe.

Parachute, 121 Wooster St., between Spring and Prince Sts. Unisex, monochrome Japanese designer clothing; scary empty spaces, lots of steel, scowling assistants and dizzying prices.

Patricia Field, 10 East 8th St., near 5th Ave. Downtown designer punk.

Polo/Ralph Lauren, 867 Madison Ave., at 72nd St. Elegant couture for both sexes, free alterations and made-to-measure suits in an Upper East Side mansion. Antiques are scattered all over the shop, and furniture and decorative accessories are sold on the top floors, in amongst old-fashioned gilt bedsteads and trunks.

Ponica, 325 East 5th St., near 2nd Ave. Transparent dresses.

Sonia Rykiel, 792 Madison Ave., at 66th St. Knitted costumes.

Victoria Falls, 451 West Broadway, between Houston and Prince Sts. Hideously expensive Victorian nightgowns, petticoats and dresses, and also some twenties and thirties evening dresses and straw boaters.

Willie Wear, 119 5th Ave., near 17th St. Bearably priced clothing, often quite tempting.

Yves St Laurent Rive Gauche, 855 Madison Ave., at 71st St. Glamorous evening dresses and comparatively staid day clothes.

Discount Labels

Aaron's, 627 5th Ave., Brooklyn. The ultimate in discount shops—a warehouse overflowing with cheap designer clothes—in Brooklyn.

Bfo, 149 5th Ave., at 21st St. For men only. Valentino, Ralph Lauren, and their likes, at about 50 per cent off usual retail prices.

Century Twenty One Department Store, 12 Cortlandt St., off Broadway. Fantastic bargains, with discounted Thierry Mugler, Genny, Gaultier Junior, Calvin Klein Sport and Perry Ellis. Also kitchenware and household goods.

Daffy's, 111 5th Ave., at 18th St. Three floors of massively reduced clothing, from run-of-the-mill casual to designer clothes.

Loehmann's, 60–06 99th St., Rego Park, Queens. Enormous reductions on designer labels, but a long trek out there on the R train.

Orchard Street Market, between Canal and East Houston Sts. Open every day except Saturday, and fit to burst with crazed discount-fanatics fighting with squalling stall-owners on Sundays. If you hunt through some really horrible offerings, there are some exceptionally good bargains on American and European designers, and especially on shoes (try the Lace-Up Shoe Shop at 110 Orchard Street).

22 Steps, 746 Madison Avenue, at 64th St. No massive reductions, but genuine Yves St Laurent and Sonia Rykiel.

Second-hand Clothes

Alice Underground, 380 Columbus Ave. All the leather and suede is of good quality.

Andy's Chee-Pees, 16 West 8th St. A bit grimy, but full of bargains.

Antique Boutique, 712–714 Broadway, between Waverly Place and Washington St. Good for leather jackets and tight satin trousers, but quite pricey.

Canal Jeans, 504 Broadway, between Spring and Broome Sts. Enormously successful warehouse selling new and old clothes at wholesale prices.

Domsey Warehouse, South 9th St., between Kent and Wyeth Aves, Williamsburg. A bit of a trek on the J train to Marcy Avenue in Williamsburg, but well worth it. There are four floors of clothes: jackets, dresses and coats for $8, shirts for $4 and vests for $2; or you can buy in bulk by the pound. In amongst a good deal of rubbish are silk dresses and cashmere coats.

Love Saves the Day, 119 2nd Ave., at East 7th St. Where Rosanna Arquette bought her jacket in *Desperately Seeking Susan*. A lot of Elvis-paraphernalia as well as clothes.

Panache, 525 Hudson St., between West 10th and Charles Sts. Expensive twenties and thirties second-hand clothes in pristine condition.

Rose's, East 9th St., between Ave. A and 1st Ave. One of the cheapest; good for fifties bathing costumes, party dresses and weird capes.

Trash & Vaudeville, 4 St Marks Pace, between 2nd and 3rd Aves. Cheap old jeans.

Unique, 718 Broadway, between Waverly Place and Washington St. An extension of Canal Jeans, with vast ground-floor second-hand clothes department.

Zoot, 734 Broadway. Fleets of fifties men's jackets in the basement.

Department Stores

A&S, Herald Square, 899 6th Ave., at West 33rd St. Manhattan's newest department store, an import from Brooklyn. Prices are good and the place is unpretentious, although some of the women's clothes are seriously afflicted by designer epaulettes and sequins.

Barney's, 106 7th Ave., between 17th and 18th Sts. Manhattan's sleekest department store, and the one with the wittiest window displays. The time to come is on the first Monday of each month when the window dressers—dressed more fashionably than catwalk models—start assembling the next month's display. The men's designer clothes department is the best in the city. Don't miss the warehouse sale in September when prices are reduced by as much as 50 per cent.

Bergdorf Goodman, 754 5th Ave., at 58th St. Once thought prissy but now resuscitated with some elegant and flattering fashions, most geared to working and older women.

Bloomingdales, 1000 3rd Ave., at East 59th St. The exhibitionist among department stores, worth visiting just to absorb all the glitz and showbiz, the petrifying scent-sprayers and the flamboyant shoppers, dressed to the nines and thrashing their way from department to department. The fourth floor has an adventurous fashion department. Closes at 9pm.

Lord & Taylor, 424 5th Ave., between 38th and 39th Sts. Worn out and a bit lacklustre compared to the other Manhattan department stores.

Macy's, Herald Square, 151 West 34th St., between Broadway and 7th Ave. Less glittery than Bloomingdales, with comparatively democratic prices. Everything is here, in purportedly the largest department store in the world—if you can find it. The Cellar has good food and kitchenware departments. Between Thanksgiving and Christmas the madhouse on the toy floor should be avoided.

Polo/Ralph Lauren, 867 Madison Ave., at East 72nd St. Expensive tweed jackets, crocodile shoes and riding gear (see Designer Clothes, above).

Saks Fifth Avenue, 611 5th Ave., between 49th and 50th Sts. 5th Avenue airs and graces, and cupcake clothes.

Discount Department Stores

Job Lot Trading, 80 Nassau St., near Broadway. Massive discounts on cosmetics, toiletries, chocolate and kitchenware.

Fabrics and Trimmings

Handblock, 487 Columbus Ave., between West 83rd and Weat 84th Sts. Handblocked Thai and Indian silks.

Garment District, between 34th and 40th Sts, and 5th and 7th Avenues. A mass of shops supplying trimmings, buttons, ribbons and hat-dummies to the fashion designers in the vicinity. Two of the best are **Gordon's Button Company** (now 50 years old), at 142 West 38th St. and **Sheru Enterprises**, 49–53 West 38th St., between 5th and 6th Aves. (see p. 179).

Tender Buttons, 143 East 62nd St., between 3rd and Lexington Aves. Millions of buttons.

Flea Markets and Auctions

New York only has a few legal and established flea markets, but everywhere you go someone is trying to flog something or other; people brush past you whispering 'Sheets from Macy's, sheets from Macy's, ten dollar!' and disappear into a shadowy sidestreet. There are 'floating' illegal flea markets outside the Cooper Union on Astor Place and down Avenue A, between East 7th and 5th Streets, filled with bric-à-brac retrieved from dustbins and bicycles with their locks still on them. In fact, sidewalks and rubbish bins, especially on the Upper East Side, are amazingly fruitful places to look out for junk. New Yorkers regularly get bored with their things and simply dump tables, filing cabinets, and even the odd antique, onto the street for passers-by to retrieve. In the spring and summer, as well, there are block fairs in neighborhoods all over the city, and often these have stalls selling junk of all shapes and sizes.

Annex Antiques Fair and Flea Market, 6th Ave., between 24th and 26th Sts. Odds and ends, jewellery and clothing (open March–Dec, 9–5).

Canal Street Casbah, near Greene and Wooster Sts. Two flea markets opposite each other, selling utter junk mostly. This end of Canal has cheap art shops, wholesale rubber and plastics dealers, and shops selling surplus surplus.

Fulton, Nassau and Chambers Streets, off Broadway. Discount electronics and hi-fi, and odd-lot surplus stores.

Greenwich Village Flea Market, PS 41, Greenwich St., at Charles St. Small and quite pricey.

P.S. 44 Flea Market, Columbus Ave., between 76th and 77th Sts, (open 10–10, Sun). Antique clothes, Art-Deco furniture and costume jewellery—interesting to pore through, but the prices are sometimes very high.

Orchard Street, on Sundays, between East Houston and Canal Streets. Turns into an outdoor clothes market, with handbags, prices slashed on designer labels. The shops on the sidestreets round about have incredible bargains in fabrics and clothes.

Police Department Auction, Pierson Warehouse, 4715 Pierson Place, Queens, tel 406 1369. Lost or confiscated goods auctioned in a fiendishly complicated procedure which involves viewing the merchandise the day before and buying a $20 paddle for making bids.

Post Office Monthly Auction, GPO, 380 West 33rd St., tel 330 2932. Mountains of undelivered year-old parcels on auction. Again, a nightmarish but rather enthralling procedure involving boisterous crowds and paddles. Arrive on the dot for the 'viewing', down in a basement labyrinth of wire cages containing a bizarre variety of amorphous packages, including vintage cookies and chocolates.

Food Markets

Throughout the year there are open-air **Farmer's Markets** all over the city. The biggest, in Union Square, is a Women's Institute orgy of stalls selling flowers, fresh eggs, vegetables and fruits, and homemade pretzels, cakes and cider. (Call 566 0990 for more information). If you have nothing better to do at 3 or 4 am, a visit to the **Fulton Street Fish Market** near South Street Seaport, or the **Gansevoort Meat Market** is

359

highly recommended. Up in a not too dangerous part of El Barrio, or Spanish Harlem, the city's most raucous and colorful market is **La Marqueta**, which takes place on Park Avenue and 110th Street under the tracks of the Penn Central railroad.

The best way of familiarizing yourself with the city's extraordinary panoply of ethnic foodstores is to walk down **Paddy's Market** , a rather grubby stretch of 9th Avenue which runs from 54th Street to 38th Street. Here you will find every kind of foodstore: fish shops, fruit and veg shops, Greek pastry shops, Pakistani rice and spice shops, Philippino grocers and Italian coffee and pasta shops, and heavenly bakeries. Every May, 9th Avenue hosts an International Food Festival attended by 750,000 New Yorkers, a street fair in which international food-sellers from all over the city set up stalls all the way down the roadside (in 1984, Bruno the King of Ravioli broke records when he sold 200,000 pasta squares).

Gourmet Delicatessens

Balducci's, 424 6th Ave., at 9th St. Prince of New York delis, with free samples for scavengers.

Dean & DeLuca, 560 Broadway, at Prince St. Food displays elevated into a shamelessly pretentious art form in SoHo.

Macy's Cellar, Herald Square, between 34th St. and 7th Ave. The most accessible part of Macy's emporium, with all kinds of foods, and excellent value kitchenware.

Russ & Daughters, 179 East Houston St., at 1st Ave. Lox, cream cheese, dried fruits and white fish, all of high quality.

Zabar's, 2245 Broadway, at 80th St. The mecca for connoisseurs of the New York delicatessen: smoked salmon, caviar, cheese and all kinds of sausages, at quite good prices too.

Specialist Food Stores

Ben's Cheese Shop, 181 East Houston St., at Allen St. The best cream cheese, farmer's cheese and pot cheese in the city—nextdoor to Russ & Daughters.

Economy Candy, 108 Rivington St. Sweeties of every description, some imported from Europe.

Empire Coffee & Tea, 486 9th Ave., at 37th St. Mayhem inside, but excellent teas and coffees at fantastic prices.

The Erotic Baker, 582 Amsterdam Ave., between 88th and 89th Sts. Unconventional cream buns and apple doughnuts.

The Italian Food Centre, 186 Grand St., at Mulberry St. Heroes stuffed with mozzarella balls and prosciutto in Little Italy.

Guss Pickles, 35 Essex St., between Grand and Hester Sts. Half-sours and sours; you can smell the pickle-whiffs from three blocks away.

Kossar's Bialys, 367 Grand St., between Norfolk and Suffolk Sts. Chewy, flour-dusted bialys and delicious bagels—some say the best in New York.

Morrone's, 324 East 116th St. Italian bakery in East Harlem which famously makes the best bread in New York and supplies gourmet food shops.

Myers of Keswick, 634 Hudson St., between Horatio and Jane Sts. For homesick Brits: Tiptree jams and marmalades, Ambrosia Creamed Rice, Marmite, HP Sauce, Ploughman's Pickle and Smarties.

Pete's Spices, 174 1st Ave., between 10th and 11th Sts. Tubs and barrels of every kind of spice.

Petrossian, 182 West 58th St., and 7th Ave. Mindbendingly expensive imported Russian caviar: *beluga*, *sevruga* and *osetra*.

Poseidon Greek Bakery, 629 9th Ave., at 44th St. Delicate, delicious fillo pastries, cherry strudels and spinach pies, or *spanakopita*, on 9th Avenue.

Yonah Schimmel, 137 East Houston St., between 1st and 2nd Aves. The best kasha, potato and spinach knishes on the Lower East Side, according to the knish cognoscenti.

A. Zito & Sons Bakery, 259 Bleecker St., at 7th Ave. Bakeries making proper bread are few and far between in the city; Zito's specializes in delicious, crusty Italian bread.

Funeral Parlors

Frank E. Campbell, 1076 Madison Ave., corner of 81st St., tel 288 3500. Funerals for the rich and famous, from Rudolph Valentino to Montgomery Clift and James Cagney.

Futons

Pillow Perfection, Stuyvesant St., between St Mark's Place and East 9th St. Single cotton futons from as little as $45, with free delivery.

Hairdressers

Astor Place Hair Designers, 2 Astor Place, near Broadway, Experimental haircuts for $10 or less, which explains the permanent queue to get in. Inside, the place is more like a social club, with lots of trendy people apparently just hanging around.

Bergdorf Goodman, 754 5th Ave., at 58th St., tel 753 7300 (see Department Stores, above). Efficient and friendly hairdressing.

Hanna, 239 East 59th St., between 2nd and 3rd Aves. Custom-made wiglets, braids, chignons and pony-tail extensions.

Household Products and Furnishings

Balducci's Outlet, 322 East 11th St., between 1st and 2nd Aves. Big reductions on beautiful ceramic bowls, kitchen utensils, cutlery and cookery books.

Conran's, Citicorp Center, 160 East 54th St., near 3rd Ave. Furnishings ranging from the functional and reasonably priced to the lavish and costly.

Hoffritz for Cutlery, 331 Madison Ave., between 42nd and 43rd Sts and Grand Central Station, 2nd Level. European kitchen knives and gold-plated nose-hair clippers.

Pottery Barn, 117 East 59th St., between Lexington and Park Aves. Basic but tasteful bowls, mugs, glasses, furniture and rugs.

Williams-Sonoma, 20 East 60th St., near Madison Ave. A branch of the smart kitchen-equipment store in San Francisco.

Hypnosis

The Hypnosis Clinic, 133 East 73rd St. Overcome problems with procrastination, shyness, phobias, public-speaking, anxiety and smoking.

Jewelry

Cartier, 2 East 52nd St., near 5th Ave. Classy, but conservative.

Robert Lee Morris, 409 West Broadway, between Spring and Prince Sts. Contemporary jewelry.

Tiffany and Co., 727 5th Ave., between 56th and 57th Sts. Even the 'At Home' cards are beyond the budgets of most people.

Lingerie

Piljo, 120 East 7th St., between 1st Ave. and Ave. A. Punk catsuits, corsets, basques and bras, sometimes shockingly racy. Very reasonable prices.

Luggage and Discount Stores

14th Street. On 14th Street, between 8th Avenue on the east side and Avenue A on the west side, is a string of discount stores and super-markets, many going into liquidation, and all with prices and styles frozen in the seventies. This is the place to shop for cheap toilet paper, T-shirts, socks and underwear in bulk, and cut-price luggage, panniers and rucksacks.

Manicure Parlors

New Yorkers frequently have manicures, probably because they are so cheap. The treatment generally includes a hand massage, wax, silk or porcelain tips, and 'sculpturing'; and the whole experience is very sooth-ing. The massage business is more or less monopolized by the city's Koreans. There are parlors all over New York, the cheapest on 14th Street and in Chinatown, where you can get the complete works, in-cluding a body massage and rub-down, for under $20.

Newsstands

Gem Spa, 131 2nd Ave., at St Mark's Place, 24 hours. Famous for its egg creams, though the newsstand itself is excellent, particularly for magazines, fanzines, comics and local community papers.
Hotalings Foreign News Depot, 1 Times Square south side, Mon–Fri 8 am–9.30 pm. 'You mention it, we got it', is the motto—and there are over 800 foreign titles stocked in New York's oldest stand.
96 News, Broadway and 96th St., 24 hours. Over a thousand magazines and papers.
Tompkins Square Newsstand, Avenue A, between 6th and 7th Sts, Mon–Sun 8 am–10 pm. Polish-run and managed by a man who always wears red leather trousers. The milk shakes are wonderful.

Opticians

Cohen's Optical, 117 Orchard St., at Delancey St. Cheapest opticians in the city, sign-posted, for the most myopic New Yorker, by a giant pair of dangling spectacles.
The Glass Eye Shop, 31st St., between 6th Ave. and Broadway. Thousands of glass eyes.

Record Shops

New York has the best collectors' record shops in the US.

Bleecker Bob's Golden Oldies, 179 Macdougal St. Rare punk, new wave and electronic music, as well as fifties and sixties oldies. The best-known of the collectors' stores.
Discophile, 26 West 8th St., near 5th Ave. Almost every imported and domestic classical recording currently available.
Footlights Records, 113 East 12th St., between 3rd and 4th Aves. Particularly good for obscure filmtracks.
St Mark's Sounds, 20 St Mark's Place, near 3rd Ave. Good deals on used records.
Tower Records & Video, 692 Broadway at East 4th St. Huge, with a good jazz department and large discounts on classical CDs.

Shoes

Manhattan has more shoe shops than seems likely or possible. Most of them are concentrated on West 34th Street between 5th and 6th Avenues, and West 8th Street between 5th and 6th Avenues.

Charles Jourdan, Trump Tower, 725 5th Ave., between 56th and 57th Sts. Elegant and well-made ladies shoes.
Lace-Up Shoe Shop, 110 Orchard St., near Delancey St. Hefty reductions on designer shoes.
Maud Frizon, 49 East 57th St., near 5th Ave. Little girl flat shoes with round toes, and cocktail party gold shoes.
McCreedy & Schreiber, 37 West 46th St., between 5th and 6th Aves. Quality men's shoes, including Lucchese boots in lizard and crocodile skins.
St Marks Leather Company, 17 St Mark's Place, between 3rd and 2nd Aves. Texas cowboy boots and Doc Marten's.

Susan Bennis/Warren Edwards, 440 Park Ave., at East 56th St. Extremely fashionable shoe designers using obscure leathers. Sandals and boots.

Tootsi Plohound, 110 and 124 Prince St., betwen Greene and Wooster Sts. Mens' shoes with rubber platform soles, and chunky styles.

Tucson Leather, 128 Thompson St., between Prince and Houston Sts. Cowboy boots from Texas and Arizona.

Tailors

There are tailors scattered all over the city, and in cheap areas they will restore an almost threadbare garment for next to nothing.

Tarot Readers

There are hundreds of tarot card, palm, tea-leaf and New Age crystal-readers, psychics, numerologists and astrologists all over the city. Many are Spanish or Latin American. The cheapest are in the East Village and on 14th Street.

Wanko's Tea Cup Readings, 136 West 34th St., near 6th Ave. Tea leaves and numerology.

Toys and Games

Big City Kite Company, 1201 Lexington Ave., between East 81st and East 82nd Sts. 150 different kites.

The Compleat Strategist, 11 East 33rd St., near 5th Ave. Wargames, board games, and windproof magnetic playing cards.

The Enchanted Forest, 85 Mercer St., between Broome and Spring Sts. Tiny SoHo toy shop filled with adults fascinated by Cow Moo Cans, glow-in-the-dark yo-yos and Slinkies.

F.A.O. Schwartz, 745 5th Ave., at 58th St. The biggest and most expensive of the New York toy shops, also filled with grown-ups hankering after stuffed toys and electronic robots.

Funchies, Bunkers, Gats & Gleeks, 1050 2nd Ave., at 55th St. Antique toys: lead soldiers, decoy ducks, money boxes and clockwork toys.

The Last Wound-Up, 290 Columbus Ave., near West 73rd St. Demented shop filled with anything that winds up, from chattering teeth to kamakaze helicopters.

Village Chess Shop, 230 Thompson St., between Bleecker and West 3rd Sts. Customers can stop in for a game of chess, and not buy anything.

Unclassifiable, Specialist and Outlandish

Aphrodisia, 282 Bleecker St. A full range of medicines, 'cures' and excitements.

Big Joe Tattooing, 27 Mount Vernon Ave., Mount Vernon. Freehand and standard designs, executed with sterilized or disposable needles.

Bowery Restaurant District, between East Houston and 4th Sts. A string of shops catering to the restaurant trade. Here you can buy the cutlery and crockery you eat and drink off in practically every New York greasy spoon: glass cruet sets, Buffalo China mugs, and monstrous kitchenware (10-gallon coffee machines and industrial-size wafflemakers and colanders), at wholesale prices. Further down the Bowery you can buy grotesque and horrible chandeliers from the stretch between Great Jones Street and SoHo known as the *lighting district*.

Bird Jungle, 401 Bleecker St., at West 11th St. Literally a jungle: toucans and mynah birds range free over the customers.

Canal Rubber, 345 Canal St., near Greene St. Disco lamps and every kind of rubber, at wholesale prices.

Canal Surplus, 363 Canal St., between Wooster St. and West Broadway. Industrial junk: reject stethoscopes, dentists' drills, defunct cauterisers, doll's limbs and a mass of objects that are unidentifiable.

Duke's, 57 Grand St. Purveyors of vintage British clothing, managed by someone called Rupert.

Famous Smoke Shop, 55 West 39th St., between 5th and 6th Aves. Imported cigars at discount prices.

Hammacher Schlemmer, 147 East 57th St., between 3rd and Lexington Aves. Idiotic gadgets: electric self-stirring saucepans, solar-activated garden-sprayers and bicycle-mowers.

H. Kauffman & Sons Saddlery & Co., 139 East 24th St., between Lexington and 3rd Aves. A full range of Western riding equipment.

International Boutique, 500 La Guardia Place. Anything military, including grenades.

Jeff's Baseball Cards, 150 2nd Ave., between 9th and 10th Sts. Baseball cards from 1910 to the present bought and sold.

Let there be Neon, 38 White St., TriBeCa. Neon lights, signs and sculptures.

Little Rickie, 49[1/2] 1st Ave., at East 3rd St. New York's 'Cathedral of

Kitsch': Pope-paraphernalia, Barbie dolls and the last black-and-white photo booth in New York City.

Maxilla & Mandible, 78 West 82nd St., on Columbus Ave. Animal, human and insect skeletons, teeth and bones in the most unconventional of Manhattan's curious shops. If you can bear the smell of camphor and relaxing fluid, there are do-it-yourself de-articulated skeleton assembly kits, human pelvises, moose antlers, porcupine prickles, and every kind of beetle.

Pearl Paint, 308 Canal St., off Broadway. The biggest discount art store in Manhattan.

Pipeworks and Wilke, 16 West 55th St., between 5th and 6th Aves. Handmade pipes and pipe-related antiques.

Pop Shop. 292 Lafayette St., near Prince St. Posters, hats, badges and magnets designed by Keith Haring.

Rent-a-Pet, 145 Nassau St., tel 374 1171. Small pets—rats, rabbits and snakes—for rent for a weekend or a week.

Star Magic, 743 Broadway, near 8th St. Caters for astronomers, dinosaur-fans (there are lots in New York), New Age scientists and the merely curious. Worth a special trip for the Read-in-the-Dark Spectacle Attachment—a gadget equipped with two torches that fits onto any pair of glasses.

Utrecht, 111 4th Avenue, near 13th St. An excellent range of cut-price art supplies, including portable drafting boards.

Sports and Activities

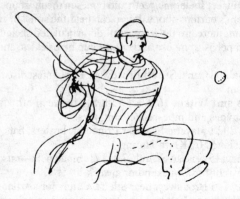

To the uninitiated, American sport is a closed and secret world. Though New Yorkers will gladly try to enlighten you, their explanations are in such copious detail and involve such complicated terminology, that they leave you in a more confused state than you were to begin with. The sports pages in the papers, filled with statistics like 'Devils have lost 4 of last 5 on road, Penguins 7 of last 9, Nuggets 10-of-41 (24 per cent) in last 6', are even more bemusing. The only solution is to take yourself off to a match, preferably with someone who knows what's what. New Yorkers are irrepressible spectators, and often the audience itself is the most entertaining spectacle of all.

Baseball

Baseball is the national obsession, and people swear that outsiders will never understand America until they have grasped the game's complexities. To newcomers from the UK, baseball looks like a dolled-up version of rounders crossed with cricket, and only the extent to which its terminology has infiltrated everyday speech ('to strike out' means 'to mess something up') gives an indication of its hold over the collective conscious. Some still insist on blaming the city's current ills and failures on the Brooklyn Dodgers and the New York Giants, who abandoned the city for greener fields in the late 1950s.

During the sixties, the Mets stepped into the gap, taking the Dodgers' blue and the Giants' orange as their colors, and since then they have been increasingly successful. Both teams attract devotion in equal measures, but the reigning monarchs of New York baseball are the Yankees whose dynasty stretches back seven decades (though currently they are the worst team in the league).

The season runs from April until October, and the best tickets to get are the 'bleachers'—unshaded seats in the rowdiest part of the stadium, which cost half the price of a regular ticket. Here you will hardly be able to see the match at all, but you're much more likely to discover a real *aficionado*—someone who goes to 50 games a year—who will be delighted to explain it all.

The Mets, Shea Stadium, 126th St., and Roosevelt Ave., Flushing, Queens, tel (718) 507 8499.

New York Yankees, Yankee Stadium, West 161st St. and River Ave., Bronx, tel 293 4300. The stadium recently lost 5000 seats when it was renovated to accommodate a corresponding increase in the size of the average New Yorker's behind.

Basketball

The Knicks have been running up bad results for the last decade or so, but they still attract fanatical followers who studiously ignore the Nets across the river in New Jersey.

There are basketball courts in parks all over the city, though getting into a game is tricky and sometimes daunting, unless you are six-foot-six and burly. Watching, however, is great fun as tempers always flare, and usually the play is quite violent with arguments and brawls over fouls and cheating. The season lasts from winter until spring.

New York Knicks, Madison Square Garden, corner of West 34th St. and 7th Ave., tel 563 8300.

New Jersey Nets, Brendan Byrne Arena, The Meadowlands, East Rutherford, New Jersey, tel (201) 935 9000.

Bicycle Hire

Cycling is probably the fastest way to get yourself flattened in New York, and most of the people who go in for it are combative or reckless spirits with a devil-may-care approach to life. On the other hand cycling is an ideal way of getting around the city, especially in the outer boroughs, where bus systems can be perplexing. On the weekends a miniature *Tour de France* ploughs up the Ramble in Central Park, though strictly speaking they are illegal. Hiring bikes can be quite pricey ($3–6 an hour, $18–30 a day).

Bicycles Metro, 1311 Lexington Ave., at East 88th St., tel 427 4450.
Loeb Boathouse, Central Park, 5th Ave., at East 72nd St., tel 861 4137.
Pedal Pusher Bicycle Shop, 1306 2nd Ave., between 68th and 69th Sts. The cheapest of the bunch.

Billiards and Pool

New Yorkers play pool and billiards round the clock, but particularly in the small hours of the morning when matches develop into full-blown battles. Most bars have pool tables, but if you don't observe the etiquette of signing your name up on a blackboard and waiting your turn, you will find yourself in a nasty pickle.

Julian Billiard Academy, 138 East 14th St., between 3rd and 4th Aves., tel 475 9338. Old-fashioned parlor filled with a fog of cigarette smoke and 29 tables, open day and night from 10 to 3.
Tekk Billiards, 75 Christopher St., between 7th Avenue South and Bleecker St., tel 463 9282. Fresh coffee, open 24 hours.
The Billiard Club, 220 West 19th St., between 7th and 8th Aves., tel 206 POOL. Open Sun–Thurs 11 to 3, Fri–Sat 11–5. Alcohol is banned.
Chelsea Billiards, 54 West 21st St., between 5th and 6th Aves., tel 989 0096. Fifty-five tables in comparatively swish surroundings.
Society Billiards, 10 East 21st St., near 5th Ave., tel 529 8600.

Beaches

Most people go to the beaches on Long Island, a 2-hour trip by car or train, and only those with a taste for the outlandish brave the 80-minute subway trip to the pongy coastline of New York City.

Coney Island, tel (718) 946 1350. A pleasant boardwalk, a petrifying roller coaster—the rickety old Cyclone—and suspiciously murky sea water.
Orchard Beach, Pelham Bay Park, Bronx, tel 885 2275. An enormous beach divided into 15 sections, at the far northeastern end of the Bronx. The green and pink rock here is curiously laval and unnatural-looking.
Rockaway Beach, Beach 1st St., to Beach 109th St., Beach 126th St., to Beach 149th St., Queens, (718) 318 4000. On a nature reserve near

370

JFK in Queens—on the way the subway passes through an extraordinary swamp village built on stilts. Best out of season when it is utterly deserted.

Boating

Loeb Boathouse, Central Park, near 5th Ave., and East 74th St., tel 517 4723. About $6 an hour for a rowing boat, with a $20 deposit.

Bocce

Youngsters, as well as crusty old Italians, play *bocce* all over the city. The courts on Roosevelt Parkway, between Canal and Houston Streets and on 2nd Avenue and Houston Street, are especially popular, and sometimes the regulars try to entice passers-by into a game.

Bowling

Bowling is great fun because it is so easy that even a novice gets a lucky strike. The only problem is scoring, which for some reason is monstrously complicated. There are only three 'alleys' left in the city but all of them stay open late.

Bowlmor Lanes, 110 University Place, near 12th St., tel 255 8188. An old-fashioned alley with 44 lanes and a bar.

New Mid City Lanes, 625 8th Ave., at 42nd St., tel 947 1829. On the west side of midtown, reasonably near Times Square.

Beacon Lanes, 344 Amsterdam Ave., at West 72nd St., tel 496 8180. Fifties alley on the Upper West Side.

Croquet

Though New Yorkers find it utterly baffling, they insist on having a go. There is even a celebrity tournament every May.

Central Park Croquet Lawn, West 67th St., and the West Drive in Central Park, tel 572 4345.

Fishing

All over Manhattan solitary fisherman doggedly plumb the sludgy waters of the East River and the Hudson. They never seem to catch anything,

371

and they probably wouldn't eat it if they did. It is the ritual of the thing that matters. If you want to catch edible fish, you are better off taking a boat out round Long Island, which you can do by calling the **Freeport Boatmen's Association**, tel (516) 378 4838.

Gyms, Weight-training and Aerobics

'Body-conditioning' is a fetish for most New Yorkers, who must punish their bodies with a tortuous work-out before they can enjoy themselves. A lot of hotels have their own private health clubs, or access to an off-premises gym. The city is seething with health clubs, but most require annual membership. You can enlist by day or by the hour at the following:

The Exercise Exchange, 236 West 78th St., at Broadway, tel 595 6475. Aerobics at standard rates.

West 72nd Street Studios, 131 West 72nd St., between Broadway and Columbus Ave., tel 799 5433. Yoga, dance, work-outs and aerobics.

Nikolaus Exercise Centers, 230 East 44th St., between 2nd and 3rd Aves., tel 986 9100. Slimming and exercising on mats. There are four different locations in Manhattan.

McBurney YMCA, 215 West 23rd St., between 7th and 8th Aves. A superb complex including a basketball court, a pool, a sauna, a running track and a gym with weights and Nautilus machines for members of the Y (membership is $468 per annum).

Football

Tickets for the Giants are sold out years ahead, and although it's slightly easier to get tickets for the less-popular Jets, you will probably end up watching American football on television. The game is stupendously violent; a kamikaze version of rugger which is thrilling to watch. The rules are fiendishly complicated and as the commentary is all in code, you will need someone to explain as you watch. The season lasts from August until Christmas.

Jets and Giants Information, Giants Stadium, Byrne Meadowlands Sports Complex, East Rutherford, New Jersey, tel (201) 935 8222.

Golf

Dyker Beach Park, 7th Ave., and 86th St., Brooklyn, tel (718) 836 9722. The biggest course in the city.

Van Courtlandt Golf Course, Van Courtlandt Park, Park South and Baily Ave., Bronx, tel 543 4595. A short but tricky course.

Handball

The name is fairly self-explanatory: basically the game is like squash and played against a wall with two goals. There are courts in Central Park, John Jay Park and Tompkins Square Park. Call the Park Rangers for more information, tel 397 3080.

Horse Racing

Racing, or rather, betting, is immensely popular throughout the US, and the *Racing Times*, a fat newspaper detailing current form and prices, is said to be the best-selling weekly in the country. If you don't make it to the racecourse, you can place a bet at any of the OTB or Off Track Betting parlors scattered all over Manhattan. Yonkers Raceway has harness racing.

Aquaduct Racetrack, 108th St., and Rockaway Boulevard, Jamaica, Queens, tel (718) 641 4700.

Belmont Park, Hempstead Turnpike and Plainfield Ave., Belmont, Long Island, tel (718) 641 4700.

Horse Riding

Claremont Riding Academy, 175 West 89th St., at Amsterdam Ave., tel 724 5100. Lessons and rentals (at around $30 per hour) for riding English-style in Central Park.

Jamaica Bay Riding Academy, 7000 Shore Parkway, Brooklyn, tel (718) 531 7000. Lessons in Western-style riding and guided trail rides.

Ice Hockey

The principal entertainment of Madison Garden ice-hockey matches is observing the Rangers' entrenched hatred for the Islanders. This stems from the fact that the Rangers haven't won a cup since 1940, while the Islanders have been staggeringly successful, their favorite taunt being 'Nineteen-forty, Nineteen-forty'.

Islanders Information, Nassau Coliseum, Hempstead Turnpike, Uniondale, tel (516) 587 9222.

Rangers Information, Madison Square Garden, 7th Ave., between 31st and 33rd Sts., tel 563 8000.

Racquetball

A kind of soft-ball game played on a squash court with racquets.
Manhattan Plaza Racquet Club, 450 West 43rd St., between 9th and 10th Aves., tel 594 0554. $20 guest fee on top of the normal rates.

Roller and Ice-skating

If you own roller-skates, bring them with you. All New Yorkers know how to roller-skate, and there are pathways that are excellent for roller-skating down the East River Park and round South Street to the new Battery Park Esplanade, along Riverside Park on the Upper West Side, and from Carl Schurz Park to John Jay Park on the Upper East Side.

On television there is an amazing event called 'Roller Games', a roller skating obstacle course featuring beefcake women who roller-skate through mud and then beat each other up in a staged skirmish.

The Impromptu Central Park Roller Skating Disco every weekend on Literary Walk near 72nd St., and 5th Ave. Some of the skaters are superb, some useless, but the whole thing is fascinating to watch, even if you can't skate.

Wollman Memorial Rink, Central Park, 830 5th Ave., at 59th St., open Oct–Mar, tel 517 4800. Trump's new outdoor skating rink in Central Park is very large and noisy, with ghetto-blasters blaring. Between April and September there is roller skating and miniature golf.

Rockefeller Center Ice Rink, 1 Rockefeller Plaza, 5th Ave., tel 757 5731/0, tel 757 5731. Open Oct–April, 9–10; Mon–Thurs 9–midnight. A lot of people will be watching as you keel over.

Lasker Pool, Harlem Meer, south of East 110th St. in Central Park, tel 397 3106. Superior to the Wollman rink: less crowded and even bigger.

Sky Rink, 450 West 33rd St., between 9th and 10th Aves., tel 695 6556. Indoor skating on the 16th floor up.

Running

New York Road Runners Club, 9 East 89th St., between 5th and Madison Aves., tel 860 4455 for advice on jogging in New York. The club organizes the New York Marathon in May.

Skiing

There are people who insist the 'slopes' of Central Park are better than those in Vermont, but unless there is a lot of snow you will want to leave the city to go skiing. The nearest resort is **Great George** in New Jersey, tel (201) 827 6000.

Softball

Baseball for cowards, using a larger, softer ball on a smaller court. There are courts on the Great Lawn and Hecksher Field in Central Park, and in Riverside Park at 102nd Street and at the Boat Basin. You should purchase a season's permit from the Parks Recreation Department before you go, however (see Tennis, below).

Squash

New York Sports Club, 404 5th Ave., at 37th St., tel 594 3120. $20 guest's fee.

Swimming

Hamilton Fish Park Play Center, Hamilton Fish Park, 130 Pitt St., between Stanton and East Houston Sts., (free). There are public outdoor swimming baths all over the city, but this monumental beaux-arts pool is one of the least well-known. Go in the morning, before the locals take it over.

John Jay Park, Cherokee Place (east of York Ave.), between East 76th and 78th Sts., (free). Very jolly outdoor pool, with lots of children, on the Upper East Side. It gets very crowded on summer weekends.

348 East, 54th Street Pool at 1st Ave., tel 397 3154. Excellent indoor pool with an annual membership fee of $2.

Carmine Street Recreation Center, Clarkson St. and 7th Ave., tel 397 3107. Annual membership costs a dollar, but you need proof that you live in the city (a letter with your name on it) and a photograph. There is also a gym.

Tennis

To play on city-owned courts you must purchase a $40 permit, which lasts for the season from April–Sept, from the Parks Department in the

Arsenal Building at 64th St. and 5th Ave., tel 360 8111. They will give you a list of courts in Central Park, East River Park, and Riverside Park. **Tennis Club**, Grand Central Terminal, 15 Vanderbilt Ave., tel 687 3841, (court fees $75 Mon–Fri, $50 weekends). It sounds bizarre, but there are four tennis courts tucked away in the roof of Grand Central Station. Using them is a pretty costly affair, although you won't find many private clubs that are significantly cheaper.

Tranquility Tanks

Tranquility Tanks, 141 5th Ave., tel 475 5225. When New York becomes really unbearable there is always total sensory deprivation – floating with your ears plugged up with wax, in a darkened room, in a tank full of salted water, for an indefinite amount of time.

Turkish Baths

Tenth Street Russian-Turkish Baths, 268 East 10th St., between 1st Ave. and Ave. A, tel 674 9250. Once there were hundreds of steam baths, or *shvitzes* ('sweats'), all over the Lower East Side; now the Tenth Street baths are practically the last in the city. There is a women-only day (Wednesday) and two men-only days (Thursday and Sunday), as well as mixed days when everyone wears loin cloths and turns a lurid pink. You will need a vodka or two from the bar upstairs before facing the Russian Radiant Heat room, the ice-cold cool-off pool and the *platzka*, a scrubbing down with a brush made of oak branches. For those that pass out entirely, there is a dormitory full of bunk beds on the first floor.

Yoga

Integral Yoga Institute, 227 West 13th St., between 7th and 89th Aves., tel 929 0586. Reasonably priced classes (about $6 a go).

Wrestling

Wrestling at the Madison Avenue Garden is perhaps the ultimate trash spectactor sport, a cross between vaudeville slapstick and war. The evening starts with red, white and blue ice-creams, and the audience cheering and singing along to the national anthem. Macho King Randy Savage, Hulk Hogan or Brutus 'The Barber' Beefcake takes to the stage, the bell goes, there is a brawl, and everyone shouts 'U-S-A!' when the goodies win.

Wrestling Information, Madison Square Garden, corner of West 34th St. and 7th Ave., tel 563 8300.

Living and Working in New York

One belongs to New York instantly. One belongs to it as much in five minutes as in five years.

—Thomas Wolfe

Millions of people, not just the annual influx of 17 million tourists, are utterly new to the city. Finding a niche—a home and a job—can take a lot of scrabbling around and quantities of stamina, resilience and downright cunning.

Finding a Job: To work legally in the States, you will need to get a relative living there, or an American company, to sponsor you in a letter. Then you have to apply for a special working visa from the American embassy or consulate in your own country before you leave. Visas are hard to come by, but it helps if you have a skill or professional qualification, for example, in architecture, engineering or academia. Students can apply for one of the **Exchange Visitor Programmes** by which you are given a social security number and a short term visa entitling you to work in the United States. These kind of visas are mostly issued through schemes like BUNAC in London tel (071) 251 3472, which charge a registration fee of about £60. In return, BUNAC gives students free accommodation for their first night in New York, followed by a morning of 'orientation'.

Picking up casual work is really quite easy, although if you get caught

378

without a visa you are liable to be deported. Most people who work illegally, make up a social security number, and many businesses are quite happy to take them on (at predictably low wages). The best places to look for work are the classified advertisements in the *Village Voice* and the *New York Times*, and on noticeboards in bars or restaurants. If you are looking for work waiting on tables, go straight to an establishment and ask. Basic jobs like baby-sitting, au-pairing, temping, dog-walking and painting and decorating are all reasonably easy to find. If you get really desperate, you can always get money working as a guinea pig in one of the cold clinics and medical research centers advertizing in the *Voice*.

Finding Somewhere to Live: This can be more of a headache. Success depends on perseverence and luck. Rented apartments go for astronomical prices, but sub-lets—which vary from a few weeks to a year or two—are usually better deals, especially if you are looking for somewhere just for the summer. For those on a low budget, one of the cheapest and nicest options is a 'share' (moving in with someone who already has an apartment), advertized in the *Village Voice* or the *New York Times*. Make sure you get hold of the *Voice* as soon as it comes out—at dawn on Wednesday morning—or you will find all the decent places have gone. In fact, there is so much demand for space that many people advertising shares get as many as 500 calls in a few days. Competition for apartments is at its most frantic at the beginning of the academic year and after Christmas: a good time to look is at the beginning of the summer when a lot of people leave the city. Expect to pay a month's rent as a deposit, plus the first month's rent in advance.

Before you start phoning people up, however, make sure you have a good idea of the kind of area you want to live in. The Upper East Side, the Upper West Side, SoHo and the West Village are generally the most expensive; the East Village, TriBeCa, the Lower East Side, Chelsea and Chinatown the least expensive, but rents are high everywhere, apart from in some of the unsmart parts of Brooklyn and Queens like Williamsburg and Long Island City. If you know where you want to live, it's an excellent idea to consult local newspapers, as well as advertisements pinned up in neighborhood bars, restaurants and on noticeboards on campuses like Cooper Union in the East Village, Columbia on the Upper West Side, and NYU in the West Village. Alternatively there are various roomate agencies, like **Roomate Finders**, **Linda Carrol's Roomates**, and **Gary's Gay Roomate Service**, who will fix you up with like-minded roomates for a yearly flat fee (between $100 and $200). Unless you are in really desperate straits you should avoid **realtors**—real estate agencies who usually charge about 15 per cent of a year's rent in return for finding an apartment.

As soon as you move in, you should think about getting **renter's insurance**. The cheapest policies are offered by Allstate and Prudential, although you may have problems taking out a policy if your building lacks fire alarms or elevators. If you have problems with your landlord you may find it helpful to get hold of the *Tenant's Handbook* which is available from the Department of Housing Preservation and Development at 100 Gold Street, New York, NY 10038. (A large number of Manhattan tenant's associations are currently on rent strike.)

Business Information: try the New York Chamber of Commerce and Industry, 200 Madison Ave., at East 35th St., tel 561 2020.

Children: the Parents League of America has advice on taking care of children in the city, and *Parentguide*, published every month, can be helpful as well. The Bureau for Day Camps and Recreation, tel 566 7763, has after-school groups for children and day trips in July and August. The Avalon Nurse Registry and Child Service, tel 245 0250, can help out with babysitters and nannies.

Cleaning and Domestic Staff: Edwona Ashton Maids Unlimited, tel 838 6282, can supply you with any kind of help, from a professional spring clean to tidy-ups after a rowdy party. Butler, bartender, maid and gardener-hire too.

Complaints: when provoked, New Yorkers aren't exactly shy about complaining, but **Rent-A-Kvetch**, tel 463 0960, takes on consumer complaints for people who don't have the time to make them in person. Alternatively call the Bella Thomas Dial-a-Philosophical Argument line on 727 2288.

Costume Hire: Animal Outfits for People, 252 West 46th St., tel 877 5085, made to measure. Universal Costumes Co., tel 239 3222, hires out more orthodox costumes.

Crime Stoppers: tel 577-TIPS, rewards for information.

Exterminators: landlords are supposed to send round exterminators to cope with New York's thriving cosmopolis of rats, squirrels, mice, cockroaches, bed bugs and termites. If you need an exterminator in an emergency, try the Roach Busters 24-hour service line on (718) 232 5507, or R. Gowers Exterminall Emergency Services on 474 3861.

Family Planning: Planned Parenthood, 380 2nd Ave., at 22nd St., tel 677 6474. Sympathetic advice on birth control, sexually transmitted diseases and abortion.

Furniture Rental: Churchill, 44 East 32nd St., tel 686 0444. Furniture rented out for up to five years.

Gay Events: are listed in the gay entertainment guide *What's Happening*, tel (201) 583 6476.

Greenpeace: tel 941 0094.

Heat Complaints: tel 960 4800.

Insurance and Medical Claims Assistance: tel (800) 232 8090. Speeds up claims payments, but takes a hefty percentage.

Laundry: National Valet, tel (1–800) 88-VALET, is a 24-hour dry-cleaning service, with free pick-up and delivery.

Libraries: New York has the most egalitarian public library in the world: anyone who is residing in the city can join, take out books and return them to any branch in Manhattan, and best of all anyone can use the magnificent Research Library on 42nd Street and 5th Avenue. Take along a letter addressed to you as proof that you live in the city, and the library will issue you with a membership card. Telephone 340 0839 to find out which is your nearest branch.

Lotto: tel 976 2020 (you pay for the service) to find out the day's winning number. The lottery is a notorious scam.

Mail Fraud: tel 330 3844 complaints, chain letters, and obscene letters.

Messenger Services: Breakaway, 368 Broadway, corner of Franklin St., room 514, tel 964 8400. Delivery within the hour using cycles, vans and motorbikes.

Parks Department: tel 860 1309 for the latest calendar of events.

Pay phone complaints: tel (800) 722 2300.

Pets: the American Society for the Prevention of Cruelty to Animals, tel (718) 272 720 has advice on strays and adoption. The North Shore Animal League, tel (516) 883 7575, has orphan pets for free adoption. The Animal Medical Center, 510 East 62nd St., tel 838 8100, is open 24 hours for veterinary problems. If you walk your dog, remember that you must clear up after him when he has done his business, or you will either get fined, or, more likely, savaged by one of those New Yorkers who take their civic duties very seriously. If you can't face walking the dog, Cammie's Critter Care, tel 481 1260, is a recommended dog-walking and pet-sitting service, and the Francine Harrison Academy and Dog-O-Rama, tel 444 7257, supervises dog obedience-training and grooming for problem breeds. Aldstate in Brooklyn takes care of pet cremations, tel 748 2104.

Private Detectives: Vincent Pargo and Christopher Ash Associates

Ltd., 210 East 35th St., tel 889 1656, specialize in 'difficult and unusual investigations' and electronic debugging.

Pothole complaints: tel POT HOLE.

Telephone Answering Services: Media Response, 314 West 53rd St., tel 246 7676. You pay someone to receive and take down messages for your business, rather than rely on an impersonal answer machine.

Theater and TV Tickets: Audience Extras, tel 989 9550, has a scheme for selling left-over seats for all kinds of events for less than $3 to members who have paid an annual registration fee of around $80. NBC has tickets for *The David Letterman Show*, *Saturday Night Live* and *The Cosby Show* on 664 3055.

Transportation: tel (718) 330 1234 for information about bus and train schedules and (800) AIR RIDE for information about transportation to airports.

Visas: Visa Express Inc., 21 East 40th St., between Madison and 5th Aves., tel 532 9437. Takes care of visas for all countries.

Day Trips From Manhattan

Coney Island

Brooklyn—Queens—The Bronx—Staten Island—Long Island—The Hudson Valley—Atlantic City and the Southern New Jersey Shore

In the boroughs outside Manhattan you find a delightful, rather quirky New York. Not the high-faluting metropolis which everyone is led to expect, but something even more disconcerting. This is a part of New York where the strange, the unexpected and the utterly charming co-exist in roughly equal quantities: where you can step from a pre-Revolutionary island of clam-diggers into beach ghettoes, and from an Italian enclave which smells like Bari in Southern Italy into an area where streets of brownstones and Els look like Manhattan did 50 years ago.

Alongside sprawling suburbia and giant co-op developments housing 200,000 people is architecture which is richer and more distinguished than anything in Manhattan. For example an English gothic castle and an Art-Deco Champs Elysées in the Bronx; a row of Greek temples, dirt tracks and Dutch farmhouses in Staten Island; the world's finest and largest collection of 19th-century brownstones in Brooklyn; New York's oldest building, its kitschest sixties ruins, and a sagging swamp village of parallelograms built on stilts in Queens.

It is out here, too, that you find the melting pot of the 1990s. It is just about to boil over. Brooklyn alone has the largest Russian, Jewish and

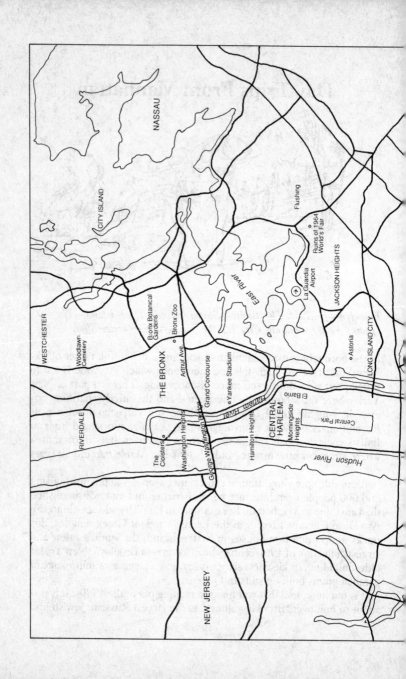

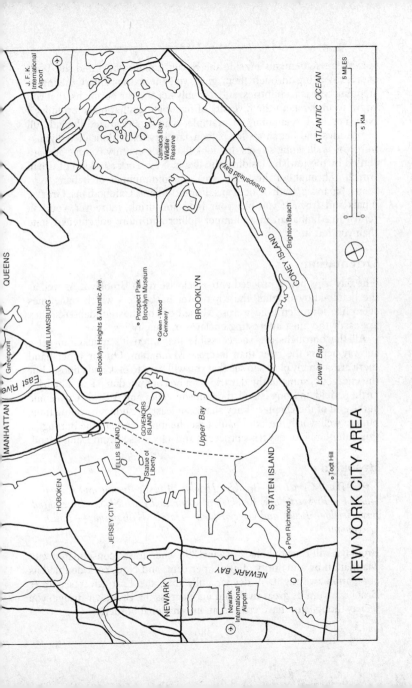

NEW YORK CITY AREA

Caribbean settlements outside the Soviet Union, Israel and the West Indies. Walking through them gives you the extraordinary feeling of stepping between countries, and it is only here, in the boroughs, that you begin to understand the diversity of nationalities that make up today's New Yorker. Greenpoint, for example, is an Americanized Poland, full of bakeries and pet shops for pigeon-fanciers. Next door in Williamsburg you walk along streets that look like 19th-century Europe and are settled by the Jewish Hasidim who live in New York as a kind of urban Amish. Throughout the whole area are communities of Italians, Koreans, Japanese, Latin Americans, Finns, Indians, Cambodians, Greeks, Thais and Irish. If you like your food and drink, moreover, you will return to Manhattan in a plumper, jollier and more enlightened state than you left it.

Orientation

The day trips below proceed anti-clockwise from Brooklyn. As well as the better-known sights, the trips cover backwaters which sometimes seem like forgotten time-warps. Missed out by most guidebooks, they are easily the most interesting enclaves in the city.

All the boroughs are so accessible that often it's quicker to get a subway across the river than to cross Manhattan. On the other hand there are so many places to see that you will have to pick and choose. For the energetic, some of the day trips can be combined in pairs. The trips farther afield, to Long Island, the Hudson Valley and Atlantic City, come at the end of the chapter. They all take at least 2¹/₂ hours traveling time, but are well worth the extra haul. Like the inner circle of the boroughs, this outer circle of day trips proceeds anti-clockwise, from Long Island.

Brooklyn

Green-Wood Cemetery—Brooklyn Heights, Atlantic Avenue and Carroll Gardens—Prospect Park, Brooklyn Museum and Park Slope—Sheepshead Bay, Brighton Beach and Coney Island—Hasidic Williamsburg—Polish Greenpoint

Brooklyn still rues the black day in 1898 when it was consolidated with Manhattan by a majority of 50.09 per cent, and New York doubled its population overnight. A deeper gully than the East River separates Brooklyn from its great rival, and once across the Brooklyn Bridge, you feel as though you have crossed an international border.

The birthplace of Bazooka bubble gum, Nathan's hot dogs and Brillo pads, Brooklyn is more than the sum of its parts, and as much a state of being as a place. 'It'd take a guy a lifetime to know Brooklyn t'roo and t'roo,' wrote Thomas Wolfe in *Only the Dead know Brooklyn*, 'An' even den, yuh wouldn't know it all'.

After Manhattan, Brooklyn comes as a revelation. Above all else, it is surprisingly big—Brooklynites proudly describe it as the Fourth Largest City in America, although as far as population goes it is actually the sixth-largest, after Los Angeles, Chicago and Detroit. With its own triumphal arch, an aristocratic park, botanical gardens and museum, Brooklyn still has the trappings of a metropolis in its own right, and to the people who live there, in spite of everything, Brooklyn is still the grandest, most important city in the world.

In the years after World War II, Brooklyn suffered more than its fair share of urban catastrophies. The Brooklyn Navy Yards, which had stood as cornerstones of the city's industrial might since the 1850s, were closed down, while Brooklyn's own newspaper *The Eagle*, which once boasted Walt Whitman on the payroll, folded after a strike. The middle classes moved out in droves, fleeing streets stricken by decay and battered by gang warfare which had been sparked off by the rise of organized crime in the borough (including Murder Inc., the syndicate of executioners headquartered in Brooklyn in 1934).

Most devastating of all, however, was the psychological blow dealt by the Brooklyn Dodgers, who abandoned their hometown for Los Angeles, just two years after winning the World Series for the first time in 1955. Often the underdogs, but always imbued with Brooklyn's fighting spirit, the Dodgers inspired a passionate following: 'Loyalty to the Dodgers,' ran a fulsome article in *Life Magazine* in 1941, 'is perhaps the most powerful emotion a man can experience'. Indeed, feelings about 'dem Bums' were so deep-seated that to this day some people blame Brooklyn's entire post-war malaise on one man: Walter O'Malley, the Dodgers' lawyer and owner, who was lured to the West Coast by the bait of real estate and oil rights.

Whatever Brooklyn may have lost, however, it has kept its nerve and gusto. New people are moving in: young couples into the largest concentration of brownstones in the country; new immigrants into Brighton Beach and Greenpoint, and East Village radicals from Manhattan to the cheaper rents of Williamsburg. Even with so much of Brooklyn looking depressingly beleaguered, it is held together by the kind of bulldog spirit that has definitely gone from Manhattan.

The day trips below cover six areas in Brooklyn, starting with the most architecturally interesting enclaves (Green-Wood, Brooklyn Heights and Park Slope) and finishing up with the main ethnic communities (Brighton Beach, Williamsburg and Greenpoint).

Green-Wood Cemetery

Getting There: take the **RR** to 25th Street and 4th Avenue and walk a block to 25th Street and 5th Avenue.

Lunch/Cafés: there are one or two coffee shops on 4th Street, but in good weather the cemetery is perfect for a picnic.

In a city which thinks it has everything, Green-Wood Cemetery counts as Heaven. Here is an arcadia of Victoriana: four times the size of Highgate Cemetery in London, with 478 acres of meticulously manicured hills, twisty paths and picturesque lakes providing a celestial dormitory for over half a million souls. The cemetery has a strangely powerful impact on the visitor, for its elegant low-rise mausoleums, its deathly hush and its scrupulously well-kept neatness make it a complete antithesis to the high-rise, noisy and untidy disorder prevailing in Manhattan.

The cemetery predates Central Park by two decades, and when it was laid out in 1838 it immediately became the most fashionable strolling ground in the city. Its developer, Henry Pierrepont (who also laid out Brooklyn Heights), hurriedly changed its title from the dour-sounding Necropolis to something more hopeful, though many of the pathways inside the cemetery retained more ambiguous names—Hemlock Path, Twilight Dell, Sunset Hill, Evergreen Ridge and Evening Cliff.

By 1850, Green-Wood was a raving success; it was one of the top ten tourist attractions in America, with a trolley ride from one end to the other, and 100,000 visitors a year. Nowadays visitors are few and far between. 'It's the most beautiful place in the world', says the lugubrious porter, whose parents used to take him for Sunday walks up to Green-Wood's **Vista Hill**—the highest promentary in Brooklyn. He makes unexpected appearances out of locked mausoleums and is practically the only animate object to be seen, except for black patrol-cars and gangster-types prowling around in silent limousines.

In fact at least three members of the New York underworld repose in secret plots somewhere in Green-Wood: 'Terrible Johnnie Torrio', the Chicago mobster who took up Al Capone as his protégé and then retired to Brooklyn; Albert Anastasia, who was responsible for hundreds of deaths as a director of the Brooklyn hit squad, Murder Inc.; and his executioner, Joey Gallo, who allegedly helped bump off Anastasia in a barber's and got himself rubbed out eating a bowl of pasta in Umberto's Clam House in Manhattan.

The **main gate** on 5th Avenue and 25th Street, tastefully signposted in black, is the best place to start. Architecturally it is Green-Wood's Gothic *pièce de resistence*. An enormous double arch, resembling an extracted molar riddled with crockets, finials, crevices and birds' nests fillings, it is by Richard Upjohn, the great English Gothic Revivalist who designed Wall Street's Trinity Church. At the gatehouse next door, it is vitally important to pick up a map, since you will almost certainly get lost without one.

Once inside, the fields of exquisitely carved mausoleums, pyramids, gravestones, cairns and obelisks, carefully placed on hills and lakesides, are just as impressive as Upjohn's extraordinary gateway. As you walk around, keep an eye out for Perpetual Care badges, like the one attached to the massive **Steinway vault** (its capacity is 200, with only 68 residents to date) signifying that the grave has been provided for indefinitely. The 19th century's most respected talents including the sculptors Augustus Saint-Gaudens and Daniel Chester French, and the architects Warren & Wetmore, who designed Grand Central Station, found commissions in the cemetery. Their work covers a whole range of different styles, although Egyptian and Gothic Revival are easily the most popular.

Green-Wood's really eminent residents have perches on hilltops. On the hill above Oak Avenue, for example, lies Horace Greeley, who founded the *New York Herald Tribune* and coined the phrase 'Go West Young Man' in the Great Depression. Of the more unorthodox monuments, there is one commemorating Julia Overington, that contains bits of her hair and a lace collar. Another on Walnut Avenue, bizarrely covered in gargoyles and frogs, depicts the 19th-century King of the Soda Fountain, John Matthews, inventing Soda Pop. The strangest thing about it, however, is that it won an award in 1870 as the country's best funerary monument. Lastly, there is the unbearably syrupy memorial to 'Precious Georgie', suitably situated on Dewy Path. On one side it is inscribed with a cameo of the dead infant and a hymn in baby language—'Hide me under de s'adow of di wing'—and on the other Georgie's soppy last words—'Does Jesus love me and what will he say when he sees me?'.

Brooklyn Heights, Atlantic Avenue and Carroll Gardens

Getting There: if you are going to do it properly, walk over the Brooklyn Bridge from Manhattan and cross over to Middagh Street from Cadman Plaza West. Otherwise take the **6** train to Borough Hall/Court Street, or the **2, 3** or **N** to Clark Street/Brooklyn Heights.

Lunch/Cafés: Montague Street is crammed with plush restaurants, as well as more down-to-earth coffee shops and Polish chains like Christine's. **Henry's End**, at 44 Henry Street, specializes in heart-attack food, including buffalo, bear and reindeer; and the venerable 1870s salon **Gage & Tollner**, at 372 Fulton Street, has recently been restored to its former glory. Absolutely the best deal of all, however, is to be had in the Middle Eastern district on **Atlantic Avenue**. Meals here are all less than $10. Take pot luck with a mass of good restaurants, or try the homely **Adnan**, or the more expensive **Morrocan Star** which boasts felafel (deep-fried spice balls), escargots and a chef from the Four Seasons in Manhattan. A little further afield, though worth the extra walk if you don't want Middle Eastern cooking, is **Joe's Luncheonette**, which dishes up a constant supply of hulky parmigiana meat buns and heroes in the Italian district of Carroll Gardens at 349 Court Street.

Perched high up on a glacial bluff, aloof from the chaos and jumble of everything below, the **Heights** are a kind of aerial bolt-hole from the turmoil of the rest of New York. No other neighborhood in the city possesses such an urbane charm. Residents proudly compare it with London's Bloomsbury, but in fact it is infinitely nicer: a tidy chessboard of brownstones, with shady trees and an esplanade romantically overlooking the harbor and Manhattan.

The quiet enclave is actually New York's first suburb. After the first ferry service to Manhattan was started up in 1814, landowners divided it up into a grid of lots, and by 1890 it was entirely filled in with what exists to this day as the finest and best preserved collection of 19th-century townhouses anywhere in New York. Before the Heights became a bastion of Victorian respectability, however, the area consisted of wild and empty highlands—inhabited by Canarsee Indians who manufactured wampum out of seashells. In the disastrous Battle of Long Island, the bluff became a brief refuge for Washington and his tattered troops as they beat a retreat to Manhattan under the cover of fog.

The neighborhood is easily seen in a day, and if you have time and guts, the grandest and most exciting way of getting to it is to tramp across the shaking walkway of the Brooklyn Bridge from Manhattan. Once across, you will find that the Heights are easy to navigate, and that they divide naturally into two with Montague Street, a busy stretch of suave shops and restaurants, bisecting it across the waist.

Runnning down the whole length of its western fringe is the **Promenade**, a stunningly beautiful walkway which rivals Brooklyn Bridge as one of the most spectacular walks in the city. From here you see the East River Bridges at their best and Manhattan at its worst, a skyline of ugly stubby skyscrapers built on Water Street in the 1960s. Far in the distance beyond Manhattan is New Jersey, and closer to are Staten Island, Governor's Island and the Statue of Liberty.

Even so, the sweep of the walkway itself and the dramatic contrast between the human-scale Heights and a Babylonian Manhattan is quite breathtaking: it inspires all kinds of romantic thoughts, and, like Venice, it is the kind of place that will make you feel quite melancholy if you have come on your own. Console yourself with the thought that you are standing on an engineering wonder—a chunk of concrete which is cantilevered for 3000 ft above two levels of the Brooklyn–Queens Expressway and a third lower level of docks at the bottom. Anyway, you will leave your melancholy behind you as soon as you set off for a distracting walk around the Heights themselves.

Here the streets are named very curiously after fruits and vegetables or city fathers. In the great Fruit Wars of the early 19th century, a Mrs Julia Middagh apparently went round tearing down street signs named after the wealthy landowners of the area and replacing them with her prettier botanical ones. A staunch anti-egotist, she nevertheless failed to eliminate a street named after her own family.

Today the fruits lord it over the north end of the neighborhood, together with **Jehovah's Witnesses** who have made the Heights their world headquarters. They have been waiting here for the Second Coming since 1909, and in the meantime have published over 43 million Bibles and goodness knows how many copies of the *Watchtower*. They are generally keener on visitors than visitors are on them, but if you are feeling brave you can join one of the day-long tours which meet at 8 in the morning at 124 Columbia Heights (tel 718 625 3600 for details).

For their dormitories, the Witnesses have colonized the 2632 rooms of the largest building on Brooklyn Heights, the massive 19th-century **St George Hotel** on the block between Hicks, Henry, Clark and Pineapple Streets. Over on Hicks Street is the hotel's annex, an anomaly for the Heights because it is actually an Art-Deco skyscraper designed in 1930 by Emery Roth. So far it has resisted the encroachment of the Witnesses and recently it was converted into private condominiums. Bluff your way up to the roof, which has a weird and wonderful Art-Deco garden sprouting brightly colored terracotta air vents resembling 2 ft-tall top hats. The tower itself is studded with discreet imitations of the Chrysler gargoyles (dragons and eagles), and the view from here of Manhattan ranks among the best in the city.

While you are in the north end of the Heights, make sure you visit **Middagh Street**, which is one of the nicest streets in the neighborhood and one of the first to be developed. It contains most of the earliest surviving wooden houses, as well as the lovely late 19th-century sweet factory which used to make Mason Mints. **24 Middagh Street**, built in 1824, is the oldest house on the block, a clapboarded Federal cottage known as the Queen of Brooklyn Heights which looks as though it is going to keel over sideways at any minute. Across the street, the rather ramshackle **No. 7** turned into a terrifying kind of cultural *bouillabaisse* during the 1940s when Carson McCullers, W. H. Auden and the literary editor of *Harpers Bazaar*, George Davis, shared the house while the likes of Dali, Benjamin Britten, Christopher Isherwood and Aaron Copland whizzed in and out with breezy regularity.

The prettiest streets in the Heights are below Montague Street. As you walk south, you might like to drop in at the **Long Island Historical Society**, a hefty Victorian pile by the architect of the New York Stock Exchange, George Post. An unattractive Viking and a handsome Indian dangle over the entrance on Pierrepont and Clinton Streets, and inside is a fascinating show of Brooklyn relics including a display of Dodgers' balls. (Open Tues–Sat 10–4.45, adm $2).

South of Montague Street are many architectural treats: the area's most attractive hidden stable yards and carriage houses, on **Hunts Lane** and **Grace Court Alley**; its best Gothic and Romanesque Revival brownstone churches (look out for **St Ann's** on the corner of Clinton and Montague Streets which had its spire amputated after a subway was built underneath); and its most imposing rows of brownstone mansions, like the rows on **Pierrepont Street** and **Columbia Heights**. There is the occasional eccentricity too—hurricane blasts puffed up through a subway ventilator disguised as a Greek Revival terraced house at **58 Joralemon Street**, and a row of beautiful colonnaded wooden houses along **Willow Place** which are in such a state of picturesque dilapidation they have lost all semblance of solidity.

By now, you may be thinking about food. Fortunately you are extremely close to **Atlantic Avenue**. The avenue itself is seemingly endless and at first it looks eerily empty, like a street from a Western just before a shoot-out (somewhere underneath it is the world's first subway, built in the 1840s and used since then by mushroom-growers).

The further east you walk, however, the more lively things become, and between Clinton and Court Streets you find yourself at the center of the main commercial strip belonging to New York's Middle Eastern community. For those with a sensitive nose, the combination of cardamon, zatar, thyme, Arabian coffee and myrrh is quite heavenly. As well as restaurants, there is a mass of bakeries and groceries which cater to anything Middle Eastern: belly-dancing suits, tasselled hoopla bras, tins of olive oil, durbeks, Armenian zither recordings and even Syrian girlie magazines. Even if you don't feel hungry, make sure you go into the **Oriental Pastry and Bakery** at 170 Atlantic Avenue, and at least look at the *halawa be aljeben*, sweet-cheese pastries which are in the ambrosia and nectar food league.

If you have the energy you can get a delicious lunch of a different sort in the neat Italian neighborhood of **Carroll Gardens**, which is well within walking distance, eight blocks south down Court Street, between Sackett and Carroll Streets. On the way, you pass the birthplace of Winston Churchill's mother at **197 Amity Street**, a truly hideous building coated from top to toe in psychedelic crazy-paving. Carroll Gardens is much nicer. All upright brownstones and deep front gardens, it was once part of the rough Red Hook district and was used as a setting for Arthur Miller's *A View from the Bridge*. The neighborhood became less hard-bitten during the sixties, and nowadays it is full of delicatessens, pasta shops, Sicilian bakeries and homely diners.

Park Slope, Prospect Park and the Brooklyn Museum
Getting there: take the **2** or **3** train to Eastern Parkway/Brooklyn Museum. The main entrance to Prospect Park is on Grand Army Plaza. **Lunch/Cafés**: As far as eating goes, take a picnic, or look for lunch in Park Slope. **Cousin John's Café** on 7th Avenue has scrumptious homemade ice cream and pastries, and **McFeely's** at 847 Union Street is a rather nice old-fashioned saloon. If you are looking for something more exotic you might try the **Terraza Restaurant** at 82 6th Avenue, near St Mark's Place. Here, everything comes with lobster, and the speciality is *pulpo enchilado*, a kind of octopus stew. Everyone slurps down *batidas*—sweet fruity milk shakes—and delicious Spanish coffees.

The area around Park Slope contains three of Brooklyn's most cherished treasures: the Brooklyn Museum, the Botanical Gardens and Prospect Park which in many ways is even more impressive than Central Park. Everything is placed so conveniently close together that it makes for a very leisurely kind of day trip.

The best place to start is at **Park Slope**, which lies along the west side of Prospect Park, on the righthand side of the the main entrance to the park at Grand Army Plaza. Once known as the Gold Coast, Park Slope boasts Brooklyn's second great belt of aristocratic brownstones. The mansions here, however, were built much later, from the 1880s onwards, and although the brownstone is unassuming enough, the façades are decked out in all the wild excesses of late Victoriana—curlicued terra-cotta bas-reliefs, extravaganzas of foliage, and any number of florid turrets, doorknockers, towers and pinnacles. One of the most exuberent palazzi of all is the **Montauk Club**, an eccentric replica of Venice's *Ca' d'Oro* covered in gargoyles and friezes of Montauk Indians, just off Grand Army Plaza, at 25 8th Avenue on the corner of Lincoln Place.

Nearby is **Montgomery Place**, an extraordinarily picturesque row of brownstones with elegantly steep stoops; and a strange anomaly, a lovely Art-Moderne apartment house, **140 8th Avenue**, at its butt end. The doorman is only too pleased to show off the lobby, which is arranged in a series of dainty drawing rooms with etched glass, mirrors and handsome light fittings.

From here, you can walk down to **7th Avenue**, a jolly street of second-hand shops, grocers, fancy bakeries and restaurants where you can get a nice lunch or a picnic if the weather is good. The original Park Slopers—a solidly upper-middle class crew of lawyers, merchants and doctors—have more or less disappeared. Nowadays in the restaurants and shops of 7th Avenue you see a rather more interesting mixture of people including Irish and Italian families who have lived in the less fashionable corners of the area since the 19th century, and young families who moved here from Manhattan and renovated battalions of brownstones in the 1970s.

They are very lucky to have **Prospect Park** more or less on their doorstep, just off Prospect Park West. Central Park will always steal the limelight, but Frederick Law Olmsted and Calvert Vaux always thought of Prospect Park as their masterpiece. It is certainly romantic: a 19th-century variation on Inigo Jones, it effaces the city, and brings off the illusion of complete rural seclusion with real panache. There are gardens, lawns, streams, and ponds—345 acres of them in all—but the loveliest part is the Long Meadow, a broad sweeping lawn with spectacular vistas across the park. Vaux and Olmsted imagined picnickers strewn across them, but nowadays you are more likely to see West Indians who come here to play cricket, and people gathering ginkgo nuts, which ripen in September and exude a potent stench of rotting game (they taste delicious when baked). If you should want a picnic, however, there is nothing to stop you plonking yourself down on one of the slopes and watching all the activity around you.

The park has its quirks too: a **Quaker burial ground** where Montgomery Clift was buried by his mother, a fervent believer; and, in Grand Army Plaza, a **triumphal arch** of preposterous proportions modeled on *L'Étoile* and topped by a monumental sculpture of a chariot drawn by four foaming horses, called a quadriga. There is also an Oriental Temple, a zoo decorated with WPA murals, a Chinese music pagoda, a Vale of Cashmere with lily ponds and weeping willows, and a series of wooded rambles where mushrooms grow in quantities.

The park is *enormous*. If you get exhausted, flag down one of the green Park Rangers vans to give you a lift to the nearest exit, though to twist their arms you might have to pretend you have a sore throat or something.

To the south of the park, between Flatbush Avenue and Washington Avenue, is a separate enclave, **Institute Park**, a triangle containing the great Brooklyn Museum, the Brooklyn Botanic Garden and the Public Library.

Open Tues 11–7.45, Wed–Sun 11–4.45, adm $3, free Tues 5–7.45, the **Brooklyn Museum** was originally intended as the largest museum in the world. The project soon ran into financial straits, however, and construction work stopped when the building, designed by McKim, Mead & White, was only a quarter complete. Even so, with five floors of shadowy galleries containing a sprinkling of everything, it seems like the world's biggest. Each floor covers a different slice of the planet, and though you need to be selective, just walking through the miles and miles of galleries is impressive.

The Indian artefacts from the Americas on the 1st floor are the best known exhibits, but the collections of Oriental, African and Polynesian Art are also splendid. If you are pressed for time, try at least to see the **Egyptian Galleries** which are the most comprehensive outside Cairo and London. The original collection was assembled by a fanatical New Yorker who gave up his printing business to forage the Nile for 14 years. His own contribution was rather paltry, but he left enough money for the museum to finance an endless series of expeditions. Upstairs, the small collection of American paintings is first class, with work by Georgia O'Keefe, members of the Hudson River School and Gilbert Stuart's 'dollar bill' portraits of Washington. Do not miss the excellent **Decorative Arts** collection on the 4th floor, with chairs by Charles Rennie Mackintosh and Frank Lloyd Wright, and a most unusual show of things called 'friggers', a kind of ornamental glass cane made in the 19th century. Lastly there is the **Museum Shop**, stuffed to the brim with sarcophagos scarves and briefcases, as well as all kinds of extraordinary reproductions, and justly famed as the best of its kind in New York.

A little way down from the museum, at 100 Washington Avenue, is the **Brooklyn Botanic Garden** (Open Apr–Sept, Tues–Fri 8–6, Sat–Sun 10–6; Oct–Mar, Tues–Fri 8–4.30, Sat–Sun 10–4.30). The garden is pleasantly small-scale. In May, New Yorkers make special trips to see the famous esplanade of Japanese cherry blossom. In winter they come for the terrific sauna-heat of a giant conservatory full of triffid-palms, banana trees and peculiar South American trees (which are culled for steroids and cortisone) as well as Dali-esque cactuses.

Coney Island, Brighton Beach and Sheepshead Bay
Getting There: take the **N** or the **B** train to Coney Island/Stillwell Avenue.
Lunch/Cafés: Charles Feltman invented the hot dog in 1867, but it is Nathan Handwerker's refreshment stand which lives on, serving Nathan's Famous from Stillwell Avenue at Coney Island for the price of a subway ride to Manhattan. (Nathan's was established in 1916 when a hot dog still cost a nickel). If you don't like hot dogs and battered seafood, however, a welcome option can be found among the raucous Russian clubs and restaurants of Brighton Beach. The three top places are the **Odessa** at 1113 Brighton Beach Avenue, the **National**, at 273 Brighton Beach Avenue, or the **Rossya**, on Neptune Avenue and West 6th Street.

> 'Fabulous and beyond conceiving, ineffably beautiful, is this fiery scintillation.'
>
> —Maxim Gorky, *Coney Island*, 1906.

Its glory days are over, but Coney Island retains the tinsel charm which once made it glitter as the most famous amusement resort in the world. Even the journey there seems slightly unreal. Halfway along the subway carriage surfaces onto elevated tracks and fills with the smell of tar and salt. Looking out of the window you find you are traveling through another country, full of seaside bungalows and neat front gardens pin-cushioned with American flags, plastic reindeers and Virgin Marys, while the skyscrapers of Manhattan float like a flimsy backdrop somewhere in the distance.

Coney is not actually an island at all but, appropriately enough for the birthplace of the hot dog, a frankfurter of land separated from Brooklyn by a small creek. It is strangely quaint: a patch of sand, a stretch of ocean, a boardwalk bleached the color of sand, and an impossibly rickety amusement park called Wonderland. The whole thing is overshadowed by the rusting ruin of the Parachute Jump which once boasted *'all the thrills of bailing out without any of the usual hazards or discomforts'*.

The jump was transported here from the World's Fair of 1939, but today it is one of the last symbols of Coney Island's heyday as a candy-colored fantasyland for the urban masses. From the turn of the century until the 1940s a million people a day flocked to Coney's frantic amusement parks, a fairytale Baghdad of fantastical architecture which immigrants sailing into New York could see gleaming some 38 miles out to sea, way before the Statue of Liberty. It was here that the roller coaster was born and developed, and the electric light and the electric train displaced gas and steam for good.

The most popular ride of all was one of the first—Steeplechase Park, where fair-goers took advantage of a rare opportunity to cuddle each other as they rode astride mechanical horses on a 25-acre artificial racecourse. Tobogganing into a lake containing 40 sea lions in 'Shoot the Chutes' was also a favorite. Otherwise visitors flocked to a city of 300 fire-fighting midgets or to reconstructions of various disasters including the Galveston Flood in Texas and the Boer War, which employed veterans who had fought in the real war five years previously. Finally there was Luna Park, a bubble-gum city composed of 1221 towers, minarets, lagoons and finials and illuminated by a necklace of 1.3 million electric lights.

In 1911, Hell caught fire and Coney Island's biggest park, Dreamland, burnt to the ground. Luna Park battled on until, during the 1940s, it was finally ravaged by a series of fires; only the Steeplechase staggered on until 1965, when it was bought by the Trump Corporation and demolished.

Today's rather melancholy **Wonderland** is a ghost of the old Coney, but even so it is great fun. In the middle are two august relics from the 1920s: the **Wonder Wheel**, a creaking ferris wheel from which you get

397

views of a spectral Manhattan, and, snaking around the whole park, the truly petrifying **Cyclone**, a clattering wooden roller coaster, whose rattles are more frightening than the whiplash ride itself. The other rides are more ordinary, except for some curious machines which tell your fortune and 'massage' your feet at the same time with a vibrating metal plate, all for 5 cents.

Next to the entrance to Wonderland is an ancient snack stand, **Gregory and Paul's**, with a two-dimensional rocket launching itself from the roof. Here you can buy fried chicken shrimp (*It's delicious!*) or blue clams. Either Gregory or Paul says he remembers Cary Grant walking up and down Surf Avenue in a clown's suit on stilts, except that in those days he was a waiter called Archie Leach. Nowadays Surf Avenue is rather frayed at the edges, but on the corner of Stillwell Avenue you can still get a hot dog from the venerable **Nathan's Famous** (see p. 396).

The nicest place on Coney Island, and one which has remained untouched since the 19th century, is of course the **Boardwalk**. Here you get a grand view of the whole scene, and of the strange mixture of pensioners and young ravers who come to parade. A little way along the boardwalk from Wonderland is the **Aquarium**, a cheery place where sea lions balance balls on their noses, dolphins shake hands, and an electric eel gives a twice-daily performance generating 650 volts at a go. (Open 10–5 Mon–Fri, 10–6 Sat–Sun, tel 718 265 FISH).

From the Aquarium it is a short, though thoroughly pleasant, walk along the boardwalk to **Brighton Beach** which nowadays houses the largest community of Russians outside the Soviet Union. After the easing of US/USSR relations in the 1970s, 90,000 Russians emigrated to America; nearly 10,000 of them to the 'Little Odessa by the Sea' at Brighton Beach.

As you get closer the Boardwalk fills with a crowd—growly old Russians wearing kipper ties, staring out to sea, and tuning into trannies. You know you have got to Brighton Beach proper, however, when you get to the disreputable-looking **Gastronom Moscow**, a boardwalk café dispensing tea and vodka. From the Gastronom, turn right off the boardwalk onto one of the streets approaching the beach, and walk a block west to the heart of the neighborhood: Brighton Beach Avenue.

Speckled by the fish spine of the El tracks, the avenue is now Brooklyn's most colorful street, lined with shops and fruit stalls and seething with shoppers, show-offs and bustle. Suddenly everything is written in Cyrillic script, no one understands English, and walking down the sidewalk turns into a battle with enormous *babushkas* wearing black scarves and laden down by shopping bags. The clothes shops sell fur coats, the newsstands *Sputnik* and *Pravda*, and delicatessens and kosher butchers are stuffed with black bread and smoked herring.

In recent years the Russians of Brighton Beach have earned a reputation for being a somewhat wild and reckless crew, who supposedly excel in the fields of forgery and fraud. Whether or not this is justified, the restaurants of Brighton Beach do little to dispel it, and if you are feeling in the least bit adventurous you should definitely stay on for an evening meal. These are raucous, rough-and-tumble affairs, for which the eaters dress to the nines in raunchy sequined evening dresses, sparklers, red tuxedos and dandy's bow ties. The evening rollocks on into the small hours. A bottle of vodka is plonked on the table, a band plays a selection of Abba, Stevie Wonder, and Polish polka medleys, and disheveled waiters serve up enough food for an army. By the end everyone seems to have lost their partner to someone else, tempers flare, and usually the meal winds up with some kind of a brawl.

If you are of a less combative temperament, there are alternatives. At the top of the avenue there is **Mrs Stahl's**, (1001 Brighton Beach Avenue), a knish parlor to which Stahl fanatics make pilgrimages from all over the world. Indeed, the knishes *are* indescribably good: the pastry crispy and chewy, and the cheese wonderfully oozy and sweet.

Rather more of a walk away, (about 15 minutes down Brighton 11), you can find a more hearty clam lunch at the outlandish fishing community of **Sheepshead Bay** a tiny port inhabited by retired people. On one side of the avenue is a mile-long lagoon of fishing boats and yachts with names like *Romance* and *Windy-Breeze*, and on the other a strip of excellent clam bars, tackle shops and ice-sellers. If you don't want to eat in one of the restaurants, you can catch your own meal by hiring a boat for the day, or buy bluefish and stripers from an old sea dog who sets up a stall near the *Firefly*.

Williamsburg

Getting There: take the **J** train to Marcy Avenue, the first stop across the East River, and then walk south down Division Avenue to Lee Avenue.

Lunch/Cafés: Williamsburg's other landmark, apart from the enormous Savings Bank, is a restaurant—the venerable **Peter Luger's**, at 178 Broadway, between Driggs and Bedford Avenues, whose steaks Alfred Hitchcock called 'the best in the universe'. On Lee Avenue itself there are several excellent Hasidic restaurants—**Landau's Glatt Kosher Deli**, at 65 Lee Avenue, and the more hectic **Williamsburg Kosher Dairy Restaurant**, just up the street, at 216 Lee Avenue near Ross Street. At tea time hundreds of school children and their parents flock to the revamped pizza parlor for huge helpings of chocolate loaf, *kugel* (a kind of sweetened potato pudding), fish balls, kosher catsup and thick soups. In one corner is a special running tap and a basin so customers can wash their hands (and pray) before eating.

Of all Brooklyn's ethnic communities, Williamsburg is the most astonishing. Since World War II it has been home to 45,000 of the Satmarer Hasidim, a Jewish sect as rigidly orthodox as the Christian Amish in Pennsylvania. Even though there are cars and computer shops, the streets of Williamsburg feel like a throwback to 19th-century Eastern Europe, and walking through them can be quite disorientating. If you come in the autumn during the harvest holiday of Sukkoth, you will see the strange sight of Williamsburg bristling with wooden prayer huts built in front gardens, on roofs, scaffolding, and fire escapes. Even the modern apartment buildings, with their specially widened balconies, sport colonies of huts, some tied together with raffia, others covered with mock-brick wallpaper; the most sophisticated decorated with striped, colored awnings and tinsel.

Historically Williamsburg began as an upper-crust resort of smart hotels, casinos and mansions. After the construction of the Williamsburg Bridge in 1903, however, the overcrowded Lower East Side swept into the enclave, and altered its character. The change is prominent in the Hasidic community's two main streets: Lee Avenue, with its rows of red-brick tenements, and Bedford Avenue, where mansions and clubs have been taken over by day schools, *yeshivas*, synagogues and other Jewish institutions. As a whole, Williamsburg now looks distinctly ramshackle, with the notable exception of its utterly incongruous beacon, the enormous leaf-green dome of the **Williamsburg Savings Bank**, a turn-of-the-century fantasy of Renaissance pillars, columns and pediments.

The most fascinating place to start a tour is on **Lee Avenue**. Here the Satmar get on with their day-to-day chores, the men wearing black coats buttoned right to left and high-sitting homburgs, and the rabbis sporting long flapping silk coats and knee breeches, and broad, sable-trimmed hats, white hose and slippers. Young boys wear *yarmulke* (skullcaps) and long curly earlocks, while the housewives, dressed in modest, long-sleeved tartan dresses and black stockings, look less unusual. All marriages are contracted, and women shave their heads and wear scarves or wigs once they are married.

The outmoded dress harks back to the foundation of the sect in the mid-19th century after a dispute blew up with the Reform Jews in Hungary over Judaic Law. Nowadays the Satmars are the most insular of all New York's Hasidic groups. They are averse to all forms of prose-lytizing, opposed to the state of Israel, and have their own newspapers, as well as bus, ambulance and car services. In business, on the other hand, the Hasidim are not quite so isolationist: they dominate computer and hi-fi retail in Manhattan, and reputedly net over $100 million a year.

Lee Avenue is Williamsburg's main shopping street. Billboards are all written in Hebrew or Yiddish and the shops sell timers that automati-cally operate electrical appliances, and keys in the form of jewelry for the Sabbath, Torah Slides and Ladders and make-your-own Synagogue kits for children. A good place to start a tour is at **Flaum Appetizers**, on 40 Lee Avenue, near Wilson Street. Outside, the street is permanently wafted with the piquant smell of homemade horseradish, smoked salmon and herring, which Flaum's pickle in steak-sized chunks. Nearby, at 65 Lee Avenue, **Landau's Glatt Kosher Deli** has thick-cut meat sandwiches and big signs in the window saying 'Assorted cold cuts for eating pleasure!', and ('Yes we have a succah for our customers!'), a public *succah* used for praying and dining.

Running parallel to Lee Avenue is **Bedford Avenue**, crammed with extremely good-looking mansions dating from the turn of the century. Once a casino, **505 Bedford Avenue** has a particularly lovely portico and a green copper cornice. Of the old mansions **559 Bedford Avenue** is one of the best, sprouting turrets at one side and covered in eccentric friezes of shells and foliage.

If you like secondhand clothes or industrial architecture, don't leave Williamsburg without visiting the Domsey Warehouse and the Dom-ino's Sugar Factory. Both are down by the river on Kent Avenue next to the Williamsburg Bridge, in an otherwise desolate area where drugs-dealers and streetwalkers are fairly permanent fixtures, along with Giando's, a sinisterly glitzy restaurant at the foot of the bridge. The **Domsey Warehouse** between Kent and Wythe Avenues at the end of South 9th Street, is a mecca for scavengers, where greatcoats and dresses cost $8, waistcoats and ties $2, and heaps of clothes are sold wholesale by weight. Further along Kent Avenue, between South 5th and 2nd Streets, the **Dominos Sugar Factory** does its refining inside a gargantuan red-brick fortress which bellows out white puffy clouds, and makes the riverside smell of caramel.

In this area, growing in the empty lots and rubbish piles which it likes best, you will see the ailanthus tree, which Betty Smith made famous in her 1943 bestseller about Williamsburg *A Tree Grows in Brooklyn*. Imported from China in 1840, the tree was introduced to graze silk moth caterpillars for the textile mills in New Jersey (they still munch away in peace and quiet), and to dispel the disease-inducing vapours that were thought to originate in low-lying swampy areas like Williamsburg.

Greenpoint

Getting There: take the **L** train from 14th Street to Lorimer Street and transfer to the **G** train for two stops north to Greenpoint Avenue.

Lunch/Cafés: the best thing to do is go to **Henryk's Delicatessen** on 105 Norman Avenue, off Manhattan Avenue, for cold fruit soup and *pirogi*. The restaurant doubles as a grocery store, a newsagent, a café and a social club, with a radio and television chattering away in the kitchen at the back. Anyone who stays on into the evening can join a fashionable crowd in the **Continental Restaurant** nightclub at 11 Newel Street, just off Driggs Avenue.

Although they know it as the birthplace of Mae West, most New Yorkers have never been to 'Greenpernt', and for most Greenpointers English is a second language. In the 19th century, Greenpoint was an industrial area, with shipbuilding down on the docks, and the 'black arts'—printing, pottery, gas, glass and iron—inland. In the 1950s, however, Poles began moving in, and now Greenpoint has the biggest Polish population in the city.

Greenpoint is the most homely of New York's communities. The main commercial drag is along **Manhattan Avenue**. Here all the shops are decked out with posters of Lech Walesa or the Pope. There are sausage shops, Polish bakeries, pigeon-fanciers' shops, and liquor stores (most with state licenses left over from Prohibition) selling 99 varieties of vodka. For those unfamiliar with Polish cooking, there are all kinds of treats.—*Kielbasa*, a kind of garlicky pork sausage, and *mysliwska*, a peppery hunter's sausage, which just slips in a jacket pocket, sold at the **Meat Market** (121 Nassau Avenue), and freshly baked challah bread and pastries from the **Honeymoon Bakery** (837 Manhattan Avenue).

Nearby, in **McCarran Park**, Poles spend sunny afternoons ensconced in men-only poker games under the shadow of the five green onion-domes of the massive **Russian Orthodox Cathedral of the Transfiguration** at 228 North 12th Street. If you can, arrange to visit the church for the Divine Liturgy on Sunday: the inside is amazing. A relatively small space, it is filled with incense, columns painted to imitate richly veined marble, iridescent stained glass, and a stupendous *iconostasis*, a wooden screen painted with icons by the monks from Kiev's Orthodox Monastery of the Caves.

Queens

The Ruins of the 1964 World's Fair—Flushing—Astoria and the Museum of the Moving Image—Roosevelt Island and the Isamu Noguchi Garden Museum

You know you are in Queens when the street signs are blue and white. The largest borough in New York and the second most populous, Queens is enormous. Six times the size of Manhattan, it begins at the old biscuit and chewing-gum factories built in the shadow of the Queensboro Bridge in Long Island City. From there it sprawls through a raggedy jumble of streets past the front lawns of 300,000 midwestern bungalows, and the suburban paradises of Forest Hills and Kew Gardens. Then it carries on, skirting past tumultuous melting pots, home to over a hundred different nationalities, towering housing projects, and endless belts of parks and cemeteries.

Eventually Queens comes to some sort of an end, at a vast and silent wildlife refuge called Jamaica Bay. Here a spit of windswept beach called the Rockaways stretches a finger out into the Atlantic and the only settlements are two depressing ghettoes, some deserted pre-war summer cottages, and a bizarre swamp village of old shacks floating on rickety piers. Inhabited by over 1000 Irish Catholics, it boasts its own subway stop.

Queens is not exactly beautiful. Settled by the Dutch in 1635 it remained relatively rural until the twenties and thirties. When development came it was swift and all-pervasive. Soon, apart from its wildlife preserves, the borough was laced by a web of highways, parks, bridges and airports all bearing the indelible mark of Robert Moses,

New York's parks commissioner and master-builder for over half a century. Crisscrossed by eight highways, two airports, and a belt of 14 cemeteries nicknamed 'terminal morraine', Queens became a place to leave, and not to visit.

Even so, it *is* a strangely fascinating place for the visitor. In Queens there is a surprise lurking behind the façade of some of the most suburban-looking semi-detached houses. The drab-looking house in Richmond Hill, for example, where Jack Kerouac lived with his mother. Or the grave of Harry Houdini, alias Erich Weiss, whose bust, coveted by spiritualists and vandals alike, does a regular disappearing act all of its own. Stranger still, is the site of New York's first supermarket, opened by King Kullen in 1930 on Jamaica Avenue. Not to mention a place named Utopia, which was planned as a 'Communistic community' for immigrants from the Lower East Side in 1905, but never materialized. Lastly, there is our first day trip, that extraordinary apogee of kitsch, and boneyard of offensively bad taste—the ruins of the 1964 Worlds Fair in Flushing Meadows Park, next to Shea Stadium.

The day trips below cover four of the most easily accessible neighborhoods. Note however that Queens has a notoriously capricious street layout. The address, 37–05 23rd Avenue, for example, ought to mean that the building is at No. 5 23rd Avenue near 37th Street, and likewise 23–05 37th Street that it is at No. 5 37th Street near 23rd Avenue. Occasionally it does not. If in doubt, ask the locals, but do not be disappointed if they are as baffled as you.

The Ruins of the 1964 Worlds Fair
Getting There: take the 7 from Manhattan to Willets Point/Shea Stadium. Walk down the boardwalk in the direction of the Unisphere, a 12-story hollow steel globe which is always in sight.
Lunch/Cafés: an ideal setting for a picnic. There are a few snack-stands in the park, but if hunger strikes, you can move on to the restaurants in the Italian enclave of Corona Avenue between 51st Avenue and 108th Street. The **Lemon Ice King of Corona** (52–02 108th Street) has the best ices in New York. Otherwise there are the Japanese, Korean, Chinese and Indian diners in Flushing's little Asia, one stop away on the 7 train at Main Street/Flushing (see below).

Flushing Meadows Park is the strangest, most surreal place you are likely to see in your travels through New York. Amongst its weeds and scrub, like the post-nuclear remains of some wrecked civilization, lie the scattered ruins and debris of the 1964 World's Fair. Like a lone archaeologist, the visitor suddenly stumbles on some lost relic—the **Whispering Column of Jerash** donated by King Hussein of Jordan, perhaps, or else an unattributed sculpture of a nude man leaping into the air with some geese.

Stage center is the 140 ft high, 380-ton **Unisphere**, a hollow globe of green steel symbolizing 'Man's aspiration towards Peace thro' Understanding'. It sits in the middle of plashing fountains and a circular pond where Queensites go for their paddles. Nearby, is the skeletal shell of Philip Johnson's **New York State Pavilion**, an enormous roofless dome with tubular concrete columns, (a technical innovation at the time), now covered by vines and moss. The floor, cracked and broken by unrecognizable plants and roots, still retains the vestiges of a mysterious 200 ft wide steel and concrete map of New York State. Next to it is a solemn concrete observation tower, adorned with smashed lights made out of blue glass, and a rusting elevator stuck halfway up.

Sixty years ago, Flushing Meadows Park didn't exist. Instead the area was a rat-infested wasteland of swampy muck, ash and filth, known properly as the 'Corona Dumps'. F. Scott Fitzgerald called it the 'valley of ashes—a fantastic farm where ashes grow like wheat into ridges and hills and grotesque gardens'. It was a perfect symbolic setting for the murder of Myrtle Wilson outside her husband's gas station in *The Great Gatsby*. Entirely man-made, the moonscape was created out of all Brooklyn's garbage: at night it glowed and reeked with burning rubbish, its landmark a 100 ft mountain known as 'Mount Corona' which stood alongside an open sewer which was once the Flushing River.

The scene of catastrophic desolation was the sort that stirred Robert Moses' imperial imagination. He looked onto the smouldering garbage and saw 1316 acres of Robert Moses Park rising like a phoenix out of the ashes. In 1934 work began on the removal of some 50 million cubic tons of garbage for the landscaping of the World's Fair. The theme of the fair was to be contained in the trylon and perisphere, an immense white needle and globe symbolizing 'democracity'.

At last, in 1939, as the rest of the world braced itself for World War II, 'the World of Tomorrow' opened with a Salute to Peace from 50,000 troops provided by the 60 participating nations. Though two of the fair's most lavish and expensive exhibition houses had been financed by Stalin and Mussolini, the pavilions of Czechoslovakia and Poland were soon shrouded in black, and after the first season the Soviet pavilion disappeared entirely. As the world keeled into war, the fair ran into debt and finally closed. The park, meanwhile, remained in a state of limbo until 1959, when Moses seized the opportunity for a second World's Fair.

While the 1939 World's Fair had been a *tour de force* of American design, 1964 materialized as a citadel of sixties kitsch. Within the square mile was a hodgepodge of colorful plastic pavilions—some shaped like tribal huts from Africa or blue pyramids and others looking sinisterly organic like gigantic caterpillar eggs and amoeba, or else futuristically domed like spaceships. The IBM Pavilion, by Eero Saarinen (who designed the famous umbilical TWA Terminal at JFK), was a huge floating white ellipsoid, supposed to resemble IBM's new typewriter ball, surrounded by steel spores and toadstools. Four hundred spectators sat in the 'People Wall', a hydraulic machine which lifted the audience into the 'Information Machine', a white egg containing a multi-screen theater. Next door was 'Dinoland', a park filled with nine life-size prehistoric monsters, and 'Progressland', a gleaming dome suspended from spiralling pipes depicting the history of electricity from its beginning up to the nuclear bang.

Nowadays in good weather the ruins are generally crowded. People come to swim in the Unisphere pool or to take part in barbecues catering to parties of 20 or more. On weekends the lawns are annexed by South American football teams, food stalls and a fanatical following, who sit at tables round the edge of the pitch munching down *enchiladas*.

At the other end of the mall from the Unisphere is the excellent **Queens Museum**, housed in the New York City Building left over from the 1939 World's Fair, (open Tues–Sat 10–5; Sun 12–5, adm $2). Its extraordinary permanent exhibit, dating from the 1964 World's Fair, is the enormous **Panorama**, a diorama of the city's 835,000 buildings which is frequently updated and changes from night to day as you watch. Downstairs there are always interesting exhibitions, as well as a good deal of memorabilia from both World's Fairs.

From the museum, it is a short walk to the **New York Hall of Science**, (open Wed–Sun 10–5, adm $2.50) at 11th Street, opposite 48th Avenue. This is housed in the most eccentric 1964 World's Fair's relic of all, a massive cement brain protected by an undulating concrete wall of blue stained-glass, with two rockets and a launcher in its carpark. Inside, the museum is arranged like a laboratory in a series of fascinating exhibits: anti-gravitational mirrors, magnified microbes, live germs and James Watt's steam engine. Children love it, especially the demonstrations of Brownian motion and how-to-dissect a cow's eye.

Flushing
Getting There: take the **7** train to Main Street, Flushing.
Lunch/Cafés: two of the nicest Chinese restaurants are the **Szechuan Hwa Yuan** (41–97 Main Street) and the **Stony Wok** (137–40 Northern Boulevard), a Taiwanese dining room, where patrons cook their own meals on a pseudo chemistry set balanced on a bunsen burner under an overhead exhaust flue. The **Cho Sun Ok** (136–73 Roosevelt Avenue) is a good Korean restaurant whose specialty is *hibachi*-based barbecue.

The 17th-century Dutch town of 'Vlissingen' or Flushing is now home to Queens' newest colonists. Nearly half its population is made up of Chinese, Korean, Indian and Japanese immigrants who gravitated to Flushing after the quota laws were eased up during the 1960s. Like most fledgling communities, Flushing is ragged and unkempt, but its energy and gusto make it exciting.

The Chinese sector is squeezed into one block on Roosevelt Avenue between Main and Prince Streets. There are gargantuan supermarkets with separate divisions for stationery, herbal medecines, rice-cookers and crockery, and no end of restaurants and bakeries including the **KY Bakery** (42–05 Main Street near Maple Avenue) which specializes in extra-long nine-tier wedding cakes.

Korean and Japanese Flushing is a few blocks away, concentrated on the stretch of Union Street between Northern Boulevard and Roosevelt Avenue. There are nail salons by the dozen, handicraft shops selling lacquered telephones at $175-a throw, and vast *sushi* emporiums with a staggering variety of toasted seaweeds, soy and *teriyaki* sauces and white noodles. Prickly sea urchins come in egg boxes, and raw octopus and salmon in transparent packs, arranged with artistic hands alongside sticks of plastic grass.

Nearby, on the corner of Bowne Street and 37th Avenue, is Queens' oldest building, **Bowne House**, a clapboard cottage used for illegal Quaker meetings in the 17th century. Peter Stuyvesant, the Dutch Governor of New York, had John Bowne clapped into prison and whipped, although he was later released after he pleaded his case with the more tolerant, commercially pragmatic Dutch West India Company.

The Indian sector is a little further away, near the Queens Botanical Gardens, on Main Street between Franklin and Holly Streets. The shops here get all their basic products, including brill cream, henna and videos, imported from Bombay, but they make Indian sweets and ice-cream on the premises. The owners of the **India Bazar** at 42–67 Main

Steet are film fanatics, and their shop is plastered from ceiling to floor in posters of Hindi movie stars. Over on 45–57 Bowne Street, between 45th and Holly Avenues, is one of the strangest sights in Queens: in amongst a row of terraced houses, the extravagant exterior of the **Hindu Temple of New York**, built in 1977 at a cost of nearly a million dollars.

Astoria and the Museum of the Moving Image
Getting There: take the N train to 30th Avenue/Grand Avenue.
Lunch/Cafés: it is hard to single out particular restaurants, but the **Nea Hellas Restaurant**, (31–15 Ditmars Boulevard, east of 31st Street), and **George's Hasapotaverna** (28–13 23rd Avenue) are especially good. As for the cafés, among the best are the **Omonia Café** (32–20 Broadway) and the **Victory Sweet Shop** (28–05 23rd Avenue), a generally empty establishment filled mostly by a long narrow bar covered with various sorts of temptations: *baklava*, *koulouvakia* (pastry cookies) and *flogera* (filo with walnuts, almonds and honey).

It takes just under 20 minutes to get from Times Square to Astoria, and the subway ride there is thrilling. At Queensboro Plaza the train suddenly slews round, and you see the whole eastern flank of Manhattan with its smudgy skyline laid out before you.

Outside of Greece, Astoria has turned into one of the largest Greek-speaking enclaves in the world. Its main spine runs down 31st Street, although there are also lively strips running along Ditmars Boulevard, Broadway and 31st Avenue. These streets are packed with Greek pastry shops (*zacharoplasteion*), cafés (*kaffenion*), restaurants and nightclubs, and it might be a good idea to visit Astoria's Museum of the Moving Image late in the afternoon and then stay on for an evening meal. If you are visiting the city at Easter, you should make a point of going to Astoria for the funeral processions that wind through the streets on the Greek Orthodox Good Friday.

But at more or less any time of the year Astoria feels festive and Mediterranean. Even the graffiti (in Greek) is daubed with zest. In shops and restaurants practically every spare surface is covered up with a picture of a Greek goddess or the Parthenon, or, failing that, an icon. In the summer life goes on outdoors, accompanied, inevitably, by bazouki players.

As well as coming here to eat, do visit **St Irene's**, one of Astoria's many Greek Orthodox churches, on 36–25 23rd Avenue, between 36th and 27th Streets. The outside, converted from two terraced houses in 1980, looks dull but the interior is stupendous, although it takes a while for the blinding gloom to wear off so you can see anything more than blackness. First of all there is the amazing smell of incense and beeswax candles, and then suddenly, at the far end of the church, you see a glimmering altarpiece and an enormous throne of red-and-gold peacocks covered by a golden canopy. In 1990, New Yorkers began making pilgrimages to St Irene's in their thousands, when it was reported that an icon of the saint, whose name means peace, had been weeping tears during the run-up to the crisis in the Gulf.

For the very determined sightseer, there is also the company town of **Steinway** north of Ditmars Boulevard. The entrepreneur and tycoon William Steinway moved his entire piano factory here in 1872, and built a park, library, gamesfields and a mansion for himself, in the hope that its inaccessability would shield his workers from union organizers. The north end of Astoria has Italian, Ukrainian and Czech communities, with the impossibly named **S&M Pork Store** (35–10 Ditmars Boulevard) functioning as a kind of Czech social club. The proprietor uses the example of the 105-year-old Ditmars resident who consumed 15lbs of sugar a month, smoked cigars and drank Thunderbird, to sell hundreds of pork sausages and salamis.

Astoria's newest attraction is the **Museum of the Moving Image** at 36–11 35th Avenue, between 36th and 37th Streets (open Wed–Thurs 1–5; Fri 1–7.30; Sat 11–7.30; Sun 11–6, adm $5). It opened in 1988 on part of the huge 13-acre site belonging to the Kaufman–Astoria Studios. The 'Big House' was founded 70 years ago under the auspices of Paramount Pictures, and in the twenties the studios became the stamping ground of Rudolph Valentino, Louise Brooks, Gloria Swanson and William Powell, the directors, Sidney Olcott and D. W. Griffith, and the Marx brothers who made *Animal Crackers* and *Cocoanuts* here.

During the War the army requisitioned the studios to make propaganda films: eventually they were abandoned until the entire compound was completely renovated in 1976, in an attempt to revive New York's film industry. Since then *The Cotton Club*, *Radio Days*, and that almighty flop, *Ishtar* have all been made in Astoria, and now the studios are the largest on the East Coast. They are not open to the public, but the museum tries to make amends with its catalogue of all aspects of film-making from silent movies to the present day. Its most important exhibits are shown in two screening rooms; the selection of films is always superb. Before you go, it is worth calling ahead (tel 718 784 4520) to ask about the current program, or consulting the listings and reviews in the *Village Voice*.

Roosevelt Island and the Isamu Noguchi Garden Museum in Queens

Getting There: by aerial tramway take the cable car from 60th Street and 2nd Avenue in Manhattan to Roosevelt Island.

Lunch/Cafés: Main Street on Roosevelt Island has coffeeshops and smart restaurants, and along the Eastwood arcade at the **Capri Restaurant** you can get good pizzas. Otherwise buy a picnic from the delicatessen at 579 Main Street, and take it to the riverside.

For $1.25 each way, an aerial tramcar whisks you up from 60th Street in Manhattan, lollops lugubriously over 1st Avenue and the East River, and deposits you in a station resembling an alpine ski slope, in the middle of Roosevelt Island. The ride takes $3^{1}/_{2}$ minutes, and once you have landed on the island itself you can board the free electric bus service which runs up and down the whole length of the $2^{1}/_{2}$ mile long, 600 ft wide sliver of land.

Today, Roosevelt Island is something like the Island of Dr Moreau. Cars are banned from the streets and stored in a huge reinforced concrete bunker called Motorgate; all the island's rubbish is sucked down pneumatic tubes to the AVAC or Automated Vacuum Collection building, where it is shredded and compressed; the 63rd Street subway, the umbilical cord connecting Roosevelt Island to Manhattan, is only just being completed. An uncanny silence looms.

The 'Instant City' was created in the 1970s from a masterplan by Philip Johnson and John Burgee, the team currently presiding over the redevelopment of Times Square. Originally the idea was to build residences for a mixed-income community of about 18,000. So far, however, fewer than half that number have moved to the island, partly due to construction delays, and partly to the financial collapse of the corporation which was overseeing the project.

You will probably want to walk along the riverside promenade which girdles the island and has superb views of Manhattan to the west and Queens to the east. At the top and bottom there are remnants of the place before it became Roosevelt Island in 1973. In the 19th century 'Blackwell's Island' was owned by the city and used for various institutions ranging from penitentiaries and workhouses to asylums and almshouses. By 1921 it was shamefully run-down. Its name was changed to Welfare

Island and various hospitals and sick homes for the terminally ill and the old were constructed.

The south end of the island is now closed off to walkers because its crumbling buildings are too dangerous. Through a fence, however, you can see the tottering remains of the old **City Hospital**, a sinister château-style building swathed in Virginia creeper. The north end is more accessible. At its very tip there is a small grey **lighthouse** curdling the East River currents, with a fancy crocketed cornice where seagulls perch. Although it was designed by the Gothic Revival architect, James Renwick Jnr., an inscription explains that: '*This is the Work / Was Done by / John McCarthy / Who built the Light / House from the Bottom to the / Top All Ye Who do Pass by May / Pray for His Soul When He Dies*'. The story goes that McCarthy, who was one of the patients from the asylum nearby, had built a fort at the end of the island to prevent an invasion by the British. Eventually he was persuaded to knock it down and replace it with a lighthouse built out of granite quarried by convicts.

From Roosevelt Island, the **Isamu Noguchi Garden Museum** in Queens is a 15-minute walk away. Make your way to the east side of the island, cross the Roosevelt Island Bridge, and then turn left onto Vernon Boulevard. The museum is five blocks to the north at 32–7 Vernon Boulevard. (Open April–Nov, Wed and Sat, 11–6).

For 30 years Noguchi used the building, originally part of a lamp factory, as his studio. He was born in Los Angeles in 1904, and trained under Gutzon Borglum, who sculpted Mount Rushmore. Borglum thought Noguchi was so bad he made him work as a model instead of apprenticing him. Nevertheless Noguchi turned out to be one of the most intrepid sculptors of his generation. His work spans many different fields, from architectural sites in Manhattan, to designs for furniture, the stage, and playground equipment. Inside the museum there are two floors of galleries devoted to his work, and outside there is one of the huge, tranquil sculpture gardens for which he is most famous. According to Noguchi, gardens were a way of including the impermanent, the intangible and the functional in sculpture.

Before you leave, have a look round the **Socrates Sculpture Park**, which is on the other side of Vernon Boulevard at Broadway. The park's 4^1/$_2$ acres of huge sculptures—giant weather vanes and oversized colored buoys – are set in an industrial wasteland on the edge of the East River. Stalking the park and using it as a kind of outdoor laboratory are the sculptors; shadowy figures wielding chainsaws, welding torches, rivets and great canisters of propane gas.

The Bronx

Grand Concourse, Arthur Avenue, Bronx Botanical Gardens and the Bronx Zoo—City Island—Woodlawn and the Bronx Hall of Fame—Riverdale

To many New Yorkers the Bronx is a great unknown. They speed through it in cars. Or else they scurry into Yankee Stadium and out again. For most, the borough is summed up by the zoo, the Bronx cheer (or raspberry), Babe Ruth and the Yankees, Trotsky's apartment on 164th Street, Miss America 1945 (Bess Myerson), and, above all, by the decimated slums that aspiring presidents descend on like a gang of *deii ex machina* during the run-up to elections. In the South and East Bronx a cheerless landscape of burnt-out walk-ups and stumpy tower blocks has become a potent symbol of urban blight. Its image has wiped the flip side of the borough off the map—5861 acres of beautiful parks, an enclave of mansions belonging to the city's most wealthy residents, a staunch Italian community and a strange collection of sailors and fishermen living in total isolation on an island in Long Island Sound.

The Bronx got its name in 1641 when Jonas Bronck, a Dane from Amsterdam, purchased 500 acres of farmland from the Dutch West India Company. Supposedly the Dutch settlers got into the way of saying 'Let's go and visit the Broncks', and the name stuck. From then until the arrival of the railroad the Bronx was a thinly populated rural backwater of country estates and farms. By the middle of the 19th century, German, Irish and Jewish immigrants began drifting in, attracted by its bucolic delights, and after World War I the newly incorporated borough became a bourgeois haven for the upwardly mobile.

The rise of the automobile, however, hailed the end of what had been a golden age for the Bronx. Residents used their motor-cars to move farther afield to Long Island and Westchester. Then, in the 1950s, Robert Moses announced the construction of the Cross-Bronx Expressway. The six-lane highway was a disaster for the Bronx. Whole neighborhoods were devastated, over 60,000 people were uprooted, and as commuters fled for the suburbs, the poor moved into the area, often under the auspices of the Welfare Department. The city withdrew capital, and buildings and services were abandoned while the infrastructure of the borough caved in. Finally, in the 1970s, the South Bronx burnt to the ground: systematic arson became big business and in 1975 alone there were 13,000 fires, costing Lloyd's a record $45 million.

412

Conditions are still intolerable, though the sightseers who come to stare at the devastation of the so-called 'Fort Apache' tend to ignore the fact that the Bronx also has solid, immigrant and working-class communities and neighborhoods: people striving against all the odds to haul the borough up by its bootstraps out of the spiral of underfunding, poverty, crime and drugs.

The day trips below cover four areas of the Bronx, including the famous Zoo and the Botanical Gardens. The districts covered are safe for those traveling on foot, but as usual you should be wary about straying off into obscure side-streets. If possible, bring a companion with you. A map of Bronx bus routes (free from information desks at Grand Central and Penn Station) is invaluable.

The Grand Concourse, Arthur Avenue, the Zoo and the Botanical Gardens

Getting there: take the **4** train to Kingsbridge Avenue/Jerome Avenue, and walk three blocks east to the Grand Concourse, or take the **D** train to Kingsbridge Avenue/Grand Concourse.

Getting Around/Lunch: the Bronx has an excellent system of bus routes, and to speed up traveling it is often a good idea to take a bus rather than walk. For lunch, Arthur Avenue has a unique selection of restaurants: for pizza, *calzone* (pizza envelopes) and pasta try **Maria & Joe's** (712 East 187th Street) or the **Full Moon Pizzeria** (602 East 187th Street). The **Caffè Cacciatore** (711 East 187th Street) takes a minimalist stance, restricting its entire menu to grappa and expresso. It does have an exercise bike in one corner, however, a photocopying machine, a picture of Etna and a couple of pieces of tinsel.

The **Grand Concourse** may not be grand anymore, but it is spectacular. The D train lands you smack in the middle, and you are bound to be bowled over. The inevitable comparison is with the Champs Elysées, although the Concourse has about as much in common with Paris as a pair of old socks. It was laid out in 1892 as the 'Speedway Concourse', with separate lanes for carriages, cyclists and walkers, so Manhattanites could zoom up to the great parks in the North Bronx. In the 1920s, after the subway linked Manhattan and the Bronx, developers built a solid wall of Art-Deco apartment houses for the well-to-do on either side of the boulevard. The buildings are now in a sorry state, but the Concourse still contains the largest, and some would say the most outstanding concentration of Art-Deco buildings in the city. The styles are a mixture of

413

twenties Art-Deco (ornamental terracotta, mosaics, ironwork and etched glass) and thirties Art-Moderne (streamlined, cantilevered corners, casement windows, industrial patterns and striped brick-work).

Next to the subway stop is the tiny **Poe Cottage**, (open Wed–Fri 9–5, Sat 10–4, Sun 1–5, adm $1), an almost ludicrously incongruous relic from the Bronx's days as a rural hinterland. Edgar Allen Poe moved into the clapboarded cottage in 1846, hoping that the country air would restore the health of Virginia Clemm, his wife and also his cousin. Virginia married Poe at the age of 13, and remained devoted despite his aberrations. She died of tuberculosis within the year, but Poe stayed on and wrote 'Ulalume' and the eulogy 'Annabel Lee', before he died two years later in bizarre circumstances in Baltimore. (Apparently he was drugged by a political gang during an election, and dragged from one polling station to another to place his vote.)

In 1913 the cottage was moved lock, stock and barrel to the other side of the Concourse. Today it is one of the more obscure New York tourist destinations, and the sociable curator who lives in a basement under-neath describes his job as a perfect situation for a misanthrope, or a criminal in hiding.

From the Poe Cottage, you can make your way south down the Grand Concourse. A few blocks down, it intersects **Fordham Road**, the main shopping drag of the Bronx, and extraordinary sight in itself. The street is a living embodiment of 20th-century consumer culture, bulging with the faces of what seems like every race and creed under the sun, and seething with a frenzy of jostling and elbowing. For five blocks Fordham Road is a solid wall of sneaker, jewelery and hi-fi shops, and Macdonalds in a variety of guises.

Two blocks further down the Concourse, on the righthand side of the street, is one of New York's last atmospheric theaters, the **Loew's Paradise**, at 2417 Grand Concourse. It was designed in 1929 by John Eberson, an Austrian architect who created the first such theater in Houston, Texas, in 1923. The Paradise has always been thought of as Eberson's masterpiece. The interior had a vast domed ceiling painted azure, which once blinked with a scintillation of tiny electric lights arranged in constellations. A machine projected moving clouds across the sky, and the walls were lined with baroque parapets, balconies and fountains, as well as panels painted with foreign landscapes. Audiences were supposed to feel as though they were sitting beneath the clear blue skies of Paradise. If you ask at the ticket office, the management will let you see the Baroque lobby inside. Sadly the auditorium was decimated in 1981 when the cinema was divided for four separate screens.

From here, a good way of seeing the rest of the Grand Concourse is to jump on the **Bx1** bus which goes down the length of the boulevard, turns round at the bottom, and loops back to Fordham Road. The Concourse gets more dangerous the further south you go, and the area to the east of its spine is known as 'Death Valley' by residents, so it isn't advisable to walk much further south than the Loew's Paradise.

By bus, the most spectacular buildings to look out for are:

The Bronx's version of the Flatiron Building, the recently restored 10-story **Mount Hope Court Apartments**, at 1882 Grand Concourse on the east corner of Monroe Avenue, at East Tremont Avenue.

1500 Grand Concourse (on the east side of the street near 172nd Street) which has a crennelated parapet carved in folds and decorated with striped brick in all kinds of beiges and browns, and has a glass tile and chrome entrance door.

The exuberent gold-mosaic entrance to **888 Grand Concourse**, on the east side near 161st Street, designed in 1937 by Emery Roth, best known for his buildings on Central Park West.

The grim Art-Deco hulk of the **Bronx County Building**, at 851 Grand Concourse, on the west side near East 161st Street, which Tom Wolfe used as a setting for Sherman McCoy's trial and drubbing in *Bonfire of the Vanities*.

A little way down East 161st Street on River Avenue is 'the house that Ruth built', the enormous **Yankee Stadium**, which was renovated in 1976 at a cost of $100-million. (The seats were widened by $2^1/_2$ inches to accommodate a corresponding enlargement in New Yorkers' behinds.)

From Fordham Road and the Grand Concourse, you can set off in search of lunch in the Bronx's **Little Italy on Arthur Avenue**. Catch the **Bx12** bus east to Arthur Avenue, or walk the 11 blocks east along Fordham Road and turn right onto Arthur Avenue.

Families have clung on in the area properly known as Belmont—a tiny square bounded by Fordham Road, the Bronx Zoo, East 187th Street and Arthur Avenue—while nearby neighborhoods have been battered into the ground by urban decay. Unlike Manhattan's Little Italy, Belmont's Italians actually live in the neighborhood, and have done so since the first Italian construction workers settled in the Bronx to build the zoo and the Jerome Park reservoir over a century ago.

Today Belmont is an incredibly friendly neighborhood. It is kept pristinely neat, and in back yards you see little shrines devoted to St Anthony and even more flamboyant ones to the Virgin Mary. The two main commercial strips are Arthur Avenue and East 187st Street. Here another kind of shrine presides, since nearly all the shops, barbers and cafés have soccer trophies in their front windows, and sports shops sell mountains of footballs. There are also fish shops (crawling with live snails), pastry shops and poultry shops (crammed with floppy-eared rabbits, bantams and white pigeons, also live).

At the hub of Belmont is the covered **Arthur Avenue Retail Market**, (2344 Arthur Avenue), New York's nicest and prettiest food market. It has its own café, decorated with pictures of the Pope, and an oil painting of the San Marco campanile, and in the stalls round about you can find mozzarella teddy bears, moulds for making ravioli, and spaghetti squash.

You can assemble a really delicious picnic from the shops on this patch of Arthur Avenue. Try **S. Calendra** at number 2314 for cheese and the **Madonia Bros Bakery** at number 2348 for peppery prosciutto bread. For pudding there are pastries in the **Caffé Margherita** (673 East 187th Street), which is decorated with a vast mural of Diana and her dogs, and an even vaster photograph of the proprietor. And if you want to sit down there are some excellent restaurants and cafés (see above).

After lunch you can easily walk to the **Bronx Park** which is adjacent to Arthur Avenue and contains the enormous Bronx Zoo as well as the Botanical Gardens. You probably won't have time to see both, but if you are visiting in May or June plump for the Botanical Gardens. To get to them, walk through the Gothic Revival campus of Fordham University to Southern Boulevard and East 200th Street. Otherwise take the **Bx22** across the Bronx Park to the Bronxdale entrance to the Bronx Zoo off Bronx Park East.

The **Bronx Botanical Gardens** (open Nov–March 8–6 and April–Oct 8–7) are immense. Taking up half the north end of the Bronx Park, about 240 acres in all, is an arboretum, a hemlock forest (the sole surviving virgin woodland in the city), a vast rock garden, a rose garden, and, best of all, an enormous conservatory inspired by Kew Gardens in

London. Inside visitors seem rather dumbfounded by the size of the greenhouse's ancient, oversized palms, banana trees and what look like triffids.

Not to be outdone, the **Bronx Zoo**, (open Nov–Jan 10–4, and Feb–Oct 10–5), is the largest in America, and its ambition—recreating the whole planet within 250 acres—is imperial. Visitors rocket through 'Wild Asia', 'Africa' and the 'Ethiopian Highlands' on a monorail, while over 3000 animals roam free. In the 'World of Birds' there is simulated weather: every day at 2 pm a 40 ft flash-flood breaks out over a fiberglass cliff in the rainforest, and next door there are twice-daily thunderstorms in the reptile house.

City Island

Getting there: take the **A** train to the terminus at 207th Street and Broadway in Manhattan, or the **1** train to 207th Street and 10th Avenue, and walk four blocks west to Broadway. Then catch the **Bx12** bus from 207th Street to City Island/Rochelle Street. The bus ride takes about 45 minutes.

Lunch/Cafés: **Rhodes**, at 233 City Island Avenue, near Fordham Street, does big sandwiches and 'surf 'n turfs'—T-bone steaks with three jumbo shrimps. At the far east end of the island is **Jimmy's Reef Restaurant**, a gargantuan diner which dishes out frankfurters, seafood (porgy, whiting, oysters and clams-in-a-basket), and chips.

City Island is the most anomalous enclave in the Bronx: an ancient maritime community which has hardly altered since the 19th century when the islanders survived by evaporating sea water to make salt. After the turn of the century the island turned from salt pans to boat-building, and in past years a good many America's Cup winners have been constructed on City Island. Today the tight little fishing community of clinking yachts and dainty New England-style clapboard houses is connected to the Bronx by a narrow causeway. Out of season, the island is so quiet that you can walk from one end to the other down the center of its main street, City Island Avenue, and not get run over. People wave and greet you with hellos. Their front lawns are covered with American flags and patriotic mail boxes, and punctually on the hour the Gothick Trinity Methodist Church chimes out electronic jingles.

The best way to see the island is to get off at the first bus stop and walk down to the end. Right at the top of the island, at 610 City Island Avenue, is the **Northward Undersea Institute Museum** (open Mon–Fri 10–5,

Sat–Sun 12–5, adm $3). The main room in this fascinating museum is constructed out of the remainders of a gaping 9 ft-wide jaw of a grey whale, inevitably nicknamed Moby Dick by the curators. Inside there are heaps of jaw bones, walrus tusks, and shark teeth, although the most interesting part of the museum is the backyard. Here in a tall cylindrical tank are three seals, the only seals in the world who work for the police force. The Institute trains them to retrieve weapons and drugs from under the water, and also to undo seat belts and haul people to the surface. If you come at the right time, you can see them fetching objects from the bottom and munching down buckets of defrosted fish.

As you make your way down to the tip of the island, do stray off onto the prettier side-streets, like King and Minnieford Avenues. On the north side of City Island Avenue, at **21 Tier Street**, is the handsome shingled house used as a setting for the 1962 film version of O'Neill's *Long Day's Journey into Night*, which starred Katherine Hepburn and Ralph Richardson. At the foot of Fordham Street is a well-kept 18th-century graveyard, the **Pelham Cemetery**, full of little obelisks and clumps of ivy. From here, you can see the sombre shape of Hart Island, the city's potter's field where prisoners set off from a special ferry at the foot of Fordham Street to bury the homeless.

All along City Island Avenue there are masses of expensive restaurants with artificial lawns and fountains, but there are also some jolly cafés, ice-cream parlors, and bars. The best and most unpretentious restaurant is Jimmy's Reef (see above), where you can look out onto Long Island Sound. Next to the restaurant is the terminus of the **Bx12** which will ferry you back to Manhattan.

Woodlawn Cemetery and the Bronx Hall of Fame
Getting there/Lunch: take the **4** train to the end of the line at Woodlawn/Jerome Avenue. Open daily, 9–4.30. Take a picnic in good weather, or eat well before you set out.

> 'High on the azure steeps
> Monody shall not wake the mariner.'
> —Hart Crane, *At Melville's Tomb*

At the end of the line, on a promontory far away from the devastation of the South Bronx, **Woodlawn Cemetery** is the comfy resting place of New York's pre-eminent 19th-century millionaires and robber barons: Woolworth, Macy, J. C. Penney and Jay Gould, the blackguardly financier and swindler, and Oliver Belmont, who founded Belmont racecourse. Their graves are all marked on a free map which you can pick up from the Porter's Lodge on the way in.

The immense Egyptian mausoleum belonging to **Frank Woolworth** stands out from all the grotesque masonry. The bronze doors in the center show a salacious Pharoah attended by several posses of maidens, and either side of the entrance are two pouting sphinxes with impossibly big bosoms. A short walk away on Catalpa Avenue is the grave of **Herman Melville** who died in penury in 1891 near the Gansevoort meat market, where he worked as a customs officer. The grave is marked, rather appropriately for a writer who eventually lost faith in words, by a blank stone scroll. Nearby, Woodlawn's most peculiar monument commemorates **George Spenser** who apparently 'Lost life by stab in falling on ink eraser, evading six young women trying to give him birthday kisses in office of Metropolitan Life Building.'

New York City's least visited and probably its strangest attraction, is another memorial, the **Bronx Hall of Fame for Great Americans**, an outdoor colonnade containing 102 famous busts, —*Mighty Men who were of old men beknown*. For the enthusiastic sightseer, however, the Hall is well worth a visit and easy to get to from Woodlawn, which is only four stops away on the Lexington Avenue *4* train. Take the *4* to Fordham Road/Jerome Avenue, walk three blocks west from the station to University Avenue, and then turn right and walk two long blocks south to the entrance to the Bronx Community College opposite West 181st Street. The Hall of Fame is spectacularly perched on a precipice overlooking the battered north end of Manhattan and the Harlem River. Designed in 1900 by New York's omnipresent architectural threesome, McKim, Mead & White, it honors luminaries such as Emerson, Poe, Whistler and Whitman, as well as soldiers, statesmen, teachers, scientists, and the occasional woman.

Riverdale: Fonthill Castle and Wave Hill
Getting There: by subway and bus, take the **A** train to the terminus at 207th Street and Broadway in Manhattan, or the **1** train to 207th Street and 10th Avenue and walk four blocks west to Broadway. Then catch the **Bx7** or the **M100** bus to Riverdale. The entrance to Fonthill inside Mount St Vincent College is at the end of the route, opposite West 161st Street, and Wave Hill is a few blocks to the west on the intersection of Independence Avenue and 249th Street.

Lunch/Cafés: Riverdale is hopeless for eating places and Wave Hill forbids picnickers. The best solution is to eat on your way at one of the pubs or bakeries near 207th Street, which is at the center of a small Irish community in Washington Heights.

Tucked away on the banks of the Hudson, Riverdale is New York City's most exclusive enclave. So exclusive that residents have adopted various ruses to ward off inquisitive sightseers: street signs are absent or confusing, roads are pot-holed and serpentine, and maps omit most of the smaller alleys and lanes. But minor impediments such as these are unlikely to put off those who are hell-bent on seeing **Fonthill Castle**, deep in the grounds of the Convent and College of Mount St Vincent on 261st Street.

Originally intended as a home for poverty-stricken actors, the barmy building was the creation of the 19th-century Shakespearean actor, Edwin Forrest, who commanded such a fanatical following that his performance of Macbeth in competition with a rival English actor sparked off the catastrophically bloody Astor Place riots in 1845. Forrest built his castle a year later in 1846, inspired by the ruins of Fonthill Abbey in England. No longer standing, the legendary English extravaganza was constructed in 1800 by William Beckford, the reclusive author of the great Gothic novel *Vathek*.

While Beckford's Fonthill was all Gothic excess, with an impossibly tall 276 ft high tower (it toppled down in 1822), the picturesque New York version looks more like an 18th-century folly. It is far more compact at only 70 ft high, with five crenellated towers grouped round an octagonal rotunda. The interior, however, which Forrest modelled more closely on the original, is exquisite, with wonderful fan vaulting, a glazed skylight, dozens of carved gargoyles, and floors and fireplaces inlaid with five kinds of wood and tessellated tiles. Although the Sisters use it for their administrative offices, they may allow you to look around.

From Fonthill, you can catch the **Bx10** or the **Bx7** to 249th Street, then walk west to Independence Avenue and the (well-sign-posted) entrance to the **Wave Hill Center for Environmental Studies** (open daily 9.30—4.30). Despite its rather drab title, Wave Hill contains some of the most beautiful gardens in the city. There are exquisite rose gardens, wild gardens, aquatic gardens, greenhouses, bowers, a pinetum and a herb garden, all with the Hudson River as a backdrop and a fine view of the Palisades behind.

In the middle is a handsome Greek Revival mansion. Built in 1844, it became a refuge for a catalogue of famous residents ranging from Theodore Roosevelt Snr., Mark Twain and William Makepiece Thackeray, to T. H. Huxley, Herbert Spencer and Toscanini. Inside is a stupendous baronial armor hall built by Dr Bashford, who was curator of reptiles at the Museum of Natural History. Around the turn of the century, the mansion was bought by a partner of J. P. Morgan who annexed the two estates next door to Wave Hill and built an underground recreation building with a bowling alley, a billiards hall and squash courts, all connected to the main building by a tunnel. If you are lucky, you will stumble on a concert in one of the drawing rooms inside.

Staten Island

Staten Island, it must be said, is not the most dynamic place on earth. Even so, like anything obscure and unfamiliar, it is strangely alluring. Spurring the curiosity is the thought that, though millions of tourists ride the ferry to the island, few of them think of getting off there.

Those who do, find a semi-suburban, semi-pastoral hinterland that boasts the steepest hills between Maine and Florida. As well as tremendous views there are the mansion retreats of a clutch of Mafia bosses (hidden behind towering walls, private driveways and clumps of fig trees), the largest rubbish dump in the world, and a breathtaking wild landscape of beaches, salty marshes, black snakes and wild pheasants that would be familiar to the Algonquin Indians who first inhabited the island.

Until 30 years ago, Staten Island was a confirmed rural backwater with a resident population comparable to that of Manhattan in 1801. While indigenous islanders worked in the fishing, oystering, farming or shipbuilding industries, wealthy New Yorkers used the island as a country retreat and made it the home of America's first lawn tennis court.

In 1964 the construction of the colossal **Verrazano-Narrows Bridge** brought suburban sprawl, a 10 per cent increase in crime and a space satellite communications center. Nowadays the bridge itself, with its swooping span of over 4000 ft, is one of the great sights of the New York. It was the last and greatest bridge engineered by the formidable Othmar Ammann, who at the age of 80 had presided over the construction of nine New York bridges. (He lived in an apartment on the 26th floor of the Hotel Carlyle where he could survey most of them through a powerful telescope.)

Secession fever has been around since the plan to turn a backwater of the island into the city's largest garbage dump in 1948. Fresh Kills is now the largest landfill in the world, and amongst Staten Island's 400,000 inhabitants there is still a powerful lobby for severance from New York, though the possibility of independence is extremely remote.

Getting There: take the Staten Island ferry from Battery Park to St George. The spectacular ride costs 50-cents, and tempts millions of people a year who are unable to resist such an obviously good deal. The journey there is usually rather serene, although in 1986 a Cuban refugee called Juan Gonzales went mad with a sword, killing two people and injuring nine others.

Getting About/Lunch: the island is $2\frac{1}{2}$ times bigger than Manhattan, and getting about on foot is difficult. From the St George ferry terminal, however, you can take Staten Island Rapid Transit to Sailors Snug Harbor, and from the same place the **S 113** bus takes passengers to Richmondtown Restoration. Ideally you should explore by car, although even so it is vital to take along a map, as roads are badly sign-posted. Richmondtown and Sailors Snug Harbor both have good cafés, and Rosebank, which is home to an Italian-American community as well as the Garibaldi Museum, has some excellent Italian restaurants.

Smelling of damp sea air and salt water, Staten Island is still sufficiently cut off from the city for it to seem like authentic countryside. Indeed a number of film-makers, including Elia Kazan and Francis Ford Coppola, have used it as a stand-in for locations ranging from Long Island and New England to the Midwest. It comes as a shock, therefore, that the first thing you find on the island is **Sailors Snug Harbor**, a row of exquisite temples set in beautiful grounds and facing the water. Built between the 1840s and the 1880s in Greek Revival style, they were originally a home for 'aged and decrepit sailors'. The complex is now being restored into a cultural center for the island, complete with art galleries, a children's museum and a theater, though the architecture is good enough to make the area worth visiting in any case. A mile to the south, in Barrett Park at 614 Broadway, is the **Staten Island Zoo**, famous for the largest collection of rattlesnakes in the world (no less than 30 varieties in all).

From the zoo, you can move on to the **Garibaldi-Meucci Museum** (open Tues–Fri 10–5; Sat–Sun 1–5), in the Italian community of Rosebank, at 420 Tompkins Avenue. Here Garibaldi lived in exile and in great poverty for three years, working as a candlemaker before he finally returned to lead his Thousand from Sicily into Rome. The museum contains 17 candles made by Garibaldi and the first telephone, invented in 1845 by his impoverished companion, Antonio Meucci.

South of Rosebank is the great precipice rising up to **Todt Hill** where Coppola shot the Corleone family residence in *The Godfather*. Just round the corner, ironically, was the base-camp of Big Paul Castellano, head of the Gambino gang and the most powerful Mafia boss in New York before he was murdered in 1985 by three men and 12 bullets on his way into Spark's Steak House in Manhattan. Constructed without a single city building permit, the mansion was dubbed 'The White House' by the feds. Some 409,239 ft above sea level, Todt Hill has always been the island's most exclusive residential area, and behind its discreetly dense thickets of rhododendrons lie scores of crumbling Victorian estates and mansions.

On the other side of the hill at 338 Lighthouse Avenue is a rather curious attraction for such a staid community: the **Jacques Marchais Center of Tibetan Art** (open Sept–May, Sat–Sun 1–5; June–Aug, Fri–Sun 1–5). The largest collection in America, it is housed in a Tibetan lamasery perched on a steep hillside and sometimes used by threadbare Buddhist monks from New Jersey.

Further south still in Latourette Park is the island's one-time capital, the **Richmondtown Restoration** (open Sept–Jun, Sat 10–5 and Sun 12–5; July–Aug, Tues–Sat 10–5 and Sun 12–5). In 1934, when the village was miserably dilapidated and deserted, the Staten Island Historical Society set about restoring the group of about 30 cottages. Now visitors can wander in and out of the houses, which date from the first Dutch settlers to the 19th century, and through an interesting museum devoted to the history of the island. The houses are quite fascinating, as long as you can ignore the obtrusive actors dressed in historical costume who accost unfortunate passers-by with griddle pancakes and faggots.

Day Trips Farther Afield

Long Island

Every summer millions of New Yorkers find a hedonistic asylum on Long Island, the 'whale' of land that Walt Whitman described as nestling its head under Manhattan and flicking its tail at Cape Cod. Reaching out 120 miles into the Atlantic Ocean east of Manhattan, the island boasts the most beautiful and wildest stretches of beach in New York State, as well as some of its most rugged and unspoilt countryside. It splits into two parts: the whale's spine, a series of craggy bluffs and wealthy estates on the **North Shore** and its belly, an endless stretch of sandy beach and beautiful cream-colored dunes along the **South Shore**. At the far eastern end of the island are the flukes of fish's tail: the remoter **North Fork** and the enclave of sophisticates wafting themselves over the beaches and cafés of the **South Fork**.

Getting There: the **Long Island Railroad** has an excellent service to most Long Island resorts from Penn Station in Manhattan, but for more remote destinations there is a good **Greyhound** network. Of course a car will get you out there faster, but bear in mind that parking rates can be high and only residents have permits.

Lunch/Cafés: For simple burgers and sandwiches etc., try the **Board-walk Restaurant** at Jones Beach, **Giovanni's** and **Flynd's** on Fire Island, **Paul's** in Southampton, and the **Sandbar** and the **Harbor View** in Sag Harbor. In Montauk, the **Plaza Restaurant** serves an excellent all-day breakfast, the **Lobster Roll** has fast seafood and **Gosman's** on West Lake Drive is the best fish restaurant.

Long Island's most popular and easily reached destinations are **Long Beach** and **Jones Beach** on the South Shore. Millions flock to Jones Beach: 2500 acres of parkland created out of a thin and inaccessible strip of sandbar in 1929, the masterpiece of Robert Moses, New York's Jupiter-like parks commissioner. Indeed, it was Moses who single-handedly transformed Long Island from a rural haven of farms spattered alongside a few estates belonging to the fantastically rich, into a metro-politan playground of 14 parks and 10,000 acres of land. Today Jones Beach has better facilities (parking for 23,000 cars, a roller rink and a theater for Broadway musicals), but Long Beach has far fewer people, although in general a little bit of walking on any of the beaches will always get you away from the crowds.

Several ferry connections from Bay Shore, Sayville and Patchogue cross the bay to **Fire Island**, a beautiful 40-mile long spit of white quartz sand that acts as a storm barrier for the south shore of Long Island. With its own wilderness and a Sunken Forest of maple, holly, Japanese cedar and sassafra down behind the dunes, the reserve is one of the last unspoilt stretches of seashore left on the Atlantic. Though cars are banned, in season the island is crowded with Manhattanites, especially the smart gay set who make for Cherry Grove, Fire Island Pines, and Point O Woods. According to holidaymakers on the island, the night-life is hot.

Like most wild places in America, Fire Island has more than its fair share of hostile flora and fauna, in particular an abundance of poison ivy, which looks like Virginia creeper but brings you out in an extremely unpleasant spreading rash. Beware also the Northern Deer tick which lurks in long grasses and can carry Lyme Disease. Signs of infection are red circles about six inches in diameter on the skin. Eventually they fade away, but left untreated the disease can cause paralysis within two years of infection. Don't let this worry you, however. Each year most visitors escape unscathed, and the sea barrier *is* one of the most beautiful spots on Long Island.

On the other side of Long Island, the North Shore is less developed than the South, with a more corrugated coast of cliffs, coves and points. The collection of lavish mansions and estates around Oyster Bay formed **'The Gold Coast'** of the twenties and thirties, and the setting of F. Scott Fitzgerald's fictional West Egg and East Egg in *The Great Gatsby*. Tourists now cruise round palaces like the Guggenheim family's *Falaise*, a 26-room manorhouse filled with French and Spanish antiques at **Sands Point** and **Old Westbury Gardens**, a strangely misfired attempt at an 18th-century English country estate built for John S. Phipps, the US Steel heir. Further along the coast at **Sagamore Hill** is Teddy Roosevelt's vast 'Summer White House', and further along still at **Centerport** is the Vanderbilts' even more bizarrely opulent Baroque Spanish-Moroccan estate. Frederick Vanderbilt Jnr. dallied at being a naturalist, and gathered an immense collection of 17,000 stuffed fishes.

Long Island's fish tail, at its far eastern end, parts into the North Fork and the South Fork. The **North Fork** is the less touristy and pretentious of the two, with the pretty 18th-century town of **Cutchogue**, its houses grouped around an English village green, and **Greenport**, a quaint fishing village. From here you can get ferry connections to **Shelter Island**, with its population of snobbish yachting fanatics. Beyond Shelter Island lies **Klawpum**, a scrubby outpost of rock named by the Indians for its gloomy remoteness, and settled in colonial times by a group of suitably despondent Latvian exiles.

The **South Fork** of Long Island is a different kettle of fish entirely, functioning as a Riviera for New York sophisticates, ranging from William de Kooning to Gloria Vanderbilt. **Southampton**, with its grand houses, sleek inhabitants, Volkswagens and prissy shops and restaurants, is the smartest of the lot, and **Westhampton** the most plebeian. In between the two **East Hampton**, once voted the prettiest town in America and filled with the holiday homes of de Kooning, Childe Hassam and Jackson Pollock, is probably the most congenial. From here, you can take route 114 to **Sag Harbor**, a quieter and less stuffy 18th-century whaling port with its own **Whaling Museum**.

Psychologically separated off from the Hamptons is **Montauk**, the farthest tip of Long Island, and an area of extreme and remote beauty. In the center is **Montauk Village**, whose beach motels and drab houses soon pale into insignificance in the salt smell and the boom of the ocean. Away from the village is an extraordinary lunar landscape of empty treeless moors, broad skies, cliffs and bleak sands battered by gales, and what amounts to the most spectacular countryside on the island.

The Hudson Valley

It doesn't seem likely from a cursory look at the Hudson River alongside Manhattan, but the sludge-colored water has got to the city along 300 miles of New York State's most mysteriously romantic scenery. So mysterious and romantic, in fact, that in the 19th century the river inspired a whole school of painters—the Hudson River School—whose scenes of the river and the Catskill Mountains initiated landscape painting in America. Nowadays Manhattan buckets out raw sewage straight into the Hudson, but above the Upper West Side lies a dramatic landscape of bluffs and woods, chasms and gorges, navigated by serpentine roads dug into sheer rock faces. Most of the Hudson Valley is easily accessible on a day trip, but you could happily spend several days exploring the towns and estates lying on both sides of the river as far up as the state capital at Albany.

Getting there: **Amtrak** travels up the East Bank to Albany, the **Hudson-Harlem** commuter train from Grand Central connects to Tarrytown, and **Trailways**, **Greyhound** and **Hudson Transit** all have bus routes which will take you to most of the smaller towns. Ideally, of course, the best way to get around is by car along **Route 9**, the old carriage road connecting the estates of Dutch New York.

Lunch/Cafés: in Tarrytown the restaurant with the best view is **Tappan Hill**, and off Route 9 near Hyde Park, the **Culinary Institute of America**, offers meals prepared by graduates from an intensive two-year training course. At West Point there is **Robert Henry**, for *cordon bleu* cooking, and **Pepe** for good pizzas.

Beyond New York City's northern boundary in the Bronx lies the executive suburbia of **Westchester County** and **Yonkers**, with its huge shopping malls, snide country clubs and dainty St Andrews Golf Course, the first in America. Drivers on Route 9, however, are shielded from the allures of this corporate paradise by leafy woods and a nice view to the west of the Hudson River.

The first proper stop, about 25 miles out of Manhattan, is **Tarrytown**, which America knows as Washington Irving's *Sleepy Hollow*, and which nowadays contains mixture of fantastically rich estates and good-looking manor houses dating from the first Dutch settlers, as well as modern condominiums and a big General Motors plant. In North Tarrytown, Irving is buried in a cemetery next to the **Old Dutch Church of Sleepy Hollow** which dates from 1697.

Here also is the **Union Church of the Pocantico Hills**, patronized by the Rockefeller family whose estate *Kykuit* lies hidden away nearby. The Rockefellers had the church's interior decorated with eight stained-glass windows by Chagall and Matisse's last work, a tiny rose window of glass cutouts. If you have time, you should also think about visiting the Georgian **Philipsburg Manor**, a working reconstruction of the Dutch mill established by the Philips family who settled in the area in the early 1650s. At the back is a garden and farm filled with stumpy cows, sheep and chickens which have been 'back-bred' to reproduce the breeds of the 18th century.

Just to the south of Tarrytown is **Sunnyside**, an endearing Dutch Colonial cottage which Washington Irving bought as a ruin in 1835 and surrounded with whimsical parks and grounds. Tours navigate people round the tiny Victorian living quarters and library which Irving called his 'snuggery'. A mile away at 635 South Broadway is an entirely different species of living quarters: **Lyndhurst**, an extravagant, fey Gothic castle with hysterical crennelations and a breathtaking view of the Hudson. It was bought by the hated robber baron, swindler and man-about-town, Jay Gould in 1880, and stands in 60 acres of handsome grounds next to the fortifications of 'Belvedere', the secluded but opulent property belonging to the Rev. Sun Myung Moon.

The Philips' lost their property after the Revolution, but the Van Courtlandt's, who backed the Americans, held on to their enormous 86,000-acre estate 10 miles to the north in Croton-on-Hudson. Now a mere 20 acres, **Van Courtlandt Manor** is the largest and most handsome of the 'Sleepy Hollow Restorations', done up in 18th-century style with lovely flower beds and orchards.

About 10 miles north of the Courtlandt Manor is an especially beautiful stretch of the river: the **Hudson Highlands**. Vertical cliffs and steep crags on either side pinch the river to an anorexic slimness, and the water runs faster and deeper than anywhere else along the Hudson channel. The drive along **Storm King Highway** past Bear Mountain (named after its barreness rather than its bears) is particularly dramatic; sometimes too dramatic, with its hair-raising hairpin twists and turns.

The chief attraction north of Bear Mountain is **West Point**, a craggy crest of land which is home to the US Military Academy. They naturally built their school in 1802 on the most strategic point of the Hudson and, quite apart from anything else, the views up and down the river are the best in the valley. Visitors are allowed to wander through the Gothic campus at will, although they are encouraged to watch a rather tedious series of recruitment films and endless parades in the Parade Ground. There is an interesting museum housing Hitler's pistol and MacArthur's dressing gown, and detailing the careers of Generals Eisenhower, Grant and Patton who all trained at the academy, as did the most unlikely cadet of all, Edgar Allan Poe, before he dropped out.

Another 25 miles or so upriver, above the town of Poughkeepsie (*pikipsy*, home of the ladies, and now the men of Vassar), are the princely palaces of Dutchess County. These are even more sumptuous than the mansions lower down. The main sight lies in **Hyde Park**, which took its name in 1741 from Edward Hyde, Viscount Cornbury, the English governor of New York who took to wearing dresses in public. The name is now synonymous with Springwood, the elegant 35-room Classical Revival mansion and shrine to Franklin D. Roosevelt, who was brought up and finally buried here, in 1945. To the north is **Olana**, an eerie Persian-Gothic castle built by the aristocratic landscape painter, Frederick Church. A few miles away is the most ostentatious of the lot: **Vanderbilt Mansion**, designed with every extravagant beaux-arts trapping by Calvert Vaux. Inside there are 54 rooms including a stomach-turning Louis XV boudoir designed for Mrs Vanderbilt Jnr.

Hyde Park is just about as far north as you could possibly get in a day, but for anyone who wants to stay on it is an ideal runway for exploring the **Catskills**. This contains a ravishing landscape: 250,000 acres of steep mountains, villages, lakes and ski resorts which the Indians called *Onteora*, or 'Land of the Sky'. In the autumn the early frosts flame, bronze and burn the leaves into colors that look almost unearthly.

428

Atlantic City and the Southern New Jersey Shore

> '...a glittering monument to the national talent for
> wholesale amusement'.
> —*Federal Writers' Project Guide*, 1939.

Atlantic City is now the tackiest, and, to the morally upstanding, the most pernicious town on the East Coast: a fascinating place for anyone who is interested in the depths as well as the heights of Americana. The national collective unconscious, of course, is thoroughly familiar with the seaside resort: in the thirties its street plan was translated to the board of the American Monopoly, and year after year, since 1921, it has hosted the Miss America Beauty Contest. What's more, since 1976, when casino gambling was legalized, 33 million Americans a year have poured into the town which has an indigenous population of 44,000.

The vote to turn Atlantic City into 'Las Vegas with a Seashore' was a last ditch attempt to rescue the New Jersey resort from utter collapse. From the 1870s onwards, Atlantic City flourished as the fount of American kitsch, giving birth to the first boardwalk, the first ferris wheel, the first Easter Parade and the first salt-water taffy (an unpleasantly colored substance which tastes horrible). By World War II, however, everything had gone to pot; the advent of Disneyland made it seem fuddy-duddy, and the resort was developing some of the worst slums in the state.

The slums are still there, but since 1976 Atlantic City has grown a green-neon skyline and it bristles with the glittering lights of 12 casino-hotels and a new hospital wing named after Frank Sinatra. Most of the hotels are uncannily alike—each with a ground-floor football-pitch sized casino which whirrs and clatters with slot machines and the shouts of crap dealers. Upstairs there are usually about five sumptuous restaurants, a couple of lounges and a showroom where stars like Frank Sinatra, Joan Rivers, Madonna and the big-name boxers draw big crowds.

The ultimate in Atlantic City tack, however, is embodied in **Caesar's Palace** with its replica of Michelangelo's *David* and Cleopatra's boat presiding over the slot machines, along with croupiers dressed in mini-togas, and an immense statue of Julius Caesar beaming onto the boardwalk. The man responsible for this monstrous bizarrity is Atlantic City's reigning supremo, Donald Trump, who is hanging on by his fingernails and praying for the success of his newest billion-dollar extravaganza, the

Trump Taj Mahal, whose pink and blue minarets and finials punctured the skyline in 1990.

Getting there: newsagents and travel-agents all over the city sell bus tickets often with meal vouchers and a roll of quarters thrown in. Sometimes the bus company, sponsored by the casinos, offer package deals in which passengers are paid back the entire cost of the fare in quarters. Every day about a 1000 buses roll up at the resort, but for those who don't like coaches, there is also an Amtrak connection from Penn Station.

Lunch/Cafés: **Carnegie Deli**, Sands Hotel on Indiana Avenue, for huge sandwiches, and **A. W. Shucks**, at Ocean One for fresh oysters, clams, mussels and chowders.

Most of the old Atlantic City resort has been replaced by casinos, but it still boasts the world's first **Boardwalk**, built along the seashore in 1870. An enterprising George Boardman came up with the notion after hotels complained that guests brought the sand in with them and ruined carpets and upholstery. The shoreline still has its five original piers including **Garden Pier**, which now houses the minimal **Atlantic City Historical Museum**, and **Steel Pier**, once used for high-diving acts by ladies who rode into a pool astride their horses, and nowadays a sad little heliport. When you tire of walking you can board one of the motorized trams, or a rolling cart, which is driver-powered, and probably even more exhausting than walking.

At the far northeastern end of the 5-mile long Boardwalk is the resort's oldest relic—the **Absecon Lighthouse** built in 1857 with a fine view for visitors from the 167 ft high top. Two less attractive sights lie at the opposite end: **Ocean One**, near Missouri Avenue, a ghastly shopping mall contained in a replica of an ocean liner, and the legendary **Convention Center** which hosts the Miss America Pageant and Contest in the second week of September.

Atlantic City is an ideal base from which to explore the curious mixture of quaint Victorian seaside resorts and fifties neon playgrounds lying to the south. **Ocean Drive** slowly weaves its way down a 40-mile length of winding road as far as Cape May and the Delaware Bay at the bottom. **Margate**, the first stop on the route, contains what must be New Jersey's most outlandish sight—**Lucy the Margate Elephant**, a six-story Victorian folly weighing 90 tons and made out of tin. Originally a gimmick to attract people to a real-estate development, the giant pachyderm has recently been saved from demolition and restored to her former shining glory. Nearby is **Ocean City**, a 'dry' Victorian resort founded in 1880 by some Methodist ministers, with its own Music Pier.

Sixteen miles further down is a very different kind of resort—the **Wildwoods**, announced by great clusters of glowing neon motels. In Wildwood proper is **Five Mile Beach**, and a vast amusement park which supposedly has more rides, arcades and amusements than Disney World, as well as a plethora of discos and nightclubs, and a free beach. You may prefer to swim, however, from **Cape May**, where you can pick up 'Cape May Diamonds', chunks of sparkling white and yellow quartz on Sunset Beach. The prettiest New Jersey resort of all, Cape May is a Victorian architectural extravaganza of hotels and houses covered in fancy 'gingerbread' woodwork. Off the cape itself is another lighthouse and the remains of the wreck of the 'Atlantus', an ill-fated *concrete* ship constructed in World War I to counter the steel shortage. Miraculously it remained afloat until it finally sank here in 1926.

Chronology

1524   Giovanni da Verrazano, an Italian working for Francis I of France, is the first European to explore New York Bay.

1609   Henry Hudson, an Englishman working for the Dutch East India Company, lands on Manhattan and explores further, sailing upriver to Albany.

1624   First 30 Dutch colonists settle in Albany and on Nut Island near Manhattan.

1625   New Amsterdam is established at the foot of Manhattan.

1626   First Governor, Peter Minuit, buys the island for 60 guilders, or $24.

1631   Minuit recalled by the Company for being too generous with the patroons.

1638   First murder: the victim, Gerrit Jansen, is brutally stabbed to death outside Fort Amsterdam.

1641   Raids on Manhattan and Staten Island, the first of a series of Indian uprisings.

1642   The island gets its first two taverns. Governor Kieft lynches Indians in the lower Hudson Valley.

1644   A wall is built (today's Wall Street) to protect the Dutch settlement from the Indians. The company frees a group of black slaves who settle on farms in SoHo.

1645   Settlements made in Flushing, Gravesend and Breukelen.

1646   Peter Stuyvesant appointed Governor.

1653   The Company insist Stuyvesant grants the city a charter establishing municipal government.

1654   First Jewish settlers arrive as refugees from Portuguese Brazil.

1656   New York has 1000 inhabitants.

1663   The city is shaken by small earthquake.

1664   In August, the *Colonel Nicholls* anchors in New York bay, three days later the Dutch surrender to the Brits without a shot, New Amsterdam becomes New York. Thomas Willet becomes mayor the following year.

1672   New York gets a postal service to Boston.

1673   Dutch recapture New York without a fight. Rename it New Orange.

1674   Dutch give New Orange back to the British.

1672   First insane asylum built in the city.

1689   Jacob Leisler leads an uprising against James II, takes over the administration of the city until 1691 when he is hanged by his so-called friends.

1725   William Bradford launches the city's first newspaper, the *New York Gazette*.

1732   A theater is built in New York.

1735   Peter Zenger, editor of the *New-York Weekly Journal*, acquitted in a libel trial which establishes freedom of the press.

1765   A rabble marches on City Hall in protest against the British Stamp Act. Congress meets in New York and denounces British policies of taxation.

1774 New York Tea Party; tea from a ship called the *London* is dumped into the harbour.

1776 Declaration of Independence, and beginning of the Revolutionary War. British smash Washington at the Battle of Long Island in Brooklyn. Patriots retreat, and by November the city has fallen into British hands.

1783 British army evacuates New York as the Treaty of Paris concludes the Revolutionary War and Britain recognizes the independence of the 13 colonies.

1785 New York City becomes the first capital of the United States for a brief five years, before Congress moves to Philadelphia.

1786 Tammany Society of New York set up by Aaron Burr.

1788 The Doctors Riot, in which an angry mob protests against dissection.

1789 Washington inaugurated outside Federal Hall.

1790 Population is 33,131.

1791 First of a series of yellow fever epidemics strikes the city.

1792 Embryonic Stock Exchange formed under a buttonwood tree on Wall Street.

1796 Black members of the Methodist Church organize the first black congregation.

1799 The Manhattan Company provides New York's first, unsanitarily piped water. The company is a front for Aaron Burr's new bank.

1803 Foundations of City Hall are laid. Population rises above 60,000.

1807 Publication of the city's first guidebook, Samuel Mitchell's *Picture of New York*.

1811 New York laid out in a grid of 2028 blocks according to a plan by John Randel Jr., even though the city only encompasses the area below City Hall.

1812 US declares war on Britain and British blockade the port. In 1814 the Treaty of Ghent ends the war.

1819 The city panicked by a financial crisis.

1825 Erie Canal opens and turns New York into America's pre-eminent port.

1832 New York and Harlem Railroad opens; carriages are drawn from Prince Street to 14th Street by horses.

1835 Disastrous fire destroys the surviving remnants of Dutch New York.

1837 Samuel Morse invents the telegraph; the first message he sends is supposedly 'What hath God Wrought!'. Another financial crisis in which $60 million is lost, 98 businesses go bankrupt and mobs storm and loot food warehouses.

1842 Dickens visits New York and hates it. The new Croton Aqueduct brings water to the city from the Catskills.

1845 Baseball founded near Madison Square Park.

1846 Irish immigrants, escaping the potato famines, arrive in great numbers.

1849 Astor Place Riots break out over the relative merits of two actors, Forest and Macready, and end in nearly 200 deaths and injuries.

1850 Garibaldi, in exile, arrives.

1851 The *New York Times* is published.

1853 A Crystal Palace built on 42nd Street for the World's Fair. It suffers the fate of its twin in London, and burns to the ground.

1857	Work starts on the construction of Central Park. Another financial panic. Riots break out between Irish gangs.
1859	Otis installs a vertical screw railway—the first steam elevator—in the Fifth Avenue Hotel.
1861	Civil War breaks out.
1863	Draft Riots against conscription effectively hijack the city for three days. Thousands are killed.
1865	Abraham Lincoln assassinated and 120,000 people file past his body in City Hall.
1868	First elevated railway opens on 9th Avenue.
1869	City's first apartment house built on 18th Street. On Black Friday, 4 September, Jim Fisk and Jay Gould corner the gold market.
1870	Work starts on Brooklyn Bridge and the first pnuematic subway.
1871	The corrupt Tammany boss, William Marcy Tweed, is arrested and sent to jail.
1873	Another Stock Exchange panic.
1880	Metropolitan Museum opens, three years after the Museum of Natural History. Sarah Bernhardt makes her American debut.
1883	Opening of the Brooklyn Bridge, in which 12 people are killed during a stampede by the crowd.
1886	Statue of Liberty is erected on Bedloe's Island.
1888	Great blizzard in which people are rescued from elevated trains upon payment of a dollar, and telegraph lines collapse under the weight of snow. The Tower Building, one of the first with a steel skeleton, is built on Broadway.
1892	Ellis Island becomes the city's immigration station.
1898	The five boroughs are consolidated into one city. New York now has a population of more than 3.1 million.
1900	Blacks begin moving into Harlem.
1907	New York gets its first metered taxi-cabs.
1913	Grand Central Terminal opens. The Woolworth Building on Broadway becomes the tallest in the world. At the Armory Show, New Yorkers have their first, horrified look at European Impressionist and Post-Impressionist paintings.
1916	Zoning laws passed, restricting the size and height of new skyscrapers.
1917	US enters World War I and 1.5 million soldiers leave New York for Europe.
1924	Jimmy Walker becomes mayor.
1929	Wall Street crashes, and the Great Depression begins.
1931	The Empire State Building and the new Waldorf-Astoria Hotel are completed a year after the Chrysler Building. Work starts on Rockefeller Center.
1933	Fiorello La Guardia becomes mayor.
1939	World's Fair opens at Flushing Meadows in Queens.
1942	Times Square blacked out during World War II. The Brooklyn Navy Yard is a hive of activity.

1946   The United Nations finds a permanent home in New York. A bomber crashes into the 58th floor of the Bank of Manhattan building on Wall Street.

1950   The population reaches an all-time high of 7.8 million.

1956   The Brooklyn Dodgers desert New York for Los Angeles, and their grounds at Ebbets Field are sold for a housing site.

1959   Work starts on Lincoln Center and the city's real estate is assessed at $32 billion.

1960   A proposal is made for building the World Trade Center. Mayor Wagner's administration is found to be inefficient and corrupt.

1964   Serious race riots in Harlem and Bedford-Stuyvesant after a young black boy is killed. The World's Fair opens. The Verrazano-Narrows suspension bridge is finished.

1965   New York's first power blackout lasts for 13 hours.

1966   Race riots in Brooklyn.

1967   Adam Clayton Powell re-elected by his Harlem constituency, even though he has been banned from Congress over a scandal involving his handling of public funds.

1968   Teachers strike over community schooling; slowdowns by police.

1970   15 per cent of New Yorkers live below the poverty line.

1971   The Giants (American Football) move to New Jersey.

1975   Mayor Beame staggers through a crisis in which New York finds itself on the brink of bankruptcy; saved by a federal loan of $2.3 billion. As the city endures drastic cutbacks in basic services, the Bronx burns and 13,000 fires devastate the area.

1977   25-hour-long power cut leads to serious looting and half of New York is trapped in elevators.

1980   Census shows that 48.1 per cent of the city's population is Hispanic or black. Hispanic immigration has increased, while the white population has fallen.

1983   Trump Tower and the AT&T Building soar up in midtown Manhattan as the city experiences an economic boom.

1986   Ed Koch elected for his third and last term as mayor. The suicide of the borough president of Queens, Donald Manes, tarnishes his administration in a bureaucratic scandal. Battery Park City, a huge complex of offices, shops and high-income apartments, is built within walking distance of Wall Street. Computer trading on Wall Street leads to a drop of 86 points on Stock Exchange.

1987   On Black Monday, the Dow Jones index falls 508 points, leading to the loss of thousands of jobs on Wall Street.

1988   Clashes between police and local residents in Tompkins Square, when police try to evict its population of homeless people. A quarter of New York lives below the poverty line.

1989   The chairman of the Municipal Assistance Corporation warns that the city may be in for another recession. The Board of Estimate, which presides over its fiscal budget, is deemed unconstitutional and abolished.

1990   In January, Democrat David Dinkins is sworn into office and becomes New York's first black mayor.

Further Reading

Asbury, Herbert, *The Gangs of New York*, (Alfred A. Knopf, Inc., 1928). An arresting account of the New York underworld, from the early gangs of the Revolution to the twenties.

Botkin, B.A. *New York City Folklore*, (Random House, 1956). A wonderfully entertaining compendium of tall stories and anecdotes about New York, compiled from diaries, gossip columns, literature and letters, as well as travel books.

Caro, Robert, *The Power Broker: Robert Moses and the Fall of New York*, (Vintage, 1975). A vast, obsessed and enthralling tome, portraying the imperious Evil Gnome, for nearly half a century the most powerful man in New York, and the one who shaped the city we see today—with $27 billion.

Charyn, Jerome, *Metropolis: New York as Myth, Marketplace and Magical Land*, (Putnam, 1986). Engaging and occasionally rather fey tour through 1980s New York, from the sex booths on Times Square to a TV supper with Ed Koch.

Chase, W. Parker, *New York: the Wonder City*, (New York Bound, 1931). A marvelous panegyric on the city—the most unconsciously funny in the genre—written in the midst of the Depression by an indefatigable showgirl-impresario.

Cohen, Barbara, Steven Heller and Seymour Chwast, *Trylon and Perisphere*, (Abrams, 1989). A glossy poster-sized encyclopaedia of a highpoint in American design, the 1939 World's Fair.

Cohen, Barbara, Steven Heller and Seymour Chwast, *New York Observed*, (Abrams, 1988). An adventurous anthology of New York from 1650 to the eighties, with a particularly good selection of illustrations ranging from Diego Rivera to Cecil Beaton and Thomas Nast.

Conrad, Peter, *The Art of the City*, (OUP, 1984). An eloquent dissection of the city using its artists and writers as scalpels.

Dos Passos, John, *U.S.A.*, (Penguin, 1938). An Olympian attempt to capture the first bewildering three decades of the century in a massive trilogy composed between 1930 and 1938.

Edmiston, Susan and Linda D. Cirino, *Literary New York* (Houghton Mifflin, 1976). Well-written and copiously researched geographical guide to historical and literary New York, from Washington Irving to the Beats.

Facaros, Dana and Michael Pauls, *Around America*, (Macdonald & Co., 1982). Definitive and sprightly guide to New York and the mid-Atlantic States.

Federal Writers' Project (including John Cheever), *New York City Guide* (Random House, 1939 and reprint Pantheon, 1982). Excellent guide to New York; compiled with great charm and insight, at a critical juncture in the history of the city, by writers subsidized by Works Progress Administration funds during the Depression.

Feininger, Andreas, and John Von Hartz, *New York in the Forties*, (Dover, 1978). Extraordinary photographs of New York taken when its serrated skyline looked its best.

Galbraith, John Kenneth, *The Great Crash*, (Penguin, 1975). Engrossing investigation into the causes of the Wall Street Crash, written with zest and panache.

Goldberger, Paul, *The City Observed* (Vintage Books, 1979). A perceptive guide to the buildings of the city by the architecture critic of the *New York Times*. Cheeky at its best, though every so often it teeters into sententiousness.

Green, Martin, *New York 1913*, (Scribners, 1988). An erudite account of pre-War radicalism in New York, focusing on the Armory Show and the Paterson Strike Pageant of 1913 as a sea-change in politics and art.

Jones, Pamela, *Under the City Streets*, (Holt, Rinehart & Winston, 1978). Crisply and intelligently written, an intriguing journey into the murk of underground New York.

Kessner, Thomas, *Fiorello H. La Guardia, and the Making of Modern New York*, (McGraw-Hill, 1989). An illuminating biography of New York's best-loved mayor, and a thorough analysis of the politics of liberalism in the thirties and forties.

Koolhaas, Rem, *Delirious New York*, (OUP, 1978). Iconoclastic, fantastical, and entirely convincing—a bracing and highly entertaining explanation of New York's predilection for insanely congested streets and delirious architecture.

Kouwenhoven, John A., *The Columbia Historical Portrait of New York*, (Harper and Row, 1972). Fascinating visual encyclopaedia of social and physical New York.

Marqusee, Mike and Bill Harris, *New York, an Anthology*, (Cadogan, 1985). An extremely well-chosen anthology of the city, with extracts from Saul Bellow, Hart Crane, Leon Trotsky, John Reed, Maxim Gorki and Le Corbusier.

Moorhouse, Geoffrey, *Imperial City*, (Hodder & Stoughton, 1981). A fresh-faced view of New York by the English travel writer.

Morris, James, *The Great Port*, (Faber, 1970). Apologetically romantic account of New York Harbor and the Port Authority.

Newfield, Jack and Wayne Barrett, *City For Sale*, (Harper & Row, 1988). An absorbing chronicle of corruption and double-dealing in the Koch administration, focusing on the dramatic suicide of Donald Manes, the Queens borough president, in 1986.

Patterson, Jerry E., *The City of New York: A History Illustrated from the Collections of the Museum of the City of New York*, (Harry N. Abrams, 1978). Thoroughly researched but somewhat dessicated history of the city from the Dutch settlement onwards.

Petronius, *New York Unexpurgated; an Amoral Guide for the Jaded, Tired, Evil, Non-conforming, Corrupt, Condemned and the Curious—Humans and Otherwise—to Underground Manhattan*, (New York, 1966). Not as salacious as it promises, but quite illuminating.

Plath, Sylvia, *The Bell Jar*, (Faber, 1963). Taut account of Esther Greenwood's visit to New York in 1953, the summer they electrocuted the Rosenbergs.

Reynolds, Donald Martin, *The Architecture of New York City*, (Macmillan, 1984). Dry and sometimes disorganized history of New York architecture, but one which covers the off-beat and virtually unheard-of, as well as the mainstream.

Salinger, J. D. *The Catcher in the Rye*, (Penguin, 1951). The story of the wry adolescent, Holden Caulfield, who runs away from a Pennsylvania boarding-school to New York, and his fears about the ducks in Central Park.

Sanders, Ronald, and Edmund V. Gillon, *The Lower East Side; a Guide to its Jewish Past*, (Dover, 1979). An unusual set of photographs and a brief history of the Lower East Side, past and present.

Smith, Matther Hale, *New York in Sunshine and Shadow*, (J. B. Burr and Co., 1869). Graphic sketches of 'High Life', 'Detectives', 'Shoddy Parties', 'Practical Jokes', 'Social Evil', 'Low-class Gambling Houses' and 'Houses of Assignation' in the Great Metropolis of the 1860s.

Snow, Richard, *Coney Island, a Postcard Journey to the City of Fire*, (Brightwaters Press, 1984). A fascinating history told in postcards of the early years of this famous and extraordinary resort.

Still, Bayard, *Mirror for Gotham*, (New York University Press, 1956). A meaty anthology of New York as contemporaries have described it from Dutch days to 1956.

Talese, Gay, *Honor Thy Father*, (Dell, 1981). Talese's gripping study of the rise and fall of the Bonanno organization, and the mafia in New York.

Trollope, Frances, *Domestic Manners of the Americans*, (Alfred A. Knopf, 1949). Terse and often very funny first-hand account of 19th-century New York.

Van Dyke, John C., *The New New York*, (Macmillan, 1909). A daring commentary on the architecture of New York in 1909, with extraordinary pencil illustrations of a wrecked Piranesian New York, by Joseph Pennell.

Van Every, Edward, *Sins of New York*, (Stokes, 1930). Sins of New York, as 'exposed' by the 19th-century *Police Gazette*, including *The Most Beautiful Illicit Love Tragedy*, *The Most Revolting Unsolved Murder Mystery*, and *Denizens and Depravities of the Deadly Dives*.

Wharton, Edith, *The Age of Innocence*, (Appleton, 1920). Set in tight-legged turn-of-the-century upper class New York, an account of Newland Archer's frustrated passion for the separated wife of a Polish count.

White, Norval, *A Physical History of New York*, (Atheneum, 1987). An extremely good architectural history including digressions on pipes and drains, transit and elevators.

White, Norval and Elliot Willensky, *AIA Guide to New York City*, (Macmillan, 1989). An indispensable geographical gazetteer of literally every single structure in the city, with brief and distinctly camp remarks on each item.

Wolf, Reinhart, *New York*, (Tuschen, 1980). A tray-sized coffee-table book of Reinhart Wolf's spectacular photographs of skyscraper crowns in dawns and sunsets, and at night.

Wright, Carol von Pressentin, *Blue Guide, New York*, (W. W. Norton, 1983). A manically comprehensive historical guide to the city, by an author whose deadpan style disguises all kinds of quirks and idiosyncrasies of taste.

A Glossary of Slang

Before very long, it will become apparent that New Yorkers speak a different language to anyone else. The fact that both you and they believe they are talking in English only makes matters more complicated. In general, New Yorkers have an unmistakably nasal accent; they speak very fast, interrupting at the slightest opportunity and drawling at the same time: they say *wassermadjawidgiu?* when you can't understand.

The so-called Brooklyn argot, which has Brooklynites referring to 'de goils on toid and toid-toidy street' and 'de toikeys in Joisey', is actually the comic creation of generations of comedians and writers: the dialect is indigenous to the entire Metropolitan area, and was originally spoken by the plug-uglies of the Bowery before the Civil War. Over scores of years it has been honed into the squawking accent heard on the streets today.

Noo Yawkers love tawking, above all else. Cecil Beaton once described their use of language as Elizabethan, and certainly to an outsider the average New Yorker's inventive use of slang is an attractive, and often infectious, blend of the robust and the florid. In recent years, apart from a strong Yiddish input, the black community has had by far the most pervasive influence on New York slang.

Like most things in the city, slang comes and goes with astonishing rapidity, but the glossary below will give you a head start. British visitors, in particular, are advised to study those problematic everyday words which have other meanings. To 'knock someone up', for example, means to get them pregnant; while to 'blow someone off' is a relatively mild phrase, meaning to cut or avoid someone.

Assawayigoze—*interj* That's life, or *c'est la vie*
Babycakes—*n* Sweetheart
Barn-burner—*n* Something sensational or exciting
Bang-up—*adj* Excellent
Bat one's gums—*v phr* Talk flippantly or frivolously
Bazoo—*n* The mouth
Belle-boy—*n* Gay prostitute
Bin-wacker—*n* A habitual drunkard
Biseeinya—*nterj* I'll be seeing you again soon
Brewskies—*n* Beers
Bronx cheer—*n phr* A lusty flatulating noise made with the tongue, cheeks and lips
Bug off—*v phr* To leave or depart
Catch some rays—*interj* A parting salutation
Caveman—*n* A masterful man
Cheesy—*adj* Lacking in taste; kitsch or shoddy
Chill—*v* Relax
Chillin out—*v phr* Relaxing
Chill out—*v phr* Relax and enjoy yourself
Chim—*n* A good fellow
Chutzpah—*n* Hubris; extreme and arrogant brashness
Clever cock—*n phr* A know-it-all
Clover hole—*n phr* Irish bar
Cool breeze—*v phr* Don't hassle me
Crib—*n* House
Crucial—*adj* Brilliant or excellent
Ditsy—*adj* Vapid and silly
Ditz—*n* A frivolous ninny; flighty or fey
Does Howdy Doody have wooden balls?—*sentence* What a stupid question to ask
Doggie—*n* A $10 bill
Don't dis me—*v phr* Don't show me any disrespect
Duhshuh-ul—*n* The shuttle connecting Times Square and Grand Central Terminal
Dyawanna brr?—*sentence* Would you like a beer?
Excuse me—*v phr* Used in the form of an expletive, meaning 'get the **** out of the way'

441

Flaky—adj Exuberantly eccentric, insane, or dizzily bewildered

Frantic—adj Excellent, cool

Funk—v To panic and fail

Funky—adj Quaint and attractively eccentric, or repulsively smelly

Futon-potato—n Yuppie stay-at-home and kill-joy

Geddowdedewai—v phr Excuse me, please

Get the matches—interj Let's have some fun

Get your gummies on—interj Move it, because the police are coming

Ginchy—adj Admirable or sexy

Gizmo—n A fellow, or 'bloke'

Glop-pads—n Marks left on a floor by sweaty feet

Go for a steak out—v phr Go out for a big meal, usually of steak

Go to business—v phr Go to work

Goof around—v phr Potter about

Goop—adj An idiotic person

Grand Central Station—n phr Anywhere excessively crowded or busy

Gumball—n The lights on top of a police-car

Gussy up—v phr Dress up in one's best, or refurbish

Gutty—adj Assertive and strong

Happy talk—n phr Informal chat among newscasters during a broadcast

Have some buttons missing—v phr To be eccentric and whimsical

Heaving—adj Excellent, wonderful or 'groovy'

Heavy duckets—n phr lots of money

Hefty—n A fat person

Helluvalot—n A large amount

Hokum—n Poppycock, nonsense

Homeboys, Hos, or *Homes—n* Neighbor, compatriot or buddy

Hootoadjadat?—sentence What you're saying is rubbish

How're you hangin?—interj How do you do?

Humpy-bumpy—n Intercourse

Jeepers creepers—interj An exclamation of surprise

Juiced up—adj phr Full of energy

Kazoo—n Backside or lavatory

Khazeray—n Odious, worthless material

Kibitz—v To give unwelcome and intrusive advice

Kishkes—n Guts or innards

KISS—sentence Keep it simple, stupid

Kissyface—n Cuddling and hugging

Kitten—n $50 bill

Klutz around—*v phr* Behave in goonish manner
Kneesies—*n* Clandestine friction of the knees
Kneesup—*n* A fun-loving person
Kvell—*v* To beam with pride or satisfaction
Kvetch—*v* To complain or be consistently pessimistic, a favorite
   occupation
Later—*interj* A casual farewell
Leg-biter—*n* A small child or infant
Let's break the cake—*interj* It's time we left this place
Let's make time—*interj* Hurry up
Love-puppet—*n* Sweet and irresistible boyfriend
Melthead—*n* Dim-witted person
Minjabak—*v phr* Please get out of my way
Momser, Mofo or *Mucker*—*n* Contemptible or despicable person
Moocher—*n* A beggar or parasite
Moosh someone—*v phr* To attack someone vigorously, to let them have it
Moxie—*n* Gumption, guts or shrewdness
My posse—*n phr* My crowd of people
No soap—*negation* Absolutely not, no way
Pesky—*adj* Irritating and annoying
Pol—*n* A politician
Rat around—*v phr* Loaf around
Ratchet-mouth—*n* A blabberer
Righteous—*adj* Excellent/genuine/the greatest
Rusty-dusty—*n* The buttocks or rump
Sass—*n* Impudence
Sausage-jock—*n* Taxi-driver
Savvy—*n* Intelligence, nous and brains
Schlemiel—*n* A victimized oaf
Schlep—*v* To carry with difficulty, or lug, or *n* a stupid person
Schlock—*n* Rubbish or shoddy, vulgar merchandise
Schlok shop—*n* Fancy-dress shop
Schlub or *Zhlub*—*n* A boorish, coarse-tongued person
Schlubette—*n* A silly girl
Schmaltz—*n* Cloying sentimentality, or a viscid substance
Schmear—*v* To bribe, flatter or soft soap, or smear on thickly,
   or *n* A scam
Schmeck—*n* A soupçon, a taste
Schmegeggy—*n* A fool
Schmendrick—*n* A gangly, inept person

443

Schmo or Joe Schmo—*n* An undistinguished or hapless character
Schmooz—*v* Cosy conversation
Schmuck—*n* An obnoxious person
Schmutter—*n* Clothes
Schnorrer—*n* A sponger or niggard
Schnozzola—*n* The nose
Shoot one's cookies—*v phr* To vomit
Shtarker—*n* A tough, a swell or a very important person
Shtick—*n* A small theatrical role, or a characteristic trait
Sissified—*adj* Timorous and spineless
Slap the plank—*v phr* To greet with mutual palm-slapping
Slooper—*n* A sneak or a gossip
Smokes—*n* Cigarettes
Snake-bitten—*adj* Hopelessly incapacitated
Spiffed-out—*adj* Dressed to the nines
Spiffy—*adj* Elegant and snazzy
Spunker-master—*n* Someone who is full of beans
Stop dissing me—*v phr* Stop distressing me
Studmuffin—*n* A gentle and attractive man with a great deal of sex-appeal, or *n* a transvestite husband
Swashle the swoosh—*v phr* Pilfer from a shop or till
Talk turkey—*v phr* Speak lucidly and candidly
Taykdiway—*v phr* I've finished, thank you
Taykadeezy—*v phr* Don't let things get on top of you
That's stupid—*interj* That's absolutely wonderful
Tittermous—*n* A giggling chatterer
Yang-allure—*n* Masculine sex appeal
Yo—*interj* Hail
You-know-what-I'm-saying?—*v phr* Do you read me?
Wannamayksumpnuvvit?—*v pht* Do you want to get involved in a brawl?
Walk heavy—*v phr* To be important
Washyerstep—*v phr* Mind where you are going
Way-hip—*adj* Very fashionable
Weenie—*n* Frankfurter, or an ineffectual person
Whadayyawant?—*v phr* Can I help you?
What can I do you for?—*interj* Hello
What gives?—*interj* What's going on? How are you?
Whazzitooyuh?—*v phr* Stop irritating me
Whazzup?—*interj* What's going on?, or hello
Whooper-dooper—*n* A wild party
Wussy—*n* A weak person

Index

Notes: *Italic* numbers indicate maps. **Bold** numbers indicate main references. Named avenues and streets are indexed by name. Numbered avenues and streets are indexed under 'Avenues' and 'Streets'.

445

INDEX

New York Marathon 16
New York Public Library 79, 163, 183, **184–5**, 320
New York State Office Building 224, 269
New York State Theater 322
New York Stock Exchange 14, 79, 103, **104–5**
New York University 164
New York Visitors and Conventions Bureau 116
New York Yacht Club 186
New Yorkers: curtness and politeness 23
New-York Historical Society 257
newspapers 28–9
newsstands 363
Nicolls, Colonel Richard 56
Nieuw Amsterdam, *see* New Amsterdam
Night Courts 225
nightclubs 341–5
Noguchi, Isamu 106, 107, 259, 411
North Wind Undersea Museum 260
Northern Dispensary 169–70
Northward Undersea Institute Museum 417–18
Nut Island 54

Ocean City 430–1
Ocean One 430
O'Dwyer, William 66
Olana 428
Old Dutch Church of Sleepy Hollow 427
Old Westbury Gardens 425
Oliver Street 226
Olmsted, Frederick Law 76, 126, 200–1, 394–5
One Astor Plaza 182
opticians 364
Orchard Street 132, 134
Orensatz, Angelo 141
Ottendorfer Library 145
Oyster Bar 247
Oyster Bay 425

packing 31
Paley Park 194
Palladium 161, 326
Pan Am Building 239, 246
Papaya King 240
Paramount Building 182
Park Avenue 66, 78, 211, 242–3, 246
La Marqueta 266
Park Coffee Shoppe 101
Park Row Building 80, 81
Park Slope 393–4
parking regulations 12
passports 3
Patchin Place 171

Paterson Strike Pageant 153
Paul, Les 159, 329
Pelham Cemetery 418
Pell Street 227–8
Pelli, Cesar 87
Penn Station 49, 79, 157
pests, animal 36–40
Peter Cooper Village 66
Petit, Philippe 108
pharmacists 349–50
Philip, Hardie 206
Philip Morris Building 248
Philipsburg Manor 427
Picasso, Pablo 243
Pierpont Morgan Library 260–1
Pierrepont, Henry 388
Pierrepont Street, Brooklyn 392
Pig-Market 138
Pine Street 106
Players Club 158, 159
Plaza Hotel 213
Poe, Edgar Allen 414, 428
Poe Cottage 414
police 22–3
    subway 50
Police Academy Museum 150, 159, 261
Polish areas 386, 402–3
pool (game) 370
population 58, 59, 62–3, 66
Post, George 79, 392
post offices 31–2
    parcel auctions 32
Powell, Adam Clayton 270
Power, Joe 144
Prince Street 231, 235
Prohibition 63
Promenade, Brooklyn 391
Prospect Park 394–5
prostitutes 161
Provincetown Playhouse 165
public holidays 32–3
Puerto Rican area 264
Puerto Rican Day Parade 19
Pulitzer, Joseph 212
Pulitzer Fountain 212
Pythian Temple 118–19

Quaker burial ground 395
Queens 62, 383, *384–5*, **403–11**
Queens Museum 261, 406
Queensboro Bridge 253

racquetball 374
Radio City Music Hall 13, **191–2**, 326
radio stations 28
Rainbow Room 190, 293
Randall, John, Jr 75
Randall Plan 58–9
rats 37
RCA Building 84–5, 188, **189–91**, 293
    Rainbow Room 190, 293
record shops 364

'Red Cube' 107
Reed & Stein 248
religious intolerance 56
religious shops 140, 267, 352
Rendons 267
Renwick, James 146
Renwick, James, Jr 411
Renwick Triangle 146–7
restaurants 282–301 *see also* beginning of Walks
    books on 305–6
Reynolds, J.R. 82
Richmond Hill 404
Richmondtown Restoration 423
Riis, Jacob 62, 138
riots 59, 60, 67
Ritz 326
Rivera, Diego 190
Riverdale 419–21
Riverside Church 276
Riverside Drive 275–6
Riverside Park 121–2
Rivington Street 140
Rizzoli's 214
Roche & Dinkeloo 202, 203, 251
Roche, Kevin 87, 211–12
Rockaways 403
Rockefeller, David 106
Rockefeller, J.D., Jr 252
Rockefeller, John D. 66, 189
Rockefeller, Michael 203
Rockefeller Center 17, 49, 84, 85, **188–92**
Rockefeller Plaza 189
Rockefellers 427
Roebling, John Augustus 109
Roebling, Colonel Washington 109–10
Rogers, Mary 107
roller-skating 374
    open-air disco 128
Roosevelt, Franklin D. 65, 428
Roosevelt Island 239–40, **410–11**
Roosevelt Island Aerial Tramway 239–40
Roosevelts 46
Rosebank 422–3
Rosenthal, Bernard 143–4
Rosenwach, Mr 46
Roth, Emery 391
Rothapfel, Samuel Lionel 'Roxy' 63–4, 191, 268
Rotunda 121
Round Table 186
Royalton Hotel 186–7
rubbish 40–3
running 374
Russian areas 383, 386, **398–9**
Russian Orthodox Cathedral of the Transfiguration 403

Saarinen, Eero 406
Sag Harbor 426
Sagamore Hill 425